Transforming English Rural Society

Between 1540 and 1920 the English elite transformed the countryside and landscape by building up landed estates which were concentrated around their country houses. John Broad's study of the Verney family of Middle Claydon in Buckinghamshire demonstrates two sides of that process. Charting the family's rise to wealth impelled by a strong dynastic imperative, Broad shows how the Verneys sought out heiress marriages to expand wealth and income. In parallel, he shows how the family managed its estates to maximise income and transformed three local village communities, creating a pattern of 'open' and 'closed' villages familiar to nineteenth-century commentators. Based on the formidable Verney family archive with its abundant correspondence, this book also examines the world of farmers, labouring families and the poor, as well as strategies for estate expansion and social enhancement. It will appeal to anyone interested in the English countryside as a dynamic force in social and economic history.

JOHN BROAD is Principal Lecturer in History at the London Metropolitan University.

Cambridge Studies in Population, Economy and Society in Past Time 40

Series Editors

RICHARD SMITH
Cambridge Group for the History of Population and Social Structure

JAN DE VRIES
University of California at Berkeley

PAUL JOHNSON
London School of Economics and Political Science

KEITH WRIGHTSON
Yale University

Recent work in social, economic, and demographic history has revealed much that was previously obscure about societal stability and change in the past. It has also suggested that crossing the conventional boundaries between these branches of history can be very rewarding.

This series exemplifies the value of interdisciplinary work of this kind, and includes books on topics such as family, kinship, and neighbourhood; welfare provision and social control; work and leisure; migration; urban growth; and legal structures and procedures, as well as more familiar matters. It demonstrates that, for example, anthropology and economics have become as close intellectual neighbours to history as have political philosophy or biography.

For a full list of titles in the series, please see end of book.

Transforming English Rural Society

The Verneys and the Claydons, 1600–1820

John Broad

London Metropolitan University

CAMBRIDGE
UNIVERSITY PRESS

PUBLISHED BY THE PRESS SYNDICATE OF THE UNIVERSITY OF CAMBRIDGE
The Pitt Building, Trumpington Street, Cambridge, United Kingdom

CAMBRIDGE UNIVERSITY PRESS
The Edinburgh Building, Cambridge, CB2 2RU, UK
40 West 20th Street, New York, NY 10011–4211, USA
477 Williamstown Road, Port Melbourne, VIC 3207, Australia
Ruiz de Alarcón 13, 28014 Madrid, Spain
Dock House, The Waterfront, Cape Town 8001, South Africa

http://www.cambridge.org

First published 2004

Printed in the United Kingdom at the University Press, Cambridge

Typeface Times 10/12 pt.   *System* LaTeX 2_ε [TB]

A catalogue record for this book is available from the British Library

Library of Congress Cataloguing in Publication data
Broad John, 1945–
Transforming English rural society : the Verneys and the Claydons, 1600–1820 /
John Broad.
   p.   cm. – (Cambridge studies in population, economy, and society in past time ; 40)
Includes bibliographical references and index.
ISBN 0 521 82933 X
1. Verney family.   2. Administration of estates – England – Buckinghamshire –
History.   3. Great Britain – History – George III, 1760–1820 – Biography.   4. Great
Britain – History – Stuarts, 1603–1714 – Biography.   5. Great Britain – History – 18th
century – Biography.   6. Gentry – England – Buckinghamshire – History.
7. Buckinghamshire (England) – Social conditions.   8. Buckinghamshire
(England) – Rural conditions.   9. Buckinghamshire (England) – Biography.
10. Buckinghamshire (England) – History.   I. Title.   II Series.
DA377.2.V5B75   2004
942.5′9 – dc22   2003055822

ISBN 0 521 82933 X hardback

Contents

List of figures

List of tables

Preface

The author of any book so long in the making has received help, advice, and encouragement from many people. My interest in early modern rural society was inspired by Sir John Habakkuk's and Joan Thirsk's undergraduate lectures and Cliff Davies's tutorial teaching. When St Edmund Hall Oxford elected me to the Gilbert Verney Senior Studentship, George Ramsay and Neville Williams supervised me with a combination of judicious promptings and enthusiastic suggestions that helped shape a doctoral thesis on Sir Ralph Verney. Joan Thirsk chaired a postgraduate seminar that was lively and thought-provoking, and helped initiate me into the intricacies and pleasures of English rural history. The decision to expand my work in time and scope was made possible by the generous help and support of three generations of the Verney family at Claydon House: Sir Harry Verney, Sir Ralph and Lady Verney, and Sir Edmund Verney gave me full access to the papers, help with accommodation to stop me freezing in the paper room and to enable me to search the eighteenth century papers systematically, and their own insights into the family history. The archivists at Buckinghamshire County Record office (now the Centre for Buckinghamshire Studies) and their staff provided help and advice on a wide range of subjects. Joan Thirsk and John Beckett many years ago provided stimulating comments on an earlier draft, making me re-think my approach during a spell of administrative duties that further delayed completion of the manuscript. I have received help and advice from so many colleagues over the years that it would be impossible to acknowledge them all, but Malcolm Airs, Penelope Corfield, Hugh Hanley, Steve Hindle, Tim Hitchcock, Richard Hoyle, Frank Melton, Roland Quinault, Richard Smith, Rachel Weil, and Susan Whyman have read and discussed various aspects to my great benefit. The Huntington Library and Scouladi Foundation made it possible for me to look at the Stowe papers in California in 1982, while the Leverhulme Foundation and the University of North London (now London Metropolitan University) provided me with the necessary time and space to bring it all to completion in 1999–2000. Students and colleagues at the University of North London were full of ideas and insights in ways they can never have anticipated or imagined. John Gibbs's help with maps in difficult circumstances has been much appreciated. My family has lived with the Verney project for so many years that they must wonder what my life and theirs will be like without it. My parents always gave me their fullest support and I feel particularly sad that my mother died knowing that it was complete, but before it could appear. Angela, David, and Ben have heard and read so much of the Verneys. David and Ben both helped with aspects of the graphs, and Angela's eagle eye has rescued me from many logical inconsistencies and textual infelicities. The responsibility for its final form remains firmly mine.

Acknowledgements

All Verney papers and letters cited in this book remain the property of the Claydon House Trust in which copyright lies. Earlier versions of some aspects of this book have previously been published in *Agricultural History Review, Bulletin of the Institute of Historical Research, Continuity and Change, Economic History Review, Historical Journal, Past and Present*, and *Records of Buckinghamshire*.

Note on editorial practice

The spelling and punctuation in so many of the Verney letters is so unfamiliar that I have taken the liberty of modernising it in the interests of clarity and readability. Quotations from printed sources have been transferred verbatim. Before 1752 the year began on 25 March, and dates between 1 January and 24 March have been put in the form 1656/7 in the footnotes. When the Verneys were abroad, dates were further complicated by differences in calendar, for example 31 Jan./10 Feb. 1646/7.

Abbreviations

BCRO	Centre for Buckinghamshire Studies, Aylesbury, formerly Buckinghamshire County Record Office
BL	British Library
Bodl.	Bodleian Library, Oxford
CJ	*House of Commons Journal*
ClH	Claydon House papers
CRO	County Record Office or archives service
HLRO	House of Lords Record Office
Huntington	H. E. Huntington Library, San Marino, California
LJ	*House of Lords Journal*
PP	Parliamentary Papers
PRO	Public Record Office (since April 2003, National Archives)
R	Reel of Verney letters microfilm

In order to prevent confusion between different members of the Verney family the following designations have been used, even when they were not the title of the person at the time. They are followed by the abbreviation used in the footnotes.

Sir Edmund Verney (d. 1642)		sev
Sir Ralph Verney (d. 1696)		srv
Edmund Verney (d. 1690)		ev
Sir John Verney, first Viscount Fermanagh	Sir John Verney	sjv
Ralph Verney, second Viscount Fermanagh	first earl	rv
Ralph Verney, second Earl Verney	second earl	rvjr
Mary Blacknall (wife of Sir Ralph Verney)		mv

The following abbreviations for frequent correspondents are used in the footnotes:

William Denton	wd
Sir Roger Burgoyne	srb
William Roades	wr

Hugh Holmes	hh
William Coleman	wc
Charles Chaloner	cc
Edward Butterfield	eb
William Butterfield (father and son)	wb

1   Introduction

This book is an extended case study of a family and its estates in midland England. It demonstrates how great landowning families and their dynastic ambitions moulded the rural economy, shaped the landscape of England, and interacted with rural society and village communities to produce effects that are still strongly visible in the twenty-first century. Modern estimates suggest that by the late nineteenth century elite landowners (the aristocracy and gentry) had accumulated estates that covered over half of the cultivable land area of the country.[1] They managed a panoply of ancient tenures involving copyholds and manorial courts that were the direct descendants of medieval villeinage. However, early modern landowners gradually altered tenures towards modern contractual arrangements especially in the south and east of England. Leases for short or medium terms (up to twenty-one years), or increasingly year-to-year tenancies, replaced lifehold arrangements, fines, heriots, and labour service requirements, and farm rents more closely reflected the real profitability of the land for those who worked it.

The long transition from medieval patterns of rural landholding and social relations to the great estates of eighteenth- and nineteenth-century England involved a variety of changes in countryside. Modernising estate management practices significantly changed landlord–tenant relationships as well as tenures. Over thirty-five years ago, Lawrence Stone demonstrated how the great Tudor landowners exploited their estates more intensively to increase income in the face of high inflation.[2] They attempted to assert new forms of property right over dormant or undefined aspects of rural land and custom. They tested local definitions of custom to increase personal control of the land at the expense of village communities, asserting their rights as manorial lords to enclose woods and commons, or brokering (with whatever necessary coercion) enclosure by

---

[1] F. M. L. Thompson, 'The social distribution of landed property in England since the sixteenth century', *Economic History Review* 2nd series, 16 (1966), pp. 505–18.

[2] L. Stone, *The Crisis of the Aristocracy* (Oxford 1965), esp. chs. 4 and 6.

mutual agreement.[3] They began the process of turning a system of tenures based on overlapping use rights over land into modern concepts of freehold landownership with fixed boundaries and few shared rights.[4] Where landowners consolidated landholdings it concentrated their power and enhanced the efficiency of estate management. Elite families' success in making this transition varied enormously. It could reflect the strength of individual vision and dynastic purpose, but chance events such as significant patterns of births, marriages, and deaths, were as important as marriage alliances and spendthrift sons.

Between the sixteenth and nineteenth centuries changes in elite lifestyles also helped to re-define the relationship between landowners and country dwellers. In the Tudor world a relatively small group of aristocratic families moved between their estates and court society. Court life was expensive, uncertain in its financial rewards, and dependent on access to networks and patrons whose favour rose and fell in political whims and winds. Kings and Queens up to and including James I made frequent progresses around the country to display themselves to their subjects. Their prime aim, apart from enjoying the hunting, was to reinforce ties of loyalty in a society without police force, standing army, or modern media, and meet many of those middling members of the elite who made up the justices and militia officers of devolved local government. The social world of the elite changed significantly after 1660. The landowning elite gained a much greater influence in politics. Although court office remained important, the expansion of government and bureaucracy, of army and navy, and above all the regular meeting of parliament and its changing role in government, broadened opportunities. There were other factors in play. London, already England's dominant city, was becoming a European metropolis. A consumer revolution brought a wide range of exotic products and novelties from distant parts of the globe to an expanding commercial entrepot. A parallel social revolution brought a wider range of landed families to spend part or all of the year in London to enjoy the 'season' with its range of entertainments, social contacts, and spectacles.[5]

These changes had significant effects on relationships in the countryside. They were expensive, demanding higher returns from the elite's major source of wealth, land. Rents were raised, contributing to the break up of crumbling feudal ties and loyalties between landowners and tenants. Hospitality and charity

---

[3] Two local microstudies of the process are S. Hindle, 'Persuasion and protest in the Caddington Common enclosure dispute, 1635–1639', *Past and Present* (1998), pp. 37–78; H. Hanley, 'The inclosure of Pitstone Common Wood, 1612', *Records of Buckinghamshire* 29 (1987).

[4] G. E. Aylmer, 'The meaning and definition of "property" in seventeenth-century England', *Past and Present* 86 (1980), pp. 87–97. Such rights are now so dominant as to be considered 'natural', and as having existed since time immemorial.

[5] The relationship of the country gentry and London's social world has been the subject of an excellent study in depth of the late seventeenth-century Verney family: S. Whyman, *Sociability and Power in late Stuart England: The Cultural World of the Verneys 1660–1720* (Oxford 1999).

became increasingly depersonalised and institutionalised in a regulated and managed rural world in which the steward or bailiff was more obviously the paid servant of the landowner than an intermediary between the farming community and their squire.[6] The role of the country house itself changed. From the eighteenth century onwards it increasingly separated the elite family and their guests from servants and local people. Parallel sets of stairs and passages made servants an invisible presence in essentially elite discourses rather than an accoutrement of local power and prestige to be displayed on public and semi-public occasions.[7] The Tudor and Stuart great house was a place where tenants came to pay their rents, exchange words with the Lord of the Manor, and perhaps attend a tenants' annual feast. The eighteenth-century mansion, surrounded by its park, gradually superseded it. Careful landscaping and tree planting were designed to minimise or exclude contact with farmers and villagers. It displayed power primarily to fellow-members of the elite, not to the population of the surrounding countryside.

Changes in elite attitudes to the localities where they concentrated their estates and built their country seats powerfully influenced the neighbourhood. Village studies suggest that over the period from 1500 to 1900 economic pressures on farmers and smallholders concentrated landownership and farming units amongst a small number of owners even in communities where elite families were not major land purchasers.[8] Small and even medium-sized units of ownership and agricultural production, those between five and forty acres, tended to diminish or even disappear widely across eastern and southern England. These changes in the size of holdings paralleled expanding market participation, and an increasing ease in transferring land.

These changes were particularly marked where great landowners and squires had significant concentrations of land. There, enclosure, the extinction of manorial rights, and conversion of tenures from copyhold to leasehold could go hand in hand with an increase in farm sizes. The scale of enlargement depended on many factors: the terrain and soil, prevalent farming patterns and labour availability, and access to markets. Landlords and agents generally preferred larger farms because there were fewer individuals to negotiate with, and tenants

[6] F. Heal, *Hospitality in Early Modern England* (Oxford 1990); D. Andrew, *Philanthropy and Police: London Charity in the Eighteenth Century* (Princeton 1989).

[7] M. Girouard, *Life in the English Country House: A Social and Architectural History* (Harmondsworth 1980).

[8] A whole range of studies has come to rather different conclusions about the timing and underlying pressures driving these changes. See particularly, W. G. Hoskins, *Midland Peasant* (1957); A. C. Chibnall, *Sherington: Fiefs and Fields of a Buckinghamshire Village* (Cambridge 1965); M. Spufford, *Contrasting Communities: English Villagers in the Sixteenth and Seventeenth Centuries* (Cambridge 1974); G. Nair, *Highley 1660–1880* (Oxford 1988); P. R. Edwards, 'The decline of the small farmer: the case of Rushock, Worcestershire', *Midland History* 21 (1996), pp. 73–100; H. R. French, and R. W. Hoyle, 'The land market of a Pennine manor: Slaidburn, 1650–1780', *Continuity and Change* 14 (1999), pp. 349–83.

with capital were more able to pay their rents regularly and punctually. Elite landowners drove through these changes primarily to maximise their income. Until the mid-seventeenth century, the word 'improvement' rarely related to the more efficient use of marginal land, or the adoption of new crops, rotations, and techniques. Although elite interest in farming innovations increased from the second half of the seventeenth century, most landowners' improvements were aimed to increase their rent rolls.

Landowners sought prosperous tenants on large farms, but larger farms meant fewer farmers in the community, and this influenced the occupational structures of villages. There are few studies of social change in communities dominated by large estates. By the nineteenth century writers on rural affairs noted divergent village typologies and the emergence of two stereotypes. There were 'closed' communities, those dominated by small numbers of owners, or a single person, and 'open' villages characterised by buoyant populations, large numbers of landowners, smaller farm sizes, and an occupational structure diversified away from agricultural to craft and service occupations. Modern analysis broadly supports these findings, but points to a range of intermediate village typologies.[9] Most research has compared village structures at one or more moments in time, but not the processes involved in creating a 'closed' village. There has been no study of the practicalities of altering tenures, enlarging farm sizes, encouraging emigration, and manipulating land and people to create the eighteenth- and nineteenth-century squire's village and park. There are examples of massive depopulation and removal of houses across the country. In Buckinghamshire, the Temples did so at Stowe and Royalist soldiers at Boarstall demolished village houses to bolster its Civil War defences. They were never rebuilt. There are famous eighteenth-century examples of new villages built away from the park and mansion in a wholesale re-modelling. The Grenvilles rebuilt Wotton Underwood, while Nuneham Courtenay in Oxfordshire and Milton Abbas in Dorset are fine examples of planned villages. There is, however, no detailed study of an estate village apart from Michael Havinden's account of the Lockinge estate in Berkshire, which is almost exclusively about the nineteenth and twentieth centuries.[10]

Village studies covering periods from the late medieval to the nineteenth century have concentrated on a variety of 'peasant' villages – agricultural, textile, and mining – all characterised by diversified landownership and a ruling

---

[9] B. A. Holderness, '"Open" and "close" parishes in England in the eighteenth and nineteenth centuries', *Agricultural History Review* 20 (1972), pp. 126–39; D. Mills, *Lord and Peasant in Nineteenth-century Britain* (1980); S. Banks, 'Nineteenth-century scandal or twentieth-century model? A new look at "open" and "closed" parishes', *Economic History Review* 41 (1989), pp. 51–73.

[10] M. A. Havinden, *Estate Villages: A study of the Berkshire Villages of Ardington and Lockinge* (London 1966).

community elite composed mainly of yeomen, farmers, and minor gentry. They are fundamental to our understanding of the structure and mentality of rural England in the sixteenth and seventeenth centuries. However, they became less typical over time and a diminishing force by the nineteenth century, when elite landownership dominated the English countryside. Those landowners did not create mansions and parks in half of England's villages. Many villages were predominantly owned by absentee great landowners who undertook similar changes in land organisation and farm size, but remained more distanced from parish issues.

This book bridges a gap in our knowledge of the dynamics of rural society, by focusing on changes in social relationships as well as in landscape and farming practice. It places them in the context of what was going on in the landowning family: the dynamics of dynastic aggrandisement, the role of demographic chance, and of external disaster in altering outlooks and planning horizons. It maps the changing relationship of the landed elite to court, parliament and the merchant and financial community, and their relative influence in decision-making over two centuries.

The book's subject is the Verney family and the three parishes of Middle, East, and Steeple Claydon in north Buckinghamshire. The period from 1600 to the early nineteenth century is covered by one of the richest archives for an upper gentry family in Great Britain. It spans the years from the first residence at Claydon of the Verney family to the extinction of the first Verney dynasty. In that time they rose from a middling gentry family with court connections, to the upper gentry with knighthoods and baronetcy, and finally into the peer-age. In the middle of the eighteenth century they were leading landowners in Buckinghamshire, vying in size of estates and political ambitions with their near-neighbours, the Temple/Grenville clan based at Stowe and Wotton Under-wood. At its height their family income brought them just within the class of great landowners who were at the pinnacle of the nation's political and social system. After the financial debacle suffered by the Verneys in the 1780s, the family recovered to retain the Claydon estate, but little other land. Their estate around Claydon in the 1820s has been substantially maintained through the nineteenth and twentieth centuries. The year 1820 is therefore a natural end point for this narrative of dynastic endeavour.

The same period also saw the transformation of the three village communities where the Verneys held sway. In 1600 all three villages had similar populations, social structures, and farming patterns, though Steeple Claydon was somewhat larger than East and Middle Claydon. East Claydon parish included the set-tlement of Botolph (often called Bottle) Claydon. All three parishes had free-holders and open fields characteristic of a majority of parishes across southern and midland England at that period. There were copyhold tenants who farmed land as their fathers had before them. There were also resident minor gentry families in all three parishes. Middle Claydon was exceptional in having a large manor house, and substantial pasture enclosures. The Giffords who built the house had been there since the 1530s, not as owners but as lessees of the manor estate.

By 1820 ownership, landscape, and village communities had been transformed. Middle Claydon House became the main seat of the Verney family in 1620. By buying out freeholders and copyholders, enclosing and converting the open fields to pasture, they turned the parish into a 'closed' village which in 1798 had only eight farming families in a parish population which had fallen from a mid-seventeenth-century peak of around 250 to only 103. East and Steeple Claydon had significantly different histories. The Verneys gained a significant foothold in East Claydon in 1662, but lost it before becoming the dominant landowners in 1729, with exclusive control from around 1765. After 1730 they began to change it as they had Middle Claydon, and by 1820 the whole parish had been divided into pasture farms held on yearly tenancies by specialist dairy farmers. After enclosure the population stabilised and did not rise at the end of the century, unlike most parishes in southern England. Steeple Claydon followed a different path. The Verneys deliberately thwarted its enclosure in the 1680s fearing the development of a rival estate close at hand. The Chaloner estates were sold in small lots to local farmers and investors, and Steeple Claydon remained an open-field village for 115 years. Its freeholders and copyholders farmed the old systems with ingenuity, in an adverse economic climate for small farms. Many diversified into trades and service occupations. They divided their houses and built new ones on common land at the edge of the parish. By 1801 the population had more than doubled to 646, and Steeple Claydon had taken on many of the characteristics of an 'open' village. Although the Verneys bought land there as it became available, they had only acquired about one third of the acreage by 1795.

The Verneys were a powerful ingredient in the formation of differentiated societies and economies in the three Claydon parishes between 1600 and 1820. Much has changed in people's breadth of experience, education, mobility, and outspokenness over the last 200 years, but patterns of social and physical development and differentiation set in the Claydons by 1800 did not substantially alter until fifty years ago.

This brief synopsis raises basic issues about the roles of landed families and the development of village societies and typologies in the transformation of English rural society between the sixteenth and the nineteenth centuries. No single microstudy can provide a model that explains the methods or timing of changes, but the Verneys experienced much that was typical of their social group. They participated in local politics and as members of parliament, but never held high political office, or gained substantial wealth from politics. However, they retained long-term connections with mercantile and financial groups that were unusual amongst their peers, but more common amongst the puritan gentry of the early seventeenth century with whom the Verneys should be grouped by tradition and education.[11] Their city links after 1640 provide a fascinating parallel with the family's fifteenth-century rise as London merchants from a Buckinghamshire gentry base. An openness to merchant ideas and knowledge was characteristic of Sir Ralph Verney's views from 1640 onwards. He maintained cordial contacts over decades with merchants who had helped him during exile in France. He was persuaded that apprenticeship to one of the great merchant companies was an acceptable career for his younger son John, who unexpectedly succeeded him.

Later contact with merchant and financial wealth came through the Verneys' unusually consistent policy of finding heiresses from non-landed families to marry their eldest sons. This major factor in their eighteenth-century expansion had two drawbacks. One was that the family's social networks locally and nationally were narrowed. They were not near the centre of fashionable groupings at court, in politics, or in aristocratic society as they had been between 1610 and 1685. The second was perhaps less predictable but devastating. Constant marriage to heiresses, themselves the products of small families, reduced family size and eventually produced a childless marriage. In 1810 the direct Verney line failed, and their estates passed to the Calverts, with whom they had strong links by marriage. They changed their names and took on the mantle of the Verney tradition in the nineteenth and twentieth centuries.

Many features of the Verneys' family history were typical of the landed upper gentry and aristocracy, but they also had their idiosyncrasies. How typical were the Claydons of English village community experience? Every village has unique qualities, but also lies in an agricultural and landscape region. The Claydons lie in a region of north Buckinghamshire that is part of that well-studied region, midland England, where the complexities of open-field agriculture and enclosure have tantalised rural historians for generations. They are some fifty miles north, and slightly west of London, well within the 100-mile radius of London considered acceptable for elite landownership in the eighteenth century. Yet the Claydons remain amongst the most rural areas of the south midlands even early in the twenty-first century, lying between the M1 and M40 motorways and not within easy commuting range of London. Only in the last thirty years has there been substantial building of modern 'infill' housing for local urban commuters.

In the seventeenth and eighteenth centuries the Claydons lay in a countryside of villages and market towns. Even Buckingham and Aylesbury struggled towards 3,000 inhabitants. Until the 1720s East and Middle Claydon lay on one of London's main arterial roads to the midlands, running through Wendover and Aylesbury to Buckingham, Brackley and Banbury to Birmingham, and clearly

---

[11] J. T. Cliffe, *The Puritan Gentry* (London 1984), pp. 108ff.

described by Ogilby in his road map of 1675.[12] There was traffic of carriers' wagons, stagecoaches, and herds and flocks of animals, while East Claydon's inn was a recognised staging post for many services. This road gave easy access to London for correspondence and goods between Verney family members and their estate officials. Two miles away, Winslow was a local market and information source for Claydon's farmers and the Verneys' stewards. However, Buckingham and Aylesbury were less important than Bicester in Oxfordshire and Leighton Buzzard in Bedfordshire for marketing the livestock and dairy produce of Claydon's tenant farmers.

The Claydons, not surprisingly given their name, lie on thick and heavy Oxford clay subsoil. Water is plentiful, with springs rising from the gentle slopes at the south, and running northwards to Padbury and Claydon brooks and onwards to the Ouse at Bedford, and out to the Wash. The woodland to the south lies on the watershed between the Thames and the Ouse. Among the thin-soiled woods are steep dips to the south and south-west with long views, and not far away the hillier Jurassic outcroppings at Quainton and Brill. The underlying clay is too heavy to produce good soil under modern soil classifications, and is not suitable for highly intensive exploitation. It had been usable for arable cultivation under the medieval open-field system, but was equally if not better suited to pastoral agriculture.

The woodlands are a reminder that in the eleventh and twelfth centuries this area was part of Bernwood Royal Hunting Forest, part of a series of linked medieval hunting reserves that stretched from Oxford to Stamford on the Lincolnshire/Northamptonshire borders. Bernwood had contracted to three parishes by the fifteenth century and was disafforested in 1632.[13] Yet many parishes in north-west Buckinghamshire retain the imprint of a forest past to the present day. They have remained well wooded over the centuries, especially where there have been elite owners. In other areas extensive commons, sometimes shared between two or more parishes, survived into the eighteenth century.

There were many deserted villages in the fifteenth and sixteenth centuries on the heavy clay of Ashendon hundred where Middle and East Claydon lay, while many other villages underwent considerable partial enclosure. Both East and Steeple Claydon had enclosed at least one third of their area before their open fields were eliminated in the eighteenth century. Much of this wooded area of north-west Buckinghamshire was gradually put down to pasture by 1800 and used for dairying – for cheese, later butter, and after the coming of the railways liquid milk and milk products. It was part of a farming region

[12] John Ogilby, *Britannia: By a Geographical and Historical Description of the Principal Roads Thereof* (London 1675).

[13] J. Broad and R. Hoyle (eds.), *Bernwood: The Life and Afterlife of a Forest* (Preston 1997).

that stretches almost thirty miles from the area around Thame in Oxfordshire, through north-west Buckinghamshire to western Northamptonshire.

The Claydons display many typical features of rural parishes in southern and midland England. No urban settlements within striking distance could compete for economic influence with London. Many parishes were suitable for conversion into the seats of the landed elite, and to the agricultural practices of a highly market-orientated rural economy. It was an area in which peasant farmers were rapidly becoming transformed in the seventeenth and eighteenth centuries into either prosperous tenant farmers, or a land-poor group of village artisans and labourers. The variety of trades and crafts that were scattered through town and countryside often disappeared under fierce competition from specialised and innovative industries in the north and the midlands, and from the sweated trades in London in the eighteenth and nineteenth centuries. Long-standing industries with local prominence and primarily regional markets, such as Brill ceramics and Long Crendon needle-making, went into terminal decline. Weaving and spinning were increasingly confined to the very poor with the roughest of materials, hemp and flax, often provided by overseers for work-fare projects. Leather working was once important, but declined with regional specialisation in the eighteenth century. Lace making flourished in the late seventeenth and eighteenth centuries, but by the mid-nineteenth century gradually lost its battle to compete with machine-made lace from Nottingham, and survived only as a 'craft' industry. These changes characterised much of southern England and can be observed in the transformation of the Claydons over 200 years.

This study is possible because of the size of the surviving archive at Claydon House, which gives both continuity and detail over long periods. Its greatest riches lie in the correspondence, which is fullest for the years from 1630 to 1745. Estate papers have survived more patchily leaving no long run of rentals or accounts. The papers after 1745 are voluminous but polyglot, covering some areas in great detail, but leaving us in ignorance of all but the basic outline of other major events. The estate charters and deeds go back to the thirteenth century, and provide a substantial record of family settlements, land purchases, and leasing agreements through the seventeenth and eighteenth centuries. The whole is a remarkable testimony to a family's interest in, and caring for, its past members and endeavours.

The Verneys and their archives have attracted historians since the middle of the nineteenth century. John Bruce edited and commented on the early papers and charters. Florence Nightingale's sister, Parthenope Verney, with great assistance from S. R. Gardiner, shaped and selected four volumes of Verney memoirs covering the seventeenth-century history of the family, and directly quoting from many of the letters. The four volumes were ably crafted and remain of great use to historians, though their focus on individuals and their activities has its limitations. Parthenope's daughter-in-law, Margaret, assisted on two volumes and produced two volumes of her own from the eighteenth-century letters. These volumes are much less digestible than their predecessors, but contain many interesting extracts from the letters and papers.[14]

In the second half of the twentieth century, Peter Verney's book, *The Standard Bearer* was a readable and lively account of Sir Edmund Verney's life and career, but added little to our knowledge. Lawrence Stone also became interested in the Verneys and produced a short article based on the archive. More importantly he set two research students to work on the papers. In the late 1960s Miriam Slater worked on family relations in the seventeenth century, though her thesis and book are almost exclusively about the 1640s. More recently Susan Whyman has researched the career of Sir John Verney, sensitively illuminating the cultural history of the late seventeenth and early eighteenth centuries, particularly the relationships of town and country, and merchant and landed society. I have benefited greatly from their research and from conversations with them, particularly with Susan Whyman, but their studies are tangential to the central themes of this book. Finally, Susan Ranson's labours under the auspices of the Claydon House Trust have recently made available for the first time a substantial and serviceable catalogue and part calendar of those parts of the Claydon House archives that have not been microfilmed.[15]

This study takes the form of parallel chapters covering family and dynastic matters, estate management and community social relationships in three periods. The first concentrates on the early seventeenth century, dealing with the family's choices and dilemmas before, during, and after the English Civil War. The chapter on the estate and community focuses primarily on Middle Claydon and its transformation, with relatively little on East and Steeple Claydon. The period closes in 1657 when Sir Ralph Verney's son Edmund came of age, and the financial crisis of the Civil War had been overcome, while at Claydon the freeholders had been bought out, copyholds extinguished, and enclosure was complete. A new era in estate management and village relationships was beginning.

The second section covers a time span from 1657 through to *c.* 1740. This period is the most fully documented from the Verney archives. The family's financial and marriage strategies and land purchases are analysed in a period when city money as well as dowries swelled the family coffers. By 1730 the family had a permanent residence close to the capital, but Middle Claydon was

---

[14] J. Bruce, *Letters and Papers of the Verney Family down to the End of the Year 1639*, Camden Society 56 (1853); F. P. Verney, and M. M. Verney, *Verney Memoirs of the Seventeenth Century* (4 vols. 1892–6); M. M. Verney, *Verney Letters of the Eighteenth Century* (2 vols. 1930); P. Verney, *The Standard Bearer: The Story of Sir Edmund Verney, Knight-Marshal to King Charles I* (1963).

[15] M. Slater, *Family Life in the Seventeenth Century: The Verneys of Claydon House* (London 1984); Whyman, *Sociability and Power*; S. R. Ranson, 'The Verney papers: a catalogue' (t.s. 1994, available at the Historical Manuscripts Commission).

still extensively used and its management carefully monitored and directed. The chapters on the village communities again highlight Middle Claydon, analysing the management and enlargement of farms, and the manipulation of the village community through control of housing, charity, and poor relief. It examines those features that made village politics considerably more than acquiescence in landlord power.

The third section covers the period from around 1700 to the early nineteenth century. The dynastic strand focuses on the life and career of the second Earl Verney who in chance circumstances found himself with a vast fortune to spend, yet left no children to inherit the Verney patrimony. It charts the expansion of his estates, the re-modelling of Claydon House, and his forays into politics, business, and finance before he fell into indebtedness and bankruptcy. His successor, the last Verney of the first line, Baroness Fermanagh, rescued the Claydon estate and re-fashioned it to its modern form. The chapter on the Claydons compares the long-term development of the three Claydon parishes from 1660 to 1820. It makes more use of parish records, taxation and militia list materials to explain important aspects not covered by the Verney archive. The conclusion examines some long-term trends for the Verneys and the Claydon villages, and marks out the key elements at the heart of the transformation of rural society.

Every village study has to make best use of available sources. At Claydon the letters and papers form an enormously rich source of detailed information. They are biased towards the landlord's point of view, but also reveal the micro-politics of village communities. The official record of Quarter Sessions, and central courts is much thinner, partly because dominant landowners discouraged litigation and themselves mediated in village disputes. However, good parish records from all three parishes have survived, lacking only the overseers' accounts at Steeple Claydon. These have made possible a reconstitution of Middle Claydon and a detailed analysis of the overseers' and churchwardens' accounts and charity records. It has often been possible to link these to the letters and trace the fortunes of families and individuals over decades. I have combined these sources with others, such as probate inventories, that have sparsely or sporadically survived, to chart the changes in the society and economy of three Buckinghamshire villages and the family that owned and influenced them profoundly over two hundred formative years.

Part I

Re-establishing a gentry family 1600–1657

2   A gentry family in county and court society 1603–1642

The Verneys established their country seat at Middle Claydon in north Buckinghamshire in 1620. They had ancient connections in the county, but only after crucial events in the first two decades of the seventeenth century did they make Claydon their county residence, taking over the existing large manor house in a parish where they were manorial lords. Over the next fifty years they consolidated their estates in the immediate neighbourhood, and then expanded them until in the third quarter of the eighteenth century they vied with the Grenvilles of Stowe and Wotton Underwood for landed and political pre-eminence in the northern or 'Vale' part of the county.

The Verney family can be traced back to around 1200, and by 1230 they had established links in the Vale of Aylesbury. By a marriage alliance they acquired Fleet Marston, some eight miles from Middle Claydon, and close to Aylesbury. It came to be their country residence for some 200 years.[1] However, in the fifteenth century the family moved to London and made vital connections in both city and court circles just as they were to do in the seventeenth century. One Ralph Verney was a London mercer who progressed through city offices to become sheriff in 1456, mayor in 1465, and was knighted and represented the City in the parliament of 1472.[2] His son John married into another city family, the Whittinghams, whose estate and house at Pendley near Tring became the family seat for over a hundred years.[3] Ralph used his wealth to purchase property in Buckinghamshire. In 1465 he acquired the manor and estate of Middle Claydon from a London draper. At Claydon there was a substantial mansion that was let to the Gifford family for the next 150 years. They rebuilt and extended the house so that in 1662 it had more hearths than any other in north Buckinghamshire.

The Verneys were drawn into the lower echelons of court life under Henry VII and Henry VIII. They were part of a circle with early Protestant views that included the Braye family and the Peckham and Cheyne families who also had Buckinghamshire property. Verneys attended the christening of Edward VI in

---

[1] Bruce, *Letters and Papers of the Verney Family*, pp. 4–6; Verneys are found amongst the Fleet Marston charters continuously in the period 1323–1401.

[2] Bruce, *Letters and Papers of the Verney Family*, pp. 13–14.

[3] L. M. Munby, *The Hertfordshire Landscape* (London 1977), pp. 133–4.

15

1537, and held office in the household of Ann of Cleves.[4] When the Catholic Queen Mary came to the throne in 1553, Edmund Verney was implicated in the Duke of Northumberland's attempts to put Lady Jane Grey on the throne. He and his brother Francis sat as MPs for Buckinghamshire in the parliament of 1555. Active in opposition to Mary and involved in the Dudley conspiracy of 1556, they were arrested but eventually reprieved.[5] Both brothers died soon after and were succeeded by another brother, also called Edmund. For the next forty years the family played a greater role in county life. In 1570 Pendley Manor was prepared for a visit from Queen Elizabeth.[6] 'Old' Sir Edmund, as he is customarily known, was sheriff for Buckinghamshire and Hertfordshire. He was knighted in 1597, and died three years later. He married three times, and his second and third wives each bore him a son. The half-brothers were named Francis and Edmund. His third wife, Mary Blakeney, also twice widowed, had a daughter by a previous marriage, and secured her future position by persuading her husband to make a settlement, confirmed by private Act of Parliament, dividing his estates equally between Francis and Edmund.[7] This broke the family practice of the two previous generations when property passed by custom or settlement to the eldest surviving male.[8] Mary Blakeney further increased her power and influence by marrying her daughter by a previous marriage, Ursula St Barbe, to her fifteen-year-old stepson, Francis Verney, in 1599.[9]

At his death in 1600, Old Sir Edmund owned property across north-west Hertfordshire and central Buckinghamshire that was substantially the same as his grandfather had held at his death in 1525.[10] Apart from his seat at Pendley near Tring, straddling the county border, he had a London residence in Drury Lane where Edmund was born. At his death Francis received the family seat at Pendley and several other properties in Hertfordshire and Buckinghamshire under the terms of the Act of Parliament, while Edmund's lands were in Buckinghamshire, at Chalfont, Mursley, and Middle Claydon. The widowed Mary Blakeney found herself coping with a difficult sixteen-year-old stepson, and a ten-year-old son. Francis soon rebelled against his arranged marriage with Ursula St Barbe, living independently in London where he ran up considerable debts. By one account he was spending at the rate of over £3,000 a year even

[4] J. Gairdner and others, *Letters and Papers, Foreign and Domestic, Henry VIII*, 21 vols. and 2 vols. of addenda (1862–1932), vol. XII, pt 2, no. 911.

[5] D. M. Loades, *Two Tudor Conspiracies* (2nd edn Bangor 1992), pp. 226, 244–5; the pardons for Edmund are in ClH 10/1 and 10/2. P. W. Hasler (ed.), *History of Parliament: The House of Commons, 1558–1603* (London 1981).

[6] Bodl. MS Rawlinson A 195 c321.   [7] ClH 2/1288–9.

[8] *LJ* i, p. 222; the Act was 39 Elizabeth private c10. In the discussion of the 1605 bill it was made plain that 'Sir Edmund Verney did follow the Bill himself and laboured divers friends in it' *CJ* i, p. 290.

[9] ClH 1/15 settlement dated 4 June 1599.

[10] Bruce, *Letters and Papers of the Verney Family*, p. 44.

before he reached his majority.[11] As soon as he reached adulthood he separated from his wife, providing her with £50 a year for the rest of her life.[12] He
also challenged his father's settlement of the family lands and unsuccessfully
tried to reverse the Act of Parliament.[13] With large debts and unable to secure
his claims he took the drastic step of selling all his lands in 1607–8. He went
abroad leaving his uncles Urian and Ralph his remaining assets and also his
debts.[14] Francis's precise activities remain uncharted until his last days but he
probably joined a band of English mercenaries, pirates, and adventurers led by
John Gifford, whose family leased Claydon House. He was admitted to hospital in Messina in Sicily on 25 August 1615, and died there on the 6 September
following.[15]

When Francis Verney sold up and left England, his brother Edmund was still
under age. He spent some time abroad, visiting the courts of France and Italy,
and seeing the war in the Low Countries before returning to England in 1610.
We do not know exactly whose patronage brought him the post of chief Sewer
in the household of Prince Henry, King James I's eldest son, and a knighthood
in the following year. However, the family had retained court connections and
one of his uncles was a royal falconer. After Prince Henry's death in November
1612, Sir Edmund's position transferred to the household of the future Charles
I, in whose service he spent the rest of his life.

Sir Edmund Verney's successful career at court spanned more than thirty
years. He rose to be Knight Marshal of the household, a close confidant of
Charles, and of the Duke of Buckingham. But the family resources supporting
his position were very limited. He had to pay jointure pensions to his mother,
and his sister-in-law (her daughter) totalling £250 a year from a much reduced
estate centred on Middle Claydon and Mursley. He also needed to support a court
lifestyle. After Francis had sold Pendley and Quainton there was no country seat
available to the family. The most lucrative parts of Middle Claydon, the manor
house and demesne were on long lease to the Gifford family which would not
end until 1634.[16]

---

[11] Bodl. MS Rawlinson B83 fo. 107b. He may have written a rather poor revenge play, and his
servant was reported to have been slain in a fight in 1604. See Bodl. MS English Poets e.5 *The
Tragedy of Antipoe*: the date on this is 1622, after his death, so it is either a later copy, or there
may have been some other Francis Verney.
[12] CIH 1/18. This was paid for the next 64 years.
[13] Bruce, *Letters and Papers of the Verney Family*, p. 94, *CJ* i, pp. 277, 286, 290; CIH 1/16–22
covering the years 1604–7.
[14] CIH 1/23–31. For aspects of the debt settlement see *Calendar of State Papers, Domestic series,
of the Reign of Charles I, 1625–1626 (1648–1649, etc.), Preserved in . . . Her Majesty's Public
Record Office (1625–38)*, ed. J. Bruce, 23 vols. (London, 1858–97) (hereafter *CSPD*), 1603–10,
p. 182.
[15] CIH 1/32 notarised documents from Sicily proving his death. *CSPD* 1611–18, p. 425, shows
government knowledge of this. Sir Francis was reported as dead 'at the galleys in Sicily'.
[16] Since 1608 the lease had been assigned by the Giffords to one Martin Lister CIH 2/45 10 May
1608.

Throughout the next thirty years, Sir Edmund Verney walked a financial tight-rope. He exploited his position at court to extract grants and perquisites, which promised future income and high returns but required immediate cash invest-ments he could ill afford. The family struggled with an increasing debt, and a range of obligations, and was eventually forced to take drastic steps to rectify the position. Sir Edmund's endeavours were greatly helped by his mother's support. Indeed, their joint efforts on a variety of fronts inculcated the intense dynastic loyalty and strong drive to consolidate and expand the family estates and income that characterised successive family heads over the next 150 years.

Sir Edmund exploited his estates and increased his landed income to compen-sate for the high inflation of the period. The family also used marriages to forge alliances and expand their estates. At the age of twenty-three, Sir Edmund mar-ried the eldest daughter of wealthy gentry neighbours with a long tradition in the law, the Dentons of Hillesden. The match was made in 1612 in the interlude be-tween Sir Edmund's service with Prince Henry and Prince Charles. Margaret's dowry of £2,300 was a worthwhile prize, particularly as Sir Edmund's income from land was probably less than £800 a year.[17] The couple lived for some time at Hillesden house with Margaret's parents, and it was there that their first child, Ralph, was born in 1613. He was the first of twelve children, six boys and six girls, ten of whom grew to adulthood. Their support was to be a major burden on the estate over the next fifty years.

Sir Edmund's access to patronage and connections expanded rapidly after Charles I's accession in 1625. Soon after, Sir Edmund was granted the office of Knight Marshal, with a salary of 10s a day, and a pension of £200 a year.[18] With the office he became titular Gaoler of the Marshalsea prison, which brought in an additional £80 to £90 a year. Verney's limited landed income was probably the reason why he received an additional pension for life of £200 a year one month later, specifically 'to enable him to wait on the King'.[19] Sir Edmund participated in projects and enterprises of various kinds, obtaining a Patent for controlling the sale of tobacco in 1619, and seeking another to license London Hackney cabs in the 1630s.[20] He petitioned for other Patents such as the enrolling of apprentices in London, and the quality control of woollen yarn.[21] Patents were politically contentious, and highly competitive, and there were endless difficulties with

[17] See CIH 1/1292–3 dated 2 December 1612 and 27 January 1612/13. The Dentons wanted a jointure of £400 a year but had to settle for less.
[18] Cal. Patent Rolls 1 Car. I pt 10 no. 1 dated 16 February 1626.
[19] PRO SP39/18 no. 125 dated 25 November 1625.
[20] CIH 9/7 shows that in 1622 the tobacco Patent was run by a London merchant, Thomas Hanson, with Sir Edmund sharing the profits with two other men. Cf. *CSPD* 1619–23, p. 47, showing that the original rent was only £100 a year; *CSPD* 1619–23, p. 138 of April 1620 shows a continuing Crown interest in the income possibilities of tobacco taxation.
[21] PRO SP16/377 fo. 1, Petition of 1637 for enrolling London apprentices; other projects included Patents for supplying turf. F. P. Verney and M. M. Verney, *Verney Memoirs*, I, pp. 108–10.

the tobacco and Hackney cab grants.[22] Verney's true income from Patents is unknown, but the Hackney cab Patent grant implies payments of £600 a year to Sir Edmund.[23] Sir Edmund's court connections also provided entry into a world of land projects; £600 was invested in 250 acres of fen lands at Deeping in Lincolnshire.[24] The Crown's disposal of various Royal Forests gave Verney the opportunity to buy lands when Bernwood was disafforested in 1632.[25] Verney's grant of 83 acres may have cost as much as £800, but he may have received concessions or discounts.[26]

Court life and contacts brought several promised gifts of money (more than was ever received) and an additional pension of £200 a year from Charles I. His steward masterminded wood sales at the disafforestation of Bernwood from which over £1,000 remained unaccounted.[27] The purchase of Bernwood lands was part of a strategy to develop a presence in Buckinghamshire and raise his profile in local political life. In 1620, he re-purchased the lease on Middle Claydon House and demesnes at a cost of £3,639, a sum he could not easily afford, to provide himself with a country seat. It was £600 more than the tenant, Lister, had paid for his sublease when it was twelve years longer in 1608. Prince Charles apparently promised to help him by paying £4,000 in four annual instalments, 'for my better maintenance and supporting myself to do my best service to the said Prince', but only £1,000 was paid, and three years later Sir Edmund simply stated 'thereby I became much in dette'.[28] The re-purchase of the lease gave the Verneys a rural seat appropriate to their county status. It was also important in enabling them to reorganise the estate and its management without undue interference.[29]

After the Verneys re-purchased Claydon House they gained county office in Buckinghamshire under the patronage of the Duke of Buckingham, who

---

[22] Bruce, *Letters and Papers of the Verney Family*, pp. 231, 233–4, 255, 258, 265–6. On the complex bids to operate cabs see K. Sharpe, *The Personal Rule of Charles I* (Newhaven, CT and London 1992), pp. 405–6. On the beginnings of tobacco licensing see M. W. Beresford, 'The beginning of retail tobacco licences 1632–41', *Yorkshire Bulletin of Economic and Social Research* 7:2 (1955), pp. 128–43. Verney was already having to fight against attempts to extract more money from him in 1634, see PRO SP16/283.

[23] CIH 7/9 unexecuted agreement dated 18 February 1640.   [24] CIH 2/1881 June 1636.

[25] On the general position see R. W. Hoyle (ed.), *The Estates of the English Crown, 1558–1640* (Cambridge 1992), pp. 353–88 and B. Sharp, *In Contempt of all Authority: Rural Artisans and Riot in the West of England, 1586–1660* (Berkeley, CA and London 1980). On Bernwood see J. Broad and R. Hoyle, *Bernwood: Life and Afterlife of a Forest* (Preston 1997).

[26] Broad and Hoyle, *Bernwood*, pp. 71–3, suggests that the Crown charged £10 an acre for the land it sold.

[27] PRO E112/161/47.   [28] Bruce, *Letters and Papers of the Verney Family*, p. 135.

[29] CIH 2/43. He borrowed the money, probably from Toby Palavicino, the heir to the rich fortunes of the Italian banking family in England. See L. Stone, *An Elizabethan: Sir Horatio Palavicino* (Oxford 1956), ch. 8, pp. 309–12. Palavicino's stepfather, Sir Oliver Cromwell, had served with Sir Edmund in Prince Henry's household, while the spendthrift Toby was moving in the Duke of Buckingham's circle in the early 1620s; see ch. 3 below.

was made Lord Lieutenant of Buckinghamshire in 1616. While the Dentons had been named amongst the Deputy Lieutenants in 1616, Sir Edmund was not added until after Charles's accession. The award of the Lieutenancy of Whaddon Chase in 1622 also raised Sir Edmund's county status. It was a prize fought over by leading county families in an earlier period, and gave Sir Edmund access to unlimited supplies of venison – a valuable commodity in the court and County worlds of patronage.[30] Sir Edmund was MP for Buckingham in 1624 and for Wycombe in 1640, when his son Ralph took one of the Aylesbury seats.

Buckinghamshire gentry politics in the 1620s and 1630s were at the centre of disputes over finance and religion that assumed national importance. Opposition to forced loans and Ship Money was fostered by powerful and articulate gentry families of national political weight in parliament and the courts. The Verneys were courtiers, dependent on royal favours and perquisites for their lifestyle. When the Duke of Buckingham moved to exclude the Crown's opponents from the magistracy in 1626, Verney's court and Country positions made him an important ally, but one who could not afford either to take too independent a stance, or offend his neighbours too deeply. Sir Edmund trod this fine line remarkably successfully. His marriage links to the Dentons enabled him to re-legitimise his connections with old county families. His Protestant credentials going back to the reigns of Henry VIII and Mary, also helped his acceptance by the Hampdens, Goodwins, and Temples who were highly influential on County society through the conflicts over forced loans and Ship Money. They were enhanced when he sent his son Ralph to Magdalen Hall Oxford, where his young brother-in-law, William Denton, was also studying, and which had a Puritan reputation. At Claydon, Sir Edmund was reprimanded for 'slackness' about following the Laudian prescription for church fittings and altar rails in the early 1630s, although the churchwardens' accounts show money spent on new altar rails in 1634.[31] His beliefs may have assisted him in winning the Long Parliament seat at High Wycombe where there had been strong local controversy over the endowment of a lectureship to promote Puritan religious values.[32] When Civil War broke out Sir Edmund stressed that his solid commitment to the Royal cause was based on personal loyalty to Charles I, not a belief in his policies. His brave death in the thick of the battle of Edgehill was in keeping with the straightforward character of the man.

---

[30] For patronage systems in Buckinghamshire before the Civil War see L. L. Peck, *Court Patronage and Corruption in Early Stuart England* (London 1990), ch. 4, and pp. 83–7. Bruce, *Letters and Papers of the Verney Family*, p. 108. On the importance of venison see S. Whyman, *Sociability and Power*, ch. 1.

[31] E. C. R. Brinkworth, 'The Laudian Church in Buckinghamshire', *University of Birmingham Historical Journal* 5 (1955), pp. 31–50. BCRO PR52/5/1.

[32] S. S. Seaver, *The Puritan Lectureships: The Politics of Religious Dissent 1560–1662* (Stanford 1970), p. 89.

However, the Verneys' finances, not their county connections, were at the heart of Sir Edmund's matchmaking for his eldest son Ralph. In 1629, at the age of sixteen, Ralph married Mary Blacknall, the thirteen-year-old heiress of an Abingdon gentry family. Her parents had died in the plague of 1625 leaving Mary property in Berkshire and Oxfordshire. A complex dispute over the wardship between four relatives led to its transfer to Sir Edmund Verney, who fended off legal action before the marriage ceremony. Even afterwards Mary's relatives (with whom she was still living) tried to persuade Mary to revoke the marriage, but it was consummated in 1631, and proved a loving and enduring relationship.[33] The Blacknall marriage exemplifies perfectly the dilemmas faced by the Verney family. During the period from 1620 to 1640 they constantly incurred debts in appropriating assets and financial opportunities of considerable long-term potential. They borrowed £1,000 to pay for Mary Blacknall's wardship, probably from Lord Dacre. The Blacknall property that came as Mary's dowry was eventually worth around £16,000.

Money that the family could ill afford was laid out in other directions. Sir Edmund did not have a suitable residence in London. In 1634 he took a long lease on two of the Earl of Bedford's fine new houses in the Piazza, Covent Garden.[34] They looked the part, but cost £160 a year in rent allowing him to accommodate his mother, and sublet rooms to the lawyer Nathaniel Hobart. Family debts rose considerably. There is no clear statement of their financial position in the 1620s and 1630s, but they never seemed to have surplus cash. London society living involved a wide range of obligations and transactions between elite families, and with the tradesmen who supplied them. A whole variety of bonds, statutes, and legal agreements show that the Verneys were simultaneously borrowers and lenders for much of the period.[35]

The family periodically needed to raise money to re-finance its obligations. The expensive re-purchase of the Middle Claydon lease in 1620 triggered one series of land sales. By 1623, it must have become obvious that Prince Charles could or would not pay more than his initial £1,000 contribution, so between 1619 and 1624 the Verneys sold all their land in Mursley to yeomen, clergymen, and one absentee gentleman, for a total of £2,885.[36] At the same time they re-leased farms in Middle Claydon for fines that raised £300, offsetting the £140 spent on purchasing small amounts of freehold land in Middle Claydon.

When Ralph Verney came of age in 1634 Sir Edmund could re-settle the estates to give the family finances greater flexibility in raising additional loans. In the spring of 1635 he made a new family settlement, declaring Ralph heir to his estates, re-establishing primogeniture, but including one major variation

<hr />

[33] Bruce, *Letters and Papers of the Verney Family*, pp. 138–45.   [34] CIH 2/1966 20 June 1634.
[35] CIH 7/10–33 give some flavour of the intermeshing of names and transactions.
[36] CIH 1/35 1 March 1622/3; CIH 2/1319–25, 2/1297. They retained the manorial rights, which they sold in 1665.

in descent by promoting his third and fourth sons, Henry and Edmund, above his black sheep second son Thomas.[37] At the same time, however, the tenants at Middle Claydon were forced to re-negotiate their leases with higher rents.[38] The real crisis came in 1638–9 when Sir Edmund raised a mortgage of £3,250 on Middle Claydon from Francis Drake, who had recently married one of Margaret Verney's sisters. The loan was carefully secured with a long lease requiring payments of £500 a year for the first ten years.[39] Sir Edmund also borrowed £1,000 from another Denton sister, Elizabeth Isham, who later told Sir Ralph 'if your father had not had my money, he must have sold some of your lands'.[40]

The £4,250 raised in 1638 was not enough, and a year later Sir Edmund raised more money by persuading his son to pay him £4,000. In return Sir Ralph gained immediate income from part of the Middle Claydon estate, and took on responsibility for paying his aunt's and grandmother's jointure payments. To raise the money, Ralph raided his wife's estates. Between 1637 and 1640 he sold off lands from the Blacknall estates to the value of over £3,500.[41] No large single item of expenditure explains the mounting debts. They probably simply reflect the cost of Sir Edmund's court lifestyle. Many London trade bills amongst the letters of the period suggest a developing credit crisis. Even after raising over £7,000 to pay off debts in the late 1630s, short-term indebtedness again rose above £7,000 at Sir Edmund's death in 1642.

The rising cost of Sir Edmund's large family was an additional burden. Thomas, the second son, was financed for two transatlantic expeditions during the 1630s, and was always in debt and asking for money. The younger sons, Edmund and Henry, tried their luck in military careers, and if less demanding were not self-supporting. However six daughters needed dowries. No respectable country gentleman, let alone high office-holder at court, could leave his daughters without dowries. The early seventeenth century saw an inflation of dowries amongst the aristocracy that brought them up to the level of £5,000 to £10,000 by 1640. Sir Edmund himself had received £2,300. Mary Blacknall's inheritance was the equivalent of £16,000, though she was an heiress. The general level of dowry amongst the upper gentry of Warwickshire in the 1620s and 1630s was around £1,000, and Sir Edmund Verney decided that all his daughters should be provided with that amount. His eldest daughter Susannah would come of age in 1642, and three others would follow within five years.[42]

---

[37] ClH 1/59–64 covering various stages of the process in the period 1634–6.
[38] See below, p. 57.
[39] ClH1/636 1–3 May 1638. The rigorous timetable for repayment was linked to Drake's marriage settlement.
[40] Elizabeth Isham to srv 9 December 1644 R6; presumably her dower money, see ClH 8/73 where Sir Edmund Verney was trustee for £1,100.
[41] ClH 1/69 26 May 1639.
[42] Stone, *The Crisis of the Aristocracy*, pp. 637–41; A. Hughes, *Politics, Society and Civil War in Warwickshire 1620–1660* (Cambridge 1987), p. 34.

Sir Edmund attempted to secure their dowries independently of his own mortality, and of the vagaries of office-holding and court favours. In the rising political tensions of 1639, when Buckinghamshire was at the forefront of opposition to Charles I's money-raising expedients, he negotiated a deal. He exchanged one of his two Exchequer annuities of £200, and his salary of £182 as Knight Marshal, for a 21-year fixed term charge of £400 a year on the chief rent of the aulnage, an ancient tax on woollen cloth. He also waived claims on the Crown for £1,500 owed him by Charles.[43] The aulnage annuity was potentially worth £8,400 and could either be used as security for his daughters' marriage portions, or reserved for any debts or liabilities. Deeds earmarked specific amounts for two daughters, and during the 1640s marriage portions and annuities for younger sons always had first call on the money.

Sir Edmund's death at Edgehill in October 1642 marked a major turning point in family fortunes. He had improved the long-term family financial position, but at a high cost. The family's income when Francis Verney left England in 1607 was probably little more than £500 a year from Claydon woods, and Mursley lands and manorial rights, with no additional court income. In 1642 landed income was substantial, but spread over Berkshire and Oxfordshire as well as Buckinghamshire, as shown in figure 1. After redeeming the Middle Claydon lease, and changing estate management practice, Sir Edmund increased its income to over £1,200 a year. The purchase of fen land brought little income, but the Brill forest properties brought in £150 a year. The Blacknall estates acquired through wardship and marriage were originally a further £800 a year, but land sales had reduced them to around £600 in 1642. Court income is likely to have been at its height in the mid-1630s when annuities of £400 a year, income of £270 a year as Knight Marshal, and whatever his various Patents produced perhaps totalled £1,000 a year.

Gross family income was perhaps as high as £3,000 a year in 1642, but realistically much less for three reasons. Firstly, Sir Edmund's court income was fragile. Much depended on his continued office, and the King's personal favour. Furthermore in the contentious political atmosphere of the years immediately before the Civil War, many of Sir Edmund's Patents, land schemes, and court perquisites were the targets of Charles I's enemies. Perhaps Sir Edmund was all too aware of this. The move to the 21-year aulnage annuity was intended to provide for his younger children even if he died. The aulnage chief rent seemed a less vulnerable source of income than many others.

[43] CIH7/4 Letters Patent 25th July 1638 surrendering the 10 shillings a day as Knight Marshal in return for the aulnage annuity is also recorded as PRO C66/2804. That Sir Edmund believed the aulnage a safe way of getting Crown money is evidenced from a later document CIH 7/7 dated 30 June 1640 in which he was granted repayment of £1,000 lent to Charles I from the same source. Sir Ralph Verney's account of the transaction is set out in a letter of srv to wd 23 January/2 February 1647/8 R8. On the aulnage of the new draperies see J. Thirsk, *Economic Policy and Projects* (Oxford 1978), pp. 59–65 and N. J. Williams, 'Two documents concerning the new draperies', *Economic History Review* 2nd series, 4 (1951–2), pp. 353–5.

Figure 1 The Verney estates *c*. 1642.

A second area of vulnerability was family annuities and non-negotiable charges. Sir Edmund's mother was still alive, claiming £200 a year. His sister-in-law's £50 a year and the widow's jointure of £400 a year that would be payable if he died before his wife, made a total of £650 annually even before providing for his children. In early 1642 none of his younger sons was financially independent, no daughter was yet married, and the youngest daughters were aged twelve and seven respectively. The potential liability amounted to £5,000 payable in cash. Finally, court life was expensive, and a courtier was required to demonstrate financial ease if not conspicuous consumption. We cannot gauge the annual or cumulative cost of this life style. Along the way, however, we can point to considerable cash sums they raised for specific investments. Overall the repurchase of Claydon, the land investments, the wardship, the Covent Garden house lease, and various Patents must have cost a minimum of £6,000. When we add the cost of journeys to Spain in 1623 and Scotland in 1639, and various loans to the Crown, the burden looks even more significant, perhaps as much as £10,000. Despite sales and mortgages that raised almost £8,000 in 1638–9 and some efforts at retrenchment, when Sir Edmund died in 1642 the debt was again significant.

After his father's death Sir Ralph took stock of the financial situation. He found debts of over £8,400 on bond or Statute, and tradesmen's bills for several hundred pounds more. Half the family's landed income of *c*. £2,200 was earmarked to pay interest and the mortgage rent charge, and considerable sums were needed to support his dependants. This last figure would have been much higher had not both Sir Edmund's wife and mother died in the space of eighteen months in 1641–2. This saved over £600 a year in widows' pensions, but at the high cost of all the connections, advice, and support the older generation could provide. At the age of twenty-nine, Sir Ralph was head of the family, with complete responsibility for sorting out its financial obligations.

The problems were considerable by contemporary standards, but not insurmountable. Lawrence Stone suggested that debt interest of one sixth of gross family income, or a total debt of twice net income, was a figure at which a family needed to take remedial action over its debts. The Verneys owed far more than that, but Sir Ralph drew up a plan that would pay it off by a series of land sales.[44] Land at Brill, and Blacknall estates in Berkshire, were earmarked for sale, as well as the remnants of the Mursley estate (the manorial rights) and Green Haylie in Monks Risborough.[45]

Sir Ralph could make these sales easily because the various family properties acquired since 1628 had not been tied into a family settlement, nor encumbered

---

[44] CIH 4/5/2/28. This list of debts and the means of paying them off is undated but must have been made between October 1642 and the summer of 1643.

[45] This was an area of commons and woodland in the Chilterns above Monks Risborough held on long lease. See CIH 2/1296 and 2/1348–51.

with mortgages, or used as security for family annuities. Sir Ralph's plan showed that the income from the Claydon estate, by far the most substantial of the family's properties, was all but swallowed up by interest and annuity payments. Perhaps he was being a little morbid in placing his wife's jointure at the top of the list, but of the Claydon gross income of *c.* £1,200 a year he reckoned £1,050 a year was already spoken for. The largest charge was the annual payment of £500 to cousin Francis Drake to pay off old debts. But Sir Edmund's will had reinforced his commitment to provide for his younger sons Henry and Edmund, leaving them and two servants annuities totalling £90 a year.[46]

The plan to restructure the family finances provides interesting insights into the ephemeral nature of the benefits of Sir Edmund's twenty-five years of court service. Sir Ralph reckoned his father was owed over £3,150 he would never recover, not counting the £1,000 promised by Charles I. Of the various schemes, he considered the Deeping fen land was valueless, despite an investment of over £1,000. None of the Patents is mentioned, but his father's lease on the Marshalsea prison still had sixteen years to run, and was worth £70 a year net. The Brill land had enduring value, as had the lands that came as Mary Blacknall's dowry with the wardship. Sir Ralph even expected to extract residual benefits from the aulnage annuity once portions and annuities had been paid.

Sir Ralph's strategy involved a period of belt tightening for perhaps five or six years, during which he would have £800 to £1,000 a year for his own family's support. Thereafter he would be debt-free and have an income approaching £2,000 a year. It was a realistic scenario for a man of sober lifestyle without high political or social ambitions. It would consolidate the real material gains made by his father's high-risk family strategy, and justify it. Ultimately, Sir Ralph was to achieve most of these goals, but only after he had survived the personal, political, and financial traumas of the English Civil War and its aftermath.

[46] Sir Edmund Verney's will (PRO PROB16/3).

3   The Civil War and Interregnum 1642–1657

The English Civil War was a time of crisis and tragedy for the Verney family. The persons and story are well known and widely quoted from the Verney memoirs. Sir Ralph Verney lost his father, mother, and grandmother in 1641 and 1642. During the 1640s he exiled himself in France because of his principled stand against a religious oath in parliament. Living in relative poverty, he lost two of his children before his wife died from breast cancer. He was separated from his younger son John for long periods, while his brothers and sisters, all in their teens and twenties, needed his guidance, influence, and money to sustain them. He saw one brother die in battle and four of his sisters marry in difficult circumstances. Yet by no means all the family problems can be laid at the door of civil commotion, and this chapter attempts to disentangle some of the parallel strands whose coincidence made it a difficult time.

The Civil War had a considerable impact on the landed classes in English society. Land was subject to very considerable increases in taxation, despite the introduction of excise duties on a variety of everyday goods. Although the first Civil War lasted only from 1642 to 1646, high taxation lasted much longer, and was compounded in many areas by the continuing cost of quartering parliament's large army. These effects were national but uneven, with taxes pressing harder on southern than northern England.[1]

Warfare was probably more economically harmful than taxation but also more sporadic and localised. Few areas of the country escaped skirmishes between assorted local forces that continued throughout the war even while the main field armies were at some distance. The counties between Oxford, where the King set up his base when he failed to enter London in the winter of 1642–3, and the London and East Anglian axis that formed the core area of parliamentary support were constantly contested and severely affected between 1643 and

---

[1] See J. Broad, 'Gentry finances and the Civil War: the case of the Buckinghamshire Verneys', *Economic History Review* 2nd series, 32 (1979), pp. 183–200, for a general view of the wider problem and C. Clay, 'Landlords and estate management in England' in J. Thirsk (ed.), *The Agrarian History of England and Wales*; vol. v, pt 2 (Cambridge 1984), pp. 119–251.

1646. Outsiders were aware of difficult conditions in Buckinghamshire and in 1644 Essex residents noted 'The sad streights of Buckinghamshire'.[2]

The Verney estates in Buckinghamshire, Berkshire, and Oxfordshire all lay in disputed areas where both sides mounted raids, skirmished, and taxed a reluctant rural population. The King's eastern outpost was at Boarstall house, just inside Buckinghamshire. Nearby Brill was garrisoned by parliament and changed hands several times. Aylesbury, to the south of Claydon, and Newport Pagnell, to the east, were garrisoned and fortified by parliament. In the spring and summer of 1643 there were skirmishes close to Claydon House at Swanbourne, Winslow, East Claydon, and Padbury, in which the Royalists had the advantage. From the beginning of 1644 parliament mounted a campaign. One target was Hillesden House, the Dentons' seat, which had been fortified. Steeple Claydon became the centre of siege operations from January to its fall on 4 March. Parliamentary troops concentrated at Buckingham and Stony Stratford in April, forcing the King to abandon Boarstall, but the tide turned in the summer, when the Royalists took Buckingham, and during the winter of 1644–5 they held large parts of north-west Buckinghamshire including Winslow, Brill, Boarstall, and Haddenham. The Royalists' small garrison at Addington, adjoining Middle Claydon, made demands that drove many of Sir Ralph's tenants to leave their lands. North Buckinghamshire was contested to the end of the first Civil War, and Boarstall House was held by Royalist forces until the summer of 1646.[3] The Blacknall lands in Berkshire and Oxfordshire were equally exposed. Abingdon, only eight miles from Oxford, was secured and held by parliamentary forces in May 1644 and harried thereafter. Longworth lay on the Thames close to the crossing at Newbridge used by Waller to move on Oxford. The other major property at Preston Crowmarsh and Benson was on the Oxford to Henley road and close to the parliamentary garrison at Wallingford. It was less than five miles from Chalgrove field where John Hampden lost his life in a skirmish in June 1643.[4]

Even sporadic warfare had dramatic effects. At the most basic level forces destroyed crops and often farm buildings during their skirmishes. They pulled down houses to make settlements defensible at Oxford and Aylesbury while at

[2] BL MS Egerton 2048, fo. 61.

[3] J. Broad, 'Sir Ralph Verney and his estates 1630–96', unpublished Oxford University DPhil thesis 1973; the clearest and most accurate account of military operations in these parts remains C. H. Firth, 'A chronological survey of the Civil War in Oxfordshire, Buckinghamshire and Bedfordshire 1642–6', *Proceedings of the Oxfordshire Archaeological Society*, new series 5 (1896–8), pp. 280–92. For contemporary accounts of some of these skirmishes see e.g. BL Thomason Tracts E59.24, E102.16 and the Earl of Clarendon, *History of the Great Rebellion*, 6 vols. (1704–6), III, pp. 233ff. For the effects of the Addington garrison see wr to srv 12 March 1644/5 R6.

[4] Firth, 'Chronological Survey', p. 285; I. A. Roots, *The Great Rebellion 1642–60* (London 1966), p. 76.

Boarstall most of the houses in the village were destroyed. Troops were badly paid and supplied, and expected to forage for their own subsistence. Troops from Oxford came into Buckinghamshire and seized cattle for supplies, a commonplace event only noted when the troops took animals from a complaining Royalist. When parliamentary forces passed through north Buckinghamshire, they seized one of Sir Alexander Denton's deer because he was a 'malignant fellow'. This kind of plunder was general and widespread in England. In Cheshire losses from plunder probably equalled the yield from direct taxation up to the summer of 1646.[5]

The widespread disruption of landed society and farming had devastating effects on farmers, particularly those who had invested in vulnerable livestock. Those with a stake in the land – freeholders and copyholders – had little alternative to staying put and waiting until the troubles subsided. Land prices fell sharply, and there were few buyers. However, in communities like Claydon with a preponderance of tenancies, farmers could sell up and leave or successfully demand rent reductions. There are many examples of landlords experiencing total loss of income from major estates, especially where estate administration broke down on outlying properties. The Bridgewater estates in Shropshire produced almost no income during the war, and the Verneys received virtually nothing from their Berkshire and Oxfordshire estates. Where estate administration remained intact, tenants could not be replaced, and farms ran wild. Examples are found everywhere – from Rutland and Somerset where warfare was sporadic, to less troubled areas such as Kent, where Sir Thomas Peyton had lands lying waste, and Henry Oxinden gave up his lease. Even in areas almost immune from warfare, such as Norfolk, rents fell substantially. The Townsends' income from their East Raynham estates fell to 50 per cent of peacetime values, at Rudham to two thirds. Rents on the Hobarts' estates at Aylsham remained at three-quarters of pre-war values.[6]

The Verneys suffered no more than neighbouring gentry families such as the Temples and Dentons. Their problems were undoubtedly exacerbated by the scale of their debts, and by Sir Ralph's religious scruples. Although he sided with parliament from 1640 to 1642, his strongly held Puritan religious views were strictly within the framework of the Church of England. He probably withdrew from active participation in parliament at an early stage. His parliamentary diary ends on 27 June 1642, and his continuing contacts with known Royalists brought

---

[5] A. A. Clark (ed.), *The Life and Times of Anthony Wood* (Oxford 1891), i, p. 71; Broad, *Gentry Finances*, p. 185; J. S. Morrill, *Cheshire 1630–60* (Oxford 1974), pp. 108–9. Two recent books confirm the general picture: P. Tennant, *Edgehill and Beyond: The People's War in the South Midlands 1642–5* (Stroud 1992), mainly concerned with Warwickshire and adjoining areas, and M. Bennett, *The Civil Wars in Britain and Ireland 1638–51* (London 1997), esp. ch. 7 which looks at the effects of war in different areas of the country.

[6] E. Hopkins, 'The Bridgewater estates in north Shropshire during the civil war', *Transactions of the Salop Archaeological Society* 56 (1961), p. 309; Broad, 'Gentry finances', pp. 186–7.

him under suspicion by the spring of 1643. When parliament sought an alliance with the Scots in the summer of 1643, one aspect of the agreement known as the Solemn League and Covenant of 17 August 1643 was the extension of Presbyterian Church organisation to England.

Sir Ralph could not accede to this, and made immediate preparations to leave England. He organised passports from both sides, and fought off an attempt to sequestrate his estates on 15 September 1643, when he was accused of absenting himself from parliament without permission. He wrote to the Parliamentary Committee for Sequestrations explaining that he was going abroad 'to inform my judgement in high things wherein I am yet doubting'. He consistently denied joining the King, and throughout his ten-year exile there is no evidence that he joined the court abroad, though he mixed with a wide spectrum of English gentry and aristocratic families in France, many of them Royalist. He left England in November 1643 with his wife Mary and eldest son Edmund, but his younger son John, aged three, was left at Claydon with Sir Ralph's younger sisters.[7] Before he left, Sir Ralph did what he could to ward off creditors and shore up the family finances. He organised a series of trust deeds, some to pay his debts, others to provide annuities for his siblings and other dependants. They lasted a total of four years, in two periods of two years, assuming that by 1647 the crisis would be over.

Sir Ralph was one of a very small number of MPs who refused to swear the Covenant in 1643, and therefore withdrew from the parliamentary cause. He attempted to stay neutral, and in doing so suffered suspicion and anger from both sides. Parliamentarians and Royalists both tried to sequestrate his lands in Buckinghamshire and Berkshire. He had some sympathy and support from moderate parliamentarians in both houses of parliament, and used their support to bolster his neutrality, but the local elites who made up the county committees were not as understanding. In Buckinghamshire the prominent parliamentary families such as Hampden, Ingoldsby, Grenville, Bulstrode, and Winwood, were all primarily engaged in national politics and directing the war from London. Local control lay with the fledgling County Committee, which became dominated by men from minor gentry families who were more radical in their views, and not the clients of the parliamentary leaders in London. In Berkshire the Verneys were absentee landowners, and their only elite connections were amongst Mary Verney's Blacknall kin. From an early stage radical parliamentarians in Buckinghamshire sought to brand him a Royalist as a prelude to seizing his land and goods for the war effort. The family's first brush with the sequestrators came in May 1643 when some of Sir Ralph's goods left at the house in London of an old family friend, Sir Edward Sydenham, were

[7] srv to Robert Gill 24 August 1643 R5 and Passport of same date; srv to Robert Reynolds n.d. c. November 1643 R5.

seized, but the parliamentary Committee for Sequestration intervened to release them.[8]

Because Sir Ralph gave principled reasons for not taking the Covenant in 1643, his friends in parliament prevented early attempts to exclude him from the House of Commons.[9] The Buckinghamshire County Committee tried to sequestrate his estates in his absence in 1644, although he was not on their list of Royalists. At Claydon, Sir Ralph's bailiff William Roades produced the deeds showing the lands were now legally in trust to pay debts and annuities. The County Committee at Aylesbury took no action, minuting the facts without comment. In 1645 however parliament and the King failed to negotiate a compromise peace at Uxbridge and Sir Ralph's position as an MP was no longer tenable. In September he was voted out of the house and declared a delinquent even though his neutral stance was respected. His friend Sir Roger Burgoyne, who attended the debate, reported that 'absence was the only cause of it, though other things were objected against, which thanks to God were proved untrue'.[10] The Commons may have been sympathetic but for the County Committee it was sufficient cause for them to treat Sir Ralph as a Royalist and sequestrate his estates. Sir Ralph's exclusion from the House of Commons had significant implications for his finances. His immunity from prosecution for debt as an MP now lapsed. This inhibited his ability to support himself and his family, to pay annuities, and to keep creditors at bay. Sequestration also meant that he could not sell land to pay creditors. If he had returned to England at that stage, he might well have found himself in jail for debt. Sequestration threatened all his income, and his capacity to plan for the future.

During 1645 and the first half of 1646 sequestration had little impact on family finances, partly because the trust deeds gave some immunity, but mainly because there was so little estate income to seize. From 1642–1646 income from the Verney estates fell steeply. Claydon produced only £600 a year in 1644–5, less than half its peacetime yield. The land at Brill, situated in the no man's land between Boarstall and Brill, produced nothing. The Berkshire and Oxfordshire land produced virtually nothing between 1642 and 1646. Gross family income fell to less than a third of peacetime levels for several years. There was a rapid turnover of tenants. Taxation was high, and demands came from both sides. East Claydon received demands from Royalists and Parliamentarians both signed by the same over-collector between December and April 1646, as did the adjoining parish of Grendon Underwood in 1644.[11] Taxes 'must be

[8] For a fuller account of the Verneys and sequestration see J. Broad, 'The Verneys and the sequestrators in the civil wars', *Records of Buckinghamshire* 27 (1985), pp. 1–9.
[9] Parliament gave those MPs who refused to swear considerable latitude and time before imposing penalties. Some were persuaded to take it as late as January 1645. See J. Cliffe, *Puritans in Conflict: The Puritan Gentry during and after the Civil War* (1988), pp. 98–9.
[10] Broad, 'The Verneys and the Sequestrators', p. 3.
[11] CIH 4/5/3; G. Eland, *Papers from an Iron Chest* (1937), p. 65.

paid, whoever goes without', wrote William Roades in April 1645, and a year later he was selling wood 'to pay taxes for if I let it run in arrears they will sell the wood themselves'.[12] The financial burden was enormous. In the two and a half years from October 1643 to March 1646 parliament raised twenty-four tax levies on Middle Claydon totalling £834, an average of £330 a year. The levies were based on a valuation of Middle Claydon at £1,440 a year, at a time when it was producing half as much rent. The effective rate of taxation was about 50 per cent of gross rent received. In the half year from Michaelmas 1644 to Lady Day 1645, when the rent roll had fallen to £311 8s 8d, some £114 10s was paid out in tax. At one point the bailiff at Claydon, William Roades, reckoned tax payments to work out at £20 a week.[13] The financial pressures on his estates brought considerable difficulties for Sir Ralph in France.

Before he left England, Sir Ralph Verney had paid his shop and trade bills, and secured many of his bond debts on land. However, William Roades's duty was, from estate income, to supply his master and mistress in France with a basic income to live on. From 1643 to 1646 this was often very small. A cash account between Sir Ralph in France, and Sir Roger Burgoyne in London, an old friend acting as his main financial agent in London between December 1643 and February 1645, shows that Burgoyne paid Sir Ralph £474 4s 7d by bill of exchange. Of this, only £60 can be show to have come from estate income. Some of the rest came from final payments from a sale of land in 1640, while much came from selling silver plate or raising loans on its security.[14] Sir Ralph took some money when he left England in 1643, probably more than the £50 he later claimed to have lived on. More plausible is his statement to William Denton that he had only been paid £90 of his income in the twenty-one months from December 1643 to September 1645.[15] Sir Ralph and his family in France lived primarily by selling assets during the first Civil War.

It was not just Sir Ralph and his immediate family who suffered. High taxation and plummeting estate income were common across the whole of landed society and made it impossible to pay annuities and debt interest. At the beginning of the war there was considerable gentlemanly forbearance. Sir Roger Pratt expressed the view that 'then 'twas almost thought a crime to ask any one of interest money'.[16] But Pratt left England in April 1643 and did not return until 1649. For those who remained, attitudes soon changed. In May 1643, Sir Ralph's aunt, Elizabeth Isham, who had lent him £1,100, had been magnanimous. She

[12] wr to srv 30 April 1645 R6, n.d. February 1645/6 R7.

[13] ClH4/5/3 wr estate account dated 24 March 1644/5 R6; wr to srv 12 March 1644/5.

[14] srb to srv 20 February 1644/5 R6; srv to Countess of Sussex 20/30 December 1644 and 3 February 1644/5 R6.

[15] srv to wd 3/13 September 1645 R6. S. R. Gardiner, *History of the Great Civil War* (1893), II, p. 209, wrongly inferred that this was the total of his disposable resources in France at the time.

[16] R. T. Gunther (ed.), *The Architecture of Sir Roger Pratt* (Oxford 1928), p. 3.

asked Sir Ralph to secure her debt on lands and congratulated herself on not
asking for security for the interest, recognising that 'it will be impossible for
you to pay according to the rate of eight for a hundred, and it would be a sin
in one to receive it, though you should freely offer it, much more to exact it at
your hands'. These cordial sentiments did not last. In December 1644 Elizabeth
pleaded destitution after her house had been pillaged; by May 1645 she was
demanding that some of the loan should be repaid, and that the capital and
arrears of interest be secured on the Middle Claydon land.[17] Verney creditors
became insistent in 1645, trying a variety of (probably genuine) hard luck stories
to get preferential treatment. By November 1646 when Mary Verney returned
to England to attempt to remove her husband's sequestration, she found that
when William Roades came to London he was assailed by creditors 'ready to
tear him in pieces'.[18]

Sir Ralph Verney made sure that close family and kin who were living on
annuities or the interest of small capital sums, suffered least. His brothers and
sisters usually received some part of their annuities on time during the Civil
War. Doll Leake, a long-time family companion and dependant, was only one
year in arrears with her interest by May 1645. Elizabeth Isham received half
interest during the whole period from 1643 to 1648.[19] Most of the Verneys'
other creditors received no interest at all. They were not unusual. Local conditions in Buckinghamshire meant that the Temples of Stowe made virtually no
interest payments from 1642 to 1647. Elsewhere matters were little better: Lord
Lovelace was seven and a half years in arrears of one rent-charge in 1649, and
claimed that no interest was paid on debts of £8,000 between 1642 and 1646,
while Sir Francis Fane in Yorkshire was three years in arrears of interest in
1646. Even in less war-torn East Anglia the Hobarts were two years in arrears
on one debt in 1647.[20]

The financial crisis that affected those with debts, living on the interest of
capital, or dependent on landed income during the Civil War had further ramifications. Most loans on bond were signed not just by the borrower but by one
or more guarantors. These were often kin, friends, or neighbours, and by definition persons (usually men) of established financial reputation. When these
debts could not be paid, the guarantors became liable. The consequences of one
man's indebtedness fell on others' shoulders. In the case of the heavily indebted
Sir Peter Temple at Stowe, his steward, James Pollard, found himself in gaol
for debt when his master used his immunity as an MP to escape.[21] Sir Ralph

---

[17] Elizabeth Isham to srv 9 May 1643 R5, 9 December 1644 R6; srv to E. Isham 23 May 1645 R6.

[18] srv to Henry Verney 4/14 April 1645 R6; mv to srv 4 December 1646 R7.

[19] D. Leake to srv 29 May 1645 R6.

[20] E. F. Gay, 'Sir Richard Temple: the debt settlement and estate litigation 1653–75', *Huntington Library Quarterly* 6:3 (1943), pp. 255–91; PRO SP 23/180, pp. 200, 216, 74–6; Bodl. MS Tanner 97, fo. 83.

[21] Gay, 'Sir Richard Temple', p. 256.

Verney's sister Susan married a Cheshire gentleman, Richard Alport, during the war, and later found him gaoled as a guarantor. She complained that 'if it were not for other people's debts I should live very handsomely'.[22] Sir Ralph's experience during the Civil War, in which he was guarantor of his father's debts, influenced his own conduct and he always refused to allow his son to act as guarantor of his debts.[23] There were many wider repercussions on elite society from the wartime financial confusion. Family and kin relationships became strained, friendships were put under pressure, high-minded forbearance was replaced by insistent demands and cries of unfair treatment. The collapse of rents and estate income was followed by a collapse in land prices. Sequestration further reduced the ability to pay interest and annuities, and made it impossible to sell assets to repay capital sums. In these circumstances interest remained unpaid, was added to capital, and rapidly increased the total sum due. Most money had been raised at 8 per cent, the maximum legal rate since 1624. By the late 1640s Sir Ralph Verney was increasingly concerned at the rate his debts were rising. In 1647 he complained of 'the great increase of my father's debts by running on of interest', and resolved 'if I pay any, to pay all; for if any is left, it may soon raise to a great sum again'. By the 1650 calculations of what was owed on various debts showed arrears of interest had increased the sum owed by figures ranging from 39 to 91 per cent, depending on how often it had been possible to pay anything during the war. As William Denton neatly put it 'interest, like any horse, will out while you sleep'.[24]

The King's headquarters at Oxford fell in June 1646. Boarstall Tower, its fortified eastern outpost in Buckinghamshire, was one of the last strongholds to concede. The agricultural economy recovered quickly and landlords soon found that they could ask for rent from tenants that by 1647 equalled and sometimes exceeded pre-war levels. This was certainly true at Claydon, and landowners elsewhere in the country such as the Nicholas and Hatton families noted the revival. Most landowners had to write off arrears of rent despite legal judgements in the central courts acknowledging their legal right to them.[25] However, farmers did not have an easy period of recovery, with poor weather, bad harvests, and severe outbreaks of animal disease in 1647 and 1648.

Peace and a reviving rural economy brought additional short-term burdens rather than benefits to the Verneys. After the war the military presence in the countryside did not suddenly melt away. At Middle Claydon, as elsewhere, taxation remained high, and it has been argued that despite the halving of the

[22] S. Alport to srv 30 June 1648 R9.   [23] srv to Thomas Stafford 2 May 1661 R17.

[24] srv to John Denton 4/14 July 1647 R7; srv to mv n.d. August 1647 R7; wd to srv 6 January 1647/8 R8.

[25] mv to srv 4 February 1646/7 R8; wd to srv 29 June 1648 R9; G. F. Warner (ed.), *The Nicholas Papers*, Camden Society, new series 40 (1886), p. 119; BL Add. MS 29550, fo. 95; Broad, 'Gentry finances', p. 193.

monthly tax in Buckinghamshire in June 1647, that year was the harshest of the 1640s for the county's inhabitants. With the war over, none of the tax was actually spent in the county, while substantial numbers of troops were quartered on towns and villages without payment.[26] The billeting of troops was unpopular throughout the country, and in Essex was the subject of popular petitioning. Troops were billeted at Middle Claydon early in 1647, and again in August, and probably at other times too.[27]

The Verneys' creditors were impatient that peace did not immediately bring instant financial recovery and the ability to repay loans. The Verney finances remained tight. In 1645–6 they found it very difficult to raise or even find security for Susan Verney's dowry of £1,000. More plate was sold. A barn at Claydon fetched £50. A suggestion that furnishings at Claydon House should be sold was rejected only because the amount raised was not expected to defray the carriage costs. Interest rates soared well above the legal maximum in 1645–6, 16 per cent was quoted in the summer of 1645, and 14 and 12 per cent in March and June the following year.[28]

There was also a bigger question. From the autumn of 1645 Sir Ralph's ability to pay his debts was hamstrung by his expulsion from parliament and sequestration. He immediately drew up a petition to have the sequestration order withdrawn, citing his poverty and his contribution to the parliamentary cause. Others had more practical concerns. His major creditor, Francis Drake, was frightened for his debt. In December 1645 Sir Ralph allowed Drake to take over the lands at Claydon used to secure his mortgage and rent charge. He took formal possession in January 1646.[29]

While the fighting was close to Sir Ralph's lands, sequestration had little practical effect. The trust deed showing that all the family's income was earmarked for debt and annuity payments was honoured. There was little income to collect, and the County Committee rarely had the power to collect it. They extracted a little money from Brill when it was in parliamentary hands between October 1645 and August 1646, but none from Claydon.[30] Attitudes changed rapidly at the end of the war. On 25 August 1646 William Roades warned Sir Ralph that the estate would probably be sequestrated at Michaelmas when rent became due, while his uncle, John Denton, warned him to draw up a particular

[26] A. M. Johnson, 'Buckinghamshire', unpublished MA thesis, University of Wales, 1760, pp. 112, 115, 130.

[27] mv to srv 18 February 1646/7, 31 August 1647 R8. E. Hockliffe (ed.), *The Diary of Ralph Josselin*, Camden Society 3rd series 15 (1908), pp. 41–3.

[28] Henry Verney to srv 30 June 1646 R7. srb to srv 16 July 1646 R7. Sir John Leake to srv 12 and 23 June 1645 R6; Henry Verney to srv 26 March 1646 R7 and 30 June 1646 R7.

[29] srv to srb 21/31 December 1645 R6; CIH 1/92 dated 25 December 1645. He had been willing to make a collusive entry since the previous August, F. Drake to srv n.d. August 1645 R6; Henry Verney to srv 1 January 1645/6 R7.

[30] PRO SP 28/207, pp. 289–91.

of his estates showing all the obligations due out of it. On 10 September 1646 the Committee at Aylesbury sequestrated the Brill property, and on 14 October William Roades was ordered to bring rents, leases, and rent rolls from Claydon to the County Committee at Aylesbury on 23 October.[31]

Sir Ralph considered making his peace with parliament and compounding for his delinquency. However, he abandoned this approach when he discovered that he still had to take the Covenant oath, holding an attitude to the sanctity of oaths unusual for the period.[32] His only alternative was to claim that his sequestration should be removed because he had never supported the King, and the oath was his only point of issue with parliament. He could not return to England for fear of imprisonment for debt, and had decided to send his wife to plead his case even before the County Committee took action in September 1646.[33] Mary Verney planned to set off in October but was delayed by illness and did not arrive until about 22 November. In England William Denton used his widespread networks in London society to coordinate an approach to parliament. Before Mary left France, Denton was telling Sir Ralph to prime her with the details of useful political and aristocratic connections.[34]

When Mary arrived in England in November 1646 she immediately fell ill, probably with the breast cancer that was to kill her, and also found that she was again pregnant. She could do little lobbying until the end of January 1647. The problem was complex. The Buckinghamshire County Committee would not lift sequestration, though they accepted the validity of the trust deeds. It argued, correctly, that the House of Commons had imposed the Sequestration Order, and must therefore lift it. Denton was uncertain whether to approach parliament through the Committee for Sequestration, or by a direct petition to the House of Commons.[35] Sir Ralph had great hopes of using his connections with the Earl of Warwick, who had married his old friend Eleanor Lee in 1646 as her third husband. They had had contacts in the 1630s over a colonising expedition to the Barbados, and Warwick had solicited Sir Ralph's assistance over the Committee of Posts in 1642, while Warwick's son Hatton Rich exchanged cordial letters with Sir Ralph in France in the autumn of 1646. But Mary found Eleanor very subdued and without much influence with her husband, and discounted her offers of help.[36]

---

[31] wd to srv 24 September 1646 R7; County Committee order dated 14th October 1646 R7.

[32] srb to srv 4 December 1645 R6 and Henry Verney to srv 8 January 1645/6 R7; see J. Spurr, 'A profane history of early modern oaths', *Transactions of the Royal Historical Society* 6th series, 9 (2001), pp. 37–64, and information from Rachel Weil.

[33] srv to Earl of Devonshire 20/30 September 1646 R7. Devonshire was a fellow exile in France.

[34] wd to srv 30 September 1646 R7 for a fuller account of the lifting of sequestration see Broad, 'The Verneys and the sequestrators in the civil wars 1642–56', *Records of Buckinghamshire*, 27 (1985), pp. 1–9.

[35] wd to srv 8, 28, 29 October 1646 R7.

[36] Earl of Warwick to srv 5, 7, 12, 15 April 1642 R4 mv to srv 11 February 1646/7 R8.

The lifting of sequestration was contested at all stages by radical elements who considered Sir Ralph a deserter to the parliamentary cause. The Committee at Aylesbury refused to provide a certificate showing why Sir Ralph had been sequestrated without an order from the Sequestration Committee in London. This was obtained early in March 1647, but when the certificate from the County Committee was taken back to the Parliamentary Committee on 16 April, they said they were powerless to hear the case because of a Parliamentary order of 23 March.[37] William Denton now had to organise a petition to the House of Commons, and to lobby for it to be heard. It was presented to the House on several occasions but ignored. Even friendly Lords and MPs who said privately that they would support it, showed no enthusiasm to have it heard by the House. The stalemate continued throughout the summer.[38]

As time slipped by, an additional crisis loomed. The trust deeds for the Verney estates covered two-year periods from November 1643 and November 1645. They would run out in November 1647, allowing the sequestrators to take possession of Claydon and other properties. The slow progress at Westminster forced Sir Ralph to ask his wife to forge new trust deeds starting from November 1647 for a further year. She was to imitate his signature and those of 'such witnesses known to be of my acquaintance but are either dead or gone beyond seas since December 1643'. Only William Denton was to know about the plan. The forged deeds were prepared and ready, but probably never used.[39]

In the autumn of 1647 the Berkshire County Committee attempted to sequestrate the Blacknall lands at Wasing. William Roades feared that the sequestrators would also cut down timber at Claydon and Wasing to raise money.[40] By early November 1647 Mary Verney despaired of her petition being heard. Her contacts told her that 'there is no hopes of doing anything in the Bas [House of Commons] but by bribery'. William Denton was already using family contacts – his cousin was Speaker Lenthall's sister-in-law – and was prepared to offer up to £50, but eventually paid £40 to receive a hearing within a week. On 25 November Mary could write that 'we are promised within a few days to have our business noticed in the House and effected there'. Despite a crowded house and urgent Scots and Army business, the motion was put on 17 December, and passed 'with some but not much regret'.[41] It simply referred the question back to the Committee for Sequestration for final decision. William Denton and Mary Verney lobbied intensively, delaying the discussion scheduled for 24 December until the 'Lords that we can make of that Committee' had returned to town.

[37] Broad, J. 'Sir Ralph Verney and his estates 1630–96', pp. 58–9.
[38] srv to wd 20/30 June 1647 R7; Sir John Trevor to mv 20 July 1647 R8.
[39] srv to mv 17/27 October 1647 R8; ClH 1/90 dated 1 December 1643 – as instructed by Sir Ralph.
[40] Broad, 'Sir Ralph Verney', pp. 62–6; wr to mv 21 October 1647 R8.
[41] wd to srv 4 and 11 November 1647 R8; mv to srv 25 November 1647 R8, 20 December 1647 R8. Certificate of the same date R8 cf. CJ v 330; wd to srv 20 December 1647 R8.

When the case was heard on 5 January the sequestration was lifted. The vote was 'eleven to three or four' after a three-hour debate in which 'those that were against us were most bitter and violent and powerful'. To achieve this result Mary had lobbied tirelessly for a week in person and writing letters, and the Earl of Warwick and his wife finally used their influence.[42] Denton acted quickly, insisting that separate certificates be sent immediately to the County Committees at Aylesbury, and in Oxfordshire and Berkshire. In Aylesbury he made sure it was presented only when Peter Dormer, a member from the old county elite was present.[43]

Sequestration was removed but the process had taken more than a year of hard work. It highlighted the tensions within the parliamentary cause between central Parliamentary Committees, with their long-standing kinship and elite networks, and County Committees with more radical agendas and attitudes. The hostility of those opposing the lifting of sequestration in London paralleled the unsympathetic attitudes of the radicals on the Aylesbury committee. It was a pattern mirrored by the experience of the Tufton family in Kent and Sussex who also used the lady of the family to plead the cause.[44] The hostility of the County Committee in Buckinghamshire reflected its desperate need to use sequestration income to pay troops when at the end of the war it had to remit its assessment taxes to London. But it was also about the deep antipathies between old and new members of the county's ruling elite. Sequestration cost the Verneys very little money directly. The deeds of trust prevented money from Berkshire and Claydon going to County Committees in almost every case. The lifting of sequestration was more important for what it prevented and enabled. Sir Ralph no longer had to compound for his estates at a cost of several thousand pounds. He did not have to make his peace with parliament or take the Covenant oath. More importantly, his freedom of manoeuvre in dealing with his creditors increased enormously.

Between 1648 and 1653 the danger that indebtedness would ruin the Verney family subsided. The debts and their effects on him and the family had understandably obsessed Sir Ralph. In October 1646 he asked his brother Henry to 'think of some way to pay my debts, for they are a most intolerable burden and torment'.[45] However Dr William Denton negotiated most debt settlements, and his correspondence with Sir Ralph in France shows the strategies employed. Denton used his network of contacts in London from his successful medical

---

[42] mv to srv 23 December 1647 R8. PRO SP20/4, p. 117 dated 24 December 1647; and p. 124 dated 5 January 1647/8. wd to srv 6 January 1647/8 R8; mv to srv 6 January 1647/8 R8.

[43] wd to wr 10 January 1647/8 R8.

[44] F. Hull, 'The Tufton sequestration papers', *A Seventeenth-century Miscellany*, Kent Records Society 17 (1960), pp. 35–6.

[45] Henry Verney to srv 1 October 1646 R7; srv to Henry Verney 30 October and 26 November 1646 R7.

practice as well as family and friends. Both he and Sir Ralph renewed contacts with Sir Orlando Bridgeman, a leading legal expert on land and family trusts of the period.[46] It was common ground between Sir Ralph, his wife, and Denton that rapid land sales were necessary to bring the debt under control. In 1646–7 Sir Ralph believed that 'unless land sells well I can never pay my debts' and that there was 'no likelihood that we should hold out two years longer . . . for we have thitherto subsisted by miracles'.[47]

A variety of schemes was discussed including a wild idea that Sir Ralph should give up responsibility for the Claydon estates to his brothers and sisters, who were clamouring for their annuities, in return for a certain annual income of £500. However, the main point of contention was between Sir Ralph and his wife over whether her Blacknall dowry lands in Berkshire and Oxfordshire should be sold. The legal position was clear. Their marriage settlement provided Mary with a jointure out of Claydon in return for Sir Ralph's ownership of her dowry lands. This was confirmed in the trust deeds of 1643.[48] The lands were at some distance from Claydon and from each other. The logic of estate building favoured their sale. Yet Mary tenaciously opposed it. Beyond any sentimental attachments to her own family and past, she used powerful, indeed unanswerable, arguments for rejection. She argued that the debts were Verney family debts, not hers or her husband's, and so should be paid from Verney lands, which effectively meant Middle Claydon. The family annuities for Sir Ralph's brothers and sisters must be paid from Claydon rents, and not from her lands, which should be retained to provide for her younger children.

The argument went back and forth between husband and wife over more than six months during 1647. Citing the cost of educating their sons and of raising dowries for their daughters over eight to ten years Sir Ralph ruled out a twenty-one year rent charge on Claydon but compromised on a ten-year rent charge and the sale of the outlying Blacknall properties and Brill. Mary conceded that she could not improve on his plan, but argued that they would be worse off than by her own plan and that Sir Ralph's proposal might still fail to pay off his debts. At one point, while the threat of sequestration was still real, she suggested that Sir Ralph should legally transfer all her lands and her jointure to her directly or to 'a friend'. However, Sir Ralph countered that he believed that the laws on women's property 'give all husbands so great an interest and so absolute a right over all wives' estates' that such a transfer would be worthless.[49] The discussion

---

[46] On Bridgeman's role see L. Bonfield, *Marriage Settlements 1601–1740: The Adoption of the Strict Settlement* (Cambridge 1983), pp. 58–70.

[47] srv to wd 13 December 1646 R7; srv to mv 24 October/3 November 1647 R8.

[48] srv to mv 14/24 October 1647 R8. ClH 1/83 dated 5 September 1643.

[49] srv to mv 20/30 May 1647 R7, 12/22 September 1647 R8; mv to srv 6, 13, 30 May 1647 R7, 15 July 1646 R7, 18 August R8, 9 December 1647 R8. On women's property rights in theory and practice at the time see A. L. Erickson, *Women and Property in Early Modern England* (London 1993).

reached stalemate. Sir Ralph was unable to persuade his wife, and unwilling to over-ride her views despite the desperate plight of the family finances. This illustrates the gulf between legal rights and practical decision-making in the deep and happy relationship between Sir Ralph and his wife. Ultimately, the Verneys' alternative piecemeal strategy successfully paid off the most pressing creditors, and mollified the remainder until land prices recovered, and interest rates on loans fell.

Sir Ralph's strategy for debt repayment was to offer creditors land at 1642 rather than current values – twenty times the estimate of the rental value before the Civil War. If creditors accepted this, he would pay the whole debt and accumulated interest during the war. Very few creditors were interested in such terms. Some wished to drive a harder bargain but for many in the late 1640s land was unattractive because difficult to sell. In 1650 William Denton stated that 'ready money makes the man, and I believe it would pay cost to take it up at the highest rate; so prevalent a thing is ready money to make easy compositions'.[50]

Some debt settlements used local contacts and attorneys. The Blacknall family's attorney, Mr Heron, negotiated one Berkshire debt settlement, while the lawyer Robert Busby of Addington near Claydon settled another. But William Denton dealt with most, including the two largest and most difficult creditors. Unlike the Temples in 1648, the Lord Saye and Sele in 1649, and the Danvers in 1652, the Verneys did not attempt to deal with their creditors as a body, or to set up a trust to pay debts over a long period. That was an expensive route and meant paying back all principal and arrears of interest. Instead Denton gave Sir Ralph's creditors two alternatives: either land at 1642 rates for the full principal and interest, or ready cash for principal but only half the accumulated interest.[51]

Most creditors chose cash. Land prices had generally fallen to anything from fourteen to eighteen years' purchase.[52] Very few creditors wanted land at twenty years' purchase with an uncertain land market, and high taxation on land. To raise cash the Verneys needed to sell land, grant a long lease for a cash sum and low or nominal rent, or raise a mortgage. All three were attempted. William Roades tried at various points to persuade Middle Claydon tenants to pay almost seven years rent up front, in return for annual rents reduced by a third for the next twenty years. Even in 1648–50 when farming conditions were adverse, two tenants were interested, but negotiations collapsed because Sir Ralph insisted that the tenants should pay all taxes.[53] It was impossible to raise a mortgage on Claydon because Francis Drake was in possession of much of the

---

[50] wd to srv 5 December 1650 R10.
[51] srv to wd 24 April 1648 R9; E. F. Gay, 'The temples of Stowe and their debts, 1603–53', *Huntington Library Quarterly* 2 (1938), pp. 434–5; Bodl. MS Rawl. D 892 fo. 23; PRO C104/85.
[52] Broad, 'Sir Ralph Verney', pp. 82–5.
[53] wr to srv 14 and 17 May 1649 R10, 26 January 1649/50 R10.

land after the Verneys' failure to pay his rent charge during the Civil War. Lady Dacre's outstanding loan under Statute Merchant (originally used to pay for Mary Blacknall's wardship) also complicated negotiations.

Denton juggled land sales and debt repayments. When he found a buyer at a reasonable price for land at Longworth in Berkshire, he simultaneously offered cash deals to Drake and Dacre. Drake would not bite, but in December 1649 the Dacre trustees, Sir Dudley North and Sir Christopher Newell, agreed to accept £1,500 in cash for their accumulated principal and interest of £1,917 10s 8d to March 1649, and almost £2,000 by December. Denton's excellent deal amounted to a reduction of interest of almost exactly one half.[54] The sale of Longworth for £1,334 was not quite enough to pay off the Dacre debt, but Denton raised an additional £200 to complete the repayment. Denton was triumphant at his success, and rightly so in the difficult conditions of the time. It was important psychologically in persuading other creditors to accept interest reductions. Only two creditors were prepared to take land (urban property in Abingdon) after two years of wearisome negotiations.[55]

Francis Drake's loan secured on Middle Claydon was a crucial barrier to the revival of the Verney finances. Drake was a kinsman of the Verneys and Dentons. He was initially helpful, and agreed to make a collusive entry on his security to prevent sequestration. But his tone suggested that he was doing his duty out of loyalty and honour rather than positive support, indeed Mary Verney found him lukewarm during her political lobbying in 1648–9. In 1648 and 1649 Denton offered him various land deals, and once almost persuaded him to take land at eighteen years' purchase. Drake's loan was secured on a large part of the Claydon estate that was needed for other debt settlements. He wanted cash and initially refused to accept that Verney could not raise such a large sum or to accept a renegotiation that transferred his debt to a straight-forward mortgage. After more than a year he eventually compromised but on harsh terms. In September 1649 land at Claydon to the value of £137 a year was pledged in a seven-year mortgage but this would become a freehold sale if the loan was not fully paid within seven years. Denton mitigated the deal's harsh terms by holding the effective interest rate to five and a half per cent.[56]

---

[54] wd to srv 12 December 1649 R10 and 22 and 23 March 1648/9 R10; ClH2/1480 and 2/1481 shows the agreement was made in July 1649, resulting in deeds of agreement in September 1649 and a final transfer in 1654. The monetary transaction took place on 29 December 1649 – receipt in R10. This is an interesting reflection on how misleading the dating of deeds can be in understanding the timing of transactions.

[55] ClH2/1446–9; wr to srv 6 July 1648 R9 and 21 February 1648/9 R9. On the other sale, to a Mrs Hyde, no deeds have survived but see wd to wr 18 July1650 R10.

[56] ClH 1/93–5; srv to Francis Drake 1/11 October 1648 R9; srv to wd 1/11 October 1648 R9; ? to wd n.d. March 1649 R9; wd to srv 10 May 1649 R10. The format of the deed follows a very ancient pattern of loan security. Drake was presumably wary of the validity of Equity of Redemption. See R. W. Turner, *Equity of Redemption* (Cambridge 1931), p. 18. Not only did

After Denton had placated Dacre and Drake he was able to settle many debts of less than £1,000 between 1648 and 1652. Some deals involved a 50 per cent reduction in interest, but occasionally, as with Mabel Willington, he had to pay full principal and interest.[57] The debt crisis gradually eased as tenants paid higher rents, and made more cash available. Creditors were experiencing the same economic improvement and were no longer in such urgent need to settle. General indebtedness made the rate of interest a political issue. Petitions were presented in both Lords and Commons in 1648 and 1649, and an act reducing the maximum rate of interest to 6 per cent was passed in August 1651.[58] When it passed, creditors still receiving 8 per cent had no incentive to demand a return of their money. Denton frequently wrote that there was plenty of money available for mortgages from 1649 onwards.[59]

In August 1650 William Denton saw no easy way through the complex maze of the remaining £4,000 to £4,500 of debts. However by the summer of 1651 Sir Ralph was persuaded that the crisis was over, and set off on an extended tour of southern France and Italy. By 1652 William Denton considered the Verney finances were no longer in crisis, although he continued his work until Sir Ralph returned to England early in 1653. Denton had achieved a great deal. Although the total principal debt had not been much reduced, creditors had compromised on arrears of interest; £3,000 principal debt incurred before 1642 was repaid between 1648 and 1652 for £4,352, when at compound interest to the end of 1650 the full cost would have been £5,550. The Verneys paid what the Hatton and Denton families paid to settle their debts, roughly principal and half interest. The Temple family's spectacular settlement in 1656 when they paid off debts of £19,468 for £6,689 was only possible because Sir Peter Temple's heir was not surety for his father's debt.[60] In 1652 the Verney debts probably still stood at over £7,000, but the estate income could well bear it.[61] Significant amounts of land set aside for sale remained, while Mary Verney's estates for her younger children remained intact.

While William Denton laboured to repair the Verney finances, Sir Ralph Verney's personal life in France was in crisis. When Mary Verney went to

Verney provide the additional security, but he was also required to install the mathematician John Kersey, at that time acting as steward for the Dentons, as tenant to collect the rent. On Kersey see Judith Curthoys, 'Land, settlement and enclosure in Hillesden, Buckinghamshire', unpublished M Studies thesis, Kellogg College, Oxford 1997, pp. 27–8.

[57] wd to srv 6 April 1650 R10.

[58] CJ II 95, 104, 108 VI 162, 197; C. H. Firth and R. S. Rait, *Acts and Ordinances of the Interregnum* (London 1911), II, pp. 548–9.

[59] Cf. H. J. Habakkuk, 'Landowners and the Civil War', *Economic History Review*, 2nd series, 18:1 (1965), p. 137.

[60] Hattons: BL Add. MS 29950 fos. 64, 66; Dentons: wd to srv 17 December 1650 R10; Gay, 'Sir Richard Temple', pp. 260–9.

[61] On the difficulties of making precise calculations of the Verney debt at this period see Broad, 'Sir Ralph Verney', pp. 94–100.

London to remove the sequestration order she was already ill. Denton believed that she had had breast cancer ever since 1636–7.[62] Mary returned to France in April 1648 with her younger son John. A happy reunion with her husband was tinged with sadness for the deaths of her young daughter and her baby boy. Blois was a backwater with little society, with few English visitors, and the contrast with the responsibilities, politics, society, and intrigue of her fifteen months in London was marked. She soon fell ill and became very weak, losing her sight for a time. Trips to Bourbon to take the waters, and to shop in Paris brought some revival in her health in 1649, but in the spring of 1650 she went into a decline, dying early in May. Sir Ralph mourned her deeply, and his letters to William Denton reveal his state of mind, full of grief and self-searching. He determined that Mary should be buried at Claydon though he did not dare return himself. He supervised the embalming of her body and sent it on its long journey home, where it was laid to rest in November 1650. When he eventually returned one of his first actions was to plan a marble funeral monument for her.[63] He never re-married in the remaining forty-six years of his life, though perhaps he once came close to doing so.

Sir Ralph Verney returned to England at the end of January 1653. After his wife had been buried in England he resolved to take his fifteen-year-old eldest son Edmund on a continental journey. The Verney archives of the time include a set of instructions for making a journey to Italy. He left Blois in March 1651, and passed through Bordeaux, Toulouse, and Carcassonne in May and June. He intended to go to northern Spain but news of plague and famine there diverted him to Lyons and Toulon in July and August. Father and son travelled to Italy in October going to Florence, Rome, and Naples, then back to Rome in January 1652, and on to Bologna and Venice in May. They returned through Frankfurt, Cologne, Rotterdam, and Amsterdam to reach Antwerp in September 1652. While in Holland Sir Ralph sought out an English tutor for Edmund, settling on Dr Robert Creighton, a former Cambridge fellow and Regius Professor of Greek, who was later to become Bishop of Bath and Wells. He was planning for his return to England, where he was still unsure of his reception, and wondered whether to come over incognito. Leaving Edmund in Holland was a classic way of protecting the family's dynastic interest by keeping his heir out of the power of the state, or of important enemies. Eventually he made a public return to England, announcing his arrival at Dover to his London friends.

Once in England, Sir Ralph set about rebuilding his life and re-moulding his country house and estate. Over the next four years he personally supervised the reconstruction of Claydon House, rectory, and almshouses to his own specification. He also built a large new walled garden, and enclosed his Middle

---

[62] wd to srv 26 April 1650 R10.
[63] L. Stone, 'The Verney tomb at Claydon', *Records of Buckinghamshire* 16 (1953–60), pp. 67–82.

Claydon estate, setting out new farmsteads and finding new tenants. The correspondence is filled with exchanges about trees, flowers, and vegetables, thronging with new ideas about husbandry. Interchanges took place with gentry friends, old and new, across the country, and also with correspondents and contacts in France and the Low Countries gained during his nine years abroad. Excluded from local and national politics, branded as a subversive Royalist and imprisoned despite all his protests during the rule of the Major-Generals, and unable this time to avoid the financial penalties of neutrality, he quite literally decided to cultivate his garden.

The family's financial crisis was over. In 1656 the Drake mortgage with its penal land-transfer terms was replaced with a standard mortgage from an old family connection, Sir Thomas Hewitt. In 1654 further land was sold at Brill.[64] There was no immediate pressure for more sales because the loss of his wife and younger children brought considerable financial benefits. No part of the estate now had to be set aside for jointure, or to raise a dowry for his daughter. With only one younger son, Sir Ralph was able to persuade himself that a substantial part of his wife's lands could safely be sold and still leave a landed estate for John. In the period up to 1660 Sir Ralph felt confident enough in his financial future to increase his debts in order to refurbish his house and garden, and improve his estate.

What then were the consequences and long-term implications of the disruption of the Civil War period for the Verney family? The financial crisis of the period hit families like the Verneys particularly hard because they began it with substantial debts. They survived by measures typical of their class – protective trusts, delaying debt payments, and coming to compromise agreements with creditors. In the medium term the legal devices invented or consolidated at that period, the strict settlement with contingent remainders, and the mortgage with equity of redemption, made a vital difference, but they were not used during the crisis. The 1651 reduction in the maximum rate of interest in part reflected low land prices, as the preamble to the Act clearly stated, but also the ready availability of money for mortgage loans. There can be no doubt that the Civil War delayed by ten or fifteen years Sir Ralph's scheme for settling his father's debts. Although indebtedness no longer posed a threat after 1650–2, it was only in the mid-1660s, after further land sales and Edmund Verney's marriage to an heiress, that Sir Ralph felt truly at ease with his financial position.

The psychological scars for all the family were considerable. When Sir Ralph returned to England in 1653 he was only forty, but the previous thirteen years had seen the loss of all his close relatives of the older generation, his wife, and two small children. He lived for ten years in lodgings abroad with little money, fighting financial ruin and political exclusion from a distance. His children

[64] CIH 1/99-100 25 July 1656; 2/1040 29 March 1654.

suffered too. John the younger son spent four years with aunts and servants in England before returning with his sick and dying mother to France, only to be left by his father and brother when they went on their eighteen-month journey to Italy and Flanders. He stayed in Blois with old family friends, was sent to school there, and did not return to England until the summer of 1653.

The effect of civil war on Sir Ralph's brothers and sisters was also significant. His brothers had nondescript military careers, and one was killed in Ireland. His sisters arguably lost more. When Sir Edmund died he left them all dowries of £1,000. This was a significant sum, but not over-generous in a period of rising elite dowries. All six had problematic marriages, with husbands of relatively lower status. Cary, the fourth daughter was only fifteen when she married Thomas Gardiner in June 1642. Her marriage had been arranged before the outbreak of war with the approval of both sets of parents. When her husband was killed fighting for the King in August 1645, Cary was pregnant. The child was a daughter 'to all our griefs' and within months, Cary felt so intimidated by her in-laws that she left their house with her daughter, and joined her sisters at Claydon. Her father-in-law was a man of high temper and a strong Royalist – the King's candidate for Speaker in 1641 – and was very hostile to Sir Ralph's support of parliament in 1642. Political animosity and Cary's failure to produce a son to further the dynastic succession made Cary a person of no standing amongst the Gardiners. Nevertheless Cary's charms had found her a suitor and husband at fifteen, before any of her elder sisters had married. They now enabled her to re-marry into the comfortable Hampshire gentry life as wife of John Stewkeley, where she lived contentedly in a world without notable elite networks and connections.

Three of Cary's sisters married in the more difficult circumstances of the Civil War. In late 1642 Lady Sussex had written to Sir Ralph: 'I am afraid in these bad times you will not match your sisters as you desire'.[65] The war circumscribed their social lives when they were in their early twenties and limited their opportunities to potential husbands. Susan, Penelope, and Margaret (Peg) spent most of the war years at Claydon House, amongst the household servants and amidst the plunder and skirmishing around them. They were deprived of London society and lacked parental guidance and authority. Their brothers (all older than they were) were their closest advisers, and Sir Ralph, the head of the family was in France and could only respond with considerable delay. There was also the problem of money. Their small allowances were often in arrears during the war and their dowries were at risk. Margaret was fortunate to have been promised a dowry by her aunt, Lady Eure, and it was promptly paid. The four remaining sisters' dowries were payable out of the twenty-one-year aulnage annuity which remained unpaid. Susan and Penelope married during

---

[65] F. P. Verney and M. M. Verney, *Verney Memoirs*, III, p. 350.

the war but their dowries were not fully paid, the rest remained promised by Sir Ralph and William Denton. Furthermore Sir Ralph firmly insisted that their dowries be paid from his father's estate and refused to raise capital sums for his sisters on his own account. However, Denton and Sir Ralph helped the sisters to petition parliament for their dowries in 1647–8, and again in February 1653.[66] Sir Ralph paid his sisters allowances of £40, sometimes £50 during their lives, but would go no further.

When Susan, Margaret, and Penelope were finding husbands in 1645–6 their dowries were still in play and an attraction to suitors. Their brothers Henry and Thomas introduced them to their future husbands, bringing them on visits to Claydon. All three were, in 1646, married to husbands from the middling gentry – Robert Alport of Cheshire, Thomas Elmes of Northamptonshire, and John Denton of Oxfordshire (a distant cousin). Promises were made about Susan and Penelope's dowries that were sufficient to allow a marriage. Susan's marriage seems to have been happy but fated. Within a few months she wrote from the Fleet prison where Robert had been incarcerated for debt, mainly other people's. She died in childbirth in 1650. Margaret's husband, Thomas Elmes, proved a very ill tempered man, and the couple badly suited. By 1657–8 Margaret was discussing a formal separation with her husband, who agreed to pay her £160 a year.[67] Penelope's husband, John Denton, could also be violent and the marriage was fraught, though some humour carried them through. In 1653 the couple signed (and had witnessed) an agreement in which John would suffer a £5 forfeit if he struck his wife with a stick or sword, or called her rude names over the following six months.[68]

By the mid-1650s all hope of the aulnage annuity had gone. The two younger daughters, Mary and Elizabeth, expected little beyond the payment of a life annuity. Their characters were very different. Mary, lively, engaging, and audacious, had boldly taken her own rooms as a single woman in London in 1653, but fell pregnant, probably by Sir Ralph Verney's secretary Robert Lloyd, failed to abort the child, and gave birth, unmarried, probably in early November 1654. Sir Ralph was horrified at the disgrace to the family, disapproved violently of Lloyd's pretensions and conduct, and opposed a marriage. Mary held out for her brother's change of heart for a year, but eventually married Robert in November 1655. Sir Ralph never again communicated with her directly, and instructed the rest of the family to ostracise her. Eventually Mary and her husband left London for his native Cheshire where his family lived. Sir Ralph did, however, pay her allowance promptly until she died in 1684.

---

[66] F. P. Verney and M. M. Verney, *Verney Memoirs*, III, pp. 431–7, print the relevant petitions and responses found in the Portland MSS; srv to Margaret Sherrard 14 February 1652/3 R11.

[67] T. Elmes settlement dated 30 January 1657/8 R15; T. Elmes to srv 9 February 1657/8 R15; srv to wd 2 March 1657/8 R15.

[68] John Denton bond to Penelope Denton dated 1 October 1654 R13.

Elizabeth, the youngest of the family by five years, remained in her sisters' orbit, particularly with Cary, until 1662 when Cary's husband objected. She was twenty-nine, and felt aggrieved that her brother had not found her a husband. He instead found her a place with a couple who kept a school at Goring in Oxfordshire, which he considered 'no ill shelter', but where Elizabeth reflected 'I think my marrying very unlikely in any place and impossible in this'.[69] She lasted only three months there, returning to London to share lodgings with another poor gentlewoman in the City. There she was swiftly wooed by a poor clergyman and married him without her brother's approval in November 1662. Charles Adams had no living, but the Verneys helped find him one at Great Baddow in Essex. Mary and Elizabeth made poor matches because they had no hopes of securing a cash dowry. Their brother also remarked that they had grown up wild without proper supervision during their formative years. Yet their allowances of £40 a year made them prizes for the poorer gentry, or those with aspirations to gentility. Both made the best of their lot in life, preferring marriage to social inferiors to the limited and demeaning alternatives of acting as poor companions in gentry households, or eking out a penurious existence in London lodgings.

The period from 1640 to 1660 brought great strains and changes to the Verney family, and profoundly influenced Sir Ralph's outlook and aspirations. He remained obsessed with debts and financial stability. He never allowed his son to stand surety for his debts, because such obligations had made his own life so much more difficult. He spent a great deal of time and energy dealing with his brothers' and sisters' difficulties over many years. He did what he felt he ought to help them and promote their interests, but never at the expense of the greater purpose of securing the succession of substantial estates to his heirs. Unable to gain a seat in parliament in 1660, he spent time and energy on his estates, reorganising them, ensuring they were well farmed and tenanted, and maximising the income he could raise from them. In this he was returning to concerns and skills first learnt in the 1630s. To understand how he was to apply them, we need to appreciate the impact of the Verneys on the village of Middle Claydon. The next chapter looks at the nature of the village society, its landscape, farming, and people, in the face of substantial change, from the beginning of the century to the completion of enclosure in 1657.

---

[69] F. P. Verney and M. M. Verney, *Memoirs of the Verney Family*, III, p. 20.

4   The creation of an enclosed estate 1600–1657

The Verneys focused their interest on their Middle Claydon estate in the early seventeenth century, particularly after Claydon House became their country residence in 1620. They quickly adopted estate policies that modernised property rights, tenures, farmsteads, and farming practices. By 1657 Middle Claydon had been transformed into a parish with a single landlord, enclosed fields without common rights, a country house with deer park, and ring-fenced farmsteads held by leaseholders or tenants-at-will at rack rents. The process had significant effects on the villagers and their relationships with their parson and landlord. Middle Claydon was one of hundreds of communities across England where analogous changes took place in the seventeenth century. But it is one of the few in which the decision-making process and human impact can be analysed in detail.

The character of Middle Claydon's landscape was heavily influenced by the heavy clayland subsoil, and the legacy of Bernwood forest. In 1600 the ancient bounds of Bernwood still contained considerable tracts of woodland and common waste which had in medieval times been shared between several parishes. That small part of Bernwood on the Oxfordshire/Buckinghamshire borders that remained Royal Forest in 1600 shared its resources with several Otmoor parishes, and also with Shabbington, several miles to the south, until these purlieu rights, as they were called, were extinguished in the 1590s. Kingswood, to the north-west, also provided shared resources. Similar patterns existed around the Claydons.[1] East Claydon had intercommoning rights over Claydon Lawn with Middle Claydon, and on Coppesley Hill with Quainton parish. Further north Hillesden and Buckingham shared rights over an area called Lenborough Wild.[2] Even where intercommoning is not formally recorded there were considerable adjoining parish-edge lands where it probably existed at an earlier date. Immediately to the south of Claydon Lawn and woods lay

---

[1] Broad and Hoyle, *Bernwood*, ch. 3.
[2] M. Reed, 'Enclosure in north Buckinghamshire, 1500–1750', *Agricultural History Review* 32:2 (1984), pp. 139–41.

the extensive area of Grendon Common, still intact in the 1760s.[3] Three Points
Lane, an ancient track well articulated in mid-seventeenth century maps, provided both a division between parishes, and an access route to grazing on both
sides. Steeple Claydon's extensive common waste on the south-west edge of
the parish adjoined the larger area of Charndon common.

In the later medieval period, settlements on north-west Buckinghamshire's
poor soils reacted sensitively to economic and social pressures. Even before the
Black Death the Nonarum Inquisitions reported uncultivated lands in a number
of vills.[4] In the later fifteenth century there was substantial depopulation, particularly in Ashendon hundred, where four 'lost villages', Fulbrook, Hogshaw,
Shipton Lee, and Doddershall, lay close to the Claydons. The land there was laid
down to grass and turned into extensive sheep runs for wool.[5] Nearer Aylesbury
a similar fate awaited Fleet Marston (once a Verney property), Quarrendon, and
Creslow, which by the late seventeenth century had become renowned for the
quality of their pastures for fattening sheep and cattle.[6]

Even where village settlements did not disappear, manorial lords took advantage of the declining demand for arable land to enclose their demesnes
into large-scale sheep runs to produce wool for home consumption and export.
Some enclosures were recorded in the 1517 depopulation returns, while those
of 1607 returns, instigated after the midland Revolt, showed substantial enclosures at Brill. Great Pollicott in Ashendon had been turned entirely to pasture.[7]
In 1620 a purveyance survey of the pastures of north Buckinghamshire listed
widespread enclosed pastures in the area, and graded their quality.[8] 'Ancient'
enclosures were exempt, but not defined, and most parishes in the hundred
reported 'several' pastures that were of recent creation. Ashendon hundred reported a much higher level of enclosure than any other hundred, and only three
parishes listed none. If we take Middle Claydon rent figures of £1 an acre for
its second-class pastures as a mean for all pastures, at least 25 per cent of the
area of the hundred was enclosed by gentry and yeoman owners in the sixty
years before 1620. This was a substantial part of the 73 per cent of the hundred
enclosed without parliamentary Act.[9]

[3] Jeffreys's map of 1770 in *Buckinghamshire in the 1760s and 1820s: The County Maps of Jeffreys
   and Bryant*, Buckinghamshire Archaeological Society 2000.
[4] A. R. H. Baker, 'Evidence from the "Nonarum Inquisitions" of contracting arable lands during
   the early fourteenth century', *Economic History Review* 2nd series, 19 (1966), pp. 518–32.
[5] M. W. Beresford, *The Lost Villages of England* (London 1954), p. 230 for relevant map.
[6] D. Defoe, *A Tour through the Whole Island of Great Britain* (London and Toronto 1928), II,
   p. 14.
[7] Reed, 'Enclosure in north Buckinghamshire, 1500–1750', p. 134.
[8] Bodl. MS Willis 30, cf. BCRO D/X49 and D/P/1/A1 for equivalent late sixteenth-century rolls
   with less information. In 1620 Ashendon hundred was surveyed twice in July and September.
[9] Reed, 'Enclosure in north Buckinghamshire, 1500–1750', p. 133.

The Verneys began to re-shape their Middle Claydon estate even before they took up residence in 1620. The 1620 Purveyance survey noted enclosed lands amongst Claydon woods where up to 150 acres of woodland had been cleared while the Giffords had 400 or 500 acres of enclosures on their demesne. An important prelude to enclosure was the agreement Edmund Verney and his mother reached with Sir Thomas Lee, manorial lord, and the freeholders of East Claydon in April 1613. This ended intercommoning on the overlawn between the two parishes, and defined a new boundary.[10] The freeholders were to lose their rights of common over the rough pasture amongst the ancient woodland, and the new boundary marked by a six-foot-wide ditch. The division took careful account of the soil quality, turning the parish boundary at that point on a tortuous and apparently illogical course to share the better soils nearer the villages. Edmund Verney and his mother did not include the other freeholders of Middle Claydon in the agreement, claiming absolute rights to the woodlands and arguing that it was recompense for the £300 they had spent on enclosure.[11] Middle Claydon now had fixed boundaries on all sides (see figure 2). It was a major pre-requisite for establishing unified ownership and control of the parish.

Sir Edmund Verney and his mother began to buy up any Middle Claydon freehold property that came available after 1608, even before they recovered the house and demesnes in 1620.[12] Information has survived on only two purchases – a strip of open field land, and a further half yardland purchased in 1610 and 1621 respectively. There were a few others, one purchased in 1632. A tax assessment for Middle Claydon in the last year of James I's reign included three taxpayers rated on their land, John Cox, Edward Deely, and Thomas Hicks, but there is no evidence of freeholders in disputes or manorial court business after 1621.[13]

Tenants on the Verneys' freehold land held leases for years, or lives and years, but there were also copyhold tenants with substantial rights exerted through a working manor court. Early seventeenth-century court rolls show a characteristic range of regulatory activities, with presentments for overstocking the commons, encroachments, sub-lettings, taking in lodgers, and not repairing fences and mounds, as well as changes in copyhold tenancies.[14] Estate correspondence between Sir Edmund Verney, his son Ralph, William Roades the bailiff, and John Aris the parson, indicates that the Verneys planned to allow manorial rights to run down, to change tenures from copyhold to leasehold, and to enclose the parish. The eighteen absentees named in the 1631 court

---

[10] CIH 2/33 and 2/34. The name 'Over Lawn' reflected the primary purpose of the medieval Royal Forests, the hunting of deer. Lawns were areas of grassland amongst the trees where deer could feed. Foresters might take a hay crop to provide winter forage for their charges.

[11] J. Aris memorandum n.d. c. 1635 R2.   [12] CIH 2/32–3 and 3/36.

[13] PRO E179/79/275 Assessment for Ashendon hundred 22 James I.   [14] CIH3/1/5–10.

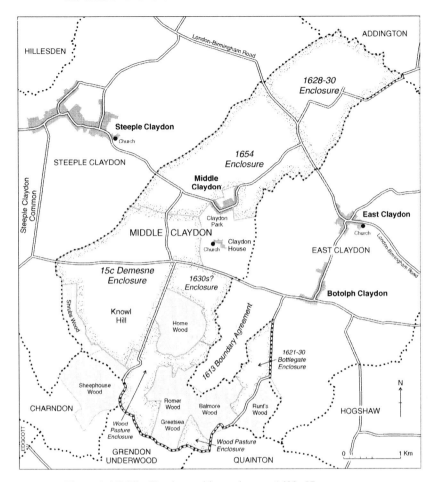

Figure 2 Middle Claydon and its enclosures 1600–57.

Roll included the Verneys' bailiff and woodman, William and Thomas Roades. In October 1632 the Manor Court held a last meeting, although some traditional functions continued and dues were collected through the 1630s. When Sir Edmund Verney threatened to call a court on one occasion it was to calm a village dispute, suggesting community collusion in the changes.[15] Without a court the Verneys increased their power over the land and community of Middle Claydon. The Manor Court had had a central place in the regulation of village farming and economic life. Without it copyholders could not lay claim to quasi-permanent rights over land, or to common rights. It is probable that after 1632

[15] sev to srv nd 1635/6 R3; sev to srv ?15 April 1639 R3.

Table 4.1 *Middle Claydon leases 1570–1669*

	1570–9	1580–9	1590–9	1600–9	1610–19	1620–9	1630–9	1640–9	1650–9	1660–9
Lives and years	0	1	0	0	0	5	4	1	2	0
=>21 years	2	4	2	0	1	5	5	0	5	1
10–20 years	0	1	0	1	2	0	5	0	0	0
5–9 years	0	0	0	3	0	0	2	0	1	0
1–4 years	0	0	0	1	0	0	0	0	1	0
Total leases	2	6	2	5	3	10	16	1	9	1

Source: 'The Verney papers: a catalogue'.

all incoming tenants either had leases or held their land on a year-to-year basis. Where open-field leases were granted after 1620, they included a clause giving the Verneys the right to undertake enclosure and exchanges of the land. The Verneys were sensitive to the rights of those copyholders whose tenancies they had converted to leases for lives and years, but once enclosure was complete they issued no more. The last long tenancy ended in 1678.

Leases for lives and years in lieu of copyholds were normally applied to lettings of open-field land and common rights, but some were also granted for enclosed lands. William Roades, the Verneys' bailiff/steward in the 1630s, held a long lease of his enclosed farm at Fimore but enclosed land was more usually let on fixed-term tenancies. Over fifty leases have survived in the period from 1570 to 1669 and analysis of their type and length by decade in table 4.1 indicates changing patterns.

Firstly, leases for years were well established in the late sixteenth century, mainly for twenty-one years and before 1600 usually involved a cash fine and reduced rent.[16] Most of those between 1600 and 1620 were for full rack rent. However, when Sir Edmund Verney bought back the lease of Claydon in 1620 he was short of cash. Between 1618 and 1621 he let five leases for lives taking a substantial fine for a nominal rent and raising £440 in advance. All but one were for open field farms. When he let newly enclosed land in 1623 and again in 1628–30, it was for twenty-one years and at rack rent.[17]

Policy was flexible, balancing immediate financial needs with strategic estate objectives. The surviving early seventeenth-century leases, however, cover only a small proportion of the land at Middle Claydon with the majority either held on a year-to-year basis without a lease, farmed directly, or held under customary tenure through the Manor court. In 1620 the mixture of farming styles, tenures, and farm organisation probably had many features in common with Richard

---

[16] E.g. CIH 4/2/1–6 1570–89.   [17] CIH 4/2/26–8, 30–4.

Grenville's nearby home parish of Wootton Underwood in 1657, which he described as:

In ye very depth of ye Vale of Aylesbury in an exceeding dirty clay soyle and although some ye enclosed pastures are indifferent good ground, yeat are ye inclosed woods very bad for wood by reason of their wetness and coldness: and common fields, common meadows, the Lawnd, and other commonable waste are generally very wett and cold lande and much annoyed with winter floodes . . . this said ville or towneshipp of Wotton consisteth: first of divers and sundry messuages, houses and cottages with small enclosed homestalls or closes to them, and of enclosed pasture grounds and enclosed woods; secondly it consisteth of five common fields . . . and theise five fields being in truth used and manured but as three fields . . . thirdly it consisteth of a large wast or common ground called the lawnd which is common all ye year long . . . also the common Moore or Cow pasture.[18]

At Claydon, the enclosed demesne lands included the best pastures in the parish. During the seventeenth and early eighteenth centuries Knowl Hill and its adjoining fields commanded the most attention from the Verneys as their flagship farm, and produced the highest rents per acre. Yet in 1620 Middle Claydon's pasture was not generally considered to be of the highest quality. The assessors for purveyance reckoned that two thirds of the demesne was of the 'second sort' of pasture, with the remainder of the 'third sort' and the lawn and wood closes were of the 'worst sort'.[19]

Enclosure was fundamental to the approach to the Verneys' land management at Middle Claydon, and across all their property in the seventeenth and eighteenth centuries. Common pasture and open field systems existed to be 'improved' wherever possible. The Verneys sought agreement and consensus whenever possible and avoided open conflict. Opposition was muted because most villagers had little access to the institutions and levers of power. Moreover, two obvious focuses for opposition were not available. The Verneys' bailiff, William Roades, was a leading member of the farming community in the village, and generally managed to maintain a balance of power and influence amongst his fellow farmers while doing the Verneys' bidding. He kept the Verneys well informed of village concerns, and they generally listened to his advice. The parson after 1630, John Aris, was intent on defending his tithes and glebe, and at odds with his fellow villagers as well as with the Verneys.

Enclosure at Middle Claydon was generally undertaken in piecemeal fashion. The enclosure of more than 500 acres of demesnes had been undertaken in the fifteenth century, affecting the south-west of the parish. The common open fields were mainly in the north and east of the parish, but including an area called Bottle Gate to the south-east of Claydon House. The woods and common waste,

[18] 'Wotton Underwood in 1657', *Records of Buckinghamshire* 14 (1942), pp. 133–48.
[19] Bodl. MS Willis 30 pp. 5, 9.

on the poorest soils in the south and south-east of the parish, were also enclosed gradually over a century or more, taking in areas as small as two or three acres at a time. Apart from the agreement between East and Middle Claydon to divide the intercommoned lawn, there are no surviving general agreements. Leases had enclosure clauses written into them, and as the Manor Court fell into disuse, enclosure took place at the will of the Lord of the Manor. Evidence before 1650 from leases, from glebe terriers, and letters and papers linked to disputes shows that the scale of enclosure was very considerable. By 1642 no more than 570 acres of Middle Claydon's area of 2,640 acres remained in the open fields.

Before 1620 the Verneys' lands in Middle Claydon lay in the woods and common waste to the south of the parish, where one of Sir Edmund Verney's uncles, Urian, lived in a substantial house of fourteen hearths 'lately built' at Fymer in 1592 – probably a hunting lodge.[20] The earliest surviving Claydon leases concern small enclosures of wood pasture carved from the waste in the 1570s and 1580s. These enclosures all included a house on the plot, but no more than three acres of land, and sometimes less than an acre. They suggest that smallholders were carving their own livings from the waste, as in many English forest and wood pasture areas in the late sixteenth and early seventeenth centuries when the rural population was expanding fast. Frequently landlords acted retrospectively to register new holdings and extract rents from well-established woodland squatters. At Claydon the Verneys were active participants, granting leases in anticipation of a new enclosure.[21] Comparison of seventeenth-century and modern large-scale maps shows some reduction in the area of Claydon Woodlands during the early modern period. Field names such as Diggins and New Grubbed Close are sure indications of wood clearance. The shape of some of the fields around Muxwell Wood make it look as if the wood had been clipped with fields like coin clippings, long and irregular in shape and following the line of the edge of the wood. While incoming farmers undertook some enclosures from the waste, the Verneys instigated those in the woods, balancing potential income against their game, timber, and firewood. The 1613 division of the waste and establishment of parish boundaries increased their control over the process by eliminating common pasture. During enclosures at Bottle Gate and in the wood grounds in the early 1620s the Verneys suppressed all common rights in the lawn and woods in return for paying the costs of enclosure.

The enclosures of 1621–3 involved the open fields as well as the lawn and woods. The late sixteenth-century farming economy of Middle Claydon was predominantly open field. Glebe terriers of 1577 and 1601 show a three-field

---

[20] ClH 4/2/9 dated 6 October 1592. This was probably a hunting lodge, and the figure of fourteen hearths comes from correspondence about the 1662 Hearth Tax.
[21] ClH4/2/2 23 January 1572; see also 4/2/1 (1570) and 4/2/3 (1584). For examples of settlement on forest and waste lands see D. G. Hey, *An English Rural Community: Myddle under the Tudors and Stuarts* (Leicester 1974) and Broad and Hoyle, *Bernwood*, ch. 3.

system in operation, mainly in the northern part of the parish, but with a small open-field area close to the lawn between East and Middle Claydon described as Bottle Gate. The three fields were called Whittard or Whitey Field, Boughton Field, and Mill Hill Field. The Bottle Gate land was managed as part of Mill Hill Field. The parish meadows lay in the northern extremity alongside the Claydon brook. The leases and glebe terriers show that the agricultural economy of Middle Claydon functioned around a group of open-field farmers whose field lands included strips, enclosures, and temporary leys and might be supplemented by enclosed pastures among the woods. They lived and worked alongside other farmers with rather larger enclosed holdings on the demesnes, which were predominantly sheep farms.

Two partial enclosures during the 1620s made considerable inroads into the open field system. Information from leases show that in 1621–3 the Verneys enclosed an area of open field (probably medieval assarting) at Bottle Gate. Two leases of 1623 specified closes of 16 and 17$\frac{1}{2}$ acres that were 'lately enclosed'. The tenants were required to build houses of at least two bays under the terms of their agreement. Seventeenth-century estate maps suggest that rather more open field land was divided into tiny closes in compensation for the copyholders' open field land and common rights. Many were of only one or two acres, but were consolidated into larger fields over the next fifty years.[22] These enclosures probably covered no more than 100 to 150 acres but the extinction of all common rights from woods and waste was vital for future estate management.[23]

In the late 1620s a more substantial enclosure was undertaken in the northern extremities of the parish, close to Addington. It involved just under 200 acres of open-field land and the meadows beside the Claydon Brook. In the mid-1630s a further small enclosure took place between Claydon House and Muxwell/Home wood. Descriptions in leases correlate with correspondence instructions on hedging and ditching, and the surveying of the area by a Mr Allen.[24] Between that date and 1654, when another survey was made for the final enclosure, the total amount of open-field land was 567 acres, rather lopsidedly divided between Whittard Field with 338 acres, Boughton Field with 226$\frac{1}{2}$ acres, and Bottle Gate with just over two acres.[25]

Surviving leases of the newly enclosed land suggest that some of the lessees had exchanged field strips for pasture closes, but others make no mention of field land, only of closes ten to twenty acres in size. One of the leases required the tenant to build a farmhouse on the land, but two others were built at Sir Edmund Verney's own cost. In a survey and rental of the land in 1650, five

[22] ClH 4/2/26, 27; 12/1/4–13.
[23] John Aris memorandum n.d. c. 1635 R2 claimed it was 100 acres.
[24] Clh 4/2/42 Lea, 4/2/41 Francklin, 4/2/45 Fitch, sev to srv 5 and 11 January, 26 February 1635/6 R3.
[25] srv memorandum n.d. c. 1653 in papers for 15 June 1653 R12.

farmsteads were noted in an area of 193 acres in that part of the parish.[26] Such re-organisation of farmsteads was particularly appropriate in a move from arable farming and into livestock, but had important additional implications for the village community. Farmers were more distant from the village centre, had fewer opportunities to meet casually to discuss village politics and gossip, and were perhaps less likely to present a common front to their landlord. When farmers lived on ring-fenced tenanted farms, they were also immediately aware of any incursions on their enclosure by those who opposed it, and had a greater incentive to preserve the new order.[27]

Sir Edmund Verney's enclosures substantially altered the landscape and farming of Middle Claydon, but were part of a wider estate strategy that scrutinised land areas, rent levels, and expectations of returns across all his property. At nearby Mursley considerable areas of commons were enclosed in 1619. An enclosure agreement was drawn up in 1611 between Sir Edmund Verney, Sir Francis Fortescue (the only other elite landowner in the parish) and the tenants and farmers. It defined the common waste to be improved, set out terms for compensating farmers and cottagers, but left all residual lands and rights in Sir Edmund's hands. A lease of 1615 included clauses allowing Sir Edmund to enclose commons and waste, exchange common field holdings, and set up arbitration procedures to determine the extent of any rent increases.[28] The enclosure of Mursley Common began in 1619 and by 1624 a substantial part of the parish had been enclosed. But as Verney enclosed and increased rents, he sold his holdings to raise money desperately needed to pay for the purchase of Middle Claydon. Some open fields remained until the parliamentary enclosure of 1819, but after the early seventeenth-century enclosure the manorial system became irrelevant as most common rights belonged to the Verneys. In 1648 the local lawyer, Robert Busby, held a court 'to no purpose in any particular whatsoever but only to receive a presentment from the Jury of yourself for not repairing the pound, although there hath been no court kept there for that Estate for these twenty-eight years'. When the Verneys sold the Lordship in 1663 the price of £100 reflected its near-titular status and negligible income.[29]

When Sir Ralph came of age in 1634 he began to exploit his wife's estate at Wasing in Berkshire in a similar fashion. Cottagers had enclosed part of the common waste and built houses on it, but Sir Ralph wanted to regulate the removal of turf for fuel and make the parson, freeholders, and tenants concede his ultimate ownership of the manorial wasteland. Control of areas subject to common and popular rights was consolidated in other ways. Sir Ralph granted Thomas Marshall a renewal of the lease of his farm in 1634, but just a few

[26] srv memorandum n.d. *c.* 1650 R11.
[27] ClH 4/2/33 Hinton, 4/2/35 William Lea, 4/2/38 William Clark and Richard Hogston.
[28] Agreement of 1611 R2; ClH 4/2/194a b 9 March 1614/15.
[29] ClH 2/1297; wr to srv 13 and 21 October 1648 R9. Robert Busby to srv 9 December 1648 R9.

months later Marshall agreed to lease an option on all his rights on the heath and common at six months' notice. Early in 1638 Verney tightened his control by taking a lease of the tithe of coneys on the heath, giving him the right to survey the warren.[30]

Practice on outlying estates confirms that the Verneys wanted the same kind of control there as at Claydon. At Claydon the Verneys took a leading part in day-to-day management, despite the fact that their estate bailiff/stewards, John, and then William Roades, lived and farmed in the parish.[31] When Sir Ralph reached adulthood in 1634 he began to run the estate under his father's guidance, and their letters show the process of policy making. The Verneys took a detailed interest in individual holdings, making decisions about incoming tenants and those in arrears and failing. Sir Edmund required precise information on a wide range of issues and even specialist matters. For instance in a letter in January 1636 he instructed his son to carry out some land exchanges between tenants, and to alter the terms of his bailiff's (William Roades's) lease. He worried over the timing of sheep sales on the home farm, and whether the ploughman was ploughing the land too early in the year, 'but because I understand it not I must leave it to them'.[32] As parts of the Claydon estate were surveyed, farms and fields could be let on the basis of rent per acre for each field. The building costs of a new house for a tenant added to rent requiring a return at the standard rate of interest: 'If he will have me bestow a house of £100 on the ground at the rent of £8 a year I will do it'.[33]

From 1600 to 1640 the Verneys actively managed their whole estate. They consolidated land rights, enclosed open-field land and waste, and gradually squeezed out manorial institutions. Their land surveying, close financial control of rentals, and detailed leases raised income and increased control of their property and the villagers who farmed it. The lack of probate inventories makes it more difficult to reconstruct the lives of farmers and estimate the impact of these policies on villagers, as John Goodacre was able to do in south-west Leicestershire.[34]

At Claydon, the estate leases provide evidence of different kinds of farming, but only partly support Goodacre's contention that there was a clear divide between open field farmers with only a few small closes of less than five acres, and the specialist livestock farmers whose land was exclusively pasture.[35] A

---

[30] CIH 4/2/2/7 lease dated 20 November 1634; 2/1538 undertaking dated 19 March 1634/5; 4/2/218 dated 10 January 1637/8 lease of tithe of coneys.

[31] John Roades appears collecting rents and keeping a rental in 1611, see CIH 4/3/1.

[32] sev to srv 4 and 5 January 1635/6 R3 and several others in the period.

[33] sev to srv 26 February 1635/6 R3, 6 April 1636 R3, 9 March 1635/6 R3.

[34] J. Goodacre, *The Transformation of a Peasant Economy: Townspeople and Villagers in the Lutterworth area 1500–1700* (Aldershot 1994), esp. pp. 93–123.

[35] *Ibid.* pp. 141–2.

number of different kinds of farming enterprise can be distinguished in Middle Claydon. On the demesnes sheep farming appears to have been the main enterprise during the 1630s, and the Verneys kept sheep on the hundred or so acres they farmed themselves. By 1652 a mixture of sheep and dairy cows were kept on an adjacent farm.[36] Most new enclosures were put down to grass and leased as pasture, which produced a much higher rent per acre than arable, but how tenants farmed their holdings is unclear. The tenants who took leases in the 1620s and 1630s were very different from the established yeomen, shepherds, and minor gentry who arrived after enclosure in the 1650s. In 1623 holdings were let to William Hall of Whitchurch, and to a partnership of Edward Hinton of Whitchurch and John Hinton of Bottle Claydon, all of them described as labourers. Both holdings were of 15 to 20 acres, and the tenants had to build a house of two bays on the grounds at their own cost. Other leases to yeomen during the early 1630s show farmhouses being built away from the village centre, on newly enclosed grounds and also on older demesne enclosures. A lease of part of the great sheep pasture of Knowl Hill in 1631 came with a house newly built by Sir Edmund. The tenants for this prime land were not just outsiders (from Swanbourne and Shipton Lee), but non-specialists whose occupations were given as a carpenter and blacksmith. Four other leases in 1634–5 went to yeomen, all but one from outside the village, and including a new farmhouse on one holding. The outsiders came predominantly from nearby open-field villages such as Whitchurch, North Marston, and East Claydon, none of which were enclosed before 1700. Their non-agricultural trades and skills suggest they could find alternative employment while they developed specialist pasture farming skills. The starting date of the leases for these small enclosed farms was Lady Day (25 March), the beginning of the farming year in pastoral areas. Most open-field leases at Claydon in the same period had a September starting date – Michaelmas – appropriate for arable enterprises.[37]

During the 1630s open-field farm leases included more enclosed pasture closes, which suggests a shift to more pastoral farming systems, perhaps because of the significant effects of early seventeenth-century enclosures on the practical workings of Middle Claydon's open field system. Terriers of 1577 and 1601 show four open-field areas, almost certainly operated on a three-year cycle with Mill Hill Field and the furlongs at Bottle Gate operating as one for the purposes of field management. However, by 1630 a two-field system had been introduced, though no field orders or court decisions mark the change. The field orders of June 1631 set out the sheep stints by field, mentioning only Whittard and Boughton fields, while Parson Aris's memoranda between 1635 and 1638

---

[36] PRO C6/15/191 Verney vs. Robert Stopp 1653.
[37] A. Kussmaul, *A General View of the Rural Economy of England 1538–1840* (Cambridge 1990), pp. 14–22.

clearly indicate a two-field system in operation. This increased the percentage of land under fallow and thus available grazing. The single field under crops grew grain crops (usually barley or oats) and pulses in roughly equal proportions. The common meadows remained, but the segments occupied by individual common right holders changed from year to year 'by lot'.[38] The shift from a three-field to a two-field system was a response used elsewhere in north Buckinghamshire, at Great Linford in the mid-sixteenth century.[39] The 1631 field orders also reduced stints for horses and cattle, banned horses from feeding in the cottagers' closes, and allowed two widows to replace their horse commons with cow commons. They indicate some of the stress points in the system. Some small holdings could not afford to keep a plough team, and others were so small that the cottager was more likely to keep a cow than plough the land. Twenty-five years earlier, the manor court had threatened a tenant with a substantial fine for not keeping a team.[40]

A series of exchanges between John Aris, the rector of Middle Claydon, and Sir Edmund Verney in the mid-1630s vividly portray the scale of change. Aris became rector in 1630 and attempted to retrieve the rights and lost income he claimed had been given up during the two enclosures of the 1620s. He used the political climate of the 1630s to support his claims. The Bishop of Lincoln appointed an enquiry soon after a visitation when he ordered Middle Claydon to provide altar rails in the church.[41] This local controversy paralleled Archbishop Laud's attempts to reinforce traditional social policies across the country including a drive to penalise depopulating enclosure and the conversion of land from arable to pasture. Fines were high and opponents of the Crown claimed that revenue take was a more important drive behind enforcement than social concern.[42] Through his political and court connections, Sir Edmund Verney avoided indictment. In March 1635 the constable of Middle Claydon, Roger Deely, was asked to make a return concerning enclosure in the parish. He certified that some thirty or forty acres of tillage had been enclosed within the

[38] CIH 3/1/9 A glebe terrier of 1639 still mentions open-field strips at Bottle Gate but without any indication of their operation, see BCRO D/A/GT/3/1/1. The system of meadow changing by lots was also used in East Claydon – see M. Reed, *Buckinghamshire Glebe Terriers 1580–1640*, Buckinghamshire Record Society 30 (1997), p. 80.

[39] A. C. Chibnall, *Sherington: Fiefs and Fields of a Buckinghamshire Village* (Cambridge 1965), p. 199. It has been argued that Steeple Claydon had a two-field system throughout the sixteenth and seventeenth centuries, and only changed to three fields in the eighteenth century; W. James and J. A. Malcolm, *General View of the Agriculture of Buckinghamshire* (1794), p. 30.

[40] CIH 3/1/6 court Roll of 1613.

[41] Bishop of Lincoln's order of 30 January 1634/5 R2 ordered three neighbouring clergy to enquire into the validity of the exchange of lands. BCRO PR52/5/1 shows new altar rails were bought in 1634.

[42] K. Sharpe, *The Personal Rule of Charles I*, pp. 471–3, points to claims in 1639 that £40,000 had been raised through fines by then. See also J. Thirsk, 'Changing attitudes to enclosure in the seventeenth century', *Festschrift for Professor Ju Hwan Oh on the Occasion of his Sixtieth Birthday* (Taegu, Korea 1991).

past thirty years, and named the current occupiers.[43] Deely probably showed
Sir Ralph Verney his draft out of deference. Sir Ralph immediately consulted
his father in London. Sir Edmund rapidly responded with a redrafted version:

I do certify that about thirteen years since Sir Edmund Verney Kt. Lord of the Manor
converted to pasture between thirty and forty acres of land by estimation which had until
then always been used in tillage, and that he is the owner and user of that land, but there
is no decay of houses in the parish.

He would not name tenants because 'if proofs should come out against so many
it would put us to great charge, for I must brave them all out in it'. He justified
his insistence on a statement that there was no decay of houses by writing that
'though there be some houses down, yet there are more erected in their place',
and ended his letter: 'I am well acquainted what is intended in this business of
conversion. Therefore let the return be made according to this direction and let
him make no other.' The tone of the letter reflects Sir Edmund's sense of his
own authority in such village matters, but probably also shock at the £4,000
fine for pulling down houses imposed by Star Chamber on Anthony Roper in
October 1634.[44]

Verney avoided indictment, but the issue became entangled with John Aris's
claim of unfair land exchanges in previous enclosures. This dispute dragged
on for years, creating friction between parson and landlord that 'the town' (as
both parties referred to the leading farmers in the community) tried to exploit
to its own advantage. The Verneys trod carefully in the dispute despite their
strong position, intent on preventing a minor dispute escalating into wider
controversy.[45]

Parson Aris argued that the Verneys and village farmers had benefited from
enclosure at his expense. To the Verneys, who had compensated themselves for
the cost of the enclosure by taking over all rights of common in the woods and
fields around them, he argued that the village farmers had done even better for

their present benefit for their share that had estates [the copyholders and long
leaseholders] was greater than his [Sir Edmund's]. Their livings for their lives were
doubled to them without any penny out of purse, whereas the lord [Verney] made a kind
purchase of that which he enclosed to himself.

Aris felt he had lost because the parson received poor-quality land while agricultural changes reduced his tithe income. He cited the reduced number of sheep on

---

[43] Warrant and Return dated 13 March 1634/5 R2. The small extent of the land mentioned in this,
and never contested by Verney, suggests either collusion in which only those enclosures disputed
by the parson were referred to, or that much of the Addington and other field enclosures were
already leys and could therefore be ignored according to the precise terms of the enquiry.

[44] sev to srv 13 March 1634/5 R2. On the Roper case see K. Sharpe, *Personal Rule*, p. 472.

[45] John Aris to sev 20 August, 29 September 1638 R2; sev to srv n.d. R2, 11 May 1639 R3; sev to
John Aris 11 April 1635 R2.

enclosed lands, lower stints on the common fields, and losses from the change from a three-field to a two-field system of working the land. His grievances are indicative of the stresses faced by the whole community in Middle Claydon.[46]

Piecemeal changes to Claydon's landscape and village community between 1600 and 1640 strengthened the Verneys' position as dominant landowners, and constricted the operation of the open fields. It is extremely difficult to document changing farm sizes, but the new lettings of ten- to twenty-acre farms to labourers or craftsmen suggest that these Claydon enclosures were not depopulating. The large pasture farms did not encroach on the newly enclosed fields. Furthermore, just as Goodacre found in the Lutterworth area, economic conditions and fashions favoured some ploughing up of old pastures and the adoption, even if briefly, of up-and-down husbandry on some land. In 1642–3 the Verneys farmed over 100 acres of land in hand which by the autumn of 1643 had produced barley, pease, and 196 sheep, but predominantly oats with almost three hundred loads harvested and in store.[47]

The piecemeal nature of changes in the first half of the seventeenth century preserved social continuity in the parish, even as Verney estate management modernised and measured every aspect of life. A few leases involved token payments in kind, and labour services on the roads (open-field farmers who needed horses and wagons to work the land had them available for road work at slack times of the year), but money rents were the norm. Land was measured and valued, even re-measured from time to time, as in 1636. Competitive bidding for farms that fell empty was normal practice, and the re-modelling of farms was only considered when prospective tenants made equal bids. Leases included clauses to ensure the land was kept 'in heart' by self-sustaining farming practices, and the correspondence confirms that these were real concerns, not routine and established wordings. Sir Edmund and his son were not just surveyors and accountants, they had a good understanding of appropriate farming techniques and practices in the area, even if they deferred to a working farmer like William Roades over details.[48]

When John Wells wrote to Sir Edmund Verney in February 1636 offering to rent a large enclosed pasture and adjoining meadow land, his letter differed very little in tone and wording from those of his successors a hundred years later. This was not simply a reflection of the co-existence of old and new ways of farming. John Aris's contemporary description of the functioning of the open fields shows how commercial considerations as well as physical constraints were altering practices. Few open-field farmers retained a permanent flock of

---

[46] John Aris memorandum *c.* 1635 R2.
[47] Goodacre, *Transformation of a Peasant Economy*, p.131; E. Kerridge, *The Agricultural Revolution* (London 1967), ch. 3. sev to srv 9 March 1635/6 R3. William Roades accounts 20 September 1643 R5.
[48] sev to srv 6 April 1636 R3; sev to Margaret Verney 27 April 1636 R3.

sheep to fold 'at the beginning and end of the year. Now they are beholding to foreigners who are long ere they come, and are gone betime'. Tithe lambs had fallen in number from thirty to seven or eight a year, and were likely to be reduced to nothing because 'they cannot winter ewes in the field, but with great loss, there being but little dry ground or harbour for them'. The tithe of wool had fallen by 75 per cent 'because few winter sheep, but keep them only one quarter before the shearer'. The constricted open-field system sparked commercially orientated animal management practices amongst farmers, similar to those found by Goodacre in Leicestershire at the same time. Within a few years open-field farmers were calling for the complete enclosure of Middle Claydon.[49]

From 1643 to 1653, the villagers of Middle Claydon experienced war damage, high taxation, a variety of human and animal epidemics, and much remoter supervision by their exiled landlord. When Sir Ralph Verney left for France in the autumn of 1643 he gave William Roades responsibility for the everyday decision-making, reporting in the first instance to William Denton in London, or other family members. From France Sir Ralph bewailed his own poverty and the lack of estate income during the war years,[50] but these were the end product of the chaos of war, plunder, and taxation directly suffered by the farmers and villagers of Middle Claydon and his other properties. How well did Middle Claydon survive in the face of these threats and demands?

William Roades's letters between 1643 and 1646 show that during the war tenants delayed paying their rent and often left their farms. When new tenants bargained for land, rent levels were reduced because they refused to pay taxation on the land. The skirmishing close to Claydon had an immediate impact. After the siege of Hillesden early in 1644, when parliamentary troops had encamped in Steeple Claydon, several tenants left. Sir Ralph commented hopefully: 'I believe they are much terrified with this last action, perhaps a month hence they may a little forget this, and be content to hold their bargains with some abatement'. He offered to offset some losses from plundering soldiers against rent, but recognised that 'it will be unsafe to stock the grounds which the tenants now leave, they may do it much safer than I can'.[50] A year later the establishment of a Royalist garrison in the adjoining parish of Addington 'makes all the 555 [tenants] remove from the place enclosed between Croton [Claydon] and that place'. The 193 acres of Addington enclosures were a substantial part of estate income. Roades believed that he would make no income from the land while the garrison was there.[51]

One tenant left a 35-acre farm to go into service, while those who remained could negotiate reduced rents at a level between one half to two thirds of

---

[49] John Aris, Memorandum n.d. c. 1635 R2; Goodacre, *Transformation of a Peasant Economy*, pp. 123–5.

[50] srv to wr 29 March 1643/4 R5.   [51] wr to srv 12 March 1644/5 R6.

pre-war levels.[52] Departing tenants did not necessarily cease farming, or leave the village. If they had cattle or sheep they could continue farming by paying to keep their animals on a daily basis at very favourable rates. Agistments, or 'joistments' as they were commonly called, became a major component of dwindling estate income during the war years. In the year from March 1644 Roades made £61 in agistments from vacant lands compared with £12 10s from hay, and £10 for the winter feeding of the grass of two fields. With so much untenanted land tenants could keep their stock very cheaply.[53] War increased farmers' risks, but those who kept solvent were in a strong position, with good local market opportunities and additional demand from garrisons. When the Verneys grew almost 300 loads of oats on their prime pasture, Knowl Hill, in 1642–3 the demand for horse fodder in war zones must have influenced their choice of crop.[54]

The war disrupted trade and brought farmers occasional seizures and losses from plundering or occupying forces, but they may not have been a greater threat to farmers than spring droughts, harvest rains, or crop and animal diseases. Some farmers, such as Richard Collins were prepared to take on large farms even at the height of war. One tenant, Thomas Kent substantially rebuilt his house as a smithy, paying the cost himself and recouping his money by paying no rent for the next five years. Roades provided stone and a substantial amount of timber, but Kent paid for other materials and for the labour, bringing in specialists from the neighbourhood, but using villagers for much of the work. He spent almost £20 in the middle of the war. Kent's profession as blacksmith required the building of a brick forge, but the reconstructed house also contained a buttery for dairying, a lean-to barn, and the refurbishment of a cow house. Kent remained in the village for at least twelve years, holding village office several times and paying taxes, but he never became tenant for any fields, despite building a dairy. He may have used agistments to sustain a small-scale farming enterprise, at least during the war years.[55]

At the end of the first Civil War there was a rapid recovery in rent levels nationally, and at Claydon no shortage of tenants for large or small farms with the capital to invest in livestock. However three village listings for 1646, 1647, and 1648 show that a high turnover of farmers continued after the war. They can be used, together with the parish register reconstitution and correspondence to reconstruct the structure of village society in the last years of the open-field

---

[52] wr to srv 9 September 1645 R6.
[53] William Roades's account 24 March 1645 R6; cf. Eleanor, Countess of Sussex, to srv 29 July 1644 R5.
[54] P. Edwards, *Dealing in Death: The Arms Trade and the British Civil Wars* (Stroud 2000).
[55] Building Account dated 1645 in papers for end 1648 R9. For a detailed account and analysis see M. Airs and J. Broad, 'The management of rural building in seventeenth-century Bucking-hamshire', *Vernacular Architecture* 29 (1998), pp. 43–56.

system. The 1646 document is a full rental of the Middle Claydon estate made at the time of Sir Ralph Verney's sequestration with reasonably accurate valuations. Fifty-nine names appear on the list, and the overwhelming majority were resident in Middle Claydon, suggesting a village population of approximately 250.[56]

Comparison with an updated tax assessment for 1647 and a parish rate assessment of 1648 reveals much about tenant turnover, the structure of tenancies, and the cottagers and poor labourers. The 1648 parish rate assessment includes fifty-three names, consistent with the omission of the very poor from the list. The 1647 tax assessment included only forty-one names, with a higher threshold for payment.[57] Some of the seven names that only appear on the rent list had rents below £1 a year, and none more than £6. Those on the rate list, but not the tax assessment predominantly paid £1 to £5 in rent, but included two paying £15 to £20 a year. Taking into account the changing circumstances of villagers, and movement in and out of the parish, the pattern is remarkably consistent.

At the end of the Civil War about two thirds of village families were above the tax threshold, while about 14 per cent were too poor to be rated. Most of the copyholders and long leaseholders who were paying nominal or low rents on their farms also paid both tax and rates which were based on a full valuation of the land. On twelve holdings there is a marked disparity between the two figures, showing some tenants on nominal rents, but about half of them on rents that were approximately half the full value. The lists also reveal tenant turnover in the post-war period. In October 1648 William Roades identified four 'livings' where the tenant had recently died (three cases) or left (one case). 'Livings' in this context appears to mean not just lifehold tenancies, but lands with a substantial proportion of open-field land. Overall between 1646 and 1648 eight rate-paying tenants appear to have left, and eight new names appear on the 1648 rate list, of whom six probably rented medium and larger farms. This turnover of approximately one in seven tenants in two years included chance elements. Three died, one, Richard King perhaps in an epidemic. He and his wife died in the same month, October 1648, when 'pox' was raging in the neighbourhood and was so bad at Mursley that William Roades would not go there to do estate business.[58]

Severe animal epidemics at this time may also have increased tenant turnover. Roades commented on stock dying of sickness in September 1645, but from 1647 to 1649 cattle murrain (probably rinderpest, known in the eighteenth century as cattle plague) and sheep rot were rife. Summer rains made the harvest of 1648 a poor one, with high grain prices. The winter of 1648/9 was particularly

---

[56] PRO SP 207 pp. 371–82.

[57] The 1647 tax assessment is PRO E179/244/9, while the 1648 rating lists are amongst papers for end June 1648 R9.

[58] wr to srv 13 October 1648 R9.

harsh with frost from mid-January to April. Six weeks without rain affected the winter corn crop and left calves and sheep dying out in the fields. Meat and butter prices rose strongly, and by September 1649 William Roades thought farmers had lost more stock from the long drought than they had lost by the rot in the previous year.[59]

One once wealthy tenant, Richard Collins asked for a moratorium on rent payments in September 1650 mainly because of animal disease. He had arrived in Middle Claydon five years earlier bringing 'a good stock', but suffered enormously from 'so much murrain and dearth that I am so much impoverished thereby (and by no other means of ill-husbandry I praise God) that makes me unable to pay your lordship my rent'. Other well-thought-of tenants such as Henry Busby had also suffered and were allowed to carry arrears for two or three years rather than leave the land untenanted.[60] When Henry Scott's lease came up for renewal in the autumn of 1648, he wanted to negotiate changes. His farm had consisted of roughly equal amounts of open-field and enclosed pasture, but he now wanted to relinquish his pasture, cutting his working capital requirements, for his cattle and sheep were almost certainly his biggest investments. At Claydon however, no farmers appear to have entered into share-cropping agreements, or 'farming to halves' although one farmer asked William Roades about the possibility, and John Duncombe, an East Claydon landlord, made one in 1651.[61]

Wealthy farmers could state their case for assistance articulately but the experience of the poor labourer and cottager during the 1640s is more difficult to reconstruct. During the first half of the seventeenth century, rural areas of England dealt with poor families in a variety of ways. Charity and exhortation remained important during the harvest crisis of 1597 in Buckinghamshire as Steve Hindle has shown, but parishes moved gradually from voluntary collections at church, and formal charities, to the raising of compulsory parish rates to support the poor before 1640. Although parishes in south-eastern Warwickshire relied more heavily on parish rates to pay for relief in the 1630s, many parishes still relied on traditional systems.[62]

The numbers of Middle Claydon's poor, and parish mechanisms for their relief, remain shadowy before 1640. The Civil War was an important catalyst

---

[59] wr to srv 9 September 1645 R6. wd to srv 1 March 1648/9 R9, 5 April 1649 R9, 26 April 1649 R9. wr to srv 18 September 1649 R10, 12 January 1649/50 R10.

[60] Richard Collins to srv 6 September 1650 R10; Henry Busby's account in papers February 1652/3 R12.

[61] wr to srv 21 December 1648 R9; Agreement dated 1 March 1651 R11. I am grateful to Elizabeth Griffiths for information about 'farming to halves'.

[62] S. Hindle, *The Birthpangs of Welfare: Poor Relief and Parish Governance in Seventeenth-Century Warwickshire*, Dugdale Society Occasional Papers 40 (2000); S. Hindle, 'Dearth, fasting and alms: the campaign for general hospitality in late Elizabethan England', *Past and Present* 172 (2001), pp. 44–86.

of change. Lists of churchwardens, sidesmen, highway supervisors, and tax collectors for the parish survive from the 1630s, but the first appointment of overseers of the poor came in April 1642. Poor rates began to be collected at some point in the 1640s, but there are no figures for expenditure until 1648. In July 1649 William Roades described twenty poor households in the village in considerable detail, and recorded the existence of an almshouse.[63] He did not think any villagers were begging though many were 'in need enough'. He clearly believed that the increase in poverty came from lack of employment: 'Tis true the poor people have not, nor can they have, the work they had in my old master's time, and that no man can help'. Increasing poverty required new kinds of assistance. In Sir Ralph's absence, the first source of help was the Town Stock. This money totalled £38, came from the accumulated gifts and legacies of gentry and villagers, and was put out at interest to support the poor.[64] During the war Roades protected the integrity of the capital sum by dividing it amongst 'every man of ability in our parish'. Each farmer took a loan of £2 10s, but they were paired and each signed a bond for £5, to cover the risk of one failing. 'In that manner it is all put forth so that at our own time we all pay the interest as need requires and where most need is'. This implied that fourteen or sixteen tenants were involved, who all paid 'full use', that is 8 per cent interest. It enabled the parish to lay out 6s 8d a week to the old and infirm, but as Roades continued 'this is nothing to our Collection'. In the previous year (1648) the poor had cost the parish £12, and Roades expected this to rise to £20 in the current year 'the reason is everything is so dear'.

    The details of these twenty poor families and their circumstances have been cross-referenced to the rentals and assessments of 1646–8, to the parish reconstitution, and the 1653 list of cottagers and their cow commons. The description covered fifteen houses, twenty families, and at least sixty-one individuals, almost one quarter of the inhabitants of Middle Claydon. Four households were receiving regular payments totalling 6s 8d a week, probably from the town stock money rather than rates. One beneficiary was 'blind' Newman, who some years earlier had been evicted from his farm holding by Sir Ralph.[65] Three widows also received regular payments, one living on her own, another with her daughter in the almshouse, and the third with her daughter and her daughter's bastard child because 'we cannot know the father from the silly fool'. None of these households were paying rent or paying taxes or rates between 1646 and 1648. Four cottager families were included, seemingly because they had three, four, or five children at home. Two of these appeared in the lists from 1646–8, and also had cow common in 1653. They were assessed for rates

[63] wr to srv 26 July 1649 R10 (misplaced in papers for 26 January 1649/50).
[64] On Town Stocks see below ch. 7.   [65] See Appendix A.

(perhaps on the cow common) in 1648. The other two households appear in none of the five sources. The remaining houses contained complex households and their problems were described in more detail. They included divided cottages and shared facilities. Two cottages contained two-generation households that had been independently identified as poor, or marginally poor from their assessments in 1647 and 1648. The one rated in 1648 had two cow commons. John Andrews lived with his wife, and was considered 'old and not able to help himself', but had lodgers, Will Lea and his wife and son. William Lea was making a living with six or seven cows, kept on another farmer's land. William Roades tried to remove them from the parish, though he also pointed out that Will Lea's contribution to the household income prevented the parish having to support John Andrews. In another house John Lea lived with his wife and two children, lodging with 'Old Gamball'. According to Roades, John Lea had 'nothing left but what his brother William Lea giveth him'. Another cottage housed two sisters, one widowed (or possibly deserted), the other caring for her bastard son. Two other properties were split and contained households of lodgers and widows.

Old age, widowhood, households with many children, and the disgrace of bastardy, characterised some of the poor families, but each had its unique story. The households of the poor were complex, and in many cases inter-dependent. They held twelve of the twenty-one cottagers' cow commons, but five of these were let out to others. In one case the widow and her (adult) son lodging in a house had let their cow commons to the man they lodged with, perhaps to pay their rent. Only four families were considered to be pensioners in need of permanent support, but others such as John Andrews and his wife, and John Lea, were little better off. Others probably required help from time to time, for they had few reserves, and no regular work.

The village community in Middle Claydon faced the pressures of farming disruption, under-employment, and high taxation during the troubled 1640s, without the guidance or direct interference of their exiled landlord. William Roades presented himself to his master as adopting a consensual approach to problems. He persuaded his fellow farmers to adopt solutions that incorporated the needs of the poor into the village's traditional institutions and mechanisms. However, Sir Ralph's absence allowed many concealed tensions in village society greater voice. Without immediate access to the ultimate source of authority, Roades had to rely more on his village and kinship networks to advance the Verney interest and maintain his position within practical parameters. He was the landlord's representative and agent, but also a farmer, two of whose daughters were married to open-field farmers in the village, Miller and Reeve. His son-in-law, Thomas Miller, came from a family of longstanding copyholders and long leaseholders. The older generation of Millers was at an age where they wanted to give up the farm to their son, and made a formal retirement agreement with him signed and witnessed.[66] These conflicting interests could be difficult to resolve in village disputes.

One example was the renewal of the tithe and glebe dispute between the parson, John Aris, the villagers, and Sir Ralph Verney. In the 1640s new factors were in play involving wider political forces. The later 1640s and 1650s were a time of national debates over such topics as tithes and a godly ministry, particularly within the independent radical elite that came to dominate politics. Radical opposition to tithes happily coincided with many farmers' self-interest.

Rumours of conflict between Roades and Parson Aris reached Sir Ralph in June 1645, who instantly recognised that 'it may much prejudice both me and him, and perhaps the parson too'. Roades broached one aspect of the conflict in October, when the parish constable was threatening to report 'our minister and some others in our parish which did not pay the assessment laid upon them'. Roades was adamant that parson Aris had not been assessed 'one penny more than their due proportionately with every man'. Aris was now in debt to the constable, and thus to 'the town', since taxes were raised as a lump sum on the community, which then had to decide how much each household paid. Aris justified his action by claiming that he and three or four (unnamed) farmers were constantly overtaxed because the old enclosures were less taxed than the new. Early in 1648 Sir Ralph optimistically believed that his arbitration would settle the matter, but a few months later the disputes were 'so high that they will hardly be reconciled' and had become personal 'especially between his wife and W[illiam] R[oades's wife] for she is most extremely violent'. One way in which villagers could respond to the parson's actions was to withhold tithes, which they threatened to do in 1650.[67]

In 1648 parliament debated the propriety of clergy holding more than one living. Aris was also incumbent of a Northamptonshire parish, but Sir Ralph hoped his farming interests in Middle Claydon (he had married the widow of the previous parson whose dowry was a copyhold farm in the village) would keep him at Claydon if he were forced to make a choice. When asked about Aris's qualities as parson, the village return, signed by William Roades and Thomas Miller, trod a dubious line of support declaring 'Mr John Aris is a preaching minister with an assistant, but of so low a voice that divers of his parishioners cannot understand him'. Those who opposed the parson attempted to have him declared a delinquent in 1651. When William Denton heard of this he wrote a very astute letter to Roades, suggesting that most of the accusations

---

[66] CIH 4/2/51 Assignment of Lease 7 October 1650 They were to move into one room of the farmhouse and receive board, lodging, and clothing, but it was a revocable agreement giving them back possession if they felt ill-treated by the deal.

[67] srv to William Brewer 20/30 June 1645 R6; wr to srv 2 October 1645 R6; srv to mv 13 February 1647/8 R8; mv to srv 2 December 1647 R8; wd to srv 4 July 1650 R7.

were 'spite and spleen'. If Aris were removed, the County Committee, not Sir Ralph, would appoint the replacement, 'a prying parson (as there are very few that are not)' who would resurrect the old claims about enclosure with more external backing, to the disadvantage of Verney and the village community. He concluded by saying that as Roades and the parson had been in dispute, Roades was the 'fittest man to fish out the knavery'.

The dispute went on. In 1652 the parson took two villagers to court in London for non-payment of tithes, but carefully chose to prosecute a non-resident tenant.[68] In May, William Denton found Thomas Miller was refusing to pay his tithes and berated him for it. This whole dispute had dragged on, and broadened, involving the courts, and threatening to bring in the County Committee. It brought home at a local level some of the national religious and social concerns and uncertainties, which many saw threatening social norms and structures of authority. In 1652, William Denton concluded one letter to Sir Ralph with a plea to Sir Ralph to return from exile: 'The main foundations and pillars of our family you and I have lived to see rooted up, the superstructure must soon follow, God knows how soon.'[69]

The social disarray in the village was exacerbated in 1650 by acute differences between William Roades and Sir Ralph Verney. Roades had been overwhelmingly loyal to the Verney family during the war years, but had always had his detractors, particularly Sir Ralph's brothers, sisters, kin, and creditors who pursued him endlessly for money. When Mary Verney was returning to her husband in France in April 1648, Sir Ralph ordered Roades to accompany her to Dieppe or Le Havre for a meeting, bringing all his accounts with him. Roades undertook what must have been a momentous journey for him, and returned to England early in May.[70]

After his return the letters between master and steward became long, more detailed, and often extremely illegible. Sir Ralph was determined to increase returns from his estate and raise rents to pay off his debts. In the autumn of 1649 he complained about the high level of rent arrears across the whole estate, but particularly at Claydon where many tenants were a year behind. Roades protested about Sir Ralph's insistence on racking up rents: 'I know you can hardly bring any of those tenants to higher rate for I protest I did what I could in it'. He openly queried the general policy thrust: 'Truly I could wish you would be pleased better to receive out of your estate one hundred pound a year too little than £50 too much. It would be a means to encourage your tenants and better enable them to maintain the poor, and they far better encourageable to pay their rents at the times so you would be sure to receive your rent at all time'.[71]

[68] PRO E112/289/46.   [69] wd to srv 20 May 1652 R11.
[70] wd to srv 6 April 1648 R9, 4 May 1648 R9.   [71] wr to srv 12 January 1649/50 R10.

In June 1650, a month after his wife died, Sir Ralph again asked Roades to travel to France with his accounts before setting off on his Italian journey. Roades begged to be excused, saying his wife had been scared to do anything in his absence last time, and had fallen ill when the present request had arrived. Sir Ralph was so displeased that he stripped Roades of much of his power. He asked his lawyer uncle John Denton to take over as rent receiver for the Claydon demesnes and wood grounds, and to supervise the estate accounts. Denton found collecting the rent no easier than Roades, and by late in the year had received less than £160 of the £414 due to him.[72] For the next year, Sir Ralph castigated Roades's disorganised accounts in letters to William Denton. But Roades's position in the community made him impossible to dismiss or ignore. John Denton found that without Roades's goodwill his powers were limited:

> for the tenants are mighty backward in paying their rents and though I cannot blame him [Roades] for it, yet I know he hath a great influence and power over them and might make them more tractable if he had a real willingness to it, but it seems you have angered him, and I am resolved some of them [the tenants] also, but that I would make them better paymasters if you will but give me power to act with authority and be able to maintain it in case of contest.[73]

William Denton tried to smooth over the quarrel before Sir Ralph's return from exile. He conceded that Roades's accounts were 'strangely disordered (even the cart before the horse) and nothing but charity can excuse him from arch-knavery', but nevertheless suggested that 'I think you are as well set up for a bailiff and solicitor as any young master in our country'.[74]

Roades and Sir Ralph discussed future estate policy in detail in their letters between 1648 and 1650. Sir Ralph was concerned to maximise rents and alleviate his debt crisis. He was also exiled, excluded from political life, and nursing a sick and dying wife. Yet he was still in his thirties and eager to set his own stamp on his world. Middle Claydon had suffered in the war but had the potential to make a quick recovery. The war had exposed the economic consequences of the enclosures and rent rises of the first half of the seventeenth century. The piecemeal enclosure of the open-field system made it less viable, forcing adaptations that integrated farmers into the market more fully. They were buying and selling for short-term needs rather than keeping sheep and cattle from breeding and over-wintering to shearing, milking, and slaughter. At the same time, higher rents made farmers cut costs, and use less labour. William Roades was clear that lack of work rather than old age or infirmity was a growing cause of recourse to charitable funds and parish doles.

---

[72] srv to wd 9/19 June 1650 R10. wr to wd 17 July 1650 R10. srv to John Denton 1/11 September 1650 R10. John Denton to srv n.d. late 1650 R11.

[73] John Denton to srv 15 July 1651 R11.   [74] wd to srv 16 September 1652 R11.

The Verneys were not present during the Civil War to distribute charitable funds or create work as they might have done before. William Roades reckoned twenty families were in poverty in 1649, but in 1654 there were only eleven cottagers with any right to cow commons in the fields and common close. The marginal families in the village had lost their rights of common in the woods at the first enclosure in the 1620s, but had always been able to gather wood for fuel after felling. In the winter of 1649/50 Sir Ralph Verney ordered the end of wood sales in Middle Claydon woods without reference to his bailiff. Roades protested that wood had always been felled in the parish and was an important source of winter employment 'besides it did relieve many poor that gathered up the small wood that now want it and are not able to buy and truly they cannot live without fire, and divers men have walls fallen down and being they cannot buy I know it will cause them to steal'. He now suggested a man should guard the woods to prevent the local poor from taking it.[75]

In this difficult conjuncture, Roades and Sir Ralph had rather different perspectives on the future. From exile, Sir Ralph tended to think along paths that he and his father had started in the 1620s and 1630s. In 1648 he asked Roades to prepare for a further piecemeal enclosure of 26 acres of common field, with full costings and details of the necessary land exchanges. Roades's letters were much more concerned for the village community and the viability of farms. Throughout the correspondence of the 1640s, and indeed before, he referred to the open-field tenancies as 'livings' approximating to the copyhold family holdings derived from villein holdings in the medieval village. With the changing scale and nature of poverty in Middle Claydon in mind, his focus was on the viability of the smaller open-field farms, those of one or two yardlands. In earlier times, two yardlands might have represented a holding of sixty to eighty acres, by 1648 a yardland was little more than seventeen acres. Roades repeatedly argued against further piecemeal enclosure, even of as small an area as twenty-six acres, because of the additional constrictions on the open-field system:

the fields are so little already that they will not keep without rutting half sheep enough to fold half the land that should be folded every year, and for soil men can make but very little by reason they keep their cattle in pastures, for there is no summering any till past harvest.

He provided Sir Ralph with the information he needed, but advised that any enclosure should eliminate the open-field system altogether: 'if I had a lease of any land there, whether for lives, or to pay a rack rent, I should be better contented that you would inclose all the fields as any of it'. Roades succeeded in preventing further piecemeal enclosure, but general enclosure was also delayed.

---

[75] wr to srv 12 January 1649/50 R10.

In the sensitive political climate of the period 1648 to 1651 enclosure would have been difficult even if Sir Ralph Verney had been in England to assert his influence and authority.[76]

Roades also stressed the need to ensure that farms were of a viable size. He was adamant that 'no man can make eight pound of any yardland in Croton [Claydon]' and that several were over-rented and would be likely to bankrupt tenants. Of the twelve farmers with open-field farms in 1648, only four had more than four yardlands, or about seventy acres, three had two to two and a quarter yardlands, and five held one or one and a half yardlands. Only three of the eight smaller holdings had additional closes. On the widely held view that rack rent paid approximated to the family income from the holding, a two yardland farm yielded a family income of no more than £16 a year, very much on the margins of economic viability by the mid-to-late seventeenth century. On the whole Claydon estate over 800 of the total of about 2,000 acres of farmland was farmed in units of less than fifty acres.[77] Roades advised Sir Ralph to take advantage of the five recent vacancies on open-field holdings to undertake consolidation, naming specific cases but enunciating the general proposition that

It is the best way for you to lay four or five yardland to every convenient house as it fall to, so that tenant that has 4 or 5 yardland may employ himself upon it and be far better able to pay his rent. For he that has but one or two yardland cannot live upon it for he cannot employ himself. Besides one team manages 4 or 5 yardland and to have a team idle is no profit.[78]

Roades's ideal farm of seventy or eighty acres made economic sense for Sir Ralph, but would also reduce the numbers of small farmers who at times might need support from their wealthier brethren and swell the cost of poor relief. Enlarging farms was central to estate policy for the next 150 years.

Sir Ralph Verney returned from exile early in 1653. Excluded from public office, widowed with teenage sons, encumbered with substantial debts, and finding his Middle Claydon House and estate dilapidated after ten years of neglect, he poured his energies into reorganisation and refurbishment. He completed the enclosure of the open-field system and its conversion from arable to pasture, and simultaneously rebuilt and remodelled Claydon House, its access roads and garden areas. Sir Ralph's actions were typical of landowners' post-war responses. Joan Thirsk's countywide study of Leicestershire points to the 1650s as a key period of enclosure activity there. Her findings have been reinforced by John Goodacre's analysis of the Lutterworth region where 28 per cent of all final enclosure, with five parishes and over 6,000 acres, took place between

[76] wr to srv 12 January 1649/50 R10; on Civil War midland enclosures see Goodacre, *Transformation of a Peasant Economy*, pp. 145–7 and J. Thirsk, 'Agrarian history 1540–1940', *VCH, Leics* II (1954), pp. 199–264.
[77] See table 6.2 below.   [78] wr to srv 21 October 1648 R10.

1620 and 1655, almost half of it between 1655 and 1665.[79] Near Claydon, Hillesden was enclosed in the same period, while John Forster of Hanslope, not far away, wrote 'there hath been of late years divers whole Lordshipps and towns enclosed and their earable land converted into pasture'.[80] The spirit of enquiry and 'improving' invention spread outward from Samuel Hartlib, Comenius, and their circle to embrace many of the gentry and aristocracy excluded from political power, whether Royalist or more conservative parliamentarian. Spending time improving one's estate became an approved, even fashionable way of reacting to exclusion. Sir Ralph's close friend the Puritan Sir Roger Burgoyne pronounced that he had entirely retired to the country in June 1653. In July he was journeying around, noticing how people's accents changed from county to county. When Sir Ralph himself made a journey to Hampshire, and then to Yorkshire to 'order' an estate there he noted the different agricultural jargon in the county. He had business in London on his own and his family's and friends' behalf but spent more time away – enough for his London landlady, Lady Ann Hobart, to tease him with the description 'country bumpkin'. He visited friends, but also corresponded with fellow gentry, seedsmen, and other contacts on a wide variety of architectural, agricultural, and particularly horticultural topics. Yet the books he recorded buying did not include any about agricultural improvement.[81]

The project to complete the enclosure of Middle Claydon was clearly conceived within months of his return but took four years to bring to fruition. In the spring of 1653 Sir Ralph ordered William Roades to draw up a list of cottagers with cow commons, and how those cow commons were currently used. It showed that while eleven cottagers held twenty-one cow commons, only four owners and their families used them themselves. One farmer, Ralph Roades, was using four sets of common rights, for a total of eight cows. Already the cottage economy based on the family and its cow was waning. Only one of the four families with common rights not considered poor by William Roades in 1648 was using its common rights directly.[82] At the same time Sir Ralph asked Roades to 'at your leisure see Cousin Smith's West Country hedges at Akeley, and tell me your opinion of them'.[83]

[79] Thirsk, 'Agrarian history', pp. 199–226; Goodacre, *Transformation of a Peasant Economy* (1994), pp. 110, 243.

[80] J. Curthoys, 'Land, settlement and enclosure in Hillesden, Buckinghamshire', Oxford University MStudies dissertation 1997; J. Forster, *England's Happiness Increased* (1664), p. 22.

[81] srb to srv 13 June and 3 July 1653 R12; srv to William Gee 8 October 1653 R12.

[82] William Roades list n.d. in papers April 1653 R12; on the declining cottager use of cow commons see L. Shaw-Taylor, 'Labourers, cows, common rights and parliamentary enclosure: the evidence of contemporary comment *c*. 1760–1810', *Past and Present* 171 (2001), pp. 95–126, and his 'Parliamentary enclosure and the emergence of an English Agricultural proletariat', *Journal of Economic History* (2001), pp. 640–62.

[83] srv memorandum 3 May 1653 R12. 'Cousin Smith' can be identified with William (later Sir William) Smith, who had married one of William Denton's nieces after meeting at the siege of

There was no general enclosure agreement for Middle Claydon because all leases since 1600 had included a clause permitting the landlord to make land exchanges to enable enclosure. During May 1653 Parson John Aris travelled to Bath and London, and Sir Ralph told Roades that he had agreed terms for an enclosure with him while in London. He now expected Roades and his son-in-law, Thomas Miller, to persuade the tenants to sign papers acknowledging their acquiescence. Sir Ralph was keen that this delicate manoeuvre should take place while John Aris was away from Claydon. Every tenant had to agree individually, and generosity and conviviality were the order of the day. For Sir Ralph, who deeply disliked immoderate drinking, the suggestion to his bailiff that

if 'tis better to brew 12 than 6 barrels at a time, and that the brewer is of that mind, then brew 12, but do it quickly and give the brewer what you think, but not under half a crown

was quite out of character.[84] Most villagers appear to have signed up to enclosure at this time. Sir Ralph now sought a surveyor to re-map the land, specifying both his preference for the Brill surveyor, George Sargeant, and how the measuring should be done.[85]

William Roades completed his tasks efficiently, but the parson proved more difficult. Aris had signed an agreement in May 1653 leasing his glebe and tithes to Sir Roger Burgoyne (undoubtedly as proxy for Sir Ralph Verney) for forty years in return for £80 a year in cash, but enclosure was not explicitly mentioned. When Aris realised that he had been out-manoeuvred he fought for a year to gain better terms. In October 1654 Edward Butterfield, a local clergyman, became a mediator in the dispute. Aris demanded £112 a year but agreed a figure of £91 a year. The agreement signed on 3 November 1654 contained twelve clauses but none compromised the enclosure.[86] One other tenant waited even longer. Thomas Edwards, a declining small farmer, exchanged his one yardland and cow common for a close, on condition that Ralph allowed a kinsman, Gibbs, to settle in Middle Claydon and lodge with him. Edwards even used John Aris to intercede, before signing his agreement and exchange on 29 December.[87]

Enclosure had been delayed by over a year. As some land had already been exchanged, Sir Ralph had open-field land in hand. On it he grew wheat, barley,

Hillesden House in 1644. Smith was a lawyer, as well as a Royalist soldier and businessman, deeply involved in property speculation and management in the third quarter of the seventeenth century. He held land at Akeley, and had a house at Ratcliffe.

[84] srv to wr 23 May 1653 R12 and letter summary covering 9–23 May 1653 R12.

[85] srv to wr 30 September 1653 R12, 23 May 1653 R12.

[86] srv memorandum in October 1654 R13. Enclosure agreement and other papers CIH 11/8/1–49. See also wd to srv 31 October 1654 R13.

[87] John Aris to srv 25 December 1654 R12; wr to srv 28 December 1654 R12; srv to wr 29 December 1654.

oats, and peas for the 1654 harvest before setting workers to construct a bank as a field division, while men were brought in from Buckingham to set up posts and rails at Bottle Gate.[88] In February 1655 a surveyor set to work measuring fields. In May two of the old-established tenants who had relinquished their leases for lives were offered newly enclosed farms on leases for lives and years that observed the fiction of continuity of custom. Ann Symonds's lease at reduced rent included traditional rent of twelve chickens payable on St John's Day, while both hers and Thomas Miller's included provisions for payment of a heriot. These were the last remnants of manorial custom, in updated form, but with no option of further renewal.[89]

Sir Ralph could not supervise the work from June to October 1655 when he was in prison in London. The Major-Generals had seized him as a potential Royalist and he remained there unnecessarily long because he refused to sign a bond for his release for several months from a sense of outraged innocence, despite the pleadings of friends and relatives.[90] Nevertheless Whittard field was enclosed and laid down by the summer of 1655, and a hay crop taken from some of the fields. Boughton field was cropped for a last time in 1655 before division and enclosure. In August posts and rails were set up across the arable land, but the different harvesting dates of the various crops made decisions about grazing the stubble difficult. The post and rails were ineffective because the undulations of ridge and furrow left gaps that allowed sheep and pigs to trample Parson Aris's corn.[91] After harvest Sir Ralph experimented with a catch crop of turnips in several small areas to provide stock with additional winter feed, finding the crop did best where weeded.[92]

The division of the old open fields was completed, but hedging continued through the winter and spring of 1655–6. In March and April 1656 outsiders were brought from Buckingham, Ratcliffe, and even Towcester in Northamptonshire, carts were hired to carry wood in June, and the fencing was eventually finished in the autumn. New tenants were not found for some time. Three 21-year leases beginning at Lady Day 1657 were agreed with tenants from outside the parish in the winter of 1656–7. Their terms included a clause allowing them to dig for springs and make ponds on their land, essential for livestock farming. Three more leases were made in the following year, well in advance of Lady Day 1658, but only one had a 21-year term. The state of the market, some experience of the newly enclosed land, and the high rents asked, made tenants increasingly wary of leases of more than ten years.[93]

---

[88] wr to srv 17 and 24 August 1654 R13; srv to wr 13 August 1654 R13.
[89] srv to wr 8 February 1654/5 R13; wr to srv 13 February 1654/5 R13. Sir Ralph Verney memorandum 4/5 February 1654 R13. CIH 4/2/53–4; wr to srv 21 May 1655 R13.
[90] srv to ev 15 June 1655 R13 srv to ? 8 October 1655 R14.
[91] wr to srv 30 July and 2 August R13. John Aris to srv 2 and 15 September 1655 R14.
[92] srv to wr 14 August 1655 R14; wr to srv 20 August 1655 R13.   [93] CIH 4/2/55–60.

The enclosure had taken almost four years and raised estate income to its full potential. At its peak valuation around 1660 the rental of Middle Claydon approached £2,000 a year. Open-field land, which William Roades generally rated at about 5s an acre, was worth around £1 an acre as enclosed pasture, such was the demand for improved grassland in the midlands. At least one farm of 125 acres was let at more than £1 an acre, and although rather more fetched around 17s 6d an acre, none of the fields leased in 1655–9 fell below 15s an acre. The total rental increase for the Verneys was somewhere between £250 and £375 a year. The improvement was achieved very cheaply. We do not have precise costings, but earlier calculations provide a good estimate. In 1648 William Roades made detailed costings for a planned enclosure of 26 acres of open field. This included prices for digging the ditches, buying 34,000 sets of hedge wood, labour and carriage costs, and allowed for some specialist work. It totalled £20 for a 26-acre area. If we add indirect costs such as drawing up leases, loss of income during the enclosure process, and even the brewing of beer to facilitate the exchange of land, then the cost in 1654–6 was probably closer to £1 an acre. This coincides with Parson Aris's estimate for Sir Edmund Verney's enclosure costs in the 1620s. If the enclosure cost Sir Ralph no more than £600 and raised his estate income by £300 a year, it implies a remarkable return on capital invested.[94]

Sir Ralph accomplished enclosure without serious opposition, but there were social consequences for individual villagers and the parish community. Those with good claim to land under customary tenure were scrupulously dealt with, to the point of including heriots and traditional rents in kind in their new leases. Cottagers on the margins of subsistence found readjustment hard. Sir Ralph granted those without farms the use of a cottagers' close in compensation for their lost cow commons, and for those with livestock a useful resource. The cottagers' close was not near the village, and inconvenient for those who used it, and their resentment at this treatment led to minor and ineffective forms of protest. In April 1656 the cottagers announced they would drive their cattle across the newly enclosed but as yet unfenced lands to get to the close morning and evening. William Roades advised an exchange of the close for one 'nearer home in lieu of that and if they refuse it they are not wise'.[95] They also protested by refusing to mend the roads – a duty on all parishioners in the era of open fields and manor court. They linked this directly to the enclosure 'since you have taken all their commons of feeding from them, and also straightened their

[94] wr to srv 13 October 1648 R9; J. Broad, 'The Verneys as enclosing landlords, 1600–1800' in J. Chartres and D. Hey (eds.), *English Rural Society, 1500–1800: Essays in Honour of Joan Thirsk* (Cambridge 1990), pp. 27–36.

[95] wr to srv 19 April 1656 R12 (in papers for 29 April 1654). Cottagers' closes were often at the parish edge on poor soil, e.g. in Brill, Boarstall, and Oakley; see Broad and Hoyle, *Bernwood* (1997), ch. 5.

ways and feeding places in their streets that they see no reason why they should mend that or any other place, for they say your straightening their streets and taking away all their feeding of either hog or other beast, they receiving no benefit are made as strangers'.[96]

Some villagers started a new life elsewhere. Thomas Tipping, one of the poor and needy in 1648, took up a job with a London brewer as drayman in 1655. He handed his key to William Roades as he left, and went with Sir Ralph Verney's approval and blessing – he thought it a suitable position for Tipping who had once been his coachman. James Lea also left for London, perhaps inspired by Tipping's example.[97] A month later one of the open-field tenants, Henry Scott, decided to leave his farm, dismantling the barn and stable he had built on the land, and selling off his stock of manure, since now he had no fallow to lay it on, to Sir Ralph. The departing tenants' empty houses were instantly requested by other families, being either larger or in better repair than their own.[98]

Enclosure raised other tensions. Sir Ralph, who was wrestling with the Protectorate regime and fighting imprisonment over Decimation tax, became exasperated with William Roades when Parson Aris complained about the enclosure fences and wandering pigs in his crops. He transferred financial control from Roades to the housekeeper (Mrs Westerholt) with hints of a deliberate attempt to humiliate Roades by putting a woman in authority over him, and describing him to the parson as a 'broken reed'. The cottagers' protests may also have provoked a further dispute involving two bastardy cases laid at the door of John Denton, Sir Ralph Verney's lawyer cousin who had acted as rent receiver in 1649–50.[99] Roades took the town's side in Denton's prosecution and sought to humiliate him by forcing him to pay maintenance. Nevertheless Roades had successfully steered through the enclosure on his master's behalf, while interpreting 'the town's' anxieties and grievances to Sir Ralph at key points. He was hardly a broken reed in 1656 and 1657, taking a full part in reorganising the estate, but his life, and that of his old sparring partner, Parson John Aris, was cut short by the severe epidemic of 1657. The new era of the enclosed estate was beginning and new key figures took up their posts from its outset.

The enclosure was an essential part of Sir Ralph's re-modelling of the estate, but the reconstruction of Middle Claydon had further social consequences. After enclosure the tenancies included newly built houses on the farmsteads, accentuating the decline of the village centre so that it became primarily a place of residence for the cottagers, labourers, and small holders. The dispute over

---

[96] wr to srv 3 June 1656 R14.
[97] srv to wr 2 and 14 August 1655 R13; wr to srv 6 August 1655 R13.
[98] wr to srv 27 August 1655 R13, 17 September, 8 October 1655 R14.
[99] Notes on case 16 November 1653 R 12; srv to Mrs Westerholt 13 September 1655 R14, srv to John Aris 13 September 1655 R14, wr to srv 17 September 1655 and 3 June 1656 R14.

road-repairs encouraged a changeover to a system of repairing the roads by raising parish rates instead of direct labour, although some farmers still carted stones in lieu of payments. Soon after his return to England Sir Ralph began construction of a block of six new brick and tiled almshouses near the church in May 1653. He made detailed plans, specifying room, door, and window sizes, but also providing gardens, and privies at the end of them.[100] The repair and re-modelling of Claydon House, church, and gardens were also extensive. The east and north fronts of the house were rebuilt and gable windows inserted in the roof. At the same time Sir Ralph rebuilt the parsonage to a higher standard. Most of the exterior work on the house was completed by July 1655 but Sir Ralph's imprisonment and the Decimation tax slowed the work, which went on through 1656.[101]

The first half of the seventeenth century saw profound changes in the landscape of Claydon and in the organisation of its farming and village life. The choices made by the Verneys were vital in most of these, and were typical of those many gentry families who modernised their estates and attempted to maximise their incomes. Underlying them was a strong ethic of economic efficiency and profit, driven by the market and its fundamental effectiveness in sharing out the benefits of hard work, and over-riding feudal concepts of stewardship and community. This is not simply a modern extrapolation from decisions made by the Verneys over fifty years. In 1650, soon after his wife's death, and in the depths of despair, Sir Ralph wrote a long 'confessional' letter to his close friend Dr William Denton which appears as Appendix A. It began conventionally enough with a recitation of various specific actions that Sir Ralph felt guilty and remorseful about. But when he meditated on the criticism that he was harsh in his dealings with his tenants, any remorse was quickly replaced with a strong and coherent account of his philosophy of business and estate dealings, and the 'rules' by which he worked. Rents were set by competitive bidding and the level determined purely by market criteria. But if tenants felt the rent was too high they could break their lease and leave before it ended. Where good but needy tenants' rents were too high they should not be reduced but instead more land should be let to them at a subsidised rent. Subsidised rents merely gave tenants higher profits at the landlord's expense, while 'a landlord is obliged to take but an equitable rent for his land, so as the tenant by God's ordinary Providence and blessing upon his honest endeavours may be a gainer by it'. Paternalism was a residual form of charity, to be applied only to those who had shown they had tried to succeed by the standards Sir Ralph set out,

---

[100] wr to srv 18 May 1656 R14, srv to wr 20 April 1654 R12; CIH 12/1/2 1654 map of the house and properties around it shows the line of new and old roads clearly; srv to wr 12 May 1653 R12. Detailed description of the almshouses in papers at end 1653 R12.

[101] For a fuller account of the transformation of Claydon House, park, and amenities see below ch. 6, pp. 118–20.

and had been prevented from achieving by circumstances rather than their own efforts.[102]

The rationale of this letter guided Sir Ralph's dealings with the farmers and cottagers of Middle Claydon for the rest of his life. Using its stern precepts Sir Ralph Verney turned the family's financial position round. He also successfully inculcated these sentiments in his successors over the next two generations. Their activities as the estate builders, estate managers, and social engineers of Middle Claydon are the subject of the next chapters.

---

[102] srv to wd 2/12 June 1650 R10. The full text of the relevant part is printed in Appendix A below.

Part II

The shaping of family and village 1657–1740

5   Land, business, and dynastic advance 1657–1736

Between the Restoration and the fall of Walpole, the Verney family successfully reversed the disasters of the Civil War period. Sir Ralph Verney outlived his eldest son and male grandchildren, so Claydon passed in 1696 to his second son John Verney, who had been apprenticed as a Levant merchant and made a respectable living from trade and finance before inheriting the estate. John married three times, raised the family to an Irish peerage, and was succeeded by his son Ralph who eventually became Earl Verney. In the eighty years spanned by this chapter the family remained an essentially middle-ranking gentry family, concerned with their estates, and with the social life of London. They participated in county politics as JPs and Deputy Lieutenants, and from 1680 to 1725 were often MPs. Their careers were worthy rather than outstanding, and they made no great fortunes from trade or office, and played no central role in government or at court. The family spent more time in London, where from the 1720s they had a permanent residence on the outskirts. Yet in 1736 they were considerably wealthier than they had been in 1657.

A sense of dynastic purpose, and a desire to make the Verneys financially strong dominated the outlook of successive heads of family. The disparate and uncertain seventeenth-century income sources were replaced by rental income from compact and improved estates, and money invested in a range of sound commercial enterprises and government bonds. Family strategy involved the careful husbanding of resources, the matching of lifestyle to income, and the adoption of improved accounting practices and detailed estate supervision. The use of city and commercial contacts enabled them to manage family finances more efficiently. In 1657, when Edmund Verney came of age, the family's gross income was approximately £2,300 a year. Indebtedness, rising towards £12,000, absorbed one third of annual income, while family annuities and taxes further reduced net income to approximately one half of the gross figure. By 1736, the estates had expanded considerably, annual gross income was between £4,000 and £5,000 a year, and the debts had all but disappeared.

At the heart of dynastic expansion was a hard-headed approach to the marriages of the heirs to the Verney estates. Between 1662 and 1736 three generations of eldest sons married substantial heiresses in arranged marriages. In no case is there any evidence of initial sentimental attachment on either part. In addition, Sir John Verney married three times, but only one of those marriages produced children. His total capital gain from the three dowries was the equivalent of marrying an heiress. All the marriage contracts after 1662 were drawn up as strict settlements with trustees for contingent remainders. This device laid down patterns of ownership and of inheritance for unborn children that prevented any individual head of the family from selling his estates to the detriment of future generations. The court of Chancery accepted such trusts from the 1650s onwards and they could not be easily broken without a private act of parliament. They made the current 'owner' of the estates no more than a tenant for life, prevented him from selling off lands included in the settlement, and ensured that the family patrimony included within the settlement passed intact to succeeding generations. Lloyd Bonfield has shown that the strict settlement did not work in the way its architects intended between 1650 and 1750, because it required that fathers lived to see their sons reach adulthood or marry to continue the process into the next generation. The high death rates amongst the elite as well as the population as a whole during that century meant that there was no guarantee that the sons of the gentry and aristocracy would be subject to a living father's influence. In practice three generations of Verney fathers lived to ensure that the system was renewed. The Verneys also avoided some of the traps that Sir John Habakkuk suggested could lead to a parallel expansion of landed estates and family debts. The estates raised few dowries for daughters, and those were relatively small. Widows' jointures were infrequently paid, and not large. Where settlements laid down that dowries were to be invested in land, the amounts involved were modest, well within family resources. Many of these factors were matters of demographic chance, but the policies pursued by the Verneys were important contributory factors.[1]

The long-term profitability of heiress marriages depended on many demographic and other factors. It was chance that in three consecutive generations of Verneys small numbers of children reached adulthood, yet the male line survived and few widows loaded the estate with heavy jointure payments. After 1630 there were more sons than daughters, and of the six daughters who reached adulthood, only four married and three were paid modest dowries. From 1660 to 1730 the Verneys' demographics followed a national trend to higher death rates and lower fertility amongst the elite, and random factors worked in the family's favour.[2] But demographic chance also worked against the dynastic interest on

[1] H. J. Habakkuk, 'Marriage settlements in the eighteenth century', *Transactions of the Royal Historical Society* 4th series, 32 (1950), pp. 15–30; Bonfield, *Marriage Settlements* and 'Marriage settlements and the "rise of great estates": the demographic aspect', *Economic History Review*, 2nd series, 32 (1979), pp. 483–93.

[2] For the demographic patterns of the aristocracy see T. H. Hollingsworth, 'The demography of the British peerage', *Population Studies*, 18:2 (supplement) (1964), pp. 1–108.

one occasion. The heiress Mary Abell brought a major land acquisition in 1662, but it was lost when her husband and all her children died between 1688 and 1697. Ultimately, the small families of earlier generations, and continuing alliances with daughters of small families, may have been a significant factor in the failure of the third generation to provide heirs and end the Verney blood line. The second Earl Verney and his wife were childless. The last Verney, Baroness Fermanagh, died unmarried.

Nevertheless the acquisition of heiress fortunes was a significant feature in the expansion of the Verney estates. The patterns of marriage settlement and their negotiation also say much about the Verneys' attitudes to social status. By choosing as partners heiresses who were by definition without strong sibling or paternal connections, the Verneys sacrificed some potential for political and social prestige. The heiresses were of lower social status than the Verneys in all cases, and were not well connected at court or in politics. Throughout our period the family moved on the fringes of high society. They had important connections at the county and business level with the Temples, Cheynes, and Dentons. However, they gradually lost contact with the wide range of court and parliamentary connections that Sir Edmund Verney's position as Knight Marshal had built up, and served Sir Ralph and the family so well during the Civil War.

In 1657, Sir Ralph Verney could look back on fifteen tumultuous years. They began with a rapid succession of deaths that left him at the age of twenty-nine without his father, mother, and grandmother. He was committed to protecting the family estates, and providing for his family and kin without advice from the older generation. In the Civil War the family debt rose alarmingly and he could not pay creditors, or adequately provide for his brothers and sisters. His forced exile in France split his family between two countries, and saw the death both of his wife and two younger children.

Unsurprisingly his outlook on his own and his children's futures was coloured by these events. He did not re-marry, though perhaps he seriously considered marrying an old friend, Vere Gaudy, in the late 1650s. His son Edmund picked up something of this in 1658 and fully understood the threat it posed: 'if she remain not barren then it may ruin me and our family'.[3] Their contemporary Sir George Sondes carefully delineated his own reasons for not re-marrying when he wrote that he had

near these twenty years kept myself a single man, and barred myself the comfort of a wife, only because I would not burden myself with more children, that you might have the more.[4]

---

[3] ev to Thomas Hyde 26 August 58 R15.
[4] 'Sir George Sondes his plain Narrative to the World of all Passages upon the Death of his two sons' (1655) reprinted in *Harleian Miscellany* x 60. See also F. Heal and C. Holmes, *The Gentry in England and Wales, 1500–1700* (London 1994), pp. 83–4.

Sir Ralph was never as explicit but the implicit threat of marriage encouraged his son's acquiescence in marriage projects for himself.

Sir Ralph saw the marriage of his elder son as the major instrument for putting the family's financial affairs on a sound footing. When he returned from France in 1653 he stabilised rather than reduced the family debt, and spent money re-modelling Claydon House and estate. He was waiting for Edmund to reach adulthood and marry to re-configure the family finances. In 1656 he wrote quite openly to his son

> when you are of age or married . . . I purpose to clear all my engagements for your Grandfather, either by a sale or portion, or by both; and then I shall know what will be left to live upon, for whilst I am thus much in debt I account myself the master of very little or nothing.[5]

He continually stressed that a profitable marriage would be 'the best and happiest way to make my family flourish'.[6] In 1656, when Edmund was only twenty, his father considered various proposals for his son, including one to match him to a rich widow. Sir Ralph responded to one possible match with a £4,000 dowry, by demanding more, or stipulating a marked reduction in jointure.[7]

When Edmund Verney came of age in 1657, Sir Ralph prepared the ground for a re-settlement of the family estates by barring entails on all the Verney lands, and thereby removing customary restraints restricting his ability to dictate the descent of his lands.[8] The search then began for a suitable bride. Edmund was an awkward young man, and soon became obese with physical weaknesses that meant he had to wear a metal brace on his shoulders and back. Sir Ralph expressed a low opinion of his son's personal qualities and described him as 'not at all nice in point of beauty or breeding, nor must that woman be so that married him'. A year earlier he had written to Edmund berating him for his lack of 'courtship and compliment, good clothes and clean linen'.[9] In these years Edmund was coached in love-letter writing and presentation by his friends, but was not particularly keen to marry. But when Sir Ralph constantly blamed the family debts for refusing to raise his son's allowance, marriage provided a reluctant Edmund with a pathway to independence. He spent much time in London and was introduced to eligible young women. His clothes were so old fashioned and ill fitting that even Sir Ralph's intimate friends pleaded with him to provide Edmund with enough money to make a good

---

[5] srv to ev 24 December 1656 R15.   [6] srv to ev 25 January 1657/8 R15.
[7] srv to Francis Drake 1 December 1656 R15; srv to Henry Verney 8 December 1656 R15.
[8] Oxfordshire CRO HIIa/43; CIH 1/106–8; cf. Sir Alexander Denton to srv 12 March 1656/7 R15. There are also draft deeds for a strict marriage settlement for Edmund that may date from this period amongst the undated papers at the end of 1660 R17. Sir Orlando Bridgeman probably oversaw this operation and his son John was a party to some of the deeds.
[9] F. P. Verney and M. M. Verney, *Verney Memoirs*, III, p. 304 quoting srv to Dorothy Leake 9 February 1656/7 R15.

impression.[10] When he fell in love, it was with Mary Eure, a cousin who had been a childhood playmate in France. She was horrified by Edmund's advances and soon rejected him. Yet Sir Ralph supported the match. The lady had a considerable dowry, and Sir Ralph mustered his own influence and that of his friends and relatives to press the cause.

Edmund remained hopeful but unrequited for three years and his father worried about the dynastic consequences. When Sir Richard Temple was reported to be ill, Sir Ralph pointed out to Edmund that 'the truth is he is to blame he doth not marry, for he may drop away on a sudden, as young as he is and then consider what a case his family is in, and all that depend on him'. Other proposals came to nothing but in the summer of 1661 a match with the heiress Mary Abell from the adjoining village of East Claydon became a possibility.[11] Mary was twenty, and had been brought up by her father and stepmother after her mother had died when she was two. Her father, William Abell, was the son of a successful city vintner who was deeply involved in the Royal wine monopoly project in 1638–40. The family owned a considerable estate in East Claydon, and a small property in Hertfordshire. Their total landed income was some £800 a year. William was High Sheriff of Buckinghamshire in 1661, and died while at Buckingham Assizes on 10 August.[12]

Sir Ralph used Edward Butterfield, the parson at Middle Claydon, to introduce the possibility of a match tactfully even as he carried Sir Ralph's condolences to Abell's widow. During the autumn and winter of 1661–2 the couple met and their relationship developed affectionately, particularly on Mary Abell's side. From the start, Edmund Verney pressed the desirability of a match because the family estates were so close. The marriage negotiations are interesting in two respects. Once it became clear that Mary Abell favoured the match and that Edmund Verney would accept it, Edmund effectively joined Mary's side of the negotiations, pressing her advisers to demand that Sir Ralph settled a larger proportion of the Middle Claydon estate on the couple. At the same time, Sir Ralph Verney was nudging his agent, Edward Butterfield, into the confidence of Mary and her stepmother. He offered to help in tiresome legal matters, but his particular aim was to ensure that the Abells did not grant Mary's stepmother too large a jointure. At the same time, the Verneys and Abells collaborated to check that Mary's father had properly broken the entail to ensure that Mary Abell was the legal heir. Otherwise her uncle, Richard Abell, would have inherited the estate.

The negotiations provide a refreshing slant on the usual story of family to family confrontation. Marriage settlements involved important inter-generational

[10] *Ibid.*, III, pp. 304–5.   [11] srv to ev 30 July 1660 R17; ev to Thomas Hyde 26 Aug 1661 R17.
[12] F. P. Verney and M. M. Verney, *Verney Memoirs* IV, p. 15 and F. C. Dietz, *English Public Finance 1558–1641* (New York 1932), p. 283.

transactions. The interests of the two dynasties had to be reconciled with those of the bride's stepmother, but the negotiations also involved the couple and their own financial interests, jointly and individually. Through months of discussions, during which Mary Abell wore her suitor's ring and picture 'openly', the couple worked in alliance to increase the proportion of the Middle Claydon estate they would immediately enjoy. Edmund Verney drafted letters for Mary to send to her advisers, one including the interesting sentence that 'I'll be no burden nor tie upon her estate because I'll be mistress of my own.' When a draft marriage settlement, drawn up by Sir Ralph Verney's lawyers, was scrutinised by the Abells' advisers they advised Mary that 'there is not anything to your advantage nor any certain provision for your children'. While Edmund had sought to advise Mary in ways that would advantage them as a couple, he had simultaneously pursued his family's interest in the future descent of the Abell estate. The Abells demanded alterations 'in another form as is convenient for us both', and a warier and wiser Mary wrote to her Edmund telling him not to pass instructions to her lawyers any more.[13]

The couple eventually married in London on 1 July 1662 and signed their marriage settlement on the same day. A £600-a-year estate in Middle Claydon became their immediate possession, and would also provide Mary's widow's pension.[14] They also drew income from Mary's land in East Claydon, which would provide Mary with a further pension during her life. Their Middle Claydon estate would pass to the couple's male heirs. If there were none, then it would descend to Edmund Verney's male heirs and in their absence then to Sir Ralph Verney and his heirs forever. The Abell lands, on the other hand, would descend to the couple's male heirs, but if there were none, then to the couple's daughters. If, finally, there were no children of the marriage then Mary Abell would have total disposition of her East Claydon estate, but if she left no instruction, such as a will, then it would pass to her heirs general.[15]

The marriage settlement was a strict settlement with contingent remainders, the first in the Verney family. They adopted the form for very natural and obvious reasons. Sir Ralph Verney lived close to the Inns of Court, lodged with a leading legal family, the Hobarts, and constantly corresponded with close kin and friends such as the Dentons who had a long legal tradition in the family. For a decade he used the legal services of Sir Orlando Bridgeman, the Restoration Lord Keeper, and one of the leading experts on the subject, and he was a good

[13] George Gaell to Mary Abell 10 April 1662 R18; Mary Abell to ev, April 1662 (received 24th) R18.
[14] The marriage licence dated 28 June 1662 was for a ceremony in King Henry VII's chapel at Westminster Abbey ClH 10/8. In the final settlement the figure of £600 a year is exactly what Sir Ralph told his aunt, Elizabeth Isham, he would settle on his son in 1655 – see srv to Elizabeth Isham 23 August 1655 R13.
[15] ClH 2/60 dated 1 July 1662.

friend of Orlando's son, John. However, the terms of the settlement were much more limited than those commonly used fifty years later. The Verneys left a considerable part of their lands out of the settlement, including only their Middle Claydon lands. The deeds carefully laid down the future descent of the land to the eldest son, but there was no provision for younger children, male or female. Although certain aspects of this reflected contemporary legal practice, Sir Ralph's wish to retain control of certain properties to clear the family debts was significant and also gave him power in any future family negotiations.[16]

Edmund manipulated Mary Abell during the courtship, and she seems to have been much more entranced by him than he by her. Before the marriage Edmund travelled with his brother to London and Gravesend as he set off to become a Levant trader and his behaviour drew the comment that if Mary had known about his activities she would have been very anxious. She nevertheless bargained marriage terms that left the Abell land in her family and at her personal disposal if her children did not survive. At an early stage in negotiations, she had shown considerable independence. She made it clear that she would only marry 'where she thinks she may be happy', and would refuse to go through any formalities until she was legally adult.[17] Furthermore, her estates would descend to her daughters if there were no sons, while Edmund's lands would go to his closest male relative. This echoed her father's insistence in his will and financial arrangements that Mary should inherit rather than his brothers and their children. On the Abell side, then, the defence of female inheritance remained strong.

Normally a marriage settlement provided the definitive statement of the descent of land for the duration of the marriage. However, within a year of the marriage there was an interesting coda which indicates how strongly the Verneys wanted to ensure that the Abell lands were merged with their own. Edmund persuaded Mary to extend the Verneys' rights if Mary died without surviving children while her husband was still living. The couple signed an agreement that the survivor would have free disposal of Mary's land. This was the closest the Verneys could get to ensuring that the Abell lands would descend to them if there were no children. It is also a statement about male power over women. The underlying assumption of this agreement was that if Mary died without issue before her husband, her first loyalty would be to him and his family. If he were to die first and childless, she would need to look to her kin for protection, since she had no responsibility for bringing up the future head of the dynasty.[18]

---

[16] Cf. Eileen Spring, *Law, Land, and Family: Aristocratic Inheritance in England, 1300 to 1800* (Chapel Hill, NC 1993), p. 143.
[17] eb to srv 15 August 1661 R17; eb to srv 18 November 1661 R18.
[18] ev to Thomas Hyde 26 August 1661 R17; CIH 2/61 dated 1 January 1662/3; cf. srv to M. Elmes 6 and 13 April 1668 R22.

The failure of the marriage settlement to provide for daughters or younger sons was partly rectified in Edmund Verney's will drawn up in 1669. In it, his household goods were to pass to his wife, his estate to his eldest son, and £1,000 only to provide a dowry for his daughter. This was very ungenerous, exactly the same as Sir Ralph had had to pay for his sisters twenty-five years earlier. The will significantly favoured his male heirs and was made under his father's influence, for Edmund consulted Sir Ralph about its contents, made him executor of the will, and charged him with guiding the education of any children. This partly reflected the fact that Mary Abell had become extremely depressed in the first year of her marriage. Her behaviour periodically required the constant attendance of nurses and helpers, and was considered 'madness' by those around her. After her husband died in 1688, Sir Ralph took out a Commission of Lunacy for her protection.[19]

Dynastic considerations undoubtedly drove Edmund Verney's marriage to Mary Abell. The marriage settlement began with a statement that it was 'for the advancement of the heirs male of the body of the said Edmund Verney which he shall beget on the body of the said Mary Abell'. The financial gain for the Verneys was considerable. Mary Abell's estate was worth some £800 a year – the equivalent of a dowry of £16,000. Yet, she received a widow's jointure of £350 a year, which at the period's normal dowry to jointure ratio of 10 to 1 was appropriate to a dowry of only £3,500. Mary had some compensating freedom in respect of the lands she brought to the marriage, but only if she survived without male heirs. By 1675, this seemed unlikely to happen. Between 1666 and 1675 she gave birth to three healthy children – two sons and a daughter.

We can consider Edmund Verney's marriage to Mary Abell from a number of points of view. For the Abell family, it provided a stable partnership for a rich but psychologically vulnerable daughter. It was in accordance with her father's wishes, and reinforced the family's place in county society by linking it to an ancient county family. For Sir Ralph Verney, his son's lucrative marriage would enable him to pay his debts, and provide for his dependants. For Edmund, the marriage meant economic independence, new status, and new responsibilities. There were further important assumptions. One was that any daughters' portions would be paid for out of Mary Abell's lands and not burden the Verney estates with future debts.[20] The Verney debt question overshadowed the whole process in Sir Ralph's mind. As he jotted down scenarios for the family finances after Edmund's marriage, Sir Ralph sought advice on how best to finance the remaining £10,000 of family debt from the £1,400 a year of Middle Claydon which he retained.[21] In November 1661, when marriage negotiations were in

[19] ev to srv 24 May 1669 R23; for the Commission of Lunacy PRO C211/26/3 dated 25 September 1688, stating that Mary Abell first became lunatic in 1671.
[20] srv to Margaret Elmes 13 April 1668 R22.   [21] srv memorandum undated at end 1660 R17.

train, he discussed a totally different approach to the debt problem with his son. Sir Ralph would give up almost all title and income to Middle Claydon leaving Edmund to take over responsibility for the family debts, and pay him £1,000 a year for life. But all the estates would revert to Sir Ralph if Edmund died and there were no male heirs from his marriage. Power lay quite overtly with the patriarchal head of the family.

While father and elder son bargained over the disposal of the estate, the younger son, John Verney, wondered how he would be provided for. Did he know of his mother's intention that her younger children should be given lands from her estates? In January 1662, at a crucial stage in Edmund's marriage negotiations, John wrote to his father tentatively asking about his own position, and received a forthright reply. Sir Ralph expected John to make money from his chosen profession, the Levant trade, and reminded him that he had paid a handsome premium for his apprenticeship. He added 'you must know children do not use to catechise their fathers what estate they intend to leave them' and made any further provision dependent on John's future conduct. Sir Ralph did not want his son to face the insecurity that his own brothers' intermittent military careers and high status expectations had brought them. The £40 a year he gave them was grudgingly given, and an important drain on family finances. At this period Sir Ralph was juggling a whole range of possibilities. His own wife's remaining lands were excluded from the marriage settlement, allowing him to sell them to pay debts. Yet he remained faithful to her wish that the Wasing estate in Berkshire should pass to their younger son John 'so that he is not like to be a great burden to his elder brother'. A month after his stern letter to John in 1662, and before John left for the Levant, Sir Ralph covenanted the small Wasing estate to John and his heirs. What he did not do was to promise John that he would enjoy the income during his lifetime.[22]

John Verney returned from twelve years in the Levant in 1674. His main assets were his merchant capital (which he estimated at around £6,000) and his gentry connections. He did not expect to inherit, but might hope to set up his own modest junior branch of the family. Yet his marriage settlement and negotiations all bear the mark of his father's guidance and reflect patriarchal and dynastic objectives, perhaps because Sir Ralph used the Wasing estate to enhance his son's assets. John married three times, and each marriage negotiation reflects the subtle shifts in his wealth and status during the intervening sixteen years.

While negotiating the first marriage with Elizabeth Palmer, the main area of contention between the two families was whether John Verney's own wealth was sufficient to match the £3,000 dowry on offer. Elizabeth's father was sceptical of the value of the Wasing estate though his agents had surveyed and valued the

[22] Berkshire CRO D/EMT T1/3 and /7 includes a confirmation of the deed made in 1649.

property, and given it a clean bill of health.[23] At one point John was required to give his own bond to secure the cash sum that was to provide the capital for any jointure. In the final document, Elizabeth Palmer retained her right to claim her third part of her husband's business and personal wealth, according to the custom of the City of London, in addition to the £2,000 cash sum she was offered. Furthermore, if the couple had surviving daughters but no sons, the daughters could refuse their share of the £4,000 laid down in the contract, in favour of their customary share of their father's wealth. John Verney did not have the resources to buy out his wife's and future daughters' rights to customary inheritance so had to make concessions. He nevertheless ensured that the Wasing estate included in the marriage settlement would only descend to the male heirs of the marriage, and would revert to Sir Ralph if John Verney's male line failed.[24]

Late in the negotiations, Sir Ralph heard that Sir Edward Chaloner, the owner of the main estate at Steeple Claydon had died, presenting the Verneys with a major opportunity to consolidate their estates. Sir Ralph immediately sounded out the possibility of altering the draft marriage contract to allow powers to sell Wasing and purchase equivalent land security for jointure. However, the negotiations had been so long, difficult, and circuitous that Sir Ralph felt he could not press for the change, and the marriage settlement went ahead without it.[25]

The final agreement gave John Verney a good dowry and suitable match. Sir Ralph maintained ultimate reversionary rights to the Wasing lands if there were no male heirs, but failed to ensure that his son's non-landed wealth would revert to the main line if the couple were childless, or produced only heiresses. Nor was he able to ensure a fixed jointure for Elizabeth Palmer in widowhood, or fixed portions for heiresses.

The terms of John Verney's second marriage in 1692 reflect the fact that after the deaths of his brother and two nephews between 1686 and 1690, John was now heir to Sir Ralph's estates. His wife had been dead six years, and he had four living children – a son and three daughters. His new bride, Mary Lawley, came from a Shropshire gentry family with London connections. John Verney first met her father in the Rainbow coffee house in August 1691, intending to broach the subject of a match 'but it being a coffee house, I did not do it'.[26] He visited the Lawleys' home for the first time in December 1691, and saw Mary, but again said nothing because of the company. After making enquiries through intermediaries, John Verney arranged for his father to meet her father,

[23] srv to Elizabeth Palmer 21 January 1679/80 R34.
[24] Berkshire CRO D/EMt T1 /14 dated 5 May 1680.
[25] sjv to srv 26 April and 1 May 1680 R34; srv to sjv 15, 23, 29 April 1680 R34.
[26] sjv to srv 4 August 1691 R45.

Sir Francis Lawley, in February 1692, and in March wrote a letter of courtship to Mary.[27] In March, he received the blessing of his first wife's father 'with thanks for your staying so long single'. Negotiations over the marriage contract were intense during April, but presumably concluded before the couple obtained a marriage licence on 11 June. The marriage articles were signed on 5 July, and the marriage celebrated a week or so later.[28]

The marriage settlement reflected John Verney's enhanced status. His wife's portion was £3,000, secured on Lawley's three-quarter share in the Rainbow coffee house and on land in Berkshire, not far from the Verneys' Wasing estate. Her jointure was agreed at £400 a year, despite Sir Ralph's objection that anything more than £300 a year was generous. The main shift in emphasis, however, was the clause requiring John Verney to complement the £3,000 dowry with £6,000 of his own money, and spend the full £9,000 on freehold land within 100 miles of London. Another clause gave John Verney the flexibility to sell lands and reinvest which had been omitted from the 1680 marriage settlement. The platform for an expanding estate was erected. The land would provide a jointure for his widow, and landed estates for the male heirs of the marriage. If there were none it would revert to John's heirs 'whosoever' with a proviso ensuring that any daughters of the marriage were properly provided with dowries. John Verney could insist on much stronger male inheritance clauses because he was putting up two thirds of the capital to make the purchases.[29]

Mary Lawley died two years later, and her only child, a son, followed her soon after. John was suitably embarrassed at the financial windfall he had acquired. The £3,000 dowry was now his without matching obligations. He sent Mary's mother £100 to pay for family mourning 'because they lose their daughter, and portion, and she hath left no children behind her'. On this occasion, John waited no more than a respectable mourning period before considering remarriage possibilities in June and July of 1695. He eventually set his cap at Elizabeth Baker, the daughter of his next door neighbour but one in Hatton Garden. Their proximity probably accounts for the relatively sparse correspondence about the marriage. The families were close politically. Daniel Baker owned property at Penn, and had been Sheriff for Buckinghamshire in 1693. During the 1696 election Baker campaigned with Verney. Yet their money was city-based, and their land at Penn little more than a house with surrounding grounds valued at less than £40 a year.[30]

---

[27] sjv to srv 10 December 1691 R45; srv to sjv 23 February 1691/2 R45.
[28] Ralph Palmer sr to sjv 9 April 1692 R45; CIH 1/125.
[29] CIH 1/125 dated 5 July 1692. John's £6,000 was currently laid out on a mortgage in Oxfordshire, suggesting that he had probably become wealthier by his business activities in the intervening years.
[30] sjv to srv 11 November 1693 R47; Daniel Baker 5 and 11 December 1696 R49.

Elizabeth and John married in April 1697, in London.[31] Elizabeth Baker's dowry was £3,500, and her jointure was potentially valued at more than £500 a year made up of various lands at Claydon and in Berkshire. The marriage contract obliged John Verney to spend a further £4,000 on land within 100 miles of London, and the income from this would supplement the jointure. These new estates would pass to any sons of the marriage, but would revert to John Verney's heirs if there were only daughters or no children. If there were daughters but no sons, these heiresses would be provided with adequate dowries (£3,500 if only one, £4,000 divided between two or more). This standard means of limiting the amount of money passing through the female line was supplemented by a clause that can only have come from the hard business-accounting streak in John Verney. The agreement laid down that if he were to pay any part of this during his lifetime, or by his will, that would be deducted from the sums set out in the settlements.

Sir John Verney's marriage settlements required increasing amounts of the couples' wealth to be invested in land, and suggest a shift in emphasis from urban to rural in their provisions. This only partly reflected Sir John's transition from city merchant to country squire. Land was still considered the safest security for wives' jointures. After Elizabeth Palmer died, there remained lasting obligations to her children that meant that John Verney could not use the land in her settlement for later jointures and dowries. The purchases of new lands under the second and third marriage settlements were a mechanism for ensuring obligations to wives and female children. But they certainly shifted money into land that John might otherwise have invested in mortgages or government stocks, if not in trade. The terms of the settlements also illustrate Eileen Spring's argument that customary inheritance rights were important zones of contention in marriage negotiations. John Verney's London citizenship gave his widow and children substantial customary rights. The three marriage settlements curbed these in proportion to John's ability to finance alternative means of provision.[32]

Similar themes dominated marriage arrangements for the next generation of Verneys. The importance of the size of fortune permeated discussions of potential matches for Ralph Verney in the five years before 1707. This was a reflection of John Verney's dynastic ambitions, but also very much the flavour of the period. It was equally true of discussions of third-party marriages in the Verney letters. At the time the marriage market was particularly favourable for eligible elder sons. In 1703 Sir John wrote of a £7,000 portion as being 'a fortune anyone may match to' and of the 'cheapness of the sex', which is illustrated by the size of dowry being asked for his daughters. There was no

---

[31] Berkshire CRO D/EMt/T1/15–7 and ClH 1/141a–c provide the legal instruments of the marriage settlement. Other aspects of their courtship and marriage are well described in Whyman, *Sociability and Power*, pp. 121–3.

[32] Spring, *Law, Land, and Family*.

single-minded search for an heiress, and Sir John emphasised Ralph Verney's part in the choice, writing 'but after all I leave this matter to your choice and pray God direct you to the best'. Nevertheless there were very considerable family pressures and influences on the young man.[33] John retained leverage in a number of ways. In June 1706 he wrote to the match-maker Ann Tregea setting out a framework for any future marriage settlement for his son. His own approval was paramount. He wrote in respect of the terms of one proposed match that 'they would have been very easy, but if they [*sic*] were but £5 a year as long as he matches with my approbation'. He also announced that he would include the whole of Middle Claydon in the settlement, with £500 a year for the immediate use of the couple, but retain all other land including the newly acquired Steeple Claydon estate 'tho' he shall have all at my death'.[34]

Ralph eventually married an heiress his father's aunt, Elizabeth Adams, found in Essex. The bride was the co-heiress of the Paschall family of Great Baddow, where Elizabeth's husband was parson.[35] The Paschalls were a declining gentry family without great social or political influence. Sir John had indicated that he expected a portion of more than £6,000 or £7,000 for his eldest son.[36] Catherine Paschall's inheritance was valued at £8,000. John Verney told his son Ralph about the match and simultaneously sent his brother-in-law, Ralph Palmer, and John Churchill, a Steeple Claydon freeholder tenant and kin to the Palmers, to value the estate in March 1707. They were to measure the land carefully, and base their valuations on an average of estate income over the previous seven years, or if possible ten. Sir John had particular doubts about the value of the estate in Baddow, Canvey Island, and Kent, and the various debts and charges secured on it, but arranged a meeting with Squire Paschall at about the same time.[37]

Several things became clear in the course of discussions of the settlement terms. Firstly, Sir John followed his father's insistence on not raising money from the core Verney property for future dowries, but looked at it from a rather different perspective when he wrote 'I do not mean to touch his wife's fortune.'[38] He would not take any of the dowry for his own use, but her lands would have to be used to finance dowries, and would also have to bear the burden of any Paschall debts. The settlement also made it more difficult to split the Paschall lands from the Verneys by stricter clauses than in Edmund Verney's marriage

---

[33] Cf. L. Stone, *The Family, Sex and Marriage in England 1500–1800* (London 1977), pp. 191, 319; M. Slater, 'The weightiest business: marriage in an upper gentry family in seventeenth century England', *Past and Present* 72 (1976), pp. 25–54; S. H. Mendelson, 'Debate', *Past and Present* 85 (1979), pp. 126–35; sjv to Thomas Cheret 16 October 1703 R52; sjv to rv 10 April 1707 R53.

[34] sjv to Ann Tregea 23 June 1706 R53.   [35] Elizabeth Adams to sjv 12 February 1706/7 R53.

[36] sjv to Tom Cherett 16 November 1703 R52.

[37] Margaret Adams to sjv 11 March 1706/7 R53.

[38] John Verney to Ann Tregea 23 June 1707 R53.

settlement of 1662. If there were no children of the marriage, but a widowed Catherine Paschall remarried, her lands would be inherited by her daughters. But if there were no daughters of a second marriage, the Paschall lands would revert to the Verneys. The importance of the ultimate destination of the Paschall lands is underlined in the series of legal questions Ralph Palmer set out for his nephew in March 1707, at the very beginning of negotiations. Question five concerned 'the final securing her inheritance unto you and your heirs, in default of issue &c. Which I perceive my Lord is very resolute to.'[39] The couple appears to have liked each other, and negotiations went on through the summer and autumn of 1707. The marriage contract was completed and signed in October 1707 but the wedding did not take place until 24 February 1708, after the separation of the inheritances of Catherine and her sister only five days earlier.[40]

Sir John Verney looked for a large dowry for his eldest son but had a different attitude to his daughters' marriages. By 1707 two of his three daughters had already married, while the third never married. Both made love matches, with the family's approval. Sir John did not attempt to use his daughters' marriages for the family's social and political advancement. Mary and Margaret married their husbands in quick succession in February and May 1703. Mary married a Colonel John Lovett who came from Ireland, but was related to an old established Buckinghamshire gentry family. His limited fortune was made up of Irish mortgages and land in reversion, but after Sir John had scrutinised them suspiciously he gave the match his approval. He promised Mary a dowry of £3,000, but no marriage settlement has survived.[41] Her younger sister, Margaret, had already married Thomas Cave, heir to the Cave estates in Stanford, Leicestershire. This love match took place against the express wishes of his father, and was briefly the talk of London. Margaret's £3,000 dowry was a respectable sum, but considerably less than Sir Roger Cave had hoped for his eldest son. In negotiations for a settlement after the marriage had taken place, he demanded a dowry of £5,000 or £6,000 in return for a jointure of £500 a year.[42] The marriage settlement was not agreed until May 1704, over a year after the wedding. Sir John Verney paid a relatively small dowry for the social connections his daughter brought him. Her jointure of about £450 a year was considerably above the standard 10:1 dowry/jointure ratio of the time.[43]

[39] Ralph Palmer to rv 10 March 1706/7 R53.
[40] CIH 1/144ab and 2/1587 dated 16 October 1707. CIH 2/1588.
[41] See J. Lovett to sjv 18 July 1702; Solicitor General Brodrick to sjv (from Dublin) 13 January 1702/3 R52 and M. M. Verney, *Verney Letters of the Eighteenth Century* (2 vols. London 1930), I, ch. 8.
[42] Cf. H. J. Habakkuk, *Marriage, Debt, and the Estates System: English Landownership 1650–1950* (Oxford 1994), p. 152. On the more general applicability of rules about jointure/portion ratios see pp. 148–9.
[43] Leicestershire CRO Braye MSS 22–23. J. Churchill to sjv 10 July 1703 R52; Tho Cheret to sjv 11 August 1703, R52.

Both Sir John Verney's daughters played an active part in choosing their husbands. Lovett eased his way into Sir John's acquiescence by his Dublin court connections, which enabled him to procure his future father-in-law an Irish viscountcy on 16 June 1703, just a month before the marriage took place on 20 July. Later marriage brokers offered to raise this to an earldom, or to convert it to an English peerage, but Sir John Verney showed no interest. Whether from gratitude, or hope of future patronage, both daughters (and presumably their husbands) decided to name their eldest sons Verney. In the mercenary spirit of the early eighteenth-century marriage market, it is worth remarking that by encouraging his daughters' love matches, Sir John was under no pressure to increase their dowries.

At every generation after 1613 the Verneys preferred brides with fortunes rather than social status and connections. In the next generation the family again benefited from the merging of two brothers' inheritances. In 1736, at the age of twenty-five, John, the elder son of Ralph Verney and Catherine Paschall, married Mary Nicholson. She was the daughter of a London businessman, Josias Nicholson of Clapham. Her dowry was £20,000, with a further £20,000 that would accrue on her father's death. The marriage settlement has not survived, but its terms can be deduced from later settlements in 1740 and 1767.[44] It ordained that her dowry should be used to buy land. Soon after the marriage, in May 1737, John Verney and his father set out to inspect a Northamptonshire estate with a view to purchase. On that journey John fell ill with a fever that worsened until he died on 5 June.[45] The dowry remained Verney property although his widow, and the daughter of the marriage born after his death, required lifetime maintenance and support from the Verneys. John's younger brother Ralph now became heir to the family fortunes. In 1740, he married Mary, the daughter of Henry Herring, a London merchant who had first made his fortune in the wine trade. She and her two sisters shared a vast fortune. Mary's dowry was initially worth £40,000, and she received at least £13,000 more at her father's death.

There is virtually no surviving correspondence about the arrangement of either John's or Ralph's marriages, but both brought wealth to the Verneys without regard to social prestige. In contrast to those of earlier generations these marriages involved much larger fortunes, and dowries that were predominantly in money and stocks, not land. However, both marriage settlements specified that the dowries should be used to buy land. This was a very substantial injection of capital into the land market. Over three generations of accumulation by marriage, the Verney family income had risen from c. £2,250 a year to £4,500 to £5,000 by 1736. When the two great dowries were invested in land, they brought the total income of the family by 1780 to close on £10,000 a year. In

[44] PRO C109/52 and ClH 1/477; the Herring marriage settlement terms are in ClH 1/474.
[45] M. M. Verney, *Verney Letters*, II, p. 145.

economic terms, the Verneys had risen from the ranks of the upper gentry to the brink of the great English landowners by marrying their sons with large dowries, irrespective of their social class. These heiresses were from less wealthy gentry or business families without important social and political connections. If they had not been heiresses, their dowries would have been much lower and the Verneys would not have been interested in them. While John Verney's marriages to City wealth reflect his status, his merchant career, and his close London connections, the Nicholson and Herring marriages of 1736 and 1740 represent a deliberate attempt to bring substantial non-landed wealth to the family. By then, the Verneys were prospering and hardly fit Sir John Habakkuk's observation that 'only landed families in very serious difficulties . . . married the daughters of moneyed men'.[46]

The heads of the family always kept substantial control of the marriages of their eldest sons, partly because after the Restoration they were never in financial difficulties and the daughter-in-law's dowry was not needed to pay their own debts. Equally importantly, some family lands always remained outside the settlement. The Verneys jealously guarded the integrity of the Claydon estate, and avoided settlements that would allow debt charges secured on that land to build up. Any legal liability for dowries was set against the wife's lands. No marriage alliances put undue burdens on estate income, or reduced the flexibility allowed to the next generation. Up until 1736 jointures were strictly limited, and wealth brought into the family was in every case channelled to provide for the male Verney line. Typically, the wife's lands could revert to her descendants or kin only in very few circumstances. The Verneys were not unique in marrying heiresses in successive generations. The Berties, Norths, Wentworths, and Cecils also used such policies to enhance their family fortunes. The Verneys must however have been one of the few families consistently able to drive such hard bargains that they avoided the pitfalls of heiress marriages up until 1740. There were no long-lived dowagers or excessively high jointures; in only one case did the death of children lead to the reversion of the lands to the heiress's family. The family thus achieved a 'really ambitious matrimonial strategy'.[47]

The Verney marriage settlements made little provision for younger sons or for the dowries of daughters except where there was no son born from the marriage. Such matters were left to lifetime discretion, and provision made in wills. Edmund Verney intended to leave his daughter a dowry of only £1,000, perhaps expecting that his wife would augment this from her own fortune. Sir John Verney's intentions are unclear from his surviving wills, but his son Ralph's attitudes are illuminated by a series of wills during the 1720s and 1730s.[48] In

---

[46] Habakkuk, *Marriage, Debt, and the Estates System*, p. 202.   [47] *Ibid.*, pp. 211–12.
[48] CIH 1/162–8 There is a sequence of seven wills between 1721 and 1737.

these, his younger son and daughters were left equal and increasing sums of money. In 1721 he left them each £3,000. This was raised to £3,300 in 1722, £3,500 in 1723 and £4,000 in 1728. In 1737 his daughters were provided with dowries of £5,000. His younger son Ralph had by this time become heir to the estate. However, Ralph had been left land in his father's earlier wills. Initially this amounted to some outlying Essex land in 1721, but as his father bought new lands and expanded the estates, small new properties in Buckinghamshire as well as Essex were added to the list. It is difficult to estimate the full annual value of the lands, but it may well have approached £300 a year by 1723. However, in 1728 (at the time of the re-purchase of East Claydon) Ralph's landed inheritance was cut back to small Essex estates, compensated for by a small increase in his cash bequest. Because Ralph, the first Earl Verney, decided such matters by will, and frequently recast his wills, he retained considerable power over his children. The wills would have dissipated some of the first earl's landed investments, but only his new purchases, not the core estate. Ralph Verney's inheritance of all his father's land provides a further example of demographic chance playing a vital part in expanding the Verney estates.

After 1650 higher mortality rates were significant in curtailing English population growth, and affected the English elite as well as the mass of the population. However, the most obvious change in the Verneys' demographic fortunes was a reduction in completed family size, and the lower fertility of Verney wives was a major part of this. It was a major factor in reducing family outgoings.[49] Sir Ralph's life was plagued by the burdens of providing for his nine brothers and sisters. Large families were also found amongst the Dentons (over two generations) and Temples in the early seventeenth century. Sir Ralph had only six children in eighteen years of marriage, of whom two died in infancy, two as young children, and two sons survived to adulthood. The younger, John, made sufficient money as a Levant merchant to be substantially independent. Edmund Verney and Mary Abell had three children, yet all died in early adulthood. Their daughter married after an elopement but died (with her child) before any dowry had been paid. Even here, the circumstances of Mary Abell's lunacy allowed Sir Ralph to ensure that her support came from the Abell estates. Sir John Verney received three dowries. He had to make provision for the children of his later wives in marriage settlement. However, all his four surviving children were born to his first wife. John was able to provide dowries for two daughters from savings without raising loans, while his third daughter never married. There

---

[49] For the demography of the elite see T. H. Hollingsworth, *The Demography of the British Peerage*, supplement to *Population Studies*, 18 (1964) and L. Stone and J. C. F. Stone, *An Open Elite?* (Oxford 1984), ch. 3, esp. pp. 95–104; E. A. Wrigley, R. S. Davies, J. E. Oeppen, and R. S. Schofield, *English Population History from Family Reconstitution 1580–1837* (Cambridge 1997), ch. 6, esp. pp. 289–98; E. A. Wrigley, and R. S. Schofield, *The Population History of England 1538–1871* (Cambridge 1981), pp. 248–53.

were two daughters in the next generation, but only one married, probably with a £5,000 dowry as laid down in her father's 1737 will.[50]

This demographic pattern strained family finances far less after 1700 than before. The Verney marriage settlements made no formal provision for younger children, unless they were heiresses, following the predominant pattern for English elite marriage settlements of the period. Although pre-emptive trusts to provide for younger children became increasingly common in strict marriage settlements after 1700, only one third of Bonfield's sample of Kent and Northamptonshire families used this legal device in marriage settlements between 1700 and 1740. Habakkuk regards the absence of provision for younger children as a means of retaining some control over them.[51] Sir Ralph Verney was obsessed with the problems of paying pre-determined annuities to his brothers and sisters and inaugurated a family belief that younger sons should find a profession. Sir John Verney was intended for the law, but persuaded his father to allow him to enter the Levant trade. Edmund Verney was keen to see that his younger son had some skill. Ralph, who became the second Earl, had his sights set on either the law or the church as a profession. Gender balance also favoured the Verneys' financial recovery in the second half of the seventeenth century. No dowries were raised between 1646 and 1703 and between 1642 and 1717 only minimal jointure was paid out of the estate. Later in the eighteenth century, the burden of portions and jointure became heavier. In several cases dowries were unpaid, but the interest on the capital sum was paid as income instead. The second earl paid a jointure of £1,600 a year to his sister-in-law Mary Nicholson for most of his life and an annuity to his sister Elizabeth instead of her dowry of £5,000.

The Verneys also improved their family finances by deciding how wide a circle of kin would receive direct support. Sir Ralph Verney had supported his nine brothers and sisters throughout his life, paying his brothers small annuities. Those sisters whose marriage portions he could not pay received an annual income based on what their dowries would have produced if lent out. They helped him keep his debt afloat during the hard Interregnum years and beyond. Their children (mainly daughters) descended into that sub-culture of poor gentlefolk who clung to their family connections and to a status their means could no longer support. Sir Ralph had paid full interest on what savings they kept with him but transferred these obligations to his son Edmund. Soon after Sir Ralph's death, Sir John Verney began to receive requests for financial help from his first cousins. He was perfectly willing to receive his poor relatives, including the son of his disgraced aunt, Mary Lloyd, whom his father had ostracised after her

---

[50] F. P. Verney, and M. M. Verney, *Verney Memoirs*, iv, ch. 10; wills 1717–37 in ClH 1/162–8.
[51] Bonfield, *Marriage Settlements 1601–1740*, pp. 111–19, especially p. 118 notes 83–4; Habakkuk, *Marriage, Debt, and the Estates System*, p. 22.

unmarried pregnancy in 1655. Within limits he would help these relatives to secure contacts and even places. Another Mary Lloyd became his third wife's companion. However, in 1704 Sir John explicitly stated that he would no longer support his cousins financially. He replied to Cary Stewkeley's request for help to pay off tradesmen's debts in Islington:

I would sooner get a livelihood by working and labour than run into debt upon uncertainties . . . I neither will nor can allow you anything . . . I pray consider the number of cousins (as near as yourselves) that I have and that they be in conditions as low as yourself . . . but if I were to maintain them and give them yearly allowances I might soon go a-begging.

As family size shrank in the later seventeenth century, and family finances improved, this problem disappeared for later generations.[52]

Family obligations declined as mortality gradually took its toll of Sir Edmund's children. Family debts were another matter and totalled £11,250 in 1661. After Edmund's marriage to Mary Abell, Sir Ralph used his wife's estates at Preston Crowmarsh and Benson in Oxfordshire to reduce his debts. They were first enclosed before selling the small farms to their occupiers, and the main farms to an outside purchaser between 1662 and 1664.[53] This raised over £8,000, reducing the debt to about £5,000 by the mid-sixties. Later debt lists show £4,750 owed in 1679, £3,900 in 1681, and £3,300 in 1685.

The annual servicing cost of the debt fell even faster. In 1661 interest had cost £691 a year, but by 1668, after land sales, only £300. Sir Ralph reduced the cost to £244 a year by 1679, £201 in 1683, and £136 in 1685, using two tactics. Falling interest rates after 1670 enabled him to pay off some old loans from income and re-finance others at lower rates of interest. In 1679–81, most of his loans were at 5 per cent, but by 1685 4 per cent was the norm. Sometimes he persuaded his creditors to reduce their rates of interest. In most cases he re-financed loans he had repaid for good reasons – as when Sir John Bridgeman needed to raise a dowry for his daughter – at a lower rate. In 1683, however, he borrowed more than he needed when offered a 4 per cent loan by John Verney's brother-in-law, Ralph Palmer. He used the surplus to pay off his poor relatives' small loans. Interest from these at 6 per cent was their prime source of income. Sir Ralph justified his decision by saying that he knew that plenty of country people and gentry were still prepared to borrow at 6 per cent. He was determined to clear his debts cheaply and quickly by tapping London finance markets, using his younger son's business and marriage connections.[54]

---

[52] Broad, 'Gentry finances', p. 199; sjv to Cary Stewkeley 24 December 1704 R52.

[53] CIH 2/2094, 2097, 2106, 2113, 2133–7.

[54] Debt lists (with interest rates): November 1661 R18; November 1679 R33; 3G May 1681 R35; Sir John Bridgeman to srv 10 Oct 1677 R30; srv to sjv 13 Aug 1683 R38.

His elder son Edmund's finances and attitudes to money make an interesting contrast. When Edmund Verney married in 1662 he had plenty of money and was lending some out for the next few years. He sold his wife's Hertfordshire property at Ayot St Peter in 1663/4 for around £3,500.[55] He consciously lived the life of an old-fashioned bountiful squire, entertaining his tenants and neighbours generously at Christmas 1664, and for a number of years afterwards providing regular cash doles to poor families. We know relatively little of Edmund's finances for the next twenty years. In 1669, his will made provision for debts of £4,000 to be settled on his estates. We have no estimate of his debts at the time but they amounted to £4,455 at his death nearly twenty years later.[56]

The structure of Edmund Verney's debts was very different from his father's. Whereas by 1685 Sir Ralph had reduced his creditors to four in number, and almost all his interest was at 4 per cent, Edmund's slightly larger debts were owed to twenty-two people. Without exception they were relatives, old family friends, family servants, and tenants. On all but £700 out of the £4,455 the interest rate was the full statutory 6 per cent, and considerable numbers of creditors were owed as little as £50 or £100. Many of the servants involved were Sir Ralph's rather than Edmund's, indicating that the expensive loans that Sir Ralph had shed during the early eighties had simply been transferred to his son. In addition, Edmund took in the poor stock from both East and Middle Claydon at different times. He seems to have had a non-economic view of his debts. They were an indication of his desire to play the paternal country gentleman and attract local goodwill. He was acting as a kind of primitive banker to the locality and wider family, and the debts reflect continuing minor overspending over the years.[57] Sir Ralph's obsession with clearing the debt led him to ask Edmund to use money from land sales to pay off more of the family debts by 'buying' a tranche of Sir Ralph's part of the Claydon estate in 1665. The extra income offered, £150 a year, almost exactly matched the sum raised by the sale of Hertfordshire land but Edmund was apparently not interested.

The improving debt situation also reflected changes in the family's lifestyles that enabled them to first consolidate and then modestly expand their estate. The heads of family adopted well-regulated domestic and estate management,

[55] CIH 2/1846–7.

[56] eb to srv 18 October 1664 and 2 and 9 January 1664/5 CIH 4/5/17; ev to Alexander Denton 24 April 1665 R20; srv to ev 30 January 1672/3 R25; ev to srv 24 May 1669 R23. CIH 1/128–9. In January 1695, Sir Ralph and John Verney secured the debts on Middle Claydon land when handing back the Abell estates and the lunatic widow Mary to her relatives. This occurred at a time when various East Claydon estate matters were being sorted out in response to the young Mary Verney's elopement. The process was confirmed and completed by Sir Ralph and his heir John in July 1696, just before Sir Ralph's death, see 1/132 dated 23 July 1696.

[57] See Debt List dated 6 September 1683 R43. After his death, John Verney noted that Sir Ralph 'would never promise to anyone to pay my brother's debts, yet he paid the interest on 'em'; sjv to P. Viccars 17 April 1704 R52.

withdrew from an expensive court life in favour of service in a variety of county roles, from JP and Deputy Lieutenant to county MP. The family revived its fortunes in part by a combination of new ties with commerce and finance, an overtly economic view of marriage, and favourable family demography. Sir Ralph Verney remained a widower and lived on until 1696. He lived on an income of about £1,000 a year, having made over about £600 a year to his son Edmund at marriage. Now that his children were grown up and financially independent, Sir Ralph found that with his naturally frugal Puritan outlook and few expensive vices, he could save money and he gradually paid off the remaining debts.

When Sir John Verney succeeded his father in 1696 the family's financial circumstances changed rapidly. The debts were almost certainly paid off immediately using the three portions that Sir John had collected between 1680 and 1694, which were only slowly invested in land. He gradually moved the money from trade into government securities, annuities, and insurance contracts, or lent on mortgage instead. He entered politics and eventually became an MP for two terms. For much of his life, Sir John was reputed to lend out money. The only occasion when he claimed not to have cash to lend was in 1703 when he had to raise portions of £6,000 for two daughters at short notice.[58]

The same was true of his son, Ralph (second Viscount Fermanagh and first Earl Verney). His comfortable prosperity is well charted in the rising amounts of land and money detailed in his wills between 1721 and 1737. His dealings with his stepmother Elizabeth Baker show his natural parsimony well. On Sir John Verney's death in 1717 he offered to pay her £220 a year as jointure free of tax, or allow her to collect the rents from her jointure lands. In her reply, Elizabeth pointedly remarked that her husband had been giving her an allowance of £500 a year during his lifetime. When she died in 1736 she left no will and her estate was divided amongst her own family. Relations between the Bakers and Verneys were strained after Verney's death.[59]

The first earl continued his father's engagement with London financial interests. He was an active investor in the South Sea flotation of early 1720, on his own behalf and also for relatives. He seems to have been reasonably shrewd, announcing at an early stage that he intended to sell off part of his holdings at a time when he had already made substantial initial gains. He did not invest in the first two subscriptions, but put sums of £3,000 and £500 in the less profitable third and fourth in the name of his younger son John. He exchanged Government lottery annuities for South Sea stock in the summer

---

[58] For a much fuller account of John Verney's networks and connections, see Whyman, *Sociability and Power, passim.*

[59] rv to Elizabeth Verney 9 September 1717 R56 and her reply 21 September 1717 R56. Catherine Verney to Mrs Stone 14 December 1736 R58. For further details of the family tensions see Whyman, *Sociability and Power*, pp. 122, 141.

of 1720, which was the undoing of many when the price of stock plummeted in the autumn. The financial impact of the South Sea Bubble on the Verneys is unclear, as there are no family accounts. Any losses cannot have been large for the family continued to buy land. Perhaps some of the poor relatives they advised were less fortunate. In March 1721 Catherine Verney wrote that she was 'so fearful of our younger children', suggesting money had been invested to boost provision for them. She planned retrenchment in the household and the renting of a smaller London house. Catherine was an ardent and shrewd observer of the financial markets throughout the episode, sending her husband sharp comments and advice clothed in obsequious phrases. When her husband failed to complete a land deal in 1719 she begged him to send the money to London quickly 'for 'tis a pity to let it lye dead any longer'. She pressed him to invest in annuities in January 1720 'for I fancy stocks won't fall till after Lady Day'.[60]

Despite his wife's fear that the number of servants they kept was ruining them, Ralph Verney had easy access to capital at least until he bought East Claydon in 1729. Between then and 1736, when the first of the great marriage portions rolled in, the Verneys may technically have been borrowers, but it did not prevent them buying further small amounts of land even as they sold outlying estates. The first Earl Verney appears to have stopped lending on mortgage after his father's death. Money was either invested in land, or in relatively liquid assets such as bank stock and government securities. Despite keeping three houses, in Little Chelsea, Essex, and Claydon, the Verneys always appear comfortably off, but without the extravagant lifestyle that was to be the second earl's undoing.[61] The first earl followed his father's politics and served as the Tory MP for Amersham from 1717 to 1727. He then left politics before building an electoral interest in Wendover from the mid-1730s onwards, serving as MP from 1741 until his death in 1752.

The money from Verney marriages fuelled the expansion of the Verney estates for eighty years. They bought to consolidate existing estates and ensure a compact and easily manageable whole. When there was no money to splash out on major purchases, they took opportunities to consolidate whenever possible. Sir Ralph Verney bought little. Between 1665 and 1700, the family probably spent only £3,750 on land, all of it to consolidate their hold on the Claydons and on Wasing. East Claydon came within their orbit but remained separately managed. Rights and jurisdictions were also important and relatively cheap. Sir Ralph bought the fee farm rents for the Claydons and Wasing in 1671. In 1674

[60] Catherine Verney to rv 12 March 1720/1 R56; 19 March 1718/9 R56; 18 January 1719/20 R56; P. G. M. Dickson, *The Financial Revolution in England* (Oxford 1967), pp. 108–9; HLRO Large Parchment Collection B62–3, and South Sea Co. Papers Box 157.
[61] sjv memorandum dated 24 July 1699 R51; Sir Thomas Tipping to sjv 15 May 1706 R53; Catherine Verney to rv 9 March 1720/1 R57.

he purchased the court Leet of Adstock for £25. As an institution it was effectively defunct, but Middle Claydon fell within its jurisdiction, and in unfriendly hands it could be a potential irritant.[62] He also bought up the advowson at Wasing.[63] But Sir Ralph also encouraged his sons to take responsibility for the long-term interests of the family. In 1674, when the Chaloner family in Steeple Claydon was preparing to enclose the common fields of the parish, Sir Ralph and his son agreed to prevent the enclosure to retain their tenants and sustain estate income at a time of falling rents. They found an opportunity to buy land and common rights, but Sir Ralph wanted his son to take the responsibility and insisted that he made the purchase, even though the cost was only £80. Yet Sir Ralph was buying Adstock Court Leet at the same time.[64] During negotiations for John Verney's first marriage in 1680, his father, rather than buy it himself, pressed John to buy the whole Steeple Claydon estate and to incorporate it into the marriage settlement.

Edmund Verney did buy a certain amount of land in East Claydon between 1662 and his death in 1688. Small farms, no bigger than twenty acres, were purchased, but the total cost of £1,545 was less than he sold his Hertfordshire land for in 1663–4.[65] When Edmund's younger son died in 1690, the Verneys had to rethink their property strategy. Now that there was no male heir, the Abell estates would revert to the couple's fifteen-year-old daughter Mary, while the main Verney estate passed to Sir John Verney. When four years later the still under-age Mary eloped with the Lord Chief Justice's son, they ensured that she obtained only an allowance. On her death in 1696, Sir Ralph and Sir John Verney relinquished custody of the lunatic Mary Abell and her East Claydon estate to her cousins in return for a renunciation of all Abell claims to Mary's jointure out of Middle Claydon.[66]

John Verney's business background gave him greater familiarity with opportunities in trade, shipping, government bonds and annuities, and mortgages than with the land market. Most of his investments in land appear to have been in mortgages, and he ignored the stipulations in his second and third marriage settlements that prescribed land purchases of £9,000 to provide for the children of the marriages. Between 1690, when he knew he was heir to the Verney estates, and his death in 1717, John spent a total of £5,581 on land, mainly between 1700 and 1707. Most was spent on acquiring the rump of the Chaloner

---

[62] CIH 2/1001; 2/1004; cf. Habbakuk, *Marriage, Debt, and the Estates System*, p. 480, citing the Child family buying up land in Middlesex to prevent manorial claims.

[63] CIH 2/1539 (1677).

[64] For the failed enclosure of Steeple Claydon see Broad, 'The Verneys as enclosing landlords', in J. Chartres and D. Hey (eds.), *English Rural Society 1500–1800* (Cambridge 1990), pp. 39–40 and below p. 234. The repercussions for Steeple Claydon are examined in J. Broad, 'The fate of the midland yeoman: tenants, copyholders, and freeholders as farmers in North Buckinghamshire, 1620–1800', *Continuity and Change* 14:3 (1999), pp. 325–47.

[65] CIH 2/1846–7; 2/184, 2/187, 2/189.   [66] CIH 1/132 ab.

estate in Steeple Claydon in 1704, including manorial rights, and a range of small farms and cottages. He made one purchase in Adstock, not far away. There were earlier modest investments in land. He made two small purchases of Steeple Claydon land in 1687 and consolidated his Wasing estate by buying a small farm for £720 in 1689. He looked at other properties close to Claydon, but was a demanding purchaser. Estate agents' property descriptions were just beginning to circulate in London society. Sir John received one about New Park farm in Boarstall (Bucks.), about ten miles from Claydon, a moated farmhouse with a dairy farm of some 134 acres. The agents' description was:

A Capital Messuage & Lands of Arable Meadow & Pasture with Barnes Stables Orchard Garden and Appurtenances, moted round. The Messuage and Barne are new built with Brick and Stone and in the Possession of one Tho Freeman and he hath 17 Years to come of his Lease.

Verney annotated the particulars in his own hand with a very modern scepticism of estate agents' wording:

Capital messuage is a very small new house and a moat just round it that you can't swing a cat in the Garden no Orchard. One Stable ready to drop down, the stable not of brick nor stone, Nor the Barn which is but one bay and a nook & the threshing floor, and if the corn were removed 'twould certainly fall; pitifully built of sallow Rafters and here is not half house room enough for the land.[67]

Sir John Verney was probably initially interested in it because it was a ring-fenced, enclosed farm in dairying country similar to Claydon.

Sir John Verney bought very little land from 1710 to 1717. His son the first earl made one small purchase in East Claydon parish for £225.[68] However, in the seven years after Sir John Verney's death in 1717 he spent a total of £5,750 – £1,855 in Steeple Claydon, £872 in East Claydon, and the rest elsewhere. The outlying properties were nearby in Adstock, in Grendon (which adjoined the Claydons), and in Bierton close to Aylesbury. The largest purchase of £1,540 was in Great Baddow (Essex), where the first earl and his wife lived for the first ten years of their married life. He was also offered property near Claydon at Marsh Gibbon, Cublington, Chalfont, and Broughton at various times.[69]

After the failure of Edmund Verney's line, the family continued its purchases in East Claydon. Some were open-market purchases but others occurred

---

[67] Miscellaneous documents of December 1690 R44. On the embryonic development of estate agency services see Habakkuk, *Marriage, Debt, and the Estates System*, pp. 66–70; F. Melton, *Sir Robert Clayton and the Origins of English Deposit Banking* (Cambridge 1986), *passim* and F. M. L. Thompson, *Chartered Surveyors, the Growth of a Profession* (London 1968), ch. 2.
[68] ClH 2/190 April 1711.
[69] D. Bradley to rv 29 November 1721 R56 (Cublington); cc to rv 15 September 1717 R56 (Broughton); N. Merwin to rv 28 September 1719 R56 (Chalfont).

where farmers sold land they had previously mortgaged to the Verneys. The Verneys had a clear interest in repurchasing the main Abell estate. When Edmund Verney's widow, Mary, finally died in 1715 John thought the Abells might sell it, and wished it might be 'to a good neighbour, or that I had money to buy it'. Six months after Ralph Verney succeeded his father in 1717 the new owner William Abell made an approach. He wrote that he was ill and lacked the energy to run an estate, and offered to 'treat with your Lordship either by myself or by my son' for East Claydon as soon as the 'ferment of money' was over.[70] Nothing came of this and in 1720 Abell took out a £4,000 mortgage on the land. In the following year, he made his will, leaving his son the land, but also making him responsible for raising £9,000 for his sister's portion. When William Abell died, his son quickly sold the land to Thomas Snow and John Paltock, a London goldsmith banking partnership, described by local people as 'stockjobbers', for £19,200. The first earl's steward later stated that his master had bid £2,000 more than the asking price, which suggests an element of antagonism in Richard Abell's decision to sell it to outsiders. The sale shocked local people. William Butterfield found new bailiffs arriving to collect arrears of rent in December 1722, and expressed consternation 'that there is no security for the perpetuating our Terra Firma in a family, which should make people not over hasty or solicitous in getting or increasing an estate'.[71]

Snow and Paltock were primarily goldsmith bankers, but they may have originated in Buckinghamshire. There is no evidence that they were regular dealers in land but once they had bought East Claydon they began a classic piece of property speculation. In 1726 they brought together the widely scattered owners of another estate in East Claydon (an Italian count, a Cornish gentleman, and a local Bledlow man). They purchased it, and the rectory and tithes of the adjoining parish of Grandborough for £4,480.[72] In the following year they bought more land adjoining East Claydon in Quainton and Grendon Underwood. Then, in April 1729, they sold the consolidated estate to the second viscount for £30,910, making a handsome profit, and providing the Verneys with a £15,000 mortgage to finance the purchase.[73] Over the next thirty years the Verneys proceeded to buy further small estates, impropriate rectory and tithes, and the remaining farms in East Claydon. They had already purchased

---

[70] sjv to rv 27 Nov 1715 R55; W. Abell to rv 3 January 1717/8 R56.
[71] CIH 2/62–9 Snow and Paltock leased back a house in East Claydon to Richard Abell in August 1722 'at no cheap rate'. I would like to thank Frank Melton for background information on Snow and Paltock. See his *Sir Robert Clayton*, pp. 211–15, 224–5. Further indirect evidence of their activities at Claydon comes in cc to rv 28 October 1722, 30 January 1722/3, wb to rv 25 December 1722 CIH 4/5/68. I also came across some evidence of their activities at this period in north-west Buckinghamshire while working on Bernwood.
[72] CIH 2/252.
[73] The manor was bought for £25,790; the rectory and Grandborough estate cost £5,000; the Christ Church College leases £210 CIH 2/72, 2/253 2/257; for the mortgage see 2/256.

the right to choose the parson in 1726. Their last major purchase was from the Duncombes in 1766.[74]

By the middle of the eighteenth century the Verneys were the dominant landowners in East and Middle Claydon, and the largest single owners in Steeple Claydon, where they held something over one third of the land. They had created the core of their estates. Their purchasing policies were typical of many English landed families in the same period. Habakkuk cites the examples of the Dukes of Kent in Bedfordshire between 1671 and 1780, the Earls of Stamford in Staffordshire after 1740, and the Duke of Kingston around Thoresby (Nottinghamshire) after 1736. In north Buckinghamshire the Temples and Grenvilles were undertaking a similar expansion during the course of the eighteenth century.[75]

The purchase of East Claydon triggered the sale of outlying Verney estates to pay off the mortgage. By 1729 these included not only Wasing, the last of the Blacknall lands which Sir John Verney had obtained from his mother's bequest, but also the valuable Paschall lands at Great Baddow. In the early years of their marriage the first Earl and his wife had lived there and farmed her ancestral estates, but nothing suggests that Catherine Verney opposed the sale of the estate in 1733. Wasing had also been sold in 1730. These two sales raised £22,604, allowing a progressive reduction in the mortgage, which they finally paid off when John Verney married in 1736.[76]

The Verneys expanded their Buckinghamshire estates between 1660 and 1736 primarily by arranging marriages to heiresses whose dowries were predominantly in land. Those estates were later sold off to pay debts, or to make purchases closer to Claydon. When Sir John Verney became head of the family, his commercial experience and contacts and moderate trading success kept the family's cash flow positive through the early eighteenth century when land tax was high. Yet purchases of land between 1660 and 1730 were few and mainly modest. Some £13,500 was spent providing an additional family income of about £600 per annum.[77] They spent about £1,100 in the 1660s, £701 in the

---

[74] 1726 Advowson purchase ClH 2/249; the Duncombe estate 2/313. A small estate belonging to Christ Church, Oxford, which was not bought until 1866, but during the eighteenth century the Verneys became the permanent leaseholders and did not even mark out the college estate separately from their own; Christ Church Archives MS Estate 7/316–41.

[75] Habakkuk, *Marriage, Debt, and the Estates System*, pp. 476–7; J. V. Beckett, *The Rise and Fall of the Grenvilles* (Manchester 1994), pp.10–11 and 32–64.

[76] The 1730 repayment came only eight days after Wasing had been sold for £8,120; Berkshire CRO D/Emt /T1 /T2; The Baddow sale is recorded in Essex CRO D/DB T105. Evidence of later eighteenth-century Verney surveys suggests that the Canvey Island property, and some woods at Baddow, remained in Verney hands.

[77] This income figure is based on an average of twenty-two years' purchase derived from C. Clay, 'The price of freehold land in the seventeenth and eighteenth centuries', *Economic History Review* 27 (1974), pp. 173–89. The true figure was probably rather smaller, since the purchases of fee farms rents, courts leet, and advowsons were more important for consolidation and protection against outside interference than for income.

1670s, £1,940 in the 1680s, and nothing, as far as can be seen, in the 1690s. Most of their purchases were small additions to existing estates. In the early eighteenth century more money was available; £5,263 was spent in the 1700s and £4,574 from 1711 to 1720.

The Verneys succeeded in their long-term estate expansion despite two major setbacks. They were unable to buy a consolidated estate from their Steeple Claydon neighbours, the Chaloners, in the 1680s. The offer came at a crucial stage in John Verney's marriage negotiations, when his finances were stretched to the limit to provide a suitable jointure for his first wife. Sir Ralph Verney still lived in terror of indebtedness, and was unwilling to borrow for an additional commitment. Edmund Verney was probably more solvent but uninterested. The Chaloners asked what seemed a very high price for the property, though their figure was very close to what the estate sold for piecemeal. Pique may have played some part on the Chaloners' side. The Verneys had used underhand tactics to prevent them enclosing the parish, but had also ensured that no major landowner could buy it and create a competing consolidated estate. Yet, it took the Verneys over a hundred years to consolidate a smaller Steeple Claydon estate once it had been broken up.

When Edmund Verney's male line failed in 1690, the project to merge the adjoining East and Middle Claydon estates collapsed. This was an even greater blow to the Verneys' plans. East Claydon remained an obvious target for purchase, but again there were enmities between the Abells and Verneys over the treatment of Mary Abell. A brief window of opportunity in 1717 when Richard Abell was dying gave way to a renewal of hostility by his successors, and the deliberate and abrupt decision to sell to Snow and Paltock despite the Verneys' substantially higher bid again delayed the project.

The Verneys often had to wait for the right property to come on the market between 1680 and 1740. They contented themselves with accumulating small farms in the neighbourhood, and kept their capital in mortgages and government investments. When they captured heiresses of lower social status but large landed dowries, they gained additional property and income without buying land. When they had cash in hand, their widespread city networks, long use of banking facilities, knowledge of alternative investment opportunities in a time of rich returns, and lack of inhibition about any social consequences of their policies, left them more profitable methods of investing their money.

At the heart of the Verneys' continuing expansion lay the firm hand of patriarchy. Successive heads of family were able to instil in their sons a commitment to the frugal management of their estates and finances, a consent to marriages that were arranged for family benefit above personal attachment, and a dynastic view of long-term estate planning. As we shall see in the next chapter, heirs to the estate expected to serve an apprenticeship in the practical management of the estate which remained a hands-on activity throughout the period from 1660 to 1740, and were groomed for their future role.

Both Sir Ralph Verney and Sir John had a continuing and controlling interest in their sons' activities. Affection was plentifully expressed in letters and
activities, but ultimately derived from paternal benevolence and calculation. A
certain distance between father and son reflected contemporary expectations
of family relations, but in the Verneys' case there were additional factors. Sir
Ralph's Civil War exile, and the loss of his wife, meant that his sons lost a
mother, and also experienced childhood separation from their father for considerable periods. Sir John did not marry until he was forty, after returning from
the Levant trade. His son was born when he was forty-three and well established
in his business career.

Family dynamics played an important part in inculcating strong and recurrent
patterns in father–son relationships, but there were vital material considerations
at stake. Sir Ralph Verney spent much of his life paying out annuities to his
brothers as set out in his father's will, and to his sisters, instead of paying their
dowries in cash. The drain on family resources during the difficult 1640 to
1660 period was considerable, yet Sir Ralph had little control over the modest
marriages his younger sisters made. He found himself paying annuities to his
brothers Tom and Henry, who had brief military careers in the 1630s and 1640s,
but no regular means of subsistence afterwards. Sir Ralph paid out Tom's annuities for many years to various remote parts of the British Isles where his
brother eked out an existence with wild projects and prospecting. He protected
him from various women who claimed they had married him and demanded
maintenance. To counterpoint the precarious lives of his brothers he had the
example of his old friend (and uncle, though close in age) William Denton,
who was the younger son of another large local gentry family who successfully
made his own way in the world as a physician. In the next three generations
fixed liabilities to kin never again hung over the Verneys. They never allowed
their children independent allowances, and encouraged the few younger sons
towards trades and professions in which they would be self-sufficient. The strict
settlements excluded sufficient land to ensure that the Verneys never lost the
power to distribute substantial amounts of the family's wealth by lifetime grant
or will in the way that Bonfield suggested.[78]

Once Sir Ralph had reduced the family debt, the Verneys remained financially
buoyant. Father never again went cap in hand to son to use a marriage settlement
to save the family finances. In this way paternal authority remained intact. This
was not only true of eldest sons. Although Sir John Verney persuaded his father
to confirm his rights in 1662 before he left for the Levant, the Wasing estate
remained Sir Ralph's. It was only when John planned marriage eighteen years
later that Sir Ralph was prepared to transfer his interest in the estates as part

[78] L. Bonfield, 'Marriage, property and the "affective family" ', *Law and History Review* 1 (1983),
p. 303.

of the negotiations for a marriage settlement. Similarly, through the 1720s and 1730s the first Earl Verney frequently changed his will to provide more for his younger son Ralph.

Paternal authority was also quietly effective in marrying heirs to the estates at a remarkably consistent age of twenty-five or twenty-six to rich brides of their own age.[79] There is little evidence of any lingering crisis in gender relationships, or even of inter-generational conflicts that challenged patriarchal power.[80] In an age when male dominance in marriage relationships was taken for granted, the Verney wives had to assert themselves by force of personality. They had little financial leverage because their marriage settlements were more than usually favourable to the Verneys. There is no evidence of any trusts that gave them economic independence from their husbands.[81] Furthermore the social dynamics of the marriages did not favour them. The Verneys married their sons for money, not for political or social status, and their brides were of inferior status and connections.[82] Thus wives did not have prized political or social networks that gave them influence over their husbands. They often played important parts in their husbands' affairs and judgements, but not by virtue of their family ties. When they produced children (and particularly sons), they fulfilled their expected role. What happened to the family estates when the male line failed and there was no clear heir is an important aspect of a later chapter.

The acquisition of consolidated estates was only the beginning of a process of re-modelling rural society. The next two chapters will unravel the ways in which the Verneys altered the farms, landscapes, and agriculture of their estates, and show how their interactions with the people whose houses and farms they owned shaped the development of a characteristic estate village society.

---

[79] Sir John Verney, who married at the age of forty, was not heir to the estates until his second marriage, and by then his own heir had been born.

[80] See A. J. Fletcher and J. Stevenson (eds.), *Order and Disorder in Early Modern England* (Cambridge 1985), articles by Underdown and Amussen; A. J. Fletcher, 'Men's dilemma: the future of patriarchy in England 1560–1660', *Transactions of the Royal Historical Society* 6th series, 4 (1994), pp. 61–81; L. Pollock, 'Rethinking patriarchy and family life', *Journal of Family History* 23 (1998), pp. 3–27.

[81] See A. L. Erickson, 'Common law versus common practice: the use of marriage settlements in early modern England', *Economic History Review* 43 (1990), pp. 21–39.

[82] Elizabeth Lawley, Sir John Verney's second wife, was an exception here, but as she lived only two years and left no heirs the marriage made little impact on family connections and female influence.

6   The making of a modern landed estate

When Sir Ralph Verney re-organised his Middle Claydon estate by enclosure in 1654–6, he simultaneously made alterations to his house and gardens, and soon after created a deer park. He was creating a country seat typical of the rural residences of the English landed elite from the sixteenth through to the late nineteenth or early twentieth centuries. These activities set a pattern for the estate for the next eighty years and were complemented by changes in estate management, and the 'improvement' of the estate. The enclosure of Middle Claydon completed the fundamental physical changes to the parish, but was only the beginning of the process of re-organising farms and farming practices. By 1660, Sir Ralph had transformed the landscape, increasing the separation of his house, with its gardens, park, and the church, from the houses and farm buildings of villagers and tenants. He introduced hedges and ring-fenced farms and fields where at the beginning of the century there had also been intercommoned rough pasture, common access to woods, and an open-field system with mutual dependence of copyhold, leasehold, and freehold tenants.

For most aristocratic and gentry estates in the seventeenth and eighteenth centuries, the policy framework within which landlords and their stewards operated is apparent in their books and letters, from rentals, surveys and leases, and from the general attitudes and demeanour.[1] The Verneys adopted a philosophy of estate management and policies based on the precepts Sir Ralph had enunciated in his letter of 1650, when he was thirty-seven.[2] They maximised immediate income from the estate but they applied this flexibly to ensure that tenants could extract a return from the land. They openly adopted rack-renting on the Claydon estates, accepting the highest bid for a farm, tempered only by some knowledge of the farming abilities of the bidder. They were initiating policies and regimes that were becoming increasingly common at this time, and

---

[1] For the general framework see Stone, *Crisis of the Aristocracy*, ch. 5 and *Family and Fortune*; G. E. Mingay, *English Landed Society in the Eighteenth Century* (London 1963), and D. R. Hainsworth, *Stewards, Lords, and People: The Estate Steward and his World in Later Stuart England* (Cambridge 1992). For the classic exposition of estate policy from the steward's point of view see Edward Laurence, *The Duty of a Steward to his Lord* (1727).

[2] See above ch. 4, p. 78.

were linked to the modernising of estate management and accountancy techniques. However, they did not develop the bureaucratised management systems and procedures that were to become standard eighteenth-century practice. This reflected the compact geographical spread of Verney lands but also their direct involvement in day-to-day decision-making throughout this period.

These policies encapsulate a fully market-orientated view of the economic life of the countryside and a complementary social policy. Sir Ralph combined a Puritan zeal for the success of the industrious poor with a hard-nosed financial view of the landlord's position. Lawrence Stone's judgement on him as 'a grasping landlord with Puritan sympathies' has great merits.[3] Tenants were expected to make a living from the land with their own resources, after paying their rent, and the landlord had no responsibility for their standard of living or for their family. The plight of the tenant of a twenty-acre farm supporting a family with ten children which he used as an example was important. It became the justification for a policy of enlarging farms, and choosing market-orientated tenants rather than the traditional village family farmers. This shift still created unease amongst bailiffs and even Parson Edward Butterfield who several times wrote: 'I hate this rack rent, 'tis worse than usury.' In his 1650 confessional letter, Sir Ralph recognised that such policy was one 'for which I know I have been very severely and perhaps too very justly censured'.[4] None of Sir Ralph's successors was as explicit, yet in general terms they followed the philosophy he set out.

From the time when Sir Ralph Verney personally ran the estates in the 1630s to the years before his great-grandson and namesake succeeded to the earldom in 1752, either the head of the family or his eldest son were active estate managers. Sir Ralph Verney was perhaps the most meticulous. During trips away from Claydon in the 1680s he demanded letters from his steward at least three times a week and often received five letters on each occasion. Each dealt with a separate aspect of estate work: household, estate management, woods, gardens, park, and deer. His steward, William Coleman laboriously pushed his pen day in, day out. Letter writing must have seriously eaten into his working day. Coleman was not the only correspondent. Sir Ralph also wrote directly to other officials, such as the woodman or housekeeper, and expected them to write directly to him. Coleman was generally kept informed of this correspondence, and often told to read the letters before passing them on. The steward had a reasonable overall view of estate management. However, the Verneys corresponded separately with their parsons throughout the later seventeenth and early eighteenth centuries. The letters sent by three generations of Butterfields covered a whole range of parish and neighbourhood topics and disputes that often overlapped those

---

[3] srv to wd, 2/12 June 1650 R10; Stone, *Crisis of the Aristocracy* (Oxford 1965), p. 330.
[4] eb to srv 18 May 1663 R19.

of William Coleman, the steward. Although there was a greater attention to neighbourhood and parish welfare concerns, the correspondence effectively gave Sir Ralph a second view of estate and parish matters and a cross-check on the steward's activities.

The Verneys had no centralised financial controller. Every employee was expected to keep running accounts and present them personally to their master. This applied to the woodman, housekeeper, and secretary (often referred to as 'my man'). The only person with a total knowledge of the financial position was the head of the family. These accounts were basic but relatively foolproof, simply noting all money that passed through the hands of each individual, whatever its purpose. The only surviving long-running set of accounts, those of the secretary, usually covered those small day-to-day transactions of a gentleman's London or country life – payments for horse-hire and carriers, or for food, books, and tips. However, in 1678 and 1686 it included four-figure sums, cash passing through his hands when mortgages were transferred. The wood accounts that survive cover only a narrow range of activities, while no more than occasional scraps of stewards' accounts are extant, covering at most a few months.[5]

The bailiff and secretary were the key members of the family entourage. But while the secretary knew most of his master's day-to-day life, travelling with him, paying his small bills, keeping personal accounts, and often writing dictated letters, the bailiff or steward was the main intermediary between the family and its rural domain. Supervision of household, garden, park, woods, estate policy and finances, made his life busy (even when he was not spending interminable hours writing about them), but he might be given additional tasks. Between 1680 and 1715, William Coleman and Charles Chaloner acted as election agents for their masters.

During this period there was a major shift in the kind of person who was employed as steward. In the period from 1620 to 1657 John Roades, and then his son William, acted as bailiff-stewards, a role that they fulfilled while also farming on the estate. Their authority in the village community drew on respect for them as yeoman farmers as much as landlord's representatives. They were good servants to the Verneys, but they came from an ancient tradition of the village headman with great practical knowledge, rather than being administrators and bookkeepers.

When Roades died in the epidemic of 1657, Hugh Holmes, a Middle Claydon farmer holding forty or fifty acres, took his place. His wife worked in some domestic capacity at Claydon House for at least part of the time. When Holmes was taken on Sir Ralph was excluded from public life and based at Claydon,

---

[5] William Coleman's accounts were almost certainly lost in the intricacies of an early eighteenth-century Chancery suit, see below p. 123.

so did not need someone of Roades's strength of character as bailiff. Holmes was a very different personality. His letters were only slightly more legible than Roades's and he had even less facility with the clerical and accounting side of the job. Sir Ralph needed his practical farming skills, in buying in and looking after stock, and used him principally for these strengths. Holmes's relationship with his master was quite different from his predecessor's. Where Roades had been a deferential but firmly influential adviser, Holmes was deeply subservient to his master. His total awe of Sir Ralph is captured in one letter in which he wrote 'it is no pleasure to displease you . . . but a terror, and you are a good master. I wish I could be a good servant.' Sir Ralph did not want someone with initiative, and Holmes had more dogged virtues. After the Restoration Sir Ralph spent more time in London and asked Parson Butterfield to report on Holmes, whom he described as 'truly . . . a very sober, diligent, careful person in your absence, as if your eye were daily upon him'.[6]

Holmes worked with Sir Ralph for ten years, but then faded from the scene. The man who succeeded him, William Coleman, had strengths in finance and accounting, and more closely matched the profile of an eighteenth-century land steward than any of his predecessors, although only described as 'steward' towards the end of his life. Coleman arrived at Claydon in November 1667. Initially his duties were confined to the supervision of all financial matters and control of the household at Claydon. He admitted to limited farming experience on arable lands only and after ten years in Sir Ralph's service he still did not know how to value a cow. Coleman and Holmes worked in tandem for Sir Ralph for eight or more years. There were conflicts. In 1671 Coleman complained that Holmes could not account accurately for the mowing. In 1675 the two men were at loggerheads over the numbers of mowers to be employed for the hay harvest. Coleman gradually eased Holmes out of the farming side. By 1675 he was finding tenants and by 1685 Sir Ralph was giving Coleman entire responsibility for letting farms in his absence.[7]

Unlike his predecessors or successors, William Coleman was an outsider from Twyford, some three miles from Claydon. The Colemans of Twyford were a large family of small freeholders, but genealogical reconstructions based on his will and parish registers leave his age and parentage unclear. None of the four William Colemans of the period corresponds closely with the family tree that can be derived from his will. The leading William of the family was one of three substantial landowners in Twyford in 1660, owning £24 per annum there and a further £10 per annum in Steeple Claydon. In 1650 he (with Edward Butterfield, the future parson of Middle Claydon) had been one of the jury for

---

[6] hh to srv 23 June 1662 ClH 4/5/15 and 3 May 1662 R18; eb to srv 21 May 1660 R17.
[7] sjv to Peter Lupart 5 July 1705 R53; William Coleman's first extant letter is dated 11 November 1667 R22; wc to srv 26 February 1676/7 ClH 4/5/29 and 10 July 1671 4/5/24 and 14 July 1675 4/5/28; srv to wc 15 October 1684 ClH 4/5/37.

Buckingham hundred when the Commonwealth surveyed church property and livings. In a 1656 Steeple Claydon deed he described himself as 'gent'. He felt sufficiently confident of his position in 1672 to write to Sir Richard Temple with details of a possible marriage alliance for Temple. How had our William Coleman come to the Verneys' attention and been selected? An early Coleman who lived in East Claydon was Sir Edmund Verney's coachman in the 1630s and may have been a relative, though Coleman is a common enough name. The Coleman property in Steeple Claydon may have provided some link. Another possibility arises from the fact that in 1657 Sir Ralph was involved in arbitrating a dispute between the two major Twyford landowners, Lord Wenman and Lady Suffolk, and that on that occasion the name William Coleman crops up in the proceedings.[8]

William Coleman was not a villager, did not farm, remained a bachelor, and lived at Claydon House rather than in the village. This separation from the village community probably contributed to a general dislike of him locally, of which he was well aware. He was Sir Ralph's man rather than a bridge between landlord and farming community. If, as Alan Everitt suggests, the social division between the gentry and their tenants was increasing in the late seventeenth century, the appointment of men like William Coleman accentuated that trend.[9]

William Coleman's origins are reflected in the occupations of his brothers. One, Francis, was also a bailiff/steward, at one time at Lee Grange in Quainton, later in Worcestershire. In 1674 he applied for the bailiff's job at Hillesden, and he periodically helped his brother find tenants for Claydon farms and made 'returns' of Verney money to London. Francis and William Coleman's careers show upward, or at least sideways, social mobility from the lesser freeholder class. Another brother, Thomas, was less successful and is occasionally to be found doing labouring work on the Claydon estate.[10]

William Coleman had been educated to a level where he wrote neat letters and kept the accurate accounts expected of the new breed of estate steward. William Coleman gained status in his role, and despite his modest wealth described himself in his will as a 'gent'. Coleman died in 1705 and was succeeded by Charles Chaloner, who entered the job from the opposite social direction. His father had been the leading landowner in Steeple Claydon. After the Restoration

[8] Huntington Library, Stowe MSS STT 522 letter dated 28 November 1672; see also STT Military Box 1(8) for a 1618 general muster in which both Francis and William Coleman are described as husbandmen; CIH 2/567 includes details of Coleman land in Steeple Claydon. The will and parish registers are in BCRO D/A/We/48/131 and PR210/1/1–26; Lambeth Palace Library MS COMM XII/3/vol. 3 fo. 86.

[9] wc to srv 21 January 1673/4 CIH 4/5/26; Alan Everitt, *Change in the Provinces: The 17th Century* (Leicester University, Department of English Local History, Occasional Papers, 2nd series, 1, Leicester 1969), pp. 48–51.

[10] wc to srv 5 Jan 1679/80 CIH 4/5/32; srv to wc 23 Nov 1674 4/5/27; wc to srv 24 Jan 1674/5 and 12 Feb 1687/8 4/5/27.

the family gradually sold off their estates with major sales in 1683–4 and a final flourish in 1704. Sir John Verney was the purchaser of the last remnants and probably wanted to use the local connection in taking on Charles Chaloner as steward in the following year. Charles was not trained for the task. Indeed Verney described him as a 'young man . . . but raw and little acquainted with my business, which gives me great fatigue'. He learnt the job as he went along, but when he died twenty-two years later the loss of 'honest Mr Chaloner' was described as 'irreparable'. Like William Coleman, Charles Chaloner was a full-time steward. In one letter in 1710 he protested that he never slept away from Middle Claydon House without Sir John Verney's permission, and never did his own business. He lived in Claydon House and his wife continued to act as housekeeper after his death.[11]

Landowners in the late seventeenth and eighteenth centuries were always nervous of cheating estate managers and other servants. The steward's prime function was to collect rent, and large sums of money passed through his hands, giving plentiful opportunities to take kick-backs from potential tenants, or from those selling to the household. The Verneys avoided many of these problems in the period from 1660 to 1730 by close supervision, by dealing directly with a variety of household and estate officials, and by scrutinising accounts regularly. Their close relationship with their parsons provided a further check. There is a marked contrast between the difficult relationship the Verneys had with John Aris, parson from the 1630s to his death in 1657, and their close partnership with the three Butterfields who were successively rectors of Middle Claydon thereafter. The Butterfields had little independence. The Verneys appointed them without outside interference and their income came directly from the Verneys rather than from tithes. The relationship began after Edward Butterfield took evidence in the village tithe dispute with John Aris, so he began with some knowledge of parish politics.[12] Edward Butterfield's letters to Sir Ralph Verney were frequent and full, a pattern that continued with his successors. The Claydon parson could exert greater weight in village matters than the steward, and was occasionally entrusted with delicate estate matters.

These control structures reflected the Verneys' active engagement and attention to detail. Claydon House was regularly occupied for substantial periods of the year during the later seventeenth century. The Verneys had no other permanent home until the 1720s when they regularly used, but never purchased,

[11] BCRO D/A/We/48/131; Deeds 1700–5 dated 31 June 1704; sjv to Ralph Palmer 12 July 1705 R53; J. Stone to rv 21 January 1727/8 R57; cc to sjv 17 December 1710 ClH 4/5/61. On the land sales at Steeple Claydon see below p. 234 and Broad, 'The fate of the midland yeoman', pp. 325–47.

[12] PRO E134/1653/4/Hil. 1. Edward Butterfield also had unfathomable connections with the Dentons, for during the 1660s the Denton trustees were paying him an annuity of £10 p.a. during the life of his son Edmund. BCRO D/X/591 e.g. p. 17.

a suburban house in Little Chelsea, close to London. This meant that Claydon was suitably furnished and embellished internally and externally for family use. On the other hand, the Verneys saw the Claydon estate primarily as a source of income from rents, and administered it with that in mind. When in London the Verneys used Claydon as a source of cash and of particular country delicacies that they wanted to enjoy in London. This chapter will look at the interactions of the Verneys' lifestyle with the Claydon estate, before examining their estate management and farming improvements.

The gentleman's country seat in the seventeenth and eighteenth centuries was a place of pleasant residence in increasingly carefully constructed surroundings, and the administrative centre of his major source of income, the farms, woods, and houses that produced crops and rent. The family's prestige was on display for fellow gentry and its power demonstrated to the neighbourhood. The layout of the house, its surrounding park and gardens, and its amenities such as woods and lakes, were an indication of the family's place in local and national society. At Claydon the relationship of the house to the world of farmers and villagers changed as the Verneys moulded the economy and society of the parish.

Sir Ralph Verney began a major re-fashioning and renovation of Claydon House and its immediate surroundings when he returned from the continent in 1653. The Giffords had probably built the gabled Tudor house that was the centrepiece of the estate. A drawing of the elevation suggesting a typical E-shaped design remains amongst the Verney papers. However, a map of the mansion and its surroundings dated 1654 shows a rambling mess of a house, roughly L-shaped, with jutting projections and wings in all directions.[13] On the south side was a rectangular formal garden, while to the north, near the present car park, was what looks like an attempt at some kind of formal entrance court with a gate. The main range of outbuildings was to the north and east, running in a line beside the entrance approach, and much of it very close to the house. Some of the buildings stood where the present stable court is, but that ground was mainly the Verneys' orchard. The rebuilding of 1654–6 was substantial, involving the house, outbuildings, and walled garden, while almshouses in the village had already been begun in 1653 and a parsonage followed in 1658. Sir Ralph supervised the design process and in August 1655 sent to France for a book of architecture by Le Muet to aid his planning.[14] He then pulled

---

[13] Elevation and perhaps a plan of what Sir Ralph wanted the house to look like with dormer windows are in R1. Map ClH 12/1/2 dated 1654.

[14] srv to Thomas Cordell (at Rouen) 30 August 1655 R14. It is not clear whether this was: Pierre Le Muet, *Traicté des Galleries, Entrées, Salles, Antichambres et Chambres, etc.* (a series of plates with descriptive text, the whole being engraved, Paris 1645), or his *Manière de bien bastir pour toutes sortes de personnes . . . Augmentée et enrichie en cette seconde edition de plusieurs figures, etc. (Augmentations de nouveaux bastimens faits en France.)* (2 pt. Chez François Langlois dict Chartres: Paris 1647). This became popular in England and was translated in 1670, going into several editions. Le Muet's translation of Palladio was the basis for late seventeenth-century English translations.

down parts of the north and east ranges of the house, put 'windows in the roof' and built two new chimney stacks. Brickmakers were brought in from St Ippolyts near Hitchin in Hertfordshire, and later from Brill, making and firing over half a million bricks and many tiles. Old brick and tile was to be used where possible, but William Allen, the Brill brickmaker, made over 300,000 bricks in a kiln close to the house and just behind the church. Stone was brought from Marsh Gibbon, or Padbury, or for more particular needs from Hornton. Various works were undertaken involving stonemasons and bricklayers, until twenty-five years later, in 1681, Sir Ralph wrote that 'all the building is done that ever I intend to do about my own house'.[15] Claydon House underwent periodic repairs and additions as successive owners made alterations to suit their tastes. In 1707 over 27,000 bricks were manufactured on site, but the purpose is not stated. In 1724–5 the summer parlour was refurbished, and a stable block built.[16]

The Verneys also distanced their seat from the village and farms. On the 1654 map the parsonage house is situated close to Claydon House but Sir Ralph decided to rebuild it at his own expense at the edge of the village, perhaps a quarter of a mile distant. The new parsonage was of four bays, wooden framed but infilled with bricks, with a tiled roof and half bays containing the porch and staircase. The 1654 map also shows a farmhouse and cottage very close to Claydon House that were probably removed at about the same time, for Sir Ralph Verney changed the line of the road linking his mansion to the village at the time of enclosure.[17]

Sir Ralph Verney also increased domestic comforts. In 1653 water from an East Claydon spring was piped through the fields to Claydon House, and the leases of newly enclosed lands included a clause permitting the laying of pipes where necessary. In 1669 Sir Ralph built an Ice House in the grounds, only a few years after the first one in England had been built in St James's Park. He wrote to a Mr Rider for help with the design, which was based on existing houses in St James and Woburn. Fishponds were stocked with teal, bream, carp, and other species and the five ponds in 1712 provided a steady supply of fresh fish.[18] A warren was set up in February 1655 to provide rabbit meat, and attempts made to prevent the colony from expanding too fast by gelding the males. Before the Restoration Sir Ralph had set up a deer park and brought

---

[15] R. Kibble to srv 19 May 1655 R13; srv agreement with Will Barker 18 January 1654/5 R13; srv to wc 27 January 1680/1 ClH 4/5/33.

[16] Brickmaker's account 18 June 1707 R53; cc to rv 27 February 1724/5 R57.

[17] Lincolnshire CRO terrier bundle 'undated' but from internal evidence before 1680 and probably *c.* 1675.

[18] On the ice house srv to Mr Rider 22 August 1669, wd to srv 1 September 1669, and plan with letters of 23 September 1669 R23; see also Monica Ellis, *Ice and Icehouses through the Ages* (Southampton University Industrial Archaeology Group 1982); on the water supply, see maps, and also srv to ev 9 June 1670 R23; on ponds, see T. Stafford to srv 14 February 1656/7 R15; srv to wc 1 February 1674/5 4/5/27; sjv to rv 16 October 1712 R54.

in deer from the regicide Sir William Monson in Northamptonshire.[19] These activities refashioned Claydon House and estate to support the country interests of the widowed but energetic Sir Ralph.

Sir Ralph's greatest interest, measured by the amount of time devoted to it in correspondence, was in his vegetable garden and orchards. Sir Ralph threw himself into various projects when he returned to England in the 1650s, and his interests endured for the rest of his life. His correspondence covered such topics as vegetable varieties, and the suitability of lime and alder trees. Fir trees were brought from Norfolk in 1654 after a long correspondence with Framlingham Gaudy. A large walled vegetable garden was constructed in the 1650s and still stands. New varieties of seeds and plants were obtained from London seedsmen, and sometimes directly from overseas, with frequent lists of seeds and plants, and great attention was paid to their cultivation and progress.

Between 1660 and 1720 the Verney household at Middle Claydon was rarely large. In 1659, when Sir Ralph and his adult son Edmund lived at Claydon, there were thirteen servants in the house – two 'men', one butler, one cook, one groom, two gardeners, three foot boys, one housekeeper, and two servant maids. In 1683 there were seven servants on the pay roll. In the 1690s the number was sometimes as few as five or six. When Sir John Verney succeeded his father, he paid five servants in 1697 and early in the following year was taxed on the same number. However, as Sir John spent more time in Buckinghamshire, his establishment increased. During an epidemic in March 1705 he wrote of '10 or 12 of our servants sick'. There are few or no precise figures but Sir John could hardly have entertained 400 guests to Christmas feasts in 1712 without a considerably greater staff. Early in the 1720s his daughter-in-law wrote of the large number of servants being ruinously expensive.[20]

Those who served the Verneys entered a way of life that marked them off from the village society from which many had come. They were, or became, better educated. They were also in a community with its own pattern of work and leisure whether or not the Verneys were in residence. The patriarchal Verneys used the terminology of the family in discussing them. In 1705 Sir John referred to the illness of William Coleman, admittedly employed for more than thirty-five years, as 'a sickness in the family'. When the gardener married a servant, he commented that the 'family is like to increase'. The Verneys expected servants to ask for their approval when they married or moved. In return, servants could

---

[19] On Monson see R. Lennard, *Rural Northamptonshire under the Commonwealth: A Study Based Principally upon the Parliamentary Surveys of Royal Estates* (Oxford Studies in Social and Legal History 5 1916), pp. 83ff.

[20] Various lists exist for 1659: 15 August 1659 R16; 1683: wage list dated 13 December 1683 R38; 1697: bill of living (at end of papers 1697), and capitation tax list February 1697/8 R50; sjv to M. Vicars 20 March 1704/5 R52; sjv to rv 8 January 1712/13 R55; Catherine Verney to rv 9 March 1720/1 R57.

expect assistance with finding a tenancy, or employment, and general benevolence during good behaviour. Sir Ralph would even pay ex-servants' full funeral expenses if the death occurred at Claydon and for the coffin if elsewhere.[21]

The steward was normally in overall charge at Claydon. There was little practical distinction between the estate servants and household servants and those living in Claydon House came from both groups. While William Roades and Hugh Holmes were farmers as well as stewards and lived on their farms, William Coleman, a bachelor, and Charles Chaloner lived in the house. Although the cook was often a living-in servant, Michael (Michel) Durant, the French cook Sir Ralph Verney had brought back from exile in 1653, married and became a farmer. Gardeners, blacksmiths, indeed all except the housekeeper, maids, and boys, could be married and living out. During Sir Ralph Verney's later years several servants were underemployed as he spent more time in London. Will Matthews, the smith, was described as 'almost out of employment' by Hugh Holmes in 1663. In 1681 Sir Ralph encouraged Coleman to find a farm for his coachman, John Banes. There were sometimes gaps in the ranks of the servants: in 1699 there was no cook, and Sir John Verney imported one from Buckingham when at Claydon.[22]

New servants were usually recruited from local villages but specialists might come from further afield. Gardeners were employed either on recommendation from other gentry or from seedsmen such as George Ball of Brentford. Cooks came from even further away. Michael Durant accompanied Sir Ralph from France, while in 1699 Edward Norgrave came from London. Several conditions went with appointment to the household. Both Sir Ralph and Sir John Verney preferred unmarried servants. The latter said he was 'unwilling to take a married man into my house (for then the maids had no hopes of him)'. Sir Ralph did not 'love to take any new servant into my house till I myself am at home to instruct him in my own way'. He also had strong views on hygiene and in 1667 gave instructions that: 'tis good to cleanse his head and hair [from lice] and let him wash himself thoroughly, let some cleanly woman see it well done, and put on his new clothes at a distance and not come near his old ones, lest he fill your house with vermin'.[23]

A servant's function in the Claydon household varied enormously according to whether the Verney family was in residence. Sir Ralph Verney spent an average of five months of the year away from Claydon between 1660 and 1680, in London or visiting friends. Sir John Verney spent up to eight or nine months in London lodgings or at Bath, Tunbridge Wells, or Epsom. From the 1720s there

[21] sjv to T. Cave, 22 March 1704/5 R52; srv to wc 9 April 1696 ClH 4/5/49.
[22] hh to srv 8 February 1663/4 & 16 March 1662/3 ClH 4/5/15; srv to wc 17 January 1680/1 4/5/33 – this was done; sjv to wc 29 March 1699 R50.
[23] E. Norgrave to Elizabeth Verney 22 July 1699 R51; wc to srv 22 July 1677 4/5/30; wd to srv 20 August 1652 R11; srv to Cary Gardiner 7 November 1670 R24; srv to ev 23 May 1667 R21.

was an established London home at Little Chelsea. There were always routine jobs and services when the family was away. The household sent provisions and country delicacies to London and in return received dirty linen to be washed at Claydon. The linen basket sometimes concealed money in transit to London. Before the family returned to Claydon the maids had to sleep in the beds to air them.

When the Verneys were away the servants were nevertheless considered under-employed, and additional tasks were set to prevent idleness. In 1675 the maids span home-produced wool. Servants were taught to read and write to enable them to write directly to their master. In 1653 Sir Ralph Verney instructed that a new cook be employed 'by learning to read or to write, lest idleness spoil him'. In 1669 William Coleman reported that he had made William Smith write and copy things and heard him read a chapter (presumably of the Bible) every day. Smith was pronounced 'very dull, but he doth read something better than he did'.[24]

There were occasional tensions, quarrels, and misdemeanours amongst the household. Henry Verney's servant fought a duel with the gardener after a violent argument at Claydon. One cook ended up at the Assizes. Some were dismissed because they were conspicuously drunk. Hugh Holmes spied on Mr Field, a butler, and discovered he often brewed beer with the villagers. Robert Kibble was sacked because 'those that love drinking cannot be long with me. From Friday morning at six o'clock till Sunday morning I could never see him.' Whatever the Verneys' ideal view of their household, the reality was less than perfect. Hugh Holmes would not go to Wasing in 1671 because the soldiers were liable to steal deer, and 'here is but a weak company about your house'. Sir John Verney's wife had some similar doubts over the state of the household in 1702 in William Coleman's dotage. The cook was often drunk, and she feared Coleman was no longer competent to look after the keys and silver plate, let alone ward off the deerstealers. For these reasons she would not join her husband at Bath.[25]

Servants could be sacked for misdemeanours or for open disagreement with their master. The bailiff, William Roades, came close to dismissal in 1650 and 1653. Robert Kibble, Sir Ralph's secretary, was sacked for drunkenness in 1655 but was reinstated, against Sir Ralph's better judgement, when no suitable replacement was found. William Coleman turned away a labourer who had gone off in a huff when criticised for slow work. Hugh Holmes and Sir Ralph agreed that one servant would have to go at the end of the year, but Holmes would not tell him because 'twill be the means to make him careless of his business'. Sir Ralph made it clear several times that 'it is against my humour to

---

[24] srv to wc 22 June 1696 CIH 4/5/49; wc to srv 14 June 1675 4/5/28; srv to wr 18/28 May 1653 R12; wc to srv 15 February 1668/9 R22.
[25] hh to srv 17 May 1663 CIH 4/5/16 and 22 June 1663 R19; srv to wr 2 August 1655 R13; hh to srv 2 December 1671 4/5/24; Elizabeth Verney to sjv 5 September 1702 R52.

keep any servant longer than he hath a mind to stay'. Although Verney servants came from other villages in the seventeenth century, there is no evidence that they were prevented from gaining settlement in Claydon.[26]

The small Claydon household of the late seventeenth century was not well paid. In 1664 the housekeeper was paid £8 a year. By 1683 her wage was £13 a year, the same as the steward's. His wage was lower than the £20 paid by the Temples and Dentons close by, and considerably less than Hainsworth's average of £40 for the late seventeenth century, and the sums of up to £100 a year paid to some eighteenth-century land stewards. Furthermore, the close supervision of stewards by the Verneys themselves and also by the Claydon parsons left few easy opportunities for frauds and perquisites. In the same year (1683) even the serving maids, gamekeeper, and gardener received £10 a year. Board and lodging were included, but were not always luxurious. When beef prices were high in 1663 the cook was ordered to serve more 'white meats' to cut down the expense. Unfortunately there are few wage figures for the eighteenth century. Work on other estates suggests that in larger households the wages of the supervising servants rose with the scale of the job. At seventeenth-century Verney wage rates, no one in the household could have expected to raise their social status to any considerable degree.[27]

William Coleman's kin in Twyford were amazed at the small size of their prestigious relative's estate at his death and sued the Verneys in Chancery in 1705. Coleman left a house, barn, and over two yardlands of land in Stewkley. He had lent £50 to William Chaloner, but owed £87 to the Verneys. Sir Ralph Verney's will left him a life annuity of £20 a year – more than his wages – making him better off in his last years than ever before. One of the family took away five guineas, three other gold pieces, three gold rings, and a watch and other possessions worth £5. However Coleman made bequests totalling £46 in his will, which presumably could not be paid. William Grosvenor, one of Sir Ralph's secretaries, accumulated more than £200 – a sum he deposited with Edmund Verney. Hugh Holmes was bailiff for almost twenty years but in 1669, while still in service, was 'so penurious that I believe he will die ere he will be at any charge to procure health'. In 1679, though ill, he was promising to pay his debts to Sir Ralph and ten years later his widow was said to be very poor.[28]

---

[26] srv to Cary Gardiner 7 September 1655 R14; wc to srv 9 January 1681/2 ClH 4/5/34; hh to srv 17 May 1663 4/5/16; srv to wc 1 January 1682/3 36; srv to ev 6 July 1674 R27. For settlement see below pp. 163–9.

[27] Hainsworth, *Stewards, Lords, and People*, pp. 30–8. G. E. Mingay, 'The eighteenth-century land steward' in J. D. Chambers and G. E. Mingay, *Land, Labour, and Population in the Industrial Revolution* (London 1967), pp. 6–12; Johnson, 'Buckinghamshire 1640–60', p. 27; G. Eland, 'A Hillesden Account Book 1661–7', *Records of Buckinghamshire* (1919–26), pp. 135–44; hh to srv 11 May 1663 ClH 4/5/16; srv to hh 10 June 1664 R19.

[28] Cf. Hainsworth, *Stewards, Lords, and People*, p. 37 on relatives' expectations that stewards were men of wealth; petition to the Lord Chancellor and reply dated 28 January 1708/9 R 53; cf PRO

Like many of the landed elite the Verneys engaged in farming only when they were left with untenanted lands. After 1660, Sir Ralph Verney's small household and long absences from Claydon made a home farm uneconomic. In normal years one or two fields of some thirty or forty acres were kept in hand to provide pasture for the horses. A few cows were sometimes kept, but rented out to tenants when Sir Ralph was away. In 1682 when cider was made at Claydon House, Coleman was told to store it in the dairy, since this was disused. Sir John Verney occasionally kept a few donkeys for their milk, and in the early eighteenth century his third wife Elizabeth had her own flock of sheep in 1700, while her daughter had her own bees in 1724.[29]

The nation-wide fall in rents after the Restoration forced tenants into bankruptcy, and the Verneys, like their neighbours the Temples and the Tyrells, occasionally responded by farming the land rather than reducing rents. Fields were stocked with cattle and sheep for fattening in 1662–4, 1672–3, 1674–5, and 1681. These enterprises were not generally profitable. Holmes's farming in 1672–3 made a profit more than twice the previous rent, the minimum acceptable return by contemporary standards, but most letters suggest that grazing in the 1660s and 1670s was only marginally profitable. These *ad hoc* farming adventures were generally meanly funded. Hugh Holmes claimed that he could not be expected to make a profit because the fields were not fully stocked. In 1662 he received money regularly, but in June the ground remained understocked and £40 was borrowed from the bailiff at Hillesden. In June 1666, again short of money, he complained that 'here might be kept in your grounds forty beast if the money was to be had to buy them'. Only in 1681, when Joseph Churchill was given £350 to spend on a trip to various fairs all over the midlands, does there seem to have been a positive commitment to running the home farm profitably. After Sir Ralph's death such episodes were less frequent. Sir John Verney and the first Earl Verney were less committed to holding rents to maximum possible levels in an era of stable or falling rent levels. The only mention of any similar enterprise was in 1728 when the first earl purchased seventeen cows, presumably for dairying, and made notes on the cost of keeping them.[30] These late seventeenth-century home farming enterprises involved cattle fattening, which became unprofitable after the Irish cattle acts, which favoured the cattle

C6/396/44 Coleman vs Verney 1710; wc's will is in BCRO D/A/We/48/131 dated 8 June 1703; eb to srv 23 May 1669 ClH 4/5/22; wc to srv 5 January 1679 and 15 December 1689 EC.

[29] srv to wc 18 September 1682 ClH 4/5/35; cc to rv 16 August 1724 4/5/70; sjv to wc 12 June 1700 4/5/53.

[30] M. G. Davies, 'Country gentry and falling rents in the 1660s and 1670s', *Midland History* 4 (1977), pp. 86–96; hh to srv 11 May 1663 ClH 4/5/16; H. King to srv 2 and 15 June 1662 R18; hh to srv 11 June 1666 4/5/19; J. Churchill's account 19 May 1681 R35; rv's notes nd. 1728 R57. 'An account that Holmes made . . . between 25th April 1672 and 7 May 1673' R25; H. Holmes to srv 3 December 1666 4/5/19; srv to M. Elmes 26 June 1667 R21.

breeders of the north and west at the expense of the fattening counties around London. But at root Sir Ralph's farming was unproductive because it was a makeshift enterprise undertaken half-heartedly to call the bluff of tenants who believed (probably rightly) that Claydon rents were too high.

An alternative approach was to plough prime pastures up for a few years, but this was more often threatened than carried out. Ploughing was a standard technique for dealing with genuinely worn-out pastures, though several eighteenth-century agricultural writers remarked that unless done skilfully it could actually worsen the land. Two prime pastures, Knowl Hill and Old Harding's Great Ground, were candidates for breaking up, but Sir Ralph's bluff was called, and the land was instead grazed. Ploughing was not a simple alternative, for the estate no longer had teams on hand to plough, and the building requirements of arable farms were quite different. Sir Ralph's preferred maxim at Claydon was: 'I had rather let it to a good tenant than plough it.' By the mid-eighteenth century the first earl was convinced that arable farms were to be disdained because they 'must need have many barns and outbuildings . . . which are great incumbrances'.[31]

Occasionally small fields on the Claydon estate were ploughed in the later seventeenth and early eighteenth centuries. The amount was usually less than ten acres and there were never more than thirty acres involved in any year. The poorest pastures were chosen, especially small fields adjoining recently grubbed woods, and they were sown with barley, oats, vetches, beans, and on two occasions wheat. This occurred in 1661/2, 1672/3, 1677/8, 1681–3, and 1710/11. Oats were the main crop and probably intended for the horses always kept at Claydon. The quality of crops seems to have been consistently mediocre or poor. The land was 'cold clay and tough hungry ground' and oats were 'much thinner than I had thought' and 'very thin' while the barley was 'poor weedy stuff'. The amount of land under the plough at Claydon remained small throughout the eighteenth century. The 1801 crop returns note just over 121 acres under crops, and Parkinson estimated 200 acres in a more rough and ready way in 1810.[32]

With no regular home farm from 1660 to 1730, the Verneys used farm labour regularly only to bring in the small hay harvest in June, and to undertake hedging, ditching, and fencing work during the rest of the year. There are many weekly lists of workmen employed, and descriptions of their tasks when Sir Ralph was absent from Claydon but very few in the eighteenth century. Before the

[31] J. Broad, 'Alternate husbandry and permanent pasture in the midlands, 1650–1800', *Agricultural History Review* 28 (1980), pp. 83–4; wc to srv 24 January 1681/2 ClH 4/5/34 and srv to wc 22 December 1686 4/5/42.

[32] wc to srv 2, 17, 24, August 1683 ClH 4/5/36; srv to wc 28 August 1686 4/5/39; M. E. Turner, 'The 1801 crop returns for Buckinghamshire', *Records of Buckinghamshire* 19:4 (1974), pp. 471–82.

Restoration women workers were often used at haymaking and harvest, but after 1660 men were used almost exclusively, though two women were employed in weeding wheat at Bottle Gate in May 1713. Normally up to ten men were employed on routine maintenance: hedging, ditching, digging drains, helping the gardener, and organising the horses. Few men worked full-time for the Verneys and there were distinct seasonal patterns. Typically, in one week in February 1664, one man worked six days, one five days, five worked four days, one three days, and one one day. The following week two men worked six days, one worked five, three worked four, and three worked two. Although two of the men who worked almost full-time did so in both weeks, the others were on a much more flexible system. One man worked three days the first week, but none the second; another did not work in the first week but worked five days in the next. The 1713 figures show a similar pattern, but a slightly smaller core of people involved. Numbers for 1739 are distorted because large numbers of people were employed planting sallow and ash trees, so in the week ending 8 December 1739 thirteen people were employed. However, the core of workers employed on routine estate work at that time may have been as low as four.[33]

The labour force was usually employed at day rates and there are only a few cases of piece rates for routine work. In 1713 John Dixon was employed fagoting at piece rates but his pay was calculated as the equivalent of six days' work. In 1672 the woodman Walter King bargained with two men to grub a hedge and beat them down to 2d a pole. The Verneys did not employ living-in servants in husbandry on annual contracts although this was common on north Buckinghamshire dairy farms. They used much less labour after enclosure, aggravating the under-employment that followed farm enlargements, conversion to pasture, and the elimination of commons where smallholders and cottagers could plant crops and keep livestock. John Poores claimed he had only one month's work between the end of September 1667 and May 1668. His daughter said that he would have starved had she not come home and earned some money by lacemaking.[34] The Verneys reduced uncertainty for a select group of Claydon labourers whom Sir Ralph Verney described as his 'constant workmen'. In November 1669 ten men were considered eligible for regular employment, six in the woods and four on the hedges. This system provided some employment

[33] The lists of 'work done' occur interleaved with the estate correspondence, and often enclosed in stewards' letters. They were usually prepared weekly, or at most fortnightly, in the later seventeenth century.

[34] srv to wc 9 December 1672 and 15 October 1684 ClH 4/5/37; 'work done' in December 1713; J. Millward to rvjr 17 May 1745 R59; for details on living-in servants see A. Kussmaul, *Servants in Husbandry* (Cambridge 1980); for local conditions in the late eighteenth century see the vivid autobiography of Joseph Mayett in BCRO D/X/371, and published by A. Kussmaul (ed.), *The Autobiography of Joseph Mayett of Quainton 1783–1839*, Buckinghamshire Record Society 21 (1986); on John Poores, hh to srv 18 May 1668 4/5/21; the family was about to be distrained for debt yet still had brass and pewter utensils in the house.

security for a small number of labouring families. Often they were failed farmers who had settlement in the parish, but no remaining capital, like Edward Dixon, while 'old' Harding asked Sir Ralph Verney to employ him when he gave up his farm.[35]

These regular estate workers had some sense of security but worked without any contract, and could be laid off at any time. Nevertheless those regularly employed were expected to show due deference and give the Verneys first call on their services. In 1675 Sir Ralph Verney complained when a 'saucy' labourer was taken on because of labour shortage. Thomas Fencutt was removed from the list in 1685 for what was considered a discourtesy. Sir Ralph wrote

As for Fencutt you may tell him I think he uses me very ill in not coming to see whether I wanted him until all his other work was almost done in all places, whereby you see he had rather work with others than with me. Therefore I shall not look upon him as a constant workman . . . I must needs confess he is a good workman, but he is too high and sturdy.

There was also a financial sacrifice involved in being a 'constant workman' at Claydon. Seasonal differentials in work availability and market wage rates were smoothed out into a summer and winter rate. In June 1662 Hugh Holmes wrote, 'the workmen, now midsummer is at hand look for their wages they use to have other years, that is ten pence a day till Michaelmas'. Two years later labourers were complaining that they were only paid 8d a day for shifting gravel at midsummer, even though it was the hay season. In this period, 8d a day was the normal constant winter wage. In 1680 William Coleman asked the estate workmen to cut a hedge on Mr Denton's estate, two miles away at Hillesden. They replied that 'they will not go thither to work for eight pence a day'.[36]

Regular winter work at 8d a day was probably satisfactory for a labourer, but 10d a day in summer was considerably less than the market rate. In 1662 mowers were demanding $16\frac{1}{2}$d a day to cut two meadows. Unless mowers were guaranteed winter work, they would be out of pocket. There were further penalties attached, as Hugh Holmes made clear in the same year:

Falkner and Whitton are afraid you will not employ them in winter, and then they shall lose much by their summer work to work for ten pence a day. They desire to know whether you will be pleased to employ them for if you should not no body would set them a work because you employed them in summer.

In 1662 prices were higher than in any year between 1650 and 1710, which made the choice between immediate cash and winter security more difficult.

[35] srv to wc 15 December 1685 ClH 4/5/38; 'work done' list 18 November 1669 R23; wb to srv 27 December 1683 4/5/36.

[36] srv to wc 18 January 1674/5 and 2 December 1685 ClH 4/5/38; hh to srv 23 June 1662 4/5/15 and 27 June 1664 4/5/17; wc to srv 23 February 1679/80 4/5/32.

Sir Ralph Verney's hard bargaining over summer wage rates produced friction and in some years mowers were reluctant to work. In 1671 Holmes that 'I shall get no mowers to cut your grass, for all that I have asked have given me but a slight answer.' But often the lure of winter work was sufficient inducement. In June 1668 the mowers were reluctant, saying 'your worship told them last year you would have better mowers' but Holmes concluded that 'I believe they will be glad to mow for you or they will want work in winter.' In the 1670s it was agreed to give the mowers a week's notice when the Verneys required them, so that they could complete other work. In Middle Claydon's pastoral economy haymaking caused the greatest demand for labour during the year.[37]

Without a substantial home farm at Claydon, the Verneys bought supplies in the neighbourhood when in residence and when they were in London. Local specialities, such as cheese and butter, were frequently bought in and dispatched to London. In April 1681 Sir Ralph Verney sent up three different sorts of cheeses to his son in London. Beef, bacon, and venison were other local products of quality. In the early eighteenth century mushrooms were cherished and regularly sent up in the late summer. Some more curious commodities made the bumpy two-day journey from Claydon to London. In 1722 kites and sparrows were shot because they were damaging crops, and the sparrows were sent up to London for the table. In June 1724, 454 spinning silk worms were dispatched.[38] Tenants on the estate were regular suppliers of cheese and butter. In 1677 the Claydon household bought in malt, oats, wheat, and beans. William Roades supplied bacon in 1723. Sir Ralph threatened to stop buying his meat from one of the Claydon farmer/butchers if he dared to brew and sell ale. Other delicacies were fetched from further afield: Bath water from Oxford in 1700, and wine to stock the cellars travelled from London with the dirty linen returning for washing at Claydon.[39]

Most commodities were sent by the regular wagon service passing along the main London to Birmingham road that cut through the eastern edge of Middle Claydon parish and East Claydon. Specified carriers were expected to call at Claydon House en route to make pick-ups. Cash also needed to pass from Claydon to London to finance the family's lifestyle there. Several alternative methods of moving money were used to counter the growing threat of highway robbery. In the seventeenth century, the Verneys frequently employed the system

---

[37] hh to srv 14 July 1662, 23,29 June 1662 CIH 4/5/15, 8 June 1668 4/5/21, 2 June 1673 4/5/26, 31 May, 19 June 1675 4/5/28. Similar patterns of fluctuating day rates for mowing are found at Hillesden nearby in the 1660s, but the highest rate shown in the accounts is 14d per day. Women were paid an unvarying 5d a day for haymaking, and children $3\frac{1}{2}$d. See BCRO D/X/591 pp. 202, 258–9, and 301–2. Piece rates were used for some fields in 1667.

[38] srv to sjv 21 April 1681 R35; hh to srv 22 December 1662 CIH 4/5/15; cc to rv 25 August 1726 R57 and 17 November 1723 4/5/69, 23 June 1724 4/5/70.

[39] srv to ev 15 March 1674/5 R28; F. Willis to sjv 8 February 1699/1700 R51; sjv to Robert Glover 12 January 1700 R51.

of 'returns' described by Mrs M. G. Davies. When country traders sold goods in London they paid their money to a landowner or his London agent. He gave them a note which entitled them to be repaid from the estate coffers, where the rents the bailiff had collected lay waiting. It was a mutually convenient arrangement: traders avoided carrying cash from London to the country, and landowners could send rent money safely in the opposite direction. Landowners were grafting their needs onto the existing credit structure of merchants, farmers and traders. The first 'return' is mentioned is in 1643 when a local woolman returned money to Sir Ralph's agents in London 'to be paid him on demand'. It was not a new device, and in 1648 a local farmer in London claimed 'he could at any time at one day's warning pay me here a hundred pound if you could help him to it in the country'. However, William Roades's accounts of 1646–7 show that money was sent by carrier as well as returned by a butcher.[40]

Between 1650 and 1670 by no means all money sent to London went by 'return', and cash sums up to £60 were occasionally sent by carrier. Small returns could be more bother than they were worth. In July 1655 Robert Kibble, Sir Ralph's secretary, wrote:

my master would not have you return any more money hereafter by Rawson, for the £20 which he should have paid me on Saturday last was sevennight is not yet paid, and it is uncertain when it will be paid, or whether it will be paid or no, and 'tis more labour to send after such uncertain people than the money is worth: such small sums as that might easily be put up in a hamper with my master's other things and sent up by the carrier without any suspicion or hazard.

Not all returns ran smoothly at either end. Sometimes farmers went to Hugh Holmes or William Coleman with their notes, to discover insufficient cash in hand to pay them. This put the Verneys' credit in the country at risk and Sir Ralph made it his rule that 'I will by no means receive more money than can be immediately repaid in the country.' Sometimes the farmer or tradesman who had promised to pay in money in London could not sell his wares. After 1670 the 'return' became normal practice on the Verney estates during Sir Ralph's lifetime. In exceptional circumstances they reverted to traditional methods: in 1672–3 and 1694–6 the financial repercussions of the Dutch war and recoinage crises forced the direct carriage of coin to London.[41]

The Verneys used lacebuyers, graziers, and butchers for 'returns' from Claydon to London in the late seventeenth century. If a 'return' were urgently required, Hugh Holmes or William Coleman would go to a local market,

[40] M. G. Davies, 'Country gentry and payments to London, 1650–1714', *Economic History Review*, 2nd series, 24 (1971), pp. 15–36; letter dated 16 May 1644 ClH 4/5/3; mv to wr 20 March 1647/8 R8. wr account dated 3 December 1646 R7.
[41] srv to wr 30 June/10 July 1653 R12; R. Kibble to wr 5 July 1655 R13; hh to srv 10 December 1663 4/5/16 and 10 May 1664 4/5/17; wc to srv 7 December 1674 4/5/27; hh to srv 14 October 1664 4/5/17; srv to wc 29 March 1693 4/5/46; eb to srv 13 January 1672/3 4/5/25.

Buckingham or Leighton Buzzard (the specialist local cattle market), to look for a butcher about to set off for London. Less commonly, Sir Ralph Verney sent his secretary to Smithfield to seek out a Buckinghamshire butcher, grazier, or drover who had not yet committed his cash to a return. The 'return' had clearly defined geographical boundaries to its operation. The furthest Sir Ralph ever took a return was from Thame, some fifteen miles from Claydon, and repaying it involved sending the cash under armed guard. The complexity of the operation convinced Sir Ralph to 'take no more at such a distance'.[42]

Between 1670 and 1696 there were regular arrangements for returns. Accounts between 1679 and 1688 allow an analysis of the participants. In those ten years, £4,141 was returned and over 70 per cent of the 'returns' were made by Verney tenants, former tenants, and their close relatives. Kinship links were important at both ends of the chain. Five members of the Churchill family carried over 42 per cent of the money. They were farming freeholders in Steeple Claydon, and sometime tenants and advisers to Sir Ralph Verney. There were also two Robinsons, two Woodfields, and two Williamses who at different times paid money to Sir Ralph in London. Comparison with the Temple and Denton estates at the same time shows virtually no overlap of those who returned money.[43]

'Returns' illustrate Verney accounting practices clearly, appearing in the accounts of Sir Ralph's secretary, William Grosvenor, but also separately in John Verney's accounts with his father when Sir Ralph was out of town. At the country end, 'returns' occur in both the steward's and woodman's accounts at Claydon. Only careful matching across several accounts brings out the full picture. One letter instructed a farmer to pay his money into Sir Thomas Fowle's bank in John Verney's absence. Although Grosvenor's London entries show £308 received by return from the end of September to the beginning of March 1684, William Coleman only repaid £248 from his own account, the rest lying in the woodman's account. The Verneys appear to have driven a hard bargain with those who made 'returns' for them and rarely paid for them. In 1652 William Denton thought William Roades 'either a fool or a knave, or a very good husband for you' when he found no payments in the estate accounts, since most other north Buckinghamshire landowners were paying 3d or 4d in the pound for the service. Mrs Davies found that charges were commonplace in the later seventeenth century, but Sir Ralph only paid them during the financial and military crisis of 1672–3, and then only 2d in the pound. The 'return' was a vital part of Sir Ralph Verney's financial system during his later years. From 1679 to 1688 more than 37 per cent of his gross rental was transmitted

---

[42] eb to srv 14 March 1663/4 R19; T. Stafford to srv 14 November 1662 R18; hh to srv 14 October 1664 CIH 4/5/17; wc to srv 7 April 1679 4/5/32; srv to wc 21 and 29 December 1683 4/5/36.

[43] For the Temples see BL Stowe MS 802 fo. 19b; equivalent evidence on the Dentons is found in BCRO M42/1.

to London and from September 1684 to March 1685 this rose to over 50 per cent. The Verneys also received rent from a number of tenants who paid them in London, and these transactions are clearly differentiated from returns.[44]

After Sir Ralph's death in 1696 'returns' gradually became less important. Sir Ralph's successors used new methods of sending money developed in the age of the 'Financial Revolution', while the changing structure of north Buckinghamshire agriculture and marketing made 'returns' less suitable. Sir John Verney had wide-ranging city investments and government securities and was never as dependent on his agricultural rents as his father. He had lines of commercial credit and used inland bills of exchange and other alternatives. His account at Hoare's bank shows some tenants paying in their rent in cash, but others used bills of exchange. Traditional 'returns' had not totally disappeared, but were only intermittently used. In 1702 Sir John wrote to the Claydon housekeeper: 'I know not when I shall get a return to London, not having returned any these twelve months.' It was not, however, extinct, and Charles Chaloner organised one in 1717 via a drover who agreed to leave his money at a Smithfield coffee house.[45]

The change from grazing to dairying in north Buckinghamshire also affected the system. The Verneys had mainly used graziers rather than lacebuyers for their 'returns.' Graziers often oversaw the selling of their own stock, but dairying for cheese, and later butter, was increasingly important, and had much lower requirements for liquidity. The butter trade was controlled by London factors who worked on long credit. The dairyman did not go to London, but waited for the butterman to collect on the farm. Grazing 'returns' were less readily available and in 1723 Charles Chaloner asked a tenant, William Webb, to ask his butterman for a return. Between February to June 1734 most of the £1,185 transferred from Claydon to London went in the 'usual way', which now meant a reversion to hiding the money in the linen basket.[46] In the eighteenth century, the Verneys were less dependent on estate income when in London, and notes of hand provided an instant means of tiding over temporary shortages of cash.[47]

After analysing the relationship between Claydon and London, we turn to examining how the Verneys raised their income from the farming tenants of Middle

---

[44] wc's account 5 March 1684/5 ClH 4/5/37; wd to srv 4 September 1652 R11; eb to srv 13 January 1672/3 4/5/25. W. Grosvenor's account books 4/6/6/1-22 entries dated 20 May 1687, 18 August 1682, 26 August 1680.

[45] sjv to P. Lupart 6 December 1704 R52; a bill drawn on a Southwark timber merchant 11 November 1714 R55; sjv to Sir Richard Hoare 23 November 1702 R52; evidence from Hoare's Bank ledgers shows that the Verneys had a moderately active account there from the turn of the century until the mid-twenties; sjv to Elizabeth Lillie 1 February 1701/2 R51; cc to rv 15 December 1717 R56.

[46] cc to rv 3 January 1722/3 4/5/60; 'book of payments' December 1733 R57. When the Verneys moved their London residence to Little Chelsea after 1721 it was not so convenient for graziers to pay them cash – it would mean carrying it right across London.

[47] For use of the excise men see Jane Hill to rv 14 December 1737 R58.

Claydon, how ideas of agricultural improvement influenced estate management, and how the farming landscape was restructured after enclosure. Enclosure at Middle Claydon in the 1650s was swiftly followed by conversion of all the land to pasture. This was a common pattern on compact enclosed estates in the south midlands, particularly in north Buckinghamshire, west Northamptonshire, east Oxfordshire (around Thame), and also in south-east Warwickshire and much of Leicestershire. It persisted until the late eighteenth century, and in many places right through to the twentieth century. The economic rationale for the agricultural switch was twofold. It made the best use of farmland on heavy midland clay of moderate natural fertility when rents were stagnant or falling between 1650 and 1750. These areas could not hope to compete with the arable improvements on the light lands of the Chilterns to the south and the northern 'redland' and limestone areas of Oxfordshire and Northamptonshire to the west and north. 'Improved' pasture – that is to say pasture that was not common waste, or rough grazing – also commanded much higher rents than any arable farming land, whether open field or enclosed. When considering the purchase of Water Stratford in 1743 the first earl asked his bailiff whether it

might be turned into Dairy bargains and hold rent, and all, or all but a trifle laid down, for surely if near half of it ploughed, or but one fourth of it, it must needs have many barns and outbuildings to it, which are great incumbrances.

The Verneys converted East Claydon to dairying at enclosure, and most of the north Buckinghamshire estates that they bought in the middle of the eighteenth century were already dominated by pasture farms, or quickly converted. After enclosing Middle Claydon, Sir Ralph initially sought graziers for his land, but within twenty years his tenants were increasingly relying on dairying, which will be discussed in more detail in chapter 9.[48] For the Verneys, pastoral agriculture meant higher rents, easier management, and lower overheads and repairs. It also had much lower labour requirements and made it easier to control in-migration and reduce poor rates.

Permanent pasture in the seventeenth and eighteenth centuries was improved in a number of ways. Although farming writers rarely wrote about pasture management, from the sixteenth century they began to accept that grass was a crop that needed nourishment with manure and other fertilisers. New drainage techniques and the provision of watercourses and ponds narrowed the distinction between feeding grounds and meadows. In improved pasture areas land

[48] On these trends see E. L. Jones, 'Agriculture and economic growth in England, 1660–1750: agricultural change', *Journal of Economic History*, 25 (1965), pp. 1–18, and Broad, 'Alternate husbandry and permanent pasture', pp. 77–89; Denton and Verney were also trying to save their pre-war investments in fen drainage in the Bedford level – what Denton called his 'fen club': see *The Humble Petition of Sir Ralph Verney, Nathaniel Hobart and Others . . .* (1660) BL C.117.g.1(29). On dairying see Joan Thirsk, *Alternative Agriculture* (Cambridge 1997), pp. 48–9 and 165–9.

was rotated between meadow and pasture, allowing more winter feed to be stored, and keeping up fertility. On the Verney estates most of these techniques were adopted in the period from 1660 to 1680. Other initiatives to improve agricultural techniques rather than farm organisation were more limited than on the lighter soils, where rapid changes were taking place. Nevertheless pasture farmers could improve their husbandry and maintain the fertility of the land by selecting the best animals, and refining butter and cheese production. Both depended on the expertise of the tenant farmer, and on his wife's dairying skills. However, Sir Ralph Verney always sought improvements and was prepared to try new crops and management techniques which he carefully monitored.[49]

Sir Ralph Verney used unlet land he was managing himself to experiment with crops and manures. Sainfoin, a fodder crop that spread very rapidly across southern England after the Restoration, was tried in 1668 and 1681. It was sown in 'the bare places in the common close and over the drain there', and its progress carefully monitored. While noting its preference for dry soils he considered ploughing up a departing tenant's largest field and sowing it with 'French grass'. The wet and heavy clays were not ideal and it did not spread fast at Claydon, but it was tried elsewhere in north Buckinghamshire. Turnips also grew poorly on heavy soils. They were commonly grown as a garden vegetable and seeds were bought in from London. However, in 1655 Sir Ralph tried them in some small closes and his bailiff noted that they did best where the gardener weeded them. Hemp was grown sporadically 'to kill the weeds and to level them'. Most experiments with crops at Claydon took place during the third quarter of the seventeenth century, a time when national interest in farming techniques was at its height, and Middle Claydon was adopting a different form of agriculture.[50]

The Verneys were also interested in new fruit, vegetable, and tree varieties. London seedsmen were regularly used, and occasionally there were direct imports from abroad. Seed was obtained from local suppliers at some distance – from Great Missenden or near Wallingford for wheat, and from Hemel Hempstead for grass seed – and contributed to the local dissemination of new varieties. However, not all innovations were diffused from above. In 1723 two farmers in Steeple Claydon were found to have sown turnips as a field crop to feed to

---

[49] Carolina Lane, 'The development of pastures and meadows during the sixteenth and seventeenth centuries', *Agricultural History Review* 28 (1980), pp. 18–30 and Broad, 'Alternate husbandry and permanent pasture', pp. 77–89.

[50] Kerridge, *The Agricultural Revolution*, p. 346; *Sainfoin Improved* (1674), pp. 1–2; sjv to srv 18 April 1689 R43; W. Denton to srv 9 April 1668 R22; srv to wc 10 February 1680/1 ClH 4/5/33; 7 July 1681 4/5/34. Turnips appear in e.g seedsmen's bills dated May 1654 R12 and 30 November 1659 R16; srv to wr 14 August 1655 R13; wr 20 August 1655 R13; hemp: srv to wr 7 April 1657 R15; hh to srv 13 January 1672/3 4/5/25.

livestock and sell, and their activities raised the question of the Verneys' right to tithes from a new crop.[51]

Permanent grassland agriculture needed fertilisers and manures to maintain the natural quality of the sward. Sir Ralph Verney experimented with potash, coal ash, and sand in the park and meadows in 1662–3. In 1664 Hugh Holmes wrote a comparison of various fertilisers:

there is good grass where the potashes were, but little where the potashes were not laid. I believe you will do very well to lay potashes in the meads so soon as they be mowed . . . the buckashes [?] . . . will do much good . . . but the coal ashes I think are best for highways . . . except they are new sifted.

Lime was brought from Brill and Water Stratford to put on the land in 1673, and Sir Ralph used sea coal and salt on the meadows in 1676 and 1678. Potashes were deemed the most successful and promoted. Sir Ralph even wanted to experiment by digging the potash deep into the clay with mould to improve the soil, following the techniques for marling suggested by seventeenth-century agricultural writers, but his bailiff was sceptical because the technique was unknown locally.[52]

'Potash' at Claydon was a by-product from local potash-makers who burnt and boiled furze, bracken, or straw, to supply the London soap boilers who mixed it with lime to make soap leas, then added tallow and olive oil to produce soap. According to William Ellis, potash was widely used in eighteenth-century Buckinghamshire, though modern soil analysis at Claydon suggests the soil is not naturally deficient in potash. Its nitrogen content was more important to the soil. The Verneys regularly sought out potash-makers as tenants, and they were highly prized. In the post-Restoration period, there were two potash-making families, the Clarkes and Grimes at Claydon for at least two generations. When William Clarke threatened to leave his land in 1695, Sir Ralph wrote 'I much desire a potash man there' and set William Coleman the task of finding another. Clarke stayed on, but his landlord insisted 'for the future I shall expect six months' warning and I would tie him to hold it for two or three years if you could'.

The potash-makers were amongst the few farmers who took long leases in the later seventeenth century, but perhaps negotiated lower rents. Thomas Grimes's agreement in 1671 was for twenty years; William Stevens's in 1720 was for a

[51] srv to wr 23 May 1653 R12; 2 June 1653 R12; rv jr to rv 2 February 1741/2 R59; cc to rv 18, 19, and 28 November 1723 ClH 4/5/69; on seedsmen see Malcolm Thick, 'Garden seeds in England before the late eighteenth century, part 2: the trade in seeds to 1760', *Agricultural History Review* 38 (1990), pp. 105–16.

[52] hh to srv 6 January 1662/3; 9 March 1662/3 ClH 4/5/15; hh to srv 27 June 1664 4/5/17; see also letter synopsis dated 10 June 1664 in July 1664 R19; hh to srv 15 June 1673 4/5/26; R. Townsend to srv 12 July 1673; 4/5/26; wc to srv 11 March 1677/8 4/5/30; 4 July 1678 4/5/31; hh to srv 23 February 1664/5 R20.

similar period. Edmund Verney wrote that his 1671 lease to Grimes was 'upon very hard terms to myself'. However, the leases included clauses giving the landlord first option on 'all the soil or dung called cast potashes if he . . . can spare them' at the going market rate. The Verneys gave potash to subsidise existing tenants who demanded lower rents, or to improve the grass as new tenants entered. By the late seventeenth century this was common, played a part in the bargaining for at least three farms let during the 1670s and 1680s, and was regularly used in the 1720s.[53]

Potash was locally available and seen as an industrial by-product that did not remove goodness from the soil. Other more traditional sources of nitrogen were used on grassland. Straw was rotted down by leaving it in the stone field drains, or in the roadway. Dung was a vital component of the natural agricultural cycle and pigeon dung was particularly renowned. There was a pigeon house at Claydon, and in 1695 Sir Ralph listed three others in north Buckinghamshire. It was laid on meadows, and in 1733 was given to a declining farmer to help him. Fertilisers were laid down in autumn or winter, to maximise their effect on the new season's grass. Occasionally, the potash-makers brought back night soil from London when they returned from delivering their potash in London.[54]

New plants and fertilisers were the areas in which the Verneys were most experimental. Other estate improvements highlight the distinction between landlord's and tenant's capital on the land, and that between repairs and improvements. The Verneys undertook water and drainage works, digging new ponds in fields for tenants, and diverting streams. In 1684 a 'straight watercourse' was dug 'from Waters Gate to the upper end of Bowden mead, as it was done a year or two ago in Markham his meadow'. Good water supply and drainage were vital to the transition to a pastoral economy, and essential in creating what North called 'upland meadows' that made it possible to mow much more pasture ground. The prevention of flooding and marshy ground was also important. Traditional stone drains were built, and in 1663 Sir Ralph used an expert recommended by Sir John Bridgeman, John Minshaw, to stop summer flooding of the meadows beside the Claydon brook rather than for any complicated system of floating meadows or irrigation.[55]

[53] J. Houghton, *Collections for the Improvement of Husbandry and Trade* (1681–3 and 1691–1703) dated 15 February 1694/5 for a detailed description of soap-making; W. Ellis, *Chiltern and Vale Farming Explained* (1733), pp. 390–2; srv to wc 6 and 7 February 1694/5 CIH 4/5/47; Grimes lease of 1671 dated 19 November 1671 CIH 4/2/64; 1720 agreement in CIH 4/5//58; ev to srv 2 February 1670/1 R24; wc to srv 17 January 1677/8 4/5/30; 13 March 1681/2 4/5/34; 10 December 1674 4/5/27; cc to rv 24 October 1722; 31 December 1723 4/5/69.

[54] srv to wc 15 May 1695 CIH 4/5/48; H. King to srv 6 March 1667/8 R22; J. Millward to rv 10 January 1737/8 4/5/78.

[55] srv to wc 15 October 1684 CIH 4/5/37; hh to srv 6 July 1663 R19; srv to Sir John Bridgeman 3 March 1664/5 R19. R. North, *An Account of the Different Kinds of Grasses Propagated in England* . . . (1759), p. 14.

None of these improvements compared with the enclosure of the open fields and laying down to pasture; indeed many of them lay in the grey area between routine maintenance and innovation. The art of keeping permanent pasture in good heart was to deal quickly with whatever threatened the deterioration of the grasslands. Ant-hills in the fields, which spoiled the turf and left the ground uneven and bare, were a particular problem. 'Banking', at first with spades, later with a specially designed plough, was the contemporary countermeasure. It was used to mollify farmers seeking rent reductions, and sometimes as an incentive to incoming tenants. Sowing grass seed on the newly banked ground enhanced the quality of the grassland.[56]

The Verneys could only test new crops and fertilisers and improve water provision when land was in hand or between leases. Without a home farm after 1660 Sir Ralph Verney could not easily promote improvement by example. Tenants on yearly tenancies did not commonly adopt new techniques unless they gave immediate returns. Careful choice of skilled tenants more easily ensured good husbandry than converting traditional farmers to new methods. But some improvement was assisted by the terms on which tenants held their farms. With few leases at Claydon after 1660, most information about farming covenants comes from references in the correspondence. Nevertheless, comparison of the terms of Verney leases with those of smaller local landowners whose land was later purchased by the Verneys shows that the Verneys were much stricter.

There were clauses forbidding sub-letting and the taking of 'inmates' or lodgers, which simply ensured that tenants sought permission, and also penalties of £5 an acre for ploughing pasture. These were genuinely intended to deter ploughing in the late seventeenth century rather than ensuring the landlord's share of quick profits from ploughing and sowing with an intensive and soil-draining crop such as hemp or woad.[57] More important at Claydon were clauses forbidding cattle from feeding on meadow grounds between 1 December and 24 February, to reduce the churning of pastures in muddy winter conditions. All animals were excluded from meadows in the month before Lady Day. A standard clause forbade farmers from selling dung or hay to outsiders, which reduced future fertility, and was particularly important in the final year of a lease. Clauses about mowing suggest that the Verneys did not fully understand rotational mowing. Leases in 1708 and 1742 both prescribed fields to be mowed and threatened £3-an-acre penalties for mowing other land. When in June 1708 John Seaton broke his mowing agreement, he was not fined, but simply asked to sign a paper acknowledging what he had done. However, several documents imply that land was alternately grazed and mown. In 1674–5 there was a discussion about the enlargement of Knowl Hill farm with an extra meadow so that it did

[56] For further details on 'banking' see Broad, 'Alternate husbandry and permanent pasture', p. 87.
[57] Cf. Kerridge, The Agricultural Revolution, pp. 191–2.

not have to be mown every year. The stipulations on mowing were probably intended to restrain tenants from cutting hay too often without allowing animals to keep up the fertility of the land by grazing it. In 1744 the future second Earl Verney wrote to his father of a 'ridiculous lease', on lands he had just bought, in which the tenant was forbidden to plough, but then given 'leave to mow the whole estate and spend nothing on it'.[58]

Pre-nineteenth-century farming in north Buckinghamshire depended on manure from animal dung on the farm, and little outside feed was bought in. Husbandry provisions in leases were primarily negative, and intended to prevent the abuse and deterioration of the land. The potential for positive initiatives to improve agricultural techniques was much less in a pastoral region than on the lighter soils. By the end of the eighteenth century, the county agricultural report writers, and men such as Arthur Young (but not so often William Marshall), depicted the south midlands as an area of poor pastoral agriculture interspersed with poorer residual open-field villages ripe for enclosure. They were perhaps too harsh on the enclosed pastoral areas, wishing to impose their own model of new crops and rotations on an environment where it had little potential. The dairy farmers and stock fatteners of the south midlands were already pressed by high rents to maximise yields from their land. They were squeezed hard between the hammer of buyer's monopoly in the London butter and cheese cartels, and the anvil of efficient estate managers seeking to maximise rentals. Without really good farming accounts to assess farm profitability accurately at this time, it is too easy to dismiss midland grazing farms as centres of poor husbandry, as R. C. Allen tends to. They simply did not fit a model of improved agriculture much better suited to lighter soils.[59]

The Verneys experimented with new crops and systems but maximised their income most effectively by letting land to farmers who were well capitalised, up to date, and therefore able to pay their rents. They encouraged farmers with good capital reserves to take on more land and expand their enterprises, thus increasing farm sizes. That process needs careful analysis, for it heralded profound social change in the community. After the enclosure of 1654–6, the Verneys were running a modern compact estate at Middle Claydon, without manorial courts or copyhold tenants, with few long leaseholds and no outside jurisdictions. Over the next twenty years Sir Ralph Verney excluded outside interference by buying the Court Leet of Adstock (whose near-redundant jurisdiction included Claydon), and the fee farm rents when they came on the

---

[58] Lane, 'Development of pastures and meadows', pp. 18–30; lease dated 1756 R60. Mary Hinton lease 1742, ClH 4/6/30a&b; paper dated 22 June 1708 4/6/28; eb to srv 18 December 1671 4/5/24; srv to wc 7 April 1688 4/5/41; wc to srv 14 April 1689 4/5/42; srv to wc 1 February 1674/5 4/5/24; rvjr to rv 18 October 1744 R59.
[59] R. C. Allen, *Enclosure and the Yeoman: The Agricultural Development of the South Midlands 1450–1850* (Oxford 1992), esp. ch. 10.

market. His estate had been mapped and surveyed at the time of enclosure, his woods had no common rights over them, and the parish boundaries were clearly physically demarcated. The enclosure had also been an important point in agricultural change. The landscape and economy of Middle Claydon now became overwhelmingly pastoral, with significant impact on local society.[60]

After 1657 the typical Middle Claydon farmer was a tenant with his own working capital, paying an annual rent that was close to the economic value of the land. Almost all were on annual tenancies or paper leases of up to three years. This system maximised rent, but the Verneys could suddenly find lands untenanted in bad years. In the inflationary years before 1660 long leases advantaged the tenant as inflation reduced his rent in real terms. As rents fell after 1660, tenants would not take land for more than two or three years at the rents he was asking. Three-year leases were only possible in favourable periods such as 1660 to 1662 and the 1690s. Short tenancies continued in the eighteenth century. Specialists such as the potash-makers received leases of up to twenty years at concessionary rents, while a market gardener in Steeple Claydon held leases of fifteen and seven years in the early eighteenth century. Short leases were formally written into Claydon estate management in 1740 when the future second Earl's marriage settlement limited leases to seven years. Verney practice is at odds with the standard advice given by land stewards and writers such as Edward Laurence who advocated slightly lower rent levels and 21-year improving leases. But yearly tenancies were typical of late seventeenth-century landed estates in south-eastern England.[61]

High rent levels rewarded farmers with capital and expertise if their farm was of an appropriate size that balanced labour requirements and overheads. The Verneys' policy after the enclosure gradually reduced the number of tenants, and increased farm sizes. The long-term impact of this process in Middle Claydon from the 1640s to the 1780s is evident from the changing farm sizes shown in table 6.1.

The overall reduction in the number of tenants in the thirty years after enclosure was considerably less than occurred in the succeeding thirty-five years when no equivalent upheaval took place. Some of the reduction between 1648 and 1688 took place during the Civil War and in the years before enclosure when the remaining copyhold and long leasehold tenancies were extinguished. Thereafter the numbers of farms mainly reduced by a slow attrition of small farms. Farmers with fewer than seventy-five acres had less access to credit, less chance of owning additional freehold property, yet had to pay the same rent per

---

[60] E.g. Thomas Cater to srv 22 December 1686 4/5/39; wc to srv 27 January 1680/1 CIH 4/5/33.
[61] Deeds 1671 dated 17 January 1671/2 CIH 4/5/24; estate correspondence 1706 4/5/58; deeds 1720–5 dated 18 March 1705/6 for 'Thomas Franklin, Gardener'; Laurence, *The Duty of a Steward to his Lord* (1727).

Table 6.1 *Changing distribution of Middle Claydon farm sizes
from rentals*

Farm size/no. of farms	Year			
	1648	1688	1722	1787
0–4 acres	6	15	7	9
5–19 acres	18	6	1	5
20–49 acres	18	6	1	5
50–74 acres	5	5	5	5
75–150 acres	4	9	12	2
150+ acres	2	2	1	8
Nos. of farms > 5 acres	47	28	20	25
Total nos.	53	43	27	34

Sources: 1648: rate dated 5 July 1648 R9; 1688 uses a combination of Middle
Claydon rental for 1688 in ClH 4/3/38-77 and Buckinghamshire CRO D/X337, East
Claydon rental of Edmund Verney, including a separate rental of his part of the
Middle Claydon estate; 1722 rental in 4/3/111/1-3; 1787 4/3/9. The dates have been
chosen because they provide the best comparative data over a period that saw the
elimination of copyholds and long leases in favour of rack-renting. The 1648 figure is
from a rating valuation that provides better evidence on farm sizes than pure rental
income at that date because it estimates the annual value of the farm rather than rent paid.

acre as those with larger farms. Their lower capital assets meant they were more
likely to understock their land, or to buy riskier cheaper stock, making them
more vulnerable to a squeeze on profits, and therefore to bankruptcy. They then
became more vulnerable to the Verneys' policy of evicting tenants who fell too
far in arrears with their rent.

The squeezing of the smaller farmer is well illustrated in table 6.1. In the
course of 150 years, successively larger farm size groups were affected. Farms
of 5 to 19 acres fell dramatically in numbers from 1648 to 1688 and had almost been eliminated by 1722, only to achieve a slight and perhaps chimerical
revival in 1787 when cottage rents were raised. These cottager and labourer
holdings, and then farms of 20 to 49 acres – the small family farms discussed
by Sir Ralph Verney in 1650 – bore the brunt of the reductions in the seventeenth and early eighteenth centuries. They were the equivalent of the half-
to two-yardland farmers of pre-enclosure times, the traditional small farmers
of midland England. In 1648 there were thirty-six such farms, but by 1722
only two.

Farms of fifty acres or more were sensitive to the changing economic size
of viable pastoral farms in the south midlands over two centuries. The group
of 50-to-74-acre farms remained stable through the later seventeenth and early
eighteenth centuries, but declined by 1787. The 75-to-150 acre grouping shows

Table 6.2 *Middle Claydon farm acreage by farm-size group using constant 2,000-acre farm area*

Farm size / acreage	Year			
	1648	1688	1722	1787
0–4 acres	19.3	22.7	45	10.12
5–19 acres	243.6	75.1	15.5	49.2
20–49 acres	544.6	339.5	160.3	98.8
50–74 acres	301.3	320.9	335.9	139
75–150 acres	381.7	936.2	1318.7	188.8
150+ acres	350.7	333.3	158.6	1701.57

Sources: as table 6.1

the greatest gains in the period from 1648 to 1722, but underwent a sharp fall in the second and third quarters of the eighteenth century. Large farms of more than 150 acres were relatively few in number in the later seventeenth and early eighteenth centuries, but predominated in 1787.

These figures suggest that before 1750 farms of 75 to 150 acres were considered the optimum size for the kind of dairy farming practised in Middle Claydon. Later in the century, larger farms were considered more viable units of production.[62] In 1648 most farmers had holdings in the 5-to-19 and 20-to-49-acre farm-size groups, and even in 1688 there were still more farmers with less than 75 acres than with 75 to 150 acres. In 1722 the biggest group of farmers rented 75-to-150-acre farms, while in 1787 farms of 150 acres or more predominated, with three farms exceeding 250 acres. The change in farm sizes can be illustrated in other ways. In table 6.2 the acreage of Middle Claydon farmed in farm units of different sizes is calculated. This assumes a constant 2,000-acre farming area in the parish, and uniform rents, though rents varied about 15 per cent from the mean. This analysis presents changes in farm sizes between 1648 and 1722 more dramatically. Small farmers with fewer than fifty acres held 40 per cent of the parish in 1648, declining to 20 per cent in 1688 and less than 10 per cent in 1787. In 1648 about 730 acres were held in farm units above 75 acres. By 1688 this had shot up to over 1,250 acres, but rose only slowly to above 1,450 in 1722. This represented about three-quarters of the parish in 1722 and more than 90 per cent in 1787. By then over 85 per cent of the parish was farmed in units of 150 acres or more. This had implications for the social fabric of the village. Although the smaller farmers of 5 to 50 acres were roughly equal in numbers in 1648 and 1688, they farmed a much smaller proportion of

[62] Cottager and labourer holdings of four acres or less have been omitted as their rent included a high element of house-rent, and from the early eighteenth century the estate used new strategies, allowing some families to live rent free, while others were paid by the parish from poor rates.

Table 6.3 *Estimates of Middle Claydon rental less woods and park 1642–1791*

Year	1642	1644–5	1648–50	1653	[1660]	1688	1722	1787	1791
Amount	£1,221	£622	c. £1,290	£1,379	c. £1,700	£1,625	£1,745	£2,313	£2,379

the land in 1688. They paid a much lower proportion of parish rates and their voice in the community was diminished as a result.

These changes are a powerful reminder of the economic forces underlying the social changes described in chapter 7. The farming community in Middle Claydon changed as tenants of smaller farms left, either from choice or because they went bankrupt. Farms rarely passed directly from father to son. Farmers moved easily between suitable tenancies, within, or away from the Claydons. Father and son occasionally farmed separate farms in Middle Claydon, but were not often in partnership, reflecting the classic English pattern of economically independent two-generation family units.

The changing pattern of late seventeenth-century tenancies at Middle Claydon reflected the Verneys' negotiating methods. The Verneys cherished competitive bidding from farmers, but there was often only one bidder and tenants became adept at coming to deals with one another to avoid competition. Sir Ralph set out his letting methodology in his 1650 'confessional' letter. He wrote

After I had received up the parcels I commonly made my demand somewhat above what I meant to take and seldom or never gave any other reasons why I value it at such a rate but that I thought others would give about that price for it, which I conceive they would not do but that it was really worth it.[63]

Sir Ralph followed this policy consistently, and his successors never modified its theory. In practical terms, obtaining the highest rent was balanced against the known skills of candidates and the need to minimise arrears. They also needed to avoid tenants shying away from a farm at the last moment and forcing them to leave land unlet, or to farm it directly.

After 1660 Verney policies had to take into account falling rents. The value of their pasture and meadow fell less than that of arable, reflecting better market prices for meat and dairy produce than for grain, but the downward pressures on rents were particularly strong in the 1670s and 1680s and again in the second quarter of the eighteenth century.[64] The overall effects can be seen in the evidence of total rental income from Middle Claydon shown in table 6.3.

This estimate shows how falling rents in the late seventeenth century put pressure on the Verneys' income. These figures include the effects of civil war,

---

[63] srv to wd, 2/12 June 1650 R10; wr to srv 12 January 1649/50 R10.
[64] M. G. Davies, 'Country gentry and falling rents', pp. 86–96.

Table 6.4 *Knowl Hill rents 1636–1722*

Year	1636	1642	1646	1648	1653	1662	1671	1674–5	1679–93	1696	1713	1722
Amount	£125	£120	£65	£100	£100	£100–10	£90	£85–6	£86	£90	£90	£90

Note: A 10–15 per cent drop after the Restoration was only partly restored after 1690.

enclosure, changing types of tenure, and alterations in the percentage of land leased out, so are not a fair reflection of fluctuations in rack rents per acre. The rent paid for one large field of *c.* 100 acres, Knowl Hill, prime old-enclosed pasture, more accurately reflects national trends on rack-rented lands. Table 6.4 shows the changing rent paid for it.

The Verneys did not hesitate to evict farmers who looked unlikely to pay their way. It was the steward's job to ensure that tenants were farming effectively, had sufficient livestock to make the profits that would pay their rent, and were not cutting corners at the expense of land quality. Throughout the later seventeenth and early eighteenth centuries there was a regular turnover of tenants with examples of farmers leaving voluntarily, and also of evictions. A particularly telling example of the Verneys' understanding of the relationship between capital availability and ability to make the farm profitable and pay rent promptly, is that of Richard Goodwin. Goodwin was tenant for about thirty acres in Middle Claydon in the early 1680s, but may have had other land in Steeple Claydon. He decided to buy land in Steeple Claydon when the Chaloners sold their estate in 1683/4. It cost £260, and Goodwin asked his landlord Sir Ralph Verney to lend him £90 to help him make the purchase. Verney refused on the grounds that if so much of his tenant's capital were tied up in land and debts, he would have to sell livestock to pay for his land purchase. He would then be unable to farm his Middle Claydon land adequately and therefore not pay his rent promptly. Goodwin bought the land but after about a year, Sir Ralph wrote

Though I think Richard Goodwin a very honest man, and one that intends not to cheat me, yet I am confident he cannot hold unless he sell both his land and his house too. Interest money must undo him.

By 1685 the Verneys felt obliged to take a mortgage to secure their back rent, and this enabled Goodwin to manage for another four years, but from 1689 he was falling into arrears again. By Michaelmas 1692 he was over two years in arrears and was forced to give up his tenancy. He still owed the Verneys money in 1695.[65]

---

[65] CIH 2/452 dated 27 March 1684; srv to wc 24 November 1684 4/5/37; CIH Rentals 4/3/38-77; 4/5/48 Joseph Churchill to srv 4 October 1695 4/5/48.

Table 6.5 *Tenant turnover at Middle Claydon at 2/3 year intervals 1679–94*

	1679–81	1681–3	1683–5	1685–8	1688–90	1690–2	1692–4
Farmers leave (name disappears)	0	4	1	3	1	2	3
New farmer (not same name)	1	4	5	1	3	3	2
Widow or son retains farm	4	2	1	0	0	0	0
Widow becomes cottager	0	0	0	1	0	1	0
Farmer becomes cottager/ pauper	2	1	0	0	0	0	1
Cottager becomes farmer	1	1	0	1	0	0	0

Table 6.6 *Late seventeenth and early eighteenth-century tenant turnover in Middle Claydon*

	1679–86	1686–94	1713–22
Farmers leaving (name disappears)	7	7	4
Farmers staying	11	16	13
Widow or son retains farm	4	0	2
Farmer becomes cottager/pauper	4	0	1

Individual cases are important for understanding these processes, but the overall picture is provided by analysis of the rent rolls from 1679 to 1694.[66] These cover approximately two thirds of the estate with Sir Ralph Verney meticulously recording in his own hand what he expected each tenant to pay in a six month period, and precisely when every penny of that rent was handed over. The results in table 6.5 compare tenant turnover at two- to three-year intervals and show only ten out of twenty-two holdings on which there was family continuity, either by the tenant, his widow, or son, between 1679 and 1694.

This turnover is almost certainly lower than during the 1660s and 1670, because after the mid-1670s Sir Ralph Verney reversed his policy of rapid eviction. He supported favoured tenants in difficulties with concealed subsidies, and occasionally allowed the parish to subsidise widowed farmers with families from the poor rate. A comparison of tenant turnover in the late seventeenth and early eighteenth centuries is possible by analysing change over longer intervals. The results, shown in table 6.6, are not dissimilar and indicate that turnover remained proportionately high.

---

[66] Claydon House rentals 1679–94; CIH 4/3/38-77; srv memorandum dated 18 November 1653 R12; The figures of incoming and outgoing tenants do not balance because farms did not remain unchanged, and land might at some points be unlet.

Figure 3 analyses the Middle Claydon rentals for the period from 1679 to 1694 to show changes in income and arrears. The rent roll was virtually static. Arrears of more than a year were almost always less than 5 per cent during the period from 1679 to 1690, but were allowed to rise significantly from 1690 to 1694, reaching over 15 per cent in the first half of 1693. Arrears of six months to one year, which from 1679–85 amounted to around 20 per cent, rose dramatically in the early 1690s. At Michaelmas 1691 they amounted to 59 per cent of rent due.

Arrears also rose between 1710 and 1720. In the year of his death, 1717, Sir John admitted that at least two tenants were more than two years in arrears. In their last years both Sir Ralph and Sir John allowed increased arrears that suggest a mellowing with age or a slackening of grip. Mounting rent arrears allowed the Verneys to bolster their nominal rent rolls for about fifty years, but was symptomatic of deeper farming problems. Rent arrears reflect inappropriate rent levels, farming disasters, or bad estate management. At Claydon the problem mainly lay with the high level of rents set. G. E. Mingay included some of the Duke of Kingston's Buckinghamshire estates in the sample supporting his 'Agricultural Depression' during the 1730s and 1740s, but there is little support from Claydon. On the Tyrells' nearby estate at Thornton, where much of the land was down to pasture, it was even possible to raise some rents during the early 1720s though they fell back after 1726. One Claydon tenant's rent account has survived for the period from 1742 to 1752 and shows no problems in paying rent, despite the cattle plague, and this supports J. V. Beckett's suggestion that pastoral areas were much less severely affected.[67]

Yet the relative stability of rentals from 1680 to 1750 does not tell the whole story. From 1680 onwards Sir Ralph provided a variety of concealed subsidies for his tenants, by occasional waiving of part arrears, and providing assistance with infrastructure and fertilisers when he could not let land easily. One technique was to allow rebates of one or two pounds at the end of the year if there was evidence of hardship. These he described as 'all one to him [the tenant] and more credit to the ground'. However they were sparingly given during the 1680s and 1690s, when an alternative approach was used. This was a system of rebate in kind designed to help the tenant improve his farm and farming. Sometimes the tenant was offered a choice of either a small cash rebate or a rather larger grant of material but usually he was simply offered help in kind. When a new tenant entered on a farm he might be offered new outbuildings to house calves or pigs, sheep pens, barns or the conversion of a room into a cheese loft. This helped farmers convert to dairying. Relatively small and cheap

---

[67] sjv to rv 21 December 1712 R54; 8 January 1712/3 R55; 31 March 1717/8 R56; BCRO D/X/596 Hester Tyrell's estate accounts for the minority of her son 1720–9, esp. pp. 1–2, 175–6. Mary Hinton's rent account 1742–52 CIH 4/6/30a, b.

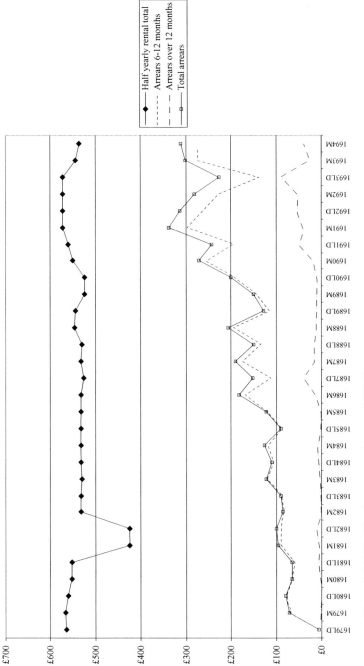

Figure 3 Middle Claydon rents and arrears 1679–94.

Legend:
- Half yearly rental total
- Arrears 6-12 months
- Arrears over 12 months
- Total arrears

improvements were preferred on the grounds that it was 'a hazard . . . for your worship to lay out money to build for a man's conveniency and then a tenant to leave it'.[68]

Other aids included the 'banking' of pasture grounds to remove large clumps of tough weeds and level mole hills, and gifts of dung and other fertilisers that would keep up the quality of the grass, and therefore the rent. Examples of 'gifts' of potash, dung, and pigeon dung are to be found throughout the period from 1650 to 1750, but they appear more systematically from 1675 to 1695 when Sir Ralph Verney was combating falling rents.[69] In 1694 Sir Ralph Verney decided to make gifts of potash to four of the seven tenants suggested to him as suitable 'for all these pay well and I must consider those most that do pay best'. Turnover rates suggest that it was only partly successful, and the letters confirm that it was not only the weak tenants who found the regime at Claydon harsh. Most landlords in the south midlands faced similar problems of weakening rent. Rent levels on the Lee estates on prime fattening lands closer to Aylesbury fell by over 11½ per cent between 1668 and 1696. Landlords kept an eye on what their neighbours were doing. Sir John Busby in neighbouring Addington gained a reputation in the 1670s as a ruthless landlord who distrained tenants' stock when they were only six months in arrears. As a result 'many people of Padbury, Adstock and Addington came and intreated Sir John on his tenants behalf . . . who is accounted a wonderful hard Landlord and all Tenants that know it cry out . . . shame on him'. Busby was even accused of deliberately driving the distrained cattle through deep water to harm them. Sir Ralph felt these reports were distorted but his neighbour's reputation may have helped to divert attention from the Verneys' own policies.[70]

Small and unprofitable farms were eliminated on the estate between 1657 and 1740 in a piecemeal, almost surreptitious, process. By 1740 there were fewer farmsteads out in the fields. Migration and tenant turnover at Claydon meant there were often empty houses that might be pulled down, converted to use as barns, or refurbished. At least two houses were pulled down immediately after the Restoration when Sir Ralph Verney tried to stop John Butcher marrying and settling in an empty house in the village. Later demolitions were more often

---

[68] srv to wc 3 April 1695 CIH 4/5/48; wc to srv 23 November 1674 4/5/27. On the conversion to dairying see below, ch. 9, cf. building works for the conversion to dairying on the Dentons' Hillesden estates in BCRO D/X/591 esp. 1662–4 payments *passim*.

[69] E.g. wc to srv 10 December 1674 CIH 4/5/27; for Thomas Grime's lease see 4/2/64; though the practice was not common other references can be found locally – see BCRO D/X723 for a 1678 Brill deed. I would like to thank Hugh Hanley for this reference. By the mid-eighteenth century, William Ellis considered potashes were over-used as a fertiliser in the Vale of Aylesbury; see W. Ellis, *Chiltern and Vale Farming Explained*, pp. 390–2.

[70] srv to wc 26 July 1694 CIH 4/5/47. Oxford CRO Dillon MSS DIL. XVIII/e/5/i. ev to srv 14 January 1677/8 R31; srv to ev 4 February 1677/8 R31.

linked to changing farm sizes and patterns. In the late 1670s and early 1680s Sir Ralph rebuilt several farmhouses at Middle Claydon to attract tenants, but demolished a number of houses in the process. In 1681 he wrote of Widow Scott's house: 'I keep up that house only for her for 'tis not wanted there' and therefore would not renovate it. In 1678 Fimore Lodge, the large old hunting lodge in the woods, was all but demolished and replaced by a more suitable farmhouse, while two if not three houses disappeared in the same period. In 1677 when William Taylor's house was burnt down Sir Ralph immediately offered to build his tenant a better house, but insisted 'I will set it where I please' and used the misfortune as an excuse for re-planning his farm with an eye to future amalgamation.[71]

A similar process took place soon after Sir John Verney succeeded his father in 1696. He ordered William Coleman 'to neglect Mrs Parrott's house, if I should have that bargain fall, for there are too many houses press upon the Park and make incursions on it'. There is no explicit underlying plan for farms on the estate. Houses were not automatically demolished when holdings were combined. When William Taylor died in 1713 with no child to inherit the farm, he wrote: 'two or three of my tenants would take it but I can't let 'em for then the house would fall down, they all having other houses to live in'. A few months later a great gale uprooted trees at Claydon, blew down Widow Delafield's house, and severely damaged a barn. Sir John Verney ordered the demolition of the house, but mended the barn.[72] Five years later a farm amalgamation was rejected on the grounds that 'if he should take it the house would soon fall'. The reduction in the number of houses on the estate was a gradual process, shaped by the changing needs of farms and farmers, and broadly in line with the falling numbers of holdings.[73]

There was no major village clearance at Middle Claydon as there had been at Stowe in the late 1630s.[74] A few houses near Claydon House disappeared as it was turned into a country seat within its own park. The fate of houses depended on their position within the ring-fenced farm, and in relation to the park and village. The gradual erosion of housing stock took place during a rolling reappraisal of individual farms, a normal part of estate management. Decisions could be swayed by potential tenants' views of what fields they

---

[71] srv to wc 10 January 1677/8 R31; 28 December 1676 ClH 4/5/28; 13 January 1680/1 4/5/33; 1 February 1676/7 4/5/29.

[72] cc to sjv 16, 21, and 25 February 1713/4 ClH 4/5/65.

[73] sjv to wc 5 December 1697 R50; 9 March 1697/8 R50; sjv to rv 1 February 1712/3 R55; cc to rv 9 February 1717/8 R56; wr to srv 21 October 1648 R9; cc to ?rv 9 February 1717/8 R56; srv to wd 2/10 June 1650 R10; srv to wc 3 December 1684 ClH 4/5/37; 29 October 1684 4/5/37; Abraham Teagle is another example of a prosperous childless farmer: see wc to srv 2 February 1695/6 4/5/48.

[74] Huntington STTM Oversize Box 2 Petition of 17 March 1640/1.

would like to rent as well as the Verneys' strategic considerations. The long-term refashioning of farms to increase their size and stabilise income from prosperous tenants was the primary consideration of estate management. Yet it had profound implications for village society and the relationship between farmers and labourers, and their landlord. These are the subject of the next chapter.

7   Power in the community – the making of an estate village 1660–1740

This chapter examines how the Verneys created an estate village at Middle Claydon by influencing a whole range of activities in the community. Middle Claydon's population fell from around 250 to 100 between 1660 and 1801. Population reconstitution data linked to a range of other sources demonstrates how landlord control of settlement, housing, marriage, and charity, worked together to reduce the number of labouring poor in the parish. It illuminates the important ways in which farmers, steward, and clergy interacted to make it a negotiated rather than a dictatorial process and demonstrates the complex nature of wider landlord control in the community in areas such as crime, healthcare, and morality.

Changes in landscape, farm layout, and agricultural practices in Middle Claydon after 1656 had important effects on the village community. Most striking was the considerable population decline which accelerated during the eighteenth century. Three measures of population in the sixty years after the Restoration all indicate a population of 40 to 50 households, or 180 to 250 people with a precise enumeration 206 in 1709.[1] By 1800 this had diminished to just over 100. Middle Claydon's population decline was greater than in any other parish in north Buckinghamshire, and was probably comparable with the greatest levels of rural depopulation nationally in that period. Wrigley and Schofield found that 14 per cent of parishes had fewer average baptisms in 1801 than in the 1660s. North Buckinghamshire's social and economic structures favoured such trends, and at least five parishes in Ashendon Hundred had roughly stable or falling populations in the period from 1660 to 1801.[2] Comparisons of the numbers of houses implied in rentals in 1646–8, the Hearth Tax, and Visitation returns

---

[1] For the Hearth Tax see PRO E179/354 (?1662) and E179/324 for the 1671 returns of exempt houses; the Compton census figures are analysed in E. A. Whiteman (ed.), *The Compton Census of 1676*, British Academy Records of Social and Economic History, new series 10 (1986), pp. 365–71; for Wake's visitation see J. Broad (ed.), *Buckinghamshire Dissent and Parish Life 1669–1712*, Buckinghamshire Record Society 28 (1993), pp. 205–6, where the number of households was estimated at 40 to 50 in 1706, and 40 in 1709.

[2] Wrigley and Schofield, *The Population History of England*, pp. 163–4. The parishes with stable or falling populations included Middle Claydon, East Claydon, Wotton Underwood, Grendon Underwood, and Chearsley.

suggest that something between five and ten households disappeared between the end of the Civil War and Queen Anne's reign.

After 1709 the pace of population decline can only be estimated from the aggregate analysis of parish registers, using a nine-year moving average of the three Claydon parishes to produce some trend indications shown in figures 4a–c.[3]

In the first half of the seventeenth century, Middle Claydon's baptism and burial totals followed rising national trends, but were below those of East and Steeple Claydon. Between 1660 and 1720, the smoothed figures fluctuate, and it is only after 1730 that there is a gradual drop in the baptismal figures which decreased fast after 1760. In general, there was a surplus of baptisms over burials in the first half of the seventeenth century, followed by a period in which they are relatively equal between 1670 and 1705. There was a surplus between 1710 and 1750, but the number of both baptisms and burials was falling, while from c. 1760 to the end of the century burials consistently equalled or exceeded baptisms.[4] It appears that the slow fall in population before 1740 was mainly the result of the attrition of farms already demonstrated from the rent rolls. The decline in the number of farm tenancies was considerably greater between 1688 and 1722 than it had been between 1648 and 1688.[5] After 1760 the decline reflects the end of a traditional village community, and a high degree of out-migration seems likely.

Comparisons of crisis mortality in the three Claydon parishes up to 1730 show significant differences, yet do not seem to have been decisive in Middle Claydon's population loss. There were mortality crises in all three parishes between 1595 and 1650 – in 1597–8, 1613–14, 1624, and 1639–41. In Middle Claydon mortality was almost three times the moving average in each, while it was closer to twice the moving average in East and Steeple Claydon. The mortality crises of 1657–8 and 1727–9 show particularly prominently in the Claydon parish registers, and dramatically in East Claydon, where the twenty-nine deaths in 1658 represented close on 10 per cent of the population. In Middle Claydon only three burials are recorded, yet in September 1657 Sir Ralph Verney described it as 'sorely visited, and particularly this very town . . . here hath been 40 or 50 sick at a time whereof the parson and eight or nine more are already dead, and at this hour many are dangerously sick and still sicken daily'. The parson and bailiff both died and most of his household had been affected, but because the parson was dead most burials went unrecorded.[6] After

---

[3] In choosing a nine-year average I have followed K. Wrightson and D. Levine, *Poverty and Piety in an English Village: Terling 1525–1700*, rev. edn (Oxford 1995) and D. Levine, *Family Formation in an Age of Nascent Capitalism* (New York 1977).

[4] See figures 4a–c. The parsons of Middle Claydon were certainly resident from the 1630s onwards, so under-registration seems to be an unlikely cause of these low baptism and burial totals.

[5] See above, p. 139.

[6] srv to Lord Warwick 17 September 1657 R15; srv to John Cary 2 October 1657 R15.

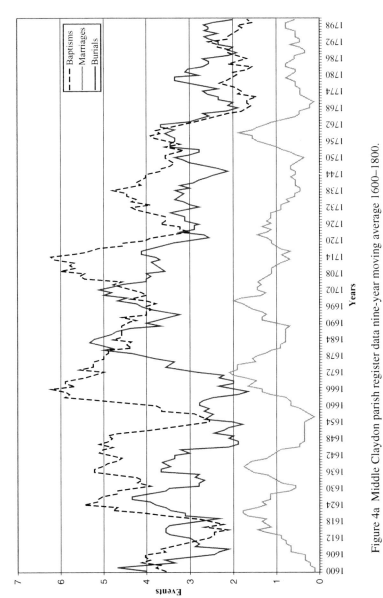

Figure 4a Middle Claydon parish register data nine-year moving average 1600–1800.

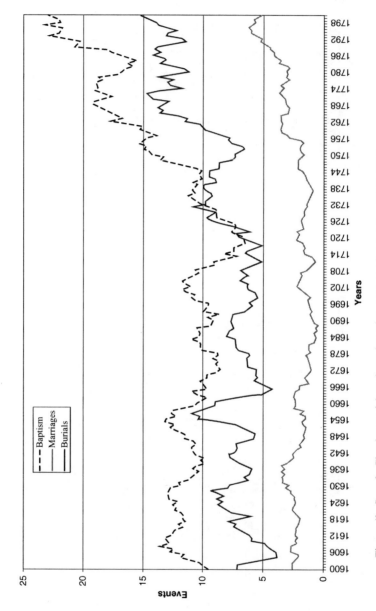

Figure 4b Steeple Claydon parish register data nine-year moving average 1600–1800.

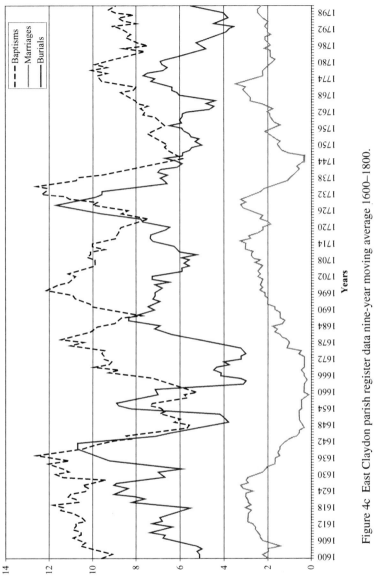

Figure 4c East Claydon parish register data nine-year moving average 1600–1800.

1657–8, baptisms in Middle and Steeple Claydon fell away quite sharply over the next twenty years, but in East Claydon recovery was rapid and sustained. In Middle Claydon this can be linked to the recent enclosure and the departure of a number of families, and a smaller influx of new tenants for the enclosed farms. In the next major epidemic years between 1727 and 1731 Middle Claydon and Steeple Claydon had significantly increased mortality, while it almost doubled in East Claydon in 1729. As in 1657 Verney's bailiff and parson both died during the epidemic, as did squire Duncombe's heir. Villagers were so busy nursing sick people that they would not pick mushrooms for their landlord as usual.[7]

The national epidemics of 1657–8 and 1727–9 were unknown fevers, perhaps influenza. Epidemics of less deadly viruses were noted in 1649 ('purple fever'), 1672 ('these new fevers'), 1696, 1705, and 1741. Plague, smallpox, and measles were more easily identified and struck fear into the population.[8] The 'great plague' of 1665 reached East Claydon in August 1665. It infected Edward Cox's house, where he and his three children died, and his wife 'hath a swelling, but is down again and goes abroad and says she is not sick . . . I hear she hath miscarried since she buried her husband and her children.' Cox was one of Edmund Verney's tenants, no other victims are named.[9] In Middle Claydon there was a panic when Jack Lea escaped London to stay with his mother. This

filled the town with so many and great fears that Holmes was forced to come to me into Oxfordshire . . . to acquaint me with ye business, upon which I resolved to come directly home, and being I did so till I see whether the town is infected by him or no, 'tis not fit for me to go to Sir Roger's.

Sir Ralph Verney's reaction was to stay at Middle Claydon writing 'the plague coming into this parish kept me about a fortnight longer here than I intended to order matters as well as I could for the security of my family and tenants'. His presence helped steady a parish in which the parson reported that 'the constable is remiss enough, but generally beggars are stopped in the county'.[10] In September plague was reported across the county 'at Hardwick, at Aylesbury but little, much at Wendover, and Bletchley and Fenny Street very sorely', and it returned in February 1666 to claim two more victims in Quainton.[11]

Isolation was normally prescribed for high infectious and dangerous diseases. In 1679, a servant at Middle Claydon with smallpox was put in an empty room

[7] wb to rv 5 November 1729 R57; cc to rv 14, 15 18, 21 September 1727; 3, 9, 12, October 1727 ClH 4/5/73.

[8] Elizabeth Isham to srv 4 June 1649 R10; wb to srv 12 April 1696 ClH 4/5/48.

[9] hh to srv 27 August 1665 ClH 4/5/17; ev to srv 27 August 1665 R20.

[10] srv to Henry Verney 16 June 1665 R20.

[11] J. Cary to srv 10 July 1665 R20; srv to Margaret Elmes 11 February 1665/6 R20; eb to srv 4 September 1665 ClH 4/5/17.

in the almshouse for the duration of his illness. Two years earlier, Sir Ralph wrote detailed instructions when his servant Tom Mathews was a suspected smallpox victim:

I absolutely command you not to come near him, but get him such a keeper or keepers as necessary and let him want for nothing for I value no charge in respect of my servants health. If Mary will be so forward as to go to him, and he so simple to suffer her, I will not absolutely forbid her, not knowing how far they are engaged, but I will advise her from it.

Sir Ralph ordered both housemaids to go and live with their parents or kin until he recovered, and paid for their board. He argued that this would prevent hysteria, for women and even men 'conceit themselves infected merely with the fear of it'. He told Mathew's girlfriend to stay with him, or to leave the Claydons, as to stay locally 'were as bad as in my house'. Sir Ralph also decided not to send down his dirty linen to be washed at Claydon, and told his bailiff not to enter his son Edmund's house in East Claydon. Sir John Verney followed similar measures during another outbreak in 1698.[12] Markets were avoided during smallpox outbreaks, and a destitute vagrant woman with an infected child was quickly provided with food and clothes and moved on.[13]

The parson was as fearful of smallpox as his parishioners and in 1722 after visiting a sick parishioner commented 'if I were to begin the world again, I think it were proper for me to be inoculated, to qualify me for the exercise of my function on those occasions'. Only a year earlier Lady Mary Wortley Montagu's daughter had been inoculated in the glare of publicity.[14] Measles caused higher mortality and anxiety in the eighteenth century, and when a child was diagnosed with it in 1674 the family burst into tears. Measles recurred every few years in the Claydons and in 1710–11 eight houses in Middle Claydon were affected and 'most of every family have them'.[15]

Epidemics were a recurrent feature of life in the three Claydon parishes, but the population generally recovered quickly. The three severest outbreaks were all unidentified 'fevers', and East Claydon sustained higher mortality than its neighbours in all three outbreaks because its position on a main road made it the first point of contact and infection from outside, and made effective preventative techniques more difficult. East Claydon suffered the only plague deaths in 1665. Middle Claydon with its more dispersed farms and population and preventative measures firmly organised by the squire appears to have suffered least from

[12] srv to ev?3 July 1679 R33; sjv to wc 24 February 1697/8 R50.
[13] srv to Margaret Elmes 15 October 1666 R21; srv to ev 7 November 1667 R22; rvjr to rv 8 September 1741 R58.
[14] wb to rv 25 December 1722 CIH 4/5/68.
[15] wc to srv 21 February 1674/5 CIH 4/5/26; Joseph Churchill to rv 18 January 1710/11 R54; cc to sjv 14 January 1710/11 CIH 4/5/62.

such crises. Steeple Claydon occupied a middle position despite its greater population.

Epidemics were not a major factor in Middle Claydon's population decline, which needs further analysis. The reconstitution of Middle Claydon's parish registers from 1580 to 1820 provides additional information, supplemented by data about the twenty-five most frequently occurring surnames in Middle Claydon from the adjoining parishes of East and Steeple Claydon, Addington, and Grendon Underwood.[16] The small size of the parish limits the statistical value of reconstitution but provides vital information about events, families, and households.

The reconstitution revealed very high levels of migration. As we saw in chapter 6, Sir Ralph Verney's leasing policy after 1656 led to high tenant turnover. The shift from mixed agriculture to pastoral farming encouraged the family to seek out tenants with specialist expertise from elsewhere. Pasture farming required a much lower workforce, accentuating mobility amongst the poorer farming and labouring groups seeking employment, amongst teenagers seeking positions as farm and domestic servants, and the 'surplus' population in general. Where experienced farmers took on leases in mid-life, they brought their wives and part-complete families with them.

When data from adjoining parishes was added, surprisingly few significant additions could be made to the reconstituted Middle Claydon families. Sometimes register entries were too imprecise, but families with common surnames found in adjoining villages were not often closely inter-connected. In some cases a surname appeared in adjoining parishes at different periods without any clear link. Moreover, a majority of those entries in East and Steeple Claydon which specifically referred to Middle Claydon inhabitants could not be linked to reconstituted families. Insofar as Middle Claydon had a resident and active parson throughout the period poor registration cannot easily be blamed. High rates of local and short-term migration are far more likely.

The persistence of surnames is a useful indicator of long-term family turnover. A comparison of surnames in the 1522–5 muster and subsidy returns with those from the Restoration Hearth Tax listings shows high population mobility even before Middle Claydon's enclosure.[17] Of thirty-three names in the early sixteenth century, only four, Verney, Hinton, Barton, and Hicks, were present after the Restoration. Comparison of rentals, rate listings, and tax assessments

---

[16] The parish registers for these parishes are all at BCRO. Those for East Claydon have some defective periods while the Steeple Claydon registers suffer from fire damage and can only be read with difficulty. They were supplemented by reference to the Bishops' Transcripts.

[17] The early Tudor listings are to be found in Buckinghamshire Record Society vols. 8 and 17; the Hearth Tax names are taken from the 1662 return, and the 1671 listing of exempt households PRO E179/354 (?1662) and E179/324.

in 1646–8 shows a 30 per cent turnover in that short period and substantial differences between all three lists. Between the Hearth Tax listings and the Posse Comitatus return of males aged 16 to 60 of 1798, only two surnames, Roades and Hinton, persist.[18] Reconstitution confirms this pattern. Analysing the 400 reconstructed marriages by family name, 148 (37%) came from families with five or more households, but only 63 (15.75%) from four surnames with more than ten households. No family surname survived in Middle Claydon throughout the period from 1560 to 1820, though some families persisted for quite long periods. The Roadeses first came into Claydon in the 1630s, and were still present in 1800 and beyond. The Kings (1562–1755), Butchers (1601–1800), Scots (1620–1721), Hintons (1618–1800), and Hicks (1588–1750) all stayed for several generations, but for a parish of 50+ households reducing to perhaps 20 to 25, this was a small percentage. A lively turnover of Middle Claydon families in the early seventeenth century accelerated with the disruption of the Civil War, and the enclosure of 1654–6 provoked further emigration. Thereafter landlord policy and use of the Settlement Act of 1662 reduced in-migration.

London was attractive as an obvious source of employment, and many individuals found service or apprenticeship there through relatives, friends, or Sir Ralph Verney's patronage. In 1707 John Hicks went to live with his brother there. More migration was local. Farmers and craftsmen commonly recruited their servants within a radius of five to ten miles of the Claydons. Farmers might well come much longer distances. In 1696, Sir Ralph Verney needed a new tenant for one of his prime pastures, Knowl Hill. Of four prospective tenants mentioned, one came from Oving (five miles), another from Stewkley (eight miles) and a third from Aylesbury (ten miles).

Widespread migration at all social levels meant that village families had long-distance connections. Edward Faulkner, an East Claydon copyholder, had a brother, who was a Brentford wharfinger. When Widow Warner died in 1683, the only relative available to look after her children was her brother, who lived in Windsor. In 1732, a Portsmouth dockyard worker who feared redundancy sought help from the Verneys because his father had kept the Swan Inn in East Claydon. Eighty years earlier, Henry Birch's settlement case shows that he was sent to Middle Claydon in 1656 claiming residence there, but the churchwardens alleged that 'he had no dwelling at our town but only by stealth and force in the time of war'. Birch had not lived in Claydon for the past year but the parish register shows five children born between 1643 and 1652, so his residence had hardly been transient. He had been born in Gloucestershire.[19]

---

[18] See I. F. W. Beckett, *The Buckinghamshire Posse Comitatus of 1798*, Buckinghamshire Record Society 22 (1985), pp. 58–9.

[19] srv to wr 19 July 1656 R14. Cf. K. Wrightson, and D. Levine, *The Making of an Industrial Society: Whickham, 1560–1765* (Oxford 1991).

Table 7.1 *Origins of parties to Middle Claydon marriages 1600–1800*

Marriage type	No.	%	No. with children	Percentage
Both Middle Claydon	29	22.8	18	62.7
Husband Middle Claydon, wife not	11	11	7	50.0
Wife Middle Claydon, husband not	66	51.9	8	12.2
Neither Middle Claydon	18	14.2	0	0.0

Local migration is most evident in the origins of marriage partners. Partners from nearby villages predominated with a good sprinkling from adjoining counties, particularly Oxfordshire and Northamptonshire. With three exceptions, all marriage partners, including out-county ones, came from within thirteen miles of Middle Claydon. Two exceptions were Butterfields, the family which provided three successive rectors of Middle Claydon, and whose social status gave them wider marriage horizons. The third, a Middle Claydon woman's marriage to a man called Plestoe from Middleton Cheney in Northamptonshire (fifteen miles away), is easily explained. He was the Verneys' regular carrier, so passed through the village four or five times a week on his journeys to London. Surprisingly, East and Steeple Claydon were not the most important sources of marriage partners. East Claydon was an important source of husbands for Middle Claydon women, but Steeple Claydon played only a minor part, and was less important than the nearby market town of Winslow.

Couples often migrated when they married and set up a separate household. Only 127 out of the 400 Middle Claydon marriages give date of marriage and place of origin of both partners. When these are analysed by type (table 7.1) they illustrate a particular problem associated with marriage customs.

In few marriages were both partners from Middle Claydon, which is not surprising in a small parish with a falling population. More importantly, most Middle Claydon marriages were in the wife's home village before she and her husband set up house elsewhere. Few of their children were baptised there, although in one or two cases, the woman came back to Middle Claydon to baptise her first child, as when John Millward of East Claydon married Ann Butterfield. Their first child was baptised in Middle Claydon, but all her other children in East Claydon.

Middle Claydon's declining population was the result of changing estate organisation and farming patterns and their repercussions on the availability of work and farming opportunities. These economic pressures had a very human dimension. The Verneys exerted many pressures on the existing population, and on those who sought to move into the parish. They operated within a framework of social responsibility as well as power to maintain social cohesion and community harmony and prevent the intervention of the law in their very personal jurisdiction. They wished to exclude other JPs, administrative supervision from Quarter Sessions, and the formal operation of the criminal and civil law, from their parishes and estates wherever possible.

Poor Law administration was regarded as a personal fiefdom on their own estates, but often extended further into the hundred or petty session area. Between 1710 and 1714 the Verneys were involved in four separate 'boundary' determinations with neighbouring landowners. A letter of 1712 expressed the underlying ethos well:

> I do not think it Civil to interfere in your parish which is the reason I did not make an order for the bearer to be relieved. I am sure you are the best judge & if you think she ought to be relieved it being your own parish no body ought to order relief to her but yourself; it has formerly been a resolution taken amongst the Gentlemen that another justice should not meddle where another inhabits it being supposed that every justice is the best judge who ought to be relieved in their respective parishes; which is the reason that I do not care to meddle in this affair.[20]

The family was as successful in excluding outsiders in criminal as well as civil and administrative matters. Certainly in the later seventeenth and early eighteenth century most thefts and affrays were dealt with directly by the Verneys and their agents. Any attempt by villagers to use other justices or Quarter Sessions to deal with crimes and disputes was considered an affront to their landlord.

There can be no doubt that the Verneys put a high priority on ensuring that Middle Claydon's population did not increase. The underlying philosophy was quite openly expressed by Middle Claydon's parson, Edward Butterfield, in 1671. At a time when pamphleteers feared that declining population threatened England's economic and military prowess he wrote: 'those that are like to multiply may do it for the King, but not for Middle Claydon'.[21] To control Middle Claydon's population the Verneys used a range of positive and negative incentives. They aimed to control attempts by outsiders to gain settlement in the parish, to encourage young people with low employment prospects to move elsewhere, and to delay and prevent what they viewed as improvident marriages. A vital aspect of this was control of housing. The Verneys owned the whole housing stock in Middle Claydon and disposed of it as they pleased. When farms were combined, or re-planned, new houses were set up, houses were moved, or where necessary pulled down.[22]

---

[20] Francis Mardston to sjv 28 June 1712, R54. The other references are: William Aubrey [of Boarstall] to sjv 14 August 1710 R54; Nicholas Merwin to sjv 15 July 1711 R54; Peter Dayrell to sjv 12 April 1714 R55; cc to sjv 23 November 1710, ClH 4/5/61.

[21] eb to srv 6 February 1670/1, ClH 4/5/23.

[22] See John Broad, 'Housing the rural poor in southern England, 1650–1850', *Agricultural History Review*, 48:2 (2000), pp. 151–70, and for particular instances ch. 6 above.

Attempts to control marriage were more subtle. The Verneys expected to be informed of the marriage plans of any villager, and to pronounce on it.[23] This was particularly true of household servants and members of the community on the edge of poverty. The Verneys frowned on what they considered imprudent marriages. Widow Durant had been married to Sir Ralph Verney's French cook, but insisted that she would only remarry if Sir Ralph approved. He made approval dependent on the successful outcome of enquiries about her suitor and insisted that until approval had been granted 'I cannot consent to his dwelling in that house.' Parson Butterfield was instructed to inform her that 'I am not against her marriage provided she see something settled on her self and children and that she chooseth an honest sober man.' Widow Durant waited until Sir Ralph had returned to the country before allowing the man to continue his advances.[24] In 1681, a Mr Mason was pursuing Sir Ralph's housekeeper at Claydon. She insisted: 'I shall do nothing without acquainting you first of all so I will be sure to follow your counsel, knowing it will be nothing but what shall be for my good.'[25] The gamekeeper at Claydon was secretive in 1695 and provoked an angry response from Sir Ralph who wrote:

The keeper now writes me word he is married 'tis strange he would not acquaint me with it before I came from home, but since 'tis so it shall be the worse for him . . . He has highly disobliged me in not acquainting me of his intended marriage before I came from Claydon.[26]

Servants had good reasons for consulting their master, hoping not just for his approval, but for help either financially or through patronage.

The Verneys also wielded their power through control of housing and charity. The case of the Butcher family shows how the Verneys could profoundly affect ordinary labouring families, but also the limitations of their power. John Butcher was born in Middle Claydon in January 1640, and his father had been born there thirty-nine years previously. In May 1660 Butcher requested permission to marry a local girl. He had nowhere to live but claimed the right to occupy his father's old house, which had been locked up. Sir Ralph refused permission but Butcher arranged a marriage ceremony in neighbouring Winslow. He called it off when he discovered that Sir Ralph had ordered the bailiff, Hugh Holmes, to pull down the chimney and removed the floorboards in the old house, making it uninhabitable. This successfully delayed the marriage.[27]

Two and a half years later the couple were reported to 'own one another in public' and remained determined to marry 'though all sober people dissuade

---

[23] Cf. S. Hindle, 'The problem of pauper marriage in seventeenth-century England', *Transactions of the Royal Historical Society* 6th series, 8 (1998), pp. 71–89.

[24] eb to srv 13 and 20 May 1672 4/5/25; srv to eb 14 May 1672 ClH 4/5/25.

[25] E. Lillie to srv 6 January 1680/1 R35; srv to E. Lillie 10 January 1680/1 R35.

[26] srv to wc 30 January 1694/5 ClH 4/5/47.

[27] eb to srv 14 May 1660, R17; eb to srv 4 June 1660, R17; hh to srv 4 June 1660, R17.

what they can, yet it does but kindle the flame'. The bailiff pulled down another empty house to prevent the couple setting up house. Those who supported the marriage egged Butcher on to 'get up her belly'. They argued that Sir Ralph would be glad of a marriage (perhaps influenced by the fact that Butcher's sister had mothered two bastards in the previous ten years). By now the girl was 'afraid if she put him off she shall never have another'. Butcher hoped Sir Ralph would relent at the time of Edmund Verney's marriage to Mary Abell and even hoped that the Verneys might help the couple in some way, such as getting them shipped to the colonies as vagrants. In April Butcher threatened a secret marriage, claiming the girl was pregnant.[28] In June Butcher's patience finally ran out and the couple married by licence away from Middle Claydon and without Sir Ralph's permission. Butcher and his wife then returned to Middle Claydon, squatting in a barn where the bailiff, Hugh Holmes, found him at work, presumably at his craft of carpentry. Sir Ralph now tried to prevent Butcher obtaining a house from Quarter Sessions by sending Holmes round to seven of the local justices to explain the case.

Sir Ralph was overruled, but his fears for what he considered an improvident marriage were fulfilled. The family had at least two children, and remained poor. Butcher was exempt from the Hearth Tax in 1671, needed money from the poor rate and village charities by at least 1680, yet their children 'live idle at home'. Butcher was the only breadwinner, and on one occasion Sir Ralph and the parson pressed the churchwardens to threaten to withhold charity unless the couple put their children into service. This cycle of poverty renewed itself at the next generation. In 1695 Parson Butterfield reported:

Jack Butcher has been asked to Mrs Verney's dairy maid thrice and nobody has been so kind as to forbid the banns and without you please suddenly to interpose he will doubtless run headlong into execution.[29]

The Verneys much preferred such couples to leave the parish and settle elsewhere before they married. In 1688 Sir Ralph Verney gave precise advice to a youth who wished to marry:

if he is resolved to go to Solebury or any other place let him first go into service there for one half year at least that he may be settled there before he marries, or else the inhabitants will not admit him there without better security than he is able to give. Therefore I pray advise him not to marry until by service he is well settled in some place lest the parish cause him to be removed.[30]

---

[28] hh to srv 16 February 1662/3, R18 and 25 June 1663, R19; eb to srv 2 March 1662/3 R18 and 26 April 1663 R19.

[29] wb to srv 22 February 1682/3; srv to wc 26 February 1682/3, CIH 4/5/35; wb to srv 31 March 1695, 4/5/48.

[30] srv to ev 11 October 1688 R43.

The Verneys were also active in seeking out the fathers of illegitimate children born in the village. They made great efforts to find husbands for pregnant servants, and opposed farmers who sent away female servants whom their sons had made pregnant. This was not simply a matter of propriety. Unmarried mothers and fatherless children were far more likely to be a burden on the rates. Thus when 'Bett's daughter' became pregnant in 1723 and her man ran off, the Verneys' steward Chaloner began to search for a likely husband and found one in Winslow.[31] Even if a bastard child died soon after birth, there could be social problems. When Widow Welhead's son fathered a child on a servant living in the family home in 1698, the Verneys tried, unsuccessfully, to prevent her being turned out of the parish. Their reasons were practical, not humanitarian: 'if she should be turned off and go begging about she may I fear hereafter be sent to the parish with a child or two at her back'. The Welheads should keep her until her year's contract was out and then place her in another parish.[32] Such policies combined a sense of moral righteousness with the successful operation of parish settlement policies. In 1681 we can see a paternity dispute from the other parish's point of view. A servant from Stowe who impregnated a Middle Claydon girl 'by Sir Ralph Verney's persuasion, or for want of security to keep him out of gaol, or both together, married her'. The child died soon after the marriage, but the couple now insisted that the husband's parish should provide a house for them.[33]

The statistical effect of these policies on population figures cannot be shown because of the small size of the Middle Claydon reconstitution sample. However, age at marriage in reconstituted families shown in table 7.2 provides some evidence. The age at marriage of only thirty-two women and twenty-four men can be determined with reasonable certainty but they are unevenly distributed over the period. A breakdown by half-century periods gives the result shown in table 7.2. It would be unwise to infer much, but women's age at first marriage appears to have been higher in the period 1650 to 1750 than before or afterwards. This conforms to national trends, but the derived figure of around twenty-eight is over two years higher than national estimates for that period. The significance of the fact that men were consistently younger than their wives at marriage before 1750 is doubtful. Most such marriages resulted in the couple moving away from Middle Claydon, and would not significantly affect the parish's demography.[34]

---

[31] cc to rv 10 November 1723 R57; 19, 24, and 28 November 1723 CIH 4/5/69.

[32] sjv to wc 19 Jan 1697/8 R50, 9 February 1697 R50.

[33] Huntington STT 1704 John Risely to Sir Richard Temple 27 June 1681. Cf. Warrants and Removal orders concerning William Matthew's pregnant servant's marriage and removal to Chetwode 31 March 1681 and 14 April 1681 R35.

[34] See Wrigley, Davies, Oeppen, and Schofield, *English Population History from Family Reconstitution 1580–1837*, table 5.3, p. 134.

Table 7.2 *Age at first marriage of Middle Claydon inhabitants by period 1601–1800*

Period	Age at first marriage of Middle Claydon inhabitants by period			
	Women	Number	Men	Number
1601–50	26.5	4	(26)	1
1651–1700	28.1	6	27.2	12
1701–50	28.0	14	26.6	7
1751–1800	25.4	8	26.6	4
1601–1800	27.2	32	26.8	24

The incidence of pre-nuptial pregnancy indicates the effects of Verney supervision of Middle Claydon. Of the fifty-six first children whose parents' date of marriage is known, twelve (21.4 per cent) were born less than eight months after the marriage. On five occasions, the marriage took place around the time of the birth of the child. Thomas May and Dorothy Flower married on the very day she gave birth to their son Thomas in 1621. Two couples married seven and ten days before a child was born, two others married six days and three weeks after the births. Of the twelve instances, four were during the seventeenth century, and eight during the eighteenth. There were only three cases between 1638 and 1746 when the Verneys were most closely supervising their estates. This conforms to national trends for the period which show lower extra-marital and pre-nuptial pregnancy associated with a near-stagnant population. In Middle Claydon the significance of high level of supervision of families and marriage is therefore unclear.[35] These direct methods of population control may have had some effect in delaying marriages, and encouraging couples to move elsewhere unless they had a prosperous livelihood. However, those who attempted to settle in the parish were a greater threat in the eyes of most landlords and parishes in the later seventeenth and early eighteenth centuries.

The settlement act of 1662 set precise parameters in contentious areas between communities and enunciated four major methods of obtaining settlement: birth, marriage, residence, and tenancy. For the poor, birth, marriage, and residency were the most relevant. It was vital to ensure that outsiders – visitors, lodgers, or vagrants – did not give birth in the village. Sir Ralph Verney was furious to discover that one his tenants, Will Symonds, had allowed Tom Harris's wife to have her baby in his house in Middle Claydon. The woman arrived late in pregnancy, and the child was born before the overseers, or more likely Sir Ralph's bailiff William Coleman, were able to notify their master. A furious Sir Ralph recalled how once before Henry Scott had allowed a beggar woman

[35] Wrigley and Schofield, *The Population History of England 1538–1871*, p. 254.

to lie in in his barn. Eleven years later the parish was faced with a bill for twenty nobles (£6 13s 4d).[36] In 1723 Bett's daughter became pregnant. When her man refused to marry her, Middle Claydon tried to get her removed to Shipton in Winslow or Addington because the girl had been in service for a year or more in both parishes. The motive was to prevent the child being able to claim settlement in Middle Claydon.[37] In 1738, the Verneys threatened to remove Tom Roades and his wife, who lived in the parish when his wife was about to give birth. Tom Roades was told to obtain a settlement certificate from his own parish to prevent any future charge on Middle Claydon.[38]

Those who obtained their settlement by marriage were grudgingly accepted. When Gamball remarried in 1670, Sir Ralph was most reluctant to let his new wife and her daughter come and live in Middle Claydon. When Richard Scarlet's widow returned to Claydon in 1674, Sir Ralph accepted that 'she cannot be refused . . . for she is an inhabitant and [if] she want the overseers of the poor must find her work'. He rather grudgingly went on 'but in strictness they are not bound to find her a house' but suggested that his son might find her somewhere to lodge 'at his pleasure'.[39]

Those who tried to return to Middle Claydon after migration found a much frostier reception and the Verneys made it impossible for any who had obtained settlement elsewhere to move back. Adult children of villagers who returned to the family home found the parish authorities in hot pursuit. In 1666, Jane Long sought approval from Parson Butterfield for her daughter to 'come down to her mother' and care for her in sickness. She was warned that 'if she came without your [Sir Ralph's] leave there was a warrant ready to send her away again, which I think will prevent that'.[40] In 1696, Betty Roades returned to Middle Claydon, but Sir Ralph remarked that 'she having served her time there [elsewhere] is an inhabitant, and cannot be forced on Middle Claydon'.[41] The Verneys put Goodwife Guttridge in a very difficult position in 1686 when her son returned to live with her. William Coleman was ordered to prepare a warrant to prevent him gaining settlement, and to discover the details of a robbery in North Marston he had been involved in, in which the boy's mother had settled with the accusers. This was technically compounding a felony and could be used as leverage over mother and son. Goodwife Guttridge found her son a servant's place in Bourton or Thornborough, but he refused it, and parish pressures forced her to send him away with ten shillings.[42]

The harsh treatment of returning apprentices, servants, and relatives contrasts ironically with the help they had been given to find opportunities elsewhere in

---

[36] wb to srv 28 August 1682 ClH 4/5/35; srv to wc 28 August 1682 4/5/35.
[37] cc to rv 8 December 1723 ClH 4/5/69.   [38] rv to J Millward 25 November 1738 R58.
[39] eb to srv 6 and 20 February 1670/1 ClH 4/5/23; srv to eb 3 December 1674 4/5/27.
[40] eb 17 December 1666 ClH 4/5/19.   [41] srv to wc 9 May 1696 ClH 4/5/49.
[42] srv to wc 4 January 1685/6 ClH 4/5/38; wc to srv 14 January 1685/6 4/5/38.

the first place. The Verneys frequently offered local people help by finding servants' places or paying apprenticeship costs away from the parish, both of which carried settlement with them. Sir Ralph Verney and his son Sir John frequently paid sums of £5 or £6 for apprenticeships, particularly when there were family problems. In one case a widow's son, in another a boy who was 'ingenious, yet he had an untoward mother', were the beneficiaries.[43] In 1700, John Bett found an apprenticeship for his younger son to a tailor in Hillesden, who demanded £5. Bett asked Sir John Verney and the parish to pay for it, which they readily did. Such money became a regular estate outgoing, and in 1675 Edmund Verney announced that he would not bind out a boy this year because his building repair costs were so high.[44]

The long-distance kinship and village networks that went with high population mobility provided information about work elsewhere. In 1668, with the help of his sister Margaret Elmes, Sir Ralph paid for an apprenticeship in London for William Scott. Six years later a twenty-year-old village youth, William Lea, wanted a London apprenticeship and William Scott was asked to 'help him to a place'.[45] Elizabeth Roades, who returned to Middle Claydon in 1695, had obtained a settlement in Shefford in Bedfordshire by apprenticeship to learn lacemaking with the sister of the poor overseer, Abraham Teagle.[46] The range of occupations into which people were placed was wide. Apart from the girls who learnt lacemaking, there were placements as tailors, ship's carpenters, and button-mould pressers, as well as the usual range of country crafts, and various unspecified trades.

The young people of Middle Claydon were encouraged to find employment and settlement elsewhere, but those who arrived in the village as servants, apprentices, or lodgers, were intensely watched to prevent them gaining settlement. In 1670 a poor sick woman, Judith May, wanted to bring a kinswoman from Buckingham to Claydon to look after her, claiming that she intended to make the girl her heir. Parson Butterfield's advice was that 'perhaps it would not be amiss to enter a complaint against her that she steal not in as an inhabitant'. In 1725 the parish was 'very uneasy' when William Hinton took in a 'foolish wench' from East Claydon 'for her victuals'. His reply was that 'he did not do it with any design of bringing her in to be a parishioner for he would turn her away at Michaelmas next'.[47] The Verneys were quite explicit about keeping servants for less than a year to prevent them gaining settlement. In 1741 the second earl wrote of his coachman '"tis now time almost Waraker was gone that he may not serve his year up'. In searching for a replacement, a failed collarmaker with a

[43] eb to srv 2 January 1664/5 ClH 4/5/17 and 6 June 1666 R22.
[44] wc to sjv 7 July 1700 ClH 4/5/53; sjv to wc 10 July 1700 4/5/53; ev to srv 1 March 1674/5 R28.
[45] srv to M. Elmes 12 June 1668 R22; wc to srv 24 December 1674 ClH 4/5/27.
[46] wc to srv 11 May 1695 ClH 4/5/48.
[47] eb to srv 9 Jan 1669/70 ClH 4/5/22; cc to rv 14 February 1724/5 R 57.

wife who earned her living and two grown sons was rejected because he might gain a settlement.[48] By the mid-eighteenth century, servants rarely stayed in their jobs in a closed parish however good their work performance.[49]

Some people did slip through the net and gained settlement. Phoebe Dunn was sent from Winslow to Claydon in 1717 because she had once been a servant there, and an appeal seems to have failed. Sarah Dunn (possibly a relative, though there are no Dunns in the parish register) wrote begging support from Towcester when she had caught smallpox. The overseers there would not relieve her because she was settled in Middle Claydon.[50] Will Holdum had been born in East Claydon, but had become an inhabitant of Swanbourne, presumably by service or apprenticeship. In 1678 he returned to East Claydon as a servant, but fell sick after eight days and returned to his father's house to be nursed for two months. Then he suddenly married and became an inhabitant of the village by residence. No one had protested against his stay while in his sickness, which as Edmund Verney wryly commented, must have been 'in his tail'.[51] The successful application of the settlement laws played a significant part in Middle Claydon's falling eighteenth-century population.

Servants and apprentices were rapidly scrutinised by the overseers and the Verneys because they rarely had significant resources of their own. A sprinkling of individuals and families attempted to enter the village as lodgers. They were not necessarily removed unless they seemed likely to fall into poverty. When John Clarke and his wife and family arrived in Claydon from London in 1673 and tried to settle there, William Coleman immediately entered a complaint against them with Justice Dormer fearing that a small sick child in the family would prove costly. Yet in 1676 Widow Clarke was living in Claydon, and herself under pressure not to bring lodgers into the village.[52]

A number of people such as the Guttridge family persistently took in lodgers. They were often poor households and widows feature prominently among them. William Symonds, who had allowed Tom Harris's wife to give birth at his house in 1682 was taken to Quarter Sessions by the overseers in 1689 in an attempt to stop him lodging beggars.[53] In 1696, Widow Mathews took in a lodger who claimed to be a travelling dealer who bought hair for wigs. William Coleman reported: 'I hear of none that know him and all eyes are on him for a suspicious person.' In 1700 a village row involved a journeyman tailor who lodged with Widow Bates. When he quarrelled with her he went to lodge with Widow Roades.[54]

[48] rvjr to rv 16 July 1741 R58.
[49] See Middle Claydon poor overseers' accounts Buckinghamshire CRO PR52/12/1–4.
[50] cc to rv 1 August and 6 October 1717 R56; Sarah Dunn to rv 30 September 1719 R56.
[51] ev to srv 30 December 1678 R32.
[52] wc to srv 16 January 1672/3 ClH 4/5/25 and 18 January 1676/7 4/5/29.
[53] Richard Harding's account, March 1688/9 R43.
[54] wc to srv 15 March 1695/6 ClH 4/5/48; wc to sjv 7 July 1700 4/5/53.

Lodgers or those they lodged with were asked to give security for their residence. In 1654, a man wanted his brother-in-law to come and live with him in Claydon. He asked Sir Ralph Verney and the parson to allow it. Sir Ralph told his steward William Roades to give the man some advice 'to meddle not . . . unless he be certain to have a considerable part of his estate to keep him . . . and tell him the Town will expect security and there he had best care to order it so as neither he nor the Town be burdened by him'.[55] When Nathaniel Holland of East Claydon asked to become tenant for an empty Middle Claydon house, William Coleman supported his application. He was a single man with property in East Claydon and Brackley who would be able to pay his rent and was unlikely to be 'burdensome to your parish'. Sir John Verney nevertheless ordered his steward to check up on this information. On the other hand, ten years later, Thomas Harding was discouraged from letting the East Claydon house he owned and coming to Middle Claydon. As the eighteenth century went on it became harder to move into Middle Claydon except as a tenant of one of the medium or larger size farms.[56]

Farmers who took on apprentices in Middle Claydon were expected to inform their landlord (preferably asking his permission), and were frequently asked to sign a document promising to take personal responsibility for the costs of the apprentice's future poverty. Wat King took on a Botolph Claydon girl to learn lacemaking for three years. He and his father had to go to Parson Butterfield to 'pass their words the child shall be no damage to the parish'. Twelve years later, Ralph Roades's wife took a Hogshaw girl as an apprentice lacemaker. She was most assertive that it was her business and not her husband's. The girl was shown to be heiress to property in Quainton, and therefore unlikely to be a charge. Not all apprentices lasted long enough to be harassed. When John Clements took on an apprentice to learn his trade of glovemaking in 1674, Sir Ralph wanted Clements to take on liability. Before this could be done it was discovered that the boy had been packed off to his parents within a week because he ate too much.[57]

Settlement through ownership of land was impossible in Middle Claydon, but renting a tenancy of more than £10 a year also gave automatic right to settlement in the parish. In Claydon, a farm of £10 a year could not support a family, or even a single man. As farms of five to twenty acres disappeared in the later seventeenth century and those between twenty and fifty acres were much reduced in the course of the eighteenth century, any tenant farmer who came into the parish automatically gained settlement.[58] This was a potential

[55] srv to wr 29 December 1654 R12.
[56] wc to srv 22 May 1701 ClH 4/5/51; cc to srv 25 January 1710/11 4/5/62.
[57] eb to srv 9, 15, and 30 December 1672 ClH 4/5/25; wc to srv 28 August 1684 4/5/37; eb to srv 20 and 27 July 1674 4/5/27.
[58] See above ch. 6, pp. 138–9.

problem when Claydon rents were high and the Verneys willing to distrain and evict tenants when they fell into difficulties. Some failed farmers such as John Hicks became a burden on the poor rates. A number of families undoubtedly became permanently settled in Middle Claydon because their farms failed. The most blatant example was Edward Dixon who arrived in Middle Claydon in March 1663 to farm one of the largest holdings. He was trading on credit, and had insufficient capital. Within a year he had been arrested for debt, and was soon farming a holding less than half the size of his original venture. He farmed for thirteen years, but by then his capital had been used up. He and his family then became dependent on wage labour, some carting, and charitable donations. Settlement might be used as a bargaining ploy when a man was near bankruptcy. In 1678 George Haynes asked Sir Ralph to let him leave the parish and start a new life elsewhere, which was mutually beneficial.[59]

Claim of settlement by tenancy could be a strategy by other parishes to force families who had at some time farmed in Middle Claydon back to that parish when they fell on hard times. Ephraim Cowdale, an East Claydon man who rented one of the new enclosures in Middle Claydon in 1658, caused great inter-parochial bitterness. He soon gave up the farm and returned to his native village. In 1669, the East Claydon overseers attempted to send Cowdale to Middle Claydon and the Verneys initially acquiesced 'since Cowdale is so simple and hath served you so ill'. In July the case went to Quarter Sessions where two East Claydon landowners (John Duncombe and John Millward) abused the Verneys so much that they insisted that Cowdale remain in East Claydon. The case went as far as the assizes where Sir Ralph used his influence with the judge. This experience soured the relationship between the Verneys and East Claydon's 'town'. Echoes of the case lingered on for years. In 1700, Sir John Verney (who had been in the Levant at the time of the case) wondered why the East Claydon overseers were again attempting to send Cowdale to Middle Claydon.[60]

The threshold figure of the £10 a year rent played its part in a fraudulent scheme to send another East Claydon inhabitant to Middle Claydon in 1711. Henry Hicks had been born in East Claydon, apprenticed in Marsh Gibbon at the age of fourteen but returned to his native village once the apprenticeship was complete. He set up as a butcher, paying forty shillings a year rent for his house, but in March 1710 his landlord evicted him, taking doors and windows off the house. The landlord then offered him a one-year lease of what purported to be Middle Claydon land for £10 a year and in November seized all his cattle and other stock. East Claydon overseers used this as a pretext for making

[59] For Haynes see wc to srv 4 February 1677/8 CIH 4/5/30.
[60] Lease dated 17 November 1658 CIH 4/2/59; srv to ev 30 June and 10 July 1669 R23; srv to ev 6 July 1669 and 2 February 1669/70 R23; sjv to wc 12 June 1700 4/5/53.

Middle Claydon pay his poor relief. The lease had no validity and when the Middle Claydon overseers complained the justices sent Hicks back to East Claydon, ordering the parish there to pay him 2s a week.[61]

In most cases the Verneys could use their economic power and social status to solve disputes without the formality of the law. Occasionally they needed the threat of an indictment and on a handful of occasions the Justices and Quarter Sessions saw cases before them. When they did involve the courts, the Verneys could be ruthless. Two well-documented examples come from Wasing in Berkshire, where they were substantial landowners, but not resident. Early in 1653, the parson at Wasing took in a lodger, against Sir Ralph Verney's wishes. William Roades was dispatched to Wasing with orders to take the Wasing overseers to see the local JP. Sir Ralph suggested that the parson should be charged 5s a week, to be levied weekly by distress, in addition to his parish rate. William Roades was also to find out if the lodger was married. If he was not, Roades was to tell the JP that the man should be given permission to marry 'and so charge the parish with a new brood at his pleasure'.[62] In a later settlement case at Wasing in 1679, Sir Ralph also went to considerable lengths. He felt that a widow and her two sons had been 'very unjustly settled at Wasing by Mr Brightwell', and fought the case at the Assizes. A letter gives full details of how the Lord Chief Justice and the other Assize judge could be influenced, the one through an acquaintance of his servant, the other by employing his 'favourite' lawyer. Sir Ralph's servant was forced to hang around the Lord Chief Justice's house for several days to discover which judge would take the trial. It was apparently normal to conceal this until the last moment so that the 'favourites are retained in all places'. Judge Atkins, the other Assize judge, appears to have had a son who travelled with him and was his 'favourite'. This attention to detail (and expense) resulted in at least a partial success with the Berkshire Justices.[63]

The strict application of the Settlement Laws and aid to migrating individuals, especially young people seeking places as servants and apprenticeships, was central to the loss of population in Middle Claydon. However, it was only part of a wider regime of control in which the compassionate side of the traditional paternal relationship was more prominent, if carefully directed. It was a contested sphere, between ancient customs and expectations from the medieval past and modern contractual relationships, between the gift and money economies. There were four participants: the landlord and his officials; the clergy and their

---

[61] cc to sjv 9, 16, 21, and 28 January 1710/11 ClH 4/5/62. Cf. Buckinghamshire Sessions Records III (1705–12), p. 264. The whole episode is encapsulated in the Quarter Sessions records as a simple confirmation of a removal warrant from Middle Claydon to East Claydon.

[62] srv to wr 1655/6 R13.

[63] srv to sjv 12th July 1679 R33; William Fall to srv 18 July 1679 R33; sjv to srv 31 July 1679 R33; cf. W. R. Prest, 'Judicial corruption in early modern England' *Past and Present*, 133 (1991), pp. 67–95.

spiritual and moral concerns; the farmers, whose views as ratepayers and parish office-holders came from a different perspective; and ordinary villagers. All had vital parts to play in village concerns such as crime, poverty, and religion.

The Verneys dominated the social structure of Middle Claydon. Their monopoly of landownership gave them the power to bring major changes to Middle Claydon's landscape and community. An analysis of the Restoration Hearth Tax returns illustrates the basic structure of the village and confirms their dominance. Middle Claydon had thirty-seven taxed households in 1662, while fourteen exempt houses were recorded in March 1671 and thirteen in the following September. There were only three houses of any size in the parish. Claydon House had forty-six hearths while the parsonage and Fimore Lodge, an old hunting lodge, had fourteen between them.[64] Claydon House was the largest building in the parish, and also in north Buckinghamshire. The parson's four-bay house had just been rebuilt by the Verneys. Fimore Lodge was now a farmhouse, where the bailiff, William Roades, had lived. The remaining houses averaged 1.44 hearths and none had more than three hearths. Even the substantial tenant farmers had small houses. Short leases gave them no incentive to invest in elaborate houses even if they were wealthy. Housing improvements accrued to the landlord who did not compensate an outgoing tenant, and many Buckinghamshire dairy farmhouses in the later seventeenth century remained small.[65]

The highly skewed social structure of Middle Claydon in the 1660s persisted through to 1820. Up until 1740 the family spent a considerable proportion of the year at their seat, and exercised power directly, or through the parson and the steward/bailiff. Two factors strengthened family influence over these omnipresent local figures. After enclosure, the Verneys paid the parson an annual salary instead of his tithes. Middle Claydon clergy now became highly dependent on their patron, and stayed for long periods. Edward Butterfield was the first of a dynasty who were rectors for over a hundred years. He was Sir Ralph Verney's confidant before he arrived at Claydon and had mediated in a quarrel between Verney and his predecessor, John Aris. He rapidly succeeded Aris and married his widow. His son and then his grandson, both called William, followed him. After a one-year interlude in 1759–60, Edward Millward followed the Butterfield dynasty and remained rector until 1806. Earlier, one of the Millwards had married William Butterfield's daughter Ann.

---

[64] The Hearth Tax assessments and exemptions are discussed above, p. 149. The assessment document is damaged and not all hearth numbers are legible, but the total and sufficient of the remaining entries remain to enable a plausible assessment of relative hearth numbers.

[65] On farmhouse building in Buckinghamshire at the time see Airs and Broad, 'The management of rural building in seventeenth-century Buckinghamshire', *Vernacular Architecture* 29 (1998), pp. 43–56.

The church reinforced traditional authority in many ways. The established religion christened, married, and buried most Englishmen. The village parson influenced his congregation by preaching, by reading out government proclamations, and by his frequent role as village schoolmaster. Most villagers paid lip-service to established religion since compulsory church attendance could be enforced in the church courts even after 1660. In Middle Claydon, absentees were easily visible since every family had its allotted place in church. A seating plan for 1674 shows how parishioners were divided both by sex – with separate men's and women's sides of the church – and by social status.[66] The richer farming families, and those holding posts under the Verneys, had pews near the front allocated according to the farm they occupied in the parish. The poor widows and those in receipt of poor relief sat towards the rear. Middle Claydon was closely regulated and most of the inhabitants attended regularly. Parson Butterfield thought it worth reporting that six days' severe snow early in March 1674 kept 'Thomas Gryme and all that dwell out of the Town from Church'.[67] Apathy and scepticism reduced church attendance in some seventeenth-century English parishes, but in response to Bishop Wake's visitation queries, William Butterfield reported 100 communicants at Easter 1709 and 150 in 1712, commenting that 'but few, if any, neglect it'. He held services twice on Sundays and on Holy and Litany days. The proportion of communicants in East and Steeple Claydon was far lower, with less than half those eligible attending, and the high figure for Middle Claydon is exceptional for Buckinghamshire, and indeed the whole diocese.[68]

Church services were social gatherings as well as acts of worship, and business and local gossip were frequently discussed there. In the later seventeenth century Middle Claydon followed a low church, Puritan tradition, in accordance with Sir Ralph Verney's beliefs. Christmas was celebrated modestly as a day of devotion, not feasting.[69] The steward wrote letters and even discussed financial matters with tenants at church as if it were a working day. On the other hand, successive parsons marked the anniversary of the execution of Charles I with respectful reverence and a day of mourning. Attitudes to older feast days were more complex. In May 1663, no workman turned up to work at Claydon House

[66] Cf. S. D. Amussen, *An Ordered Society: Gender and Class in Early Modern England* (Oxford 1988), pp. 137–44 and R. Gough, *The History of Myddle*, ed. D Hey (Harmondsworth 1981), pp. 80–4.
[67] eb to srv 2 March 1673/4 CIH 4/5/26.
[68] Broad, *Buckinghamshire Dissent*, pp. xxxv, 90–1, 204–6. By this stage, Butterfield's patron was Sir John Verney, whose views were far more partisan in their Tory and Anglican attachments. Butterfield's figure of 150 is probably a zealous exaggeration. His precise population figure of 1706 of 206 would imply that only just over 25 per cent of parishioners were under sixteen. This is possible but unlikely for a parish with a declining population in a period when nationally the ageing population structure gives a figure closer to 30 per cent of young people. See Wrigley and Schofield, *The Population History of England and Wales*, p. 35.
[69] srv to ? 9 December 1685 CIH 4/5/38.

on Ascension Day or on the following day, the King's birthday. When Sir Ralph Verney berated his bailiff on the subject he received a reply that invoked urban and rural differences. Holmes wrote: 'I doubt you forget Easter holy days and St George and St Mark now you are at London, but when you are at Claydon you will think of them as soon as anybody, therefore you cannot expect your business to be done as if there were no holy days.'[70] Nevertheless, Sir Ralph Verney's Puritan zeal influenced other traditional village observances. There are no references to a village feast in the village, though they remained in the other Claydons and elsewhere in the area, and in 1712 William Butterfield declared that there were no processions in Middle Claydon.

Sir Ralph Verney and his son Sir John both strongly upheld the Anglican church in Middle Claydon. Sir John Verney was very straightforward in his antipathy to non-conformity, but his father was much more ambiguous. Sir Ralph's Puritan views were well known in a locality where non-conformist ideas remained powerful in the later seventeenth century. Benjamin Leach of Winslow preached there after the Restoration and underwent a well-publicised trial for his beliefs in 1664. The Vicar of Water Stratford in the 1680s, John Mason, attracted crowds to his parish with his mystical visions and prophecies, and twenty years later still had a group of adherents meeting in Adstock. However, very few meeting houses from the area were registered at Quarter Sessions during the early eighteenth century.[71]

Middle Claydon's 1676 Compton census return lists only one dissenting family, and in 1706 and 1709 none were recorded there. However, dissent was more influential locally than these figures suggest. In East Claydon, the 1676 returns gave two names, yet in 1673 Thomas Deverell of East Claydon became a Quaker, and in 1678 three East Claydon men were excommunicated for their beliefs.[72] By 1706, there was just one Anabaptist in the village, and two in Steeple Claydon. Sir Ralph tolerated non-conformists among his tenants and villagers provided they did not proselytise or disturb the social order. Non-conformists considered him a sympathetic member of the elite, and appealed to him when under attack on several occasions. He was not active in enforcing the Conventicle Acts.[73]

Whenever non-conformity threatened the established order, Sir Ralph was hostile to it. In 1661 there were rumours of rebellion among the 'fanaticks' including Anabaptists and Quakers in Haddenham, Cuddington, and Long

---

[70] hh to srv 4 May 1663 ClH 4/5/16; 'work done May 1663' 4/5/16.

[71] See Broad, *Buckinghamshire Dissent*, Introduction. A printed account of Benjamin Leach's trial is found amongst the Verney papers for September 1664 R19.

[72] sjv to srv 19 May 1678 R31. In 1683 there was a Quarter Sessions order against dissenters in Claydon srv to ?ev 25 January 1682/3 ClH 4/5/35.

[73] A. J. Fletcher, 'The enforcement of the Conventicle Acts 1664–1679' in *Persecution and Toleration*, Studies in Church History, 21, ed. W. J. Sheils (Oxford, 1984), pp. 235–46. See also Broad, *Buckinghamshire Dissent*, pp. xvi–xviii.

Crendon, south of Claydon. Verney supported the raising of a gentry posse in anticipation of armed insurrection. He also kept notes of North Marston and East Claydon men who held meetings instead of attending church.[74] Within Middle Claydon, he forbade one of his tenants in the 1670s, Robert Stopp, from preaching in the parish but made no objection to his activities elsewhere. He greatly respected another tenant, Abraham Teagle, who was poor overseer for many years and ran the scheme for spinning and weaving hemp. Yet Teagle was probably a non-conformist. When Jane Bates was depressed and 'doubting', the housekeeper at Claydon reported that 'Mr Butterfield often visits her, but I fear Teagle doth endeavour to convert her to his principles.'[75] Fear of conversion also led to a long debate as to whether a renowned Quaker midwife should attend Edmund Verney's wife's childbirth, for women were considered more susceptible to conversion when distracted during labour.[76] William Grosvenor, Sir Ralph Verney's secretary, recorded notes of his vision and 'conversion' in 1681.[77] Sir Ralph permitted such privately held beliefs provided they did not threaten public order or established ways in the parish.

Edward Butterfield and later rectors also acted as agents for the Verneys, sometimes collecting rents, and sorting out local squabbles when the Verneys were away. They kept a watchful eye on the bailiff and household at Claydon, and reported independently on matters of interest in the neighbourhood. Their fortunes were closely tied to those of the Verneys and the Claydon estate. They offered frank advice, but never seriously quarrelled with their patrons. Together with a new breed of loyal stewards who stayed for a lifetime – William Coleman for thirty-eight years Charles Chaloner for twenty-two – they formed a new layer in the community, above the tenants in social rank.[78] Parson and steward enabled the Verneys to exert influence in Middle Claydon throughout the year. They were intermediaries in the processes of controlling lands, farms, and tenants but their relationship with the parish officers was particularly important. The parson supervised the selection of churchwardens, overseers of the poor, overseers of the highways, and parish constables. He sent lists with several names to the Verneys, and his own preference. These posts usually rotated between more substantial tenants and were drawn alternately from different parts of the parish to balance local interests. At the beginning of the eighteenth century, the office of churchwarden was reserved for tenants of the large farms out in the 'pastures'. The inhabitants of 'the town' – the village centre – provided constables and overseers. In theory, parish officers acted independently

[74] W. Bury to srv 29 January 1660/1 R17, srv memorandum dated 20 January 1660/1 R17.
[75] srv to wc 17 January 1677/8 R31; E. Lillie to srv 31 January 1680/1 R35.
[76] srv to ev 12 December 1666 R21; ev to srv 19 and 21 January 1666/7 R21.
[77] Two versions of this exist, one in the papers for May 1681 R35, the other amongst papers at the end of 1648 R9.
[78] Cf. Hainsworth, *Stewards, Lords, and People.*

of the landlord, but all were Verney tenants and under constant supervision. The Verneys rarely intervened directly, preferring to pass general comments to their agents. Through these officers the Verneys influenced village matters including poor relief payment, migration patterns, the distribution of charity moneys and of places in their almshouse.

One result was that the voice of ordinary villagers is muted after 1660. The sense of 'the town' as a collective entity had played an important role in village decision making during the Civil War and Interregnum but now disappeared. It lacked the semi-independent leadership of the parson, and to a lesser extent of the bailiff, that had existed before the Restoration. Abram Teagle's fifteen-year reign as poor overseer, with its emphasis on finding work for the unemployed, provides evidence that the Puritan 'better sort' had a continuing part to play in the later seventeenth century. 'The town' still influenced disputes over parish rates and poor relief. The overseers occasionally refused to pay as much relief as the Verneys suggested and sometimes reduced payments. On one occasion several farmers combined to subsidise a widow with a large family rather than see her evicted and become dependent on the rates. It was increasingly a ratepayers' rather than a village interest that made itself felt. The Verneys could not ignore it because the prosperous farmers undertook unpaid parish office, ensured that rates were paid, administered the poor law, and raised national taxes. Above all, they provided the Verneys with their major source of income. But a ratepayer's interest that was also a tenant interest was more generally supportive of the existing social order.

Middle Claydon's unified landownership and dependent elite and tenants made it easy to govern. When challenged on their estate, the Verneys could wield the powers that went with the offices of Justice of the Peace, Deputy Lieutenant, and Member of Parliament, and use the influence that long residence in the county gave them with so many other county families. Such unity made it difficult for conflicts to erupt in the village in the later seventeenth and eighteenth centuries. Sir Ralph once boasted that he was proud that he had never taken a man to court and Middle Claydon's inhabitants were indeed rarely involved in litigation. There is a paradox in all this. The sources for the history of Middle Claydon come predominantly from the landlord's side. The absence of alternative perspectives such as those from court cases reinforces the sense of local harmony and unity the Verneys so much wished to instil.

Informal controls ranged from the upholding of good name and reputation, to the settlement of intra-village disputes, and of breaches of the criminal law. The resident parson and bailiff at Middle Claydon communicated the views of the parish officers, and the mood of tenants and villagers. There were always people willing to report disloyalty amongst their neighbours. In 1693 Sir Ralph Verney heard that a tenant had told his bailiff that another tenant, Tom Matthews, had 'spoken ill' of Verney at Bicester fair. Matthews was immediately berated by

William Butterfield, and forced to make a special trip to London to explain himself to Sir Ralph (and presumably do secular penance). In the early eighteenth century, an informer in the East Claydon alehouse told the steward of a conversation about a poaching expedition in the Verneys' deer park. They were summoned and warned not to carry out their plan.[79]

The Verneys' attempts to extend their influence over tenants to landownership and politics showed the limits of their power. Tenants were expected not to criticise their landlord publicly. The Verneys also expected first refusal if a tenant intended to sell local land. A tenant who owned freehold land was entitled to vote in elections for parliament, but when Sir John Verney stood for election he could not automatically expect his tenants' support. Joseph Churchill was not just an ally but claimed distant kinship, and acted as an agent and adviser. Sir John may have felt aggrieved in 1702 when Churchill did not vote for him, but commented: 'I reckon when a freeholder rents land of me one voice is partly my due, though not altogether for my land.' In 1713, Verney wrote to Lord Cheyne that he could not rely on tenants to give him even one of their two votes.[80]

Recent research has reinforced the idea that parishes acted as little kingdoms, especially in parishes with elites below gentry level.[81] Landlord power extended beyond the boundaries of the parish, but could not openly threaten ancient ideas of freeholder independence, or indeed the rights of neighbouring gentry and JPs. Local administration was a personal fiefdom, extending out from their own estates into the hundred or petty session area. Boundaries between fellow justices and landowners have already been noted for poor law administration, but were also true of the judicial system.[82]

Within the petty sessions area a JP exerted a great deal of power and influence without reference to any court of record before the late eighteenth century. Very few criminal indictments refer to Middle Claydon in the late seventeenth- and early eighteenth-century Buckinghamshire Quarter Sessions. There are few Claydon court cases in Exchequer or Chancery in the same period. A JP had many opportunities for avoiding the formal legal processes. Alehouse licensing and poor law disputes were settled between friends and neighbours. JPs settled many disputes by arbitration and intervened to cool tempers in

[79] srv to wc ? January 1692/3 ClH 4/5/45.

[80] sjv to wc 13 May 1702 ClH 4/5/54; sjv to W. Cheyne 5 December 1714 R55; see also Whyman, *Sociability and Power*, ch. 6, on the Verneys in politics, as well as J. Broad, 'Sir John Verney and Buckinghamshire elections, 1696–1715', *Bulletin of the Institute of Historical Research* 61 (1983), pp. 195–204 and W. A. Speck, *Tory and Whig: The Struggle in the Constituencies 1701–15* (London 1970).

[81] Joan R. Kent, 'The centre and the localities: state formation and parish government in England circa 1640–1740', *Historical Journal* 38 (1995), pp. 363–404; S. Hindle, 'Power, poor relief, and social relations in Holland fen, *c.* 1600–1800', *Historical Journal* 41 (1998), pp. 67–96; D. Eastwood, *Government and Community in the English provinces, 1700–1870* (London and Basingstoke 1997); Eastwood, 'The republic in the village'.

[82] See page 159, n. 20 above.

informal ways recorded only in justices' notebooks, such as those of Sir Roger Hill, Henry Norris, and William Hunt.[83] The Verneys frequently intervened to minimise disputes and litigation in the interests of community peace. Attitudes changed subtly over time. Sir Ralph Verney frequently boasted that he never took people to court, and legal problems play a small part in his correspondence. Occasionally he threatened to go to law over rent arrears or in settlement cases but at Claydon few cases went further than the issue of writs and judgements, or beyond the lower courts.

From the moment he succeeded his father Sir John Verney threatened exemplary prosecutions to deter potential offenders for a number of possible reasons. He had lived in London, with its less personal and informal attitudes to crime and justice. He also wished to assert himself on his estates after living most of his adult life as the younger son of the family. Early in 1698, he insisted that the thief who had taken a furnace from Claydon House needed to be caught and punished to set an example. The following Christmas Sir John was most concerned that a man who was caught stealing a turkey was allowed to get away with it. Three years later he was intent on prosecuting a blatant and provocative poacher and wrote: 'I have a mind to make an example of him to deter others from poaching in my woods.' Yet the case was probably dropped when William Coleman pointed out that the miscreant's father was a local freeholder who supported Sir John in his political aspirations.[84] Ultimately Sir John and his successors, the eighteenth-century Verneys, pressed prosecutions no more vigorously than Sir Ralph had.

The Verneys settled most disputes by arbitration. Villagers referred a dispute over payments for washing clothes to Sir Ralph in 1662. In 1672 'Wat King and Thomas Miller were going to Law in all haste for some broad scandalous words spoken against honest Betty upon the Ale bench, but I have stopped it till your coming down.'[85] Sometimes villagers could settle such disputes themselves. In 1661 two villagers met for a duel with rapiers, but neighbours intervened to part them. On the other hand, Sir Ralph Verney arbitrated in other parishes such as Sir Richard Temple's parish of Finemere on the Oxfordshire border in 1681.[86]

---

[83] J. A. Sharpe, 'Enforcing the law in the 17th century English village' in V. A. C. Gatrell, B. Lanman, and G. Parkar (eds.), *Crime and the Law, The Social History of Crime in Western Europe since 1500* (London *c.* 1980); K. Wrightson, 'Two concepts of order' in J. Brewer, and J. Styles (ed.), *An Ungovernable People: The English and their Law in the Seventeenth and Eighteenth Centuries* (1980); Ruth Paley (ed.), *Justice in 18th Century Hackney: The Justicing Notebook of Henry Norris and the Hackney Petty Sessions Book*, London Record Society 28 (London 1991); E. Crittall (ed.), *The Justicing Notebook of William Hunt, 1744–9*, Wiltshire Record Society 37 (1982).

[84] sjv to wc 19 January 1697/8 R50; Elizabeth Verney to wc 27 December 1698 R50; sjv to wc 11 June 1701 CIH 4/5/54; wc to sjv 15 June 1701 4/5/54.

[85] hh to srv 23 December 1662 CIH 4/5/14; eb to srv 25 November 1672 4/5/25.

[86] eb to srv 24 June 1662 R17; Butterfield commented 'Now judge you whether you had not need take up the Commission to keep the peace.'

The Verneys intervened to keep village disputes out of the courts. One night in June 1700, three young villagers who had been drinking in the alehouse until past midnight wandered through the village on their way home. Richard Crawley was a journeyman tailor who had once lodged with Widow Bates but had quarrelled with the family. As he passed her house he hurled a stone through the dairy window and frightened the widow. Accompanied by her son and brother-in-law, she rushed to the JP in the next village, Captain Piggott, who bound the lads over to appear at Quarter Sessions. Sir John Verney was annoyed that they had immediately gone to law and wrote: 'I believe she prosecuted him out of spite' and his intervention apparently cooled tempers. When the Quarter Sessions met on 18 July the quarrel had been settled out of court, and recognisances were discharged.[87]

Many disputes were settled entirely within the community, as two examples show. In December 1674 some sheep were stolen in Middle Claydon. The victim applied for a search warrant from Sir John Busby in the adjoining parish of Addington. A notorious tenant, Dixon, was discovered to have mutton in his house, and an argument ensued. Both parties appealed to Edmund Verney in East Claydon, who referred them to his father. The case was due to be heard at Sessions in January but collapsed because no one was willing to prosecute Dixon, presumably because he had agreed to make restitution.[88] A case of wood stealing in 1711 was settled very simply. Sir John Verney's steward caught two twelve-year-old boys from Bottle Claydon and punished them by ordering them to clear up snow on various parts of the estate. Significantly, their fathers were required to make a formal apology at Claydon House.[89]

If the Verneys were unaware of a developing situation, informal methods were less effective. On one occasion, village feeling became overwhelmingly hostile to one party in a dispute and invoked the very potent sanction of ostracism. Anne Warner came from an old Claydon family. She had one brother who lived in East Claydon and another who was a prosperous farmer in Old Windsor. Her husband, John Warner came from another local family. Five children were christened in Middle Claydon during the 1670s and there was at least one other child, probably born in 1667 or 1668. John Warner died early in 1683 and his widow continued to farm to support her six children, none of whom was yet adult. Perhaps she was under financial strain when in

[87] On recognisances see R. B. Shoemaker, *Prosecution and Punishment: Petty Crime and the Law in London and Rural Middlesex 1660–1725* (Cambridge 1991), chs. 2, 3, 5; the discharge is noted in W. Le Hardy and G. Ll. Reckitt, *Calendar of Buckinghamshire Quarter Sessions Records*, vol. ii (Aylesbury 1936), p. 261 Crawley's companions, Henry King and William Webb, were both described as 'dairyman'.

[88] Robert Parrott to srv 3 December 1674 ClH 4/5/27; wc to srv 3 December 1674 4/5/27 and 4 January 1674/5 5/5/27. In another instance in 1711, separate thefts by different people of a 3d loaf and a bottle of ale were settled by an agreement by the thief to recompense to full value and pay the costs of the warrant (1s) that had been taken out: cc to sjv 3 June 1711 4/5/62.

[89] cc to sjv 1 February 1710/11 ClH 4/5/62.

January 1684 she was accused of stealing £60 from her sister's chest in East Claydon.[90]

Sir Ralph Verney was in London. He considered that a piece of milled money and a handkerchief found at her house, and other circumstantial evidence, would weigh heavily against her in court. She had paid off various debts before they were due. She had bought new clothes at Winslow with cash where before she had always used credit. Her son had bought a gun for 12s, which was more than the money that he claimed to have. Appearing before the magistrates at Brill in January 1684, she had only one surety, and asked William Coleman to be the other.[91]

Sir Ralph Verney ordered William Coleman to get her the best defence he could and to try and find villagers to testify to her good character and past honesty. He even wanted him to discover whether her sister would offer a general release. Verney was going out of his way to see fair play in a difficult situation in which Widow Warner was completely isolated. On 17 February, the case took a dramatic turn. As the trial loomed, Widow Warner fell ill and two weeks later was found dead in her bed. The extent of village ostracism now became apparent. No one was willing to lay out the corpse. Coleman had to order the poor overseers to organise it. No villager would play any part in burying her.[92]

The ostracism extended to her four orphaned children. Local relatives would not come and look after them, so they were left in the house with the body overnight. Eventually their uncle in Windsor provided help, but they remained a long-term problem for the parish. The strength of village reaction to the case even after Widow Warner's death seems startling, but makes it plausible that village ostracism was an important factor in her sudden and unexpected demise.

In the later seventeenth and early eighteenth century crime detection was based on the traditional assumption that most crimes were carried out by people within the neighbourhood, or at least the market area of local towns. This was successful in two cases at the turn of the seventeenth century. Early in 1698 a furnace was stolen from Claydon House and Sir John Verney ordered William Coleman to send round a description of the article to all the braziers in the district with instructions to report any rumours they heard. He added 'it must be some neighbour and I should be very glad to find him out, for if he gets off of this it will encourage him to do more and worse', and again 'I wish I could find him out not for the value of the thing but to make an example of him to deter others.' Sir John used similar methods when a thief stripped the lead from Middle Claydon church roof in 1711, sending word to plumbers in Bicester and Brill. An ex-soldier married to a Middle Claydon woman had

---

[90] Information from Middle Claydon reconstitution.

[91] wc to srv 13 January 1683/4 ClH 4/5/39.

[92] srv to wc 6 and 20 February 1683/4 ClH 4/5/39; wc to srv 17, 22, 24, and 25 February 1683/4 4/5/39.

stolen it, as well as five pounds from a Bottle Claydon house. He had sold the lead to a Winslow plumber to repay a debt and was detected because a farmer remembered carrying a letter to the plumber earlier and bringing back 4s. In neither case is there any evidence that the matter went beyond Petty Sessions.[93]

From the later seventeenth century improved communications increased the number and range of crimes involving outsiders from further afield. Highwaymen operated on the main Buckinghamshire roads throughout the period as well as on the approach roads to London. The Verneys monitored their activities because they often sent cash to London by the carriers, who were frequent victims.[94] Robberies took place from farmhouses, or even from a farmer on his own land. In 1664 Robert Scott went to Leighton Buzzard market on a Tuesday and returned to find that £14 had been stolen from his house. In 1678, James Stevens of nearby Hogshaw was robbed of £50 in his own grounds. In 1695, £12 and gold rings were stolen from a house, while two years later Joseph Miller was robbed of £100. The gentry and nobility were not exempt. Sir Richard Temple's house was robbed while he visited the Dormers at Rousham in 1702.[95] There were other tales to report. In 1701 Millie Lea, the Claydon gardener, went to Winslow with all the money he could raise – £3 11s – to buy a cow, and lost it all to a pickpocket. Sir John Verney sent him 10s to help him, but commented: 'I fear he got into some crowd a listening to some ballad singers or sellers of penny Godly books, for pickpockets have some of their gang always selling such things to make country folks crowd together.'[96]

These outsiders, and local gangs and bands that enforced silence by terror, presented a different problem that could not be dealt with so easily by traditional means. In 1701 there were rumours of gangs of up to sixty carrying out robberies and housebreaking. Late in 1710 there was a spate of robberies linked to fairs – at Northampton on 23 November, Lambourn on 26, and at Woodstock on 9 December where the men were chased across country before hiding in woods. At the same time, there were robberies totalling over £100 in the Winslow area. The steward and gardener at Claydon kept loaded guns in their rooms at night for self-defence. One night just after Christmas, when the steward was on estate business at Wasing, the household panicked. Imagining a break-in, they fired a gun and rang the bell, bringing men running from the village to search the house.[97]

Yet these crimes were either unsolved, or did not go to court – there is no mention of any Winslow robberies in the Quarter Session records for 1710–11.

---

[93] sjv to wc 19 January 1697/8 R50; cc to sjv 16 January and 8, 20, 22 February 1710/11 CIH 4/5/62.
[94] Incidentally, they had a distant relative, Richard Hals, who took up highway robbery.
[95] eb to srv 21 October 1664 CIH 4/5/17; wc to srv 3 January 1677/8 4/5/30; Elizabeth Verney to sjv nd September 1702 R52.
[96] wc to sjv 18 May 1701 CIH 4/5/54; sjv to wc 21 and 25 May 1701 4/5/54.
[97] wc to sjv 8 June 1702 CIH 4/5/54; cc to sjv 23, 26 November and 9 December 1710 4/5/61; sjv to rv 4 January 1710/11 R54.

There are also few references to poaching and deer stealing in the court records from 1660 to 1740 although it was a chronic irritant, and a significant problem at some periods. E. P. Thompson linked deer stealing in Windsor Forest between 1718 and 1723 to the passing of the Black Act, but poaching was concurrently prevalent in north Buckinghamshire, and dealt with rather differently. Deer were introduced to Claydon after Sir Ralph Verney's return from the continent in the 1650s, a keeper employed, and in 1682 there were fifty-five deer. Deer stealers were first mentioned in 1671 but only in passing. Local gentry – and particularly their young sons like Sir John Busby's and Mr Duncombe's in 1689 – might take an occasional buck, and villagers who took the odd hare or even shot a buck – like Richard Crawley in 1700 – could be dealt with by informal means.[98]

In the early eighteenth century poaching 'gangs' began to operate over a wide area and regularly took deer. They disguised themselves, used dogs and guns, and worked in groups of eight to a dozen. Intimidation was their stock in trade and they were happy to fire guns and threaten retaliation if their dogs or equipment were confiscated. They were active in the Claydon neighbourhood in 1701–2, and at various times through to the 1730s.[99] Gangs used local superiority in numbers to intimidate keepers and household staff. Landowners could prosecute under a whole range of statutes passed during the seventeenth and early eighteenth centuries, but the deer-stealing gangs were fluid in composition and drawn from village communities, not some criminal subculture. It was difficult to find people who would inform on them.

The activities of the 'new set-up deer stealers at Steeple Claydon' who raided Judge Denton's park at Hillesden in February 1723 illustrate the problems of prosecution. One of the gang, John East, was captured and Denton ordered his prosecution and imprisonment to await trial.[100] This raised tensions in the village communities. The Verneys' keeper was cursed by Steeple Claydon men for informing on the leader of the gang. Chaloner pressured the Claydon gardener into breaking his links with the man with whom he used to 'keep company'.[101] As the trial approached the villagers of Steeple Claydon drew up a petition to free East, and according to Chaloner 'got most of the townspeople's hands to it'. At the Assizes, East was found guilty and sentenced to transportation but Denton then did a remarkable volte-face and petitioned the Regency Council for a pardon.[102]

---

[98] For a fuller account of these activities and their context see J. Broad, 'Whigs and deer-stealers in other guises: a return to the origins of the Black Act', *Past and Present* 119 (1988), pp. 56–72, esp. pp. 58–65.

[99] wc to sjv 3 and 4 July 1701 R52; Elizabeth Verney to sjv 5 September 1702 R52.

[100] cc to sjv 3 and 7 March 1722/3 ClH 4/5/69.

[101] cc to rv 12, 14, 24, 26, 28 February 1722/3 ClH 4/5/61.

[102] cc to rv 28, 31 November and 8 December 1723 ClH 4/5/61; cf. E. P. Thompson, *Whigs and Hunters* (London 1975), pp. 77–9.

There is no grant of pardon in the Privy Council register, but by November 1723 East was back in Steeple Claydon a free man. A twelve-man raid on Middle Claydon Park followed his return, and the deer stealers issued the keeper with a death threat. Raids took place all over north and central Buckinghamshire during 1724. Wing, Winchenden, Winslow, Doddershall, Hillesden, and Tring parks were all subject to attacks. Mrs Piggott at Doddershall House was held at gunpoint at her front door. Landowners who actively pursued the deer stealers were subject to retaliation. Captain Chapman had his horses mutilated, while Mr Lowndes of Winslow was attacked at ten o'clock at night on his way back from Buckingham.[103]

Verney's response was dramatic. In December 1723 he conceded victory to the deer stealers by selling his deer. Other landowners' response was to buy them off, as Turnham, the purchaser of the Claydon herd, did as he moved his animals to their new home. Lord Northampton took compensation from the Olney gang who raided his park. Lord Cobham at Stowe had two offenders prosecuted and hanged in the 1740s, but this put huge pressure on his estate servants. His steward committed suicide after a deerstealer was convicted at the Assizes in 1741.[104]

Deer-stealing activities help to delineate the limits of a substantial landowner's power, and the practical limits of the application of the criminal law. Such gangs operated over whole swathes of the county. The world of the estate and closed parish, where landowners like the Verneys were so powerful, could not isolate itself from the wider neighbourhood. In parishes where power was more diffuse, and the power of custom and traditional rights were stronger, individuals could more easily express a wider range of ideas and approaches to social and political problems. At the end of the eighteenth century, landowners and farmers set up prosecution associations to pursue thieves and compensate victims. In 1793–4 the Grenvilles founded one covering communities from Waddesdon to Quainton, centred on their Wotton Underwood estate. Lady Fermanagh and the Lowndes family organised another based on Winslow, covering the Claydons, Horwood, and Whaddon Chase. Those who joined included thirteen farmers from East Claydon and eight from Middle Claydon, but only three from Steeple Claydon, all of whom had close links to the Verneys.[105]

Within Middle Claydon the Verneys held more extensive power from a dominant social and economic position. The workings of the poor law exemplify the

---

[103] cc to rv 8, 12, and 15 December 1723 ClH 4/5/69 and 2, 5, and 21 July 1724 4/5/70 and 23 February 1724/5 R57, and 24 July and 14, 21 August 1726 R57 4/5/70.

[104] cc to rv 8, 12,15 December 1723 ClH 4/5/69; cc memorandum n.d. 1723 R57; cc to rv 25 April 1724 4/5/70.

[105] Peter J. R. King, 'Prosecution associations and their impact in eighteenth-century Essex', in D. Hay and F. Snyder (eds.), *Policing and Prosecution in Britain, 1750–1850* (Oxford 1989), pp. 171–210; Huntington STG Manorial Boxes 10 and 14.

tensions between modern economic estate policy and social paternalism, but also the ways in which different social groups within the parish defended their own interests to put limits on Verney power. During the seventeenth century village society moved away from dependence on neighbourly charity and recip-rocal help towards more impersonal forms of assistance. This was a response to the rising scale of poverty nationally, the increasing mobility of population, and the numbers of people in the countryside who no longer had land sufficient to make them even partially self-sufficient. Within the estate village, the landlord had traditional charitable obligations towards the poor on a continuing basis, not just in times of crisis. Changes in village society, and in the relationship between charitable giving and the support of the poor through the poor rate, influenced landowners' perceptions of their role in the relief of the poverty.[106]

The declining population of Middle Claydon benefited landlords and tenant farmers alike. By reducing the number of poor householders, the Verneys kept the poor rate low, and the numbers of permanent recipients remained small. This reduced farmers' costs, enabling them to pay the high rents asked by the Verneys. Poor rates were first raised regularly by the parish overseers in Middle Claydon during the Civil War, and after the Restoration became a permanent feature of the parish economy. The poor law became a point of collision between landlord and farming tenants, but also between old and new values.

The scale of poverty in Middle Claydon was never high, indeed probably remained lower than that in East and Steeple Claydon throughout the period from 1600 to 1820. The Verneys' estate policies reduced the number of the more vulnerable small farmers at risk, and encouraged out-migration to decrease the numbers of labouring families in the village. At the Restoration 27 per cent of Middle Claydon houses were exempt from the Hearth Tax. This figure was lower than either of its neighbouring parishes and much lower than a parish like Brill, ten miles away, where 67 per cent of households were exempt. By 1800 Middle Claydon had the lowest poor rates in Buckinghamshire.[107]

Poverty in Middle Claydon tended to reflect the changing economic structure of the parish, or was the result of economic, harvest, and life-cycle crises. The post-enclosure economy of Middle Claydon after 1656 reduced employment prospects for smallholders and labourers and removed access to common waste and woodland. The switch to pastoral farming reduced demand for agricultural labour, while the Puritan widower, Sir Ralph Verney rarely employed more than seven permanent staff. The thriving lace industry provided reasonable work

---

[106] Paul Slack, *Poverty and Policy in Tudor and Stuart England* (London 1988); Hindle, 'Power, poor relief, and social relations in Holland fen, *c.* 1600–1800', pp. 67–96; and *The Birthpangs of Welfare: Poor Relief and Parish Governance in Seventeenth-century Warwickshire*, Dugdale Society Occasional Papers no. 40 (2000).

[107] See PP 1803–4 (175); St J. Priest, *A General View of the Agriculture of Buckinghamshire* (London 1810), pp. 400ff.; on Brill see Broad and Hoyle, *Bernwood*, esp. chs. 4 and 5.

opportunities for women and children, but there were few alternative jobs for men locally. It was not difficult for Edward Butterfield to describe his relatively well-provided parish as 'such a poor town as ours'.[108]

Sir Ralph's estate policy of enlarging farms reflected a social policy that placed commercially successful farming above the needs of families, thrusting responsibility for poverty squarely with individual farming families. His views on the place of ordinary working men on the margins of poverty as revealed in his 1650 letter did not allow them to be subsidised for social reasons. It was a very modern vision of a high-productivity, high-wage economy very much at odds with the tradition of parish neighbourliness and mutual help.

Traditionally, the landlord, or lord of the manor, had a central role in providing help to individuals in time of need. Food from the kitchen of the great house, help with gifts of money in times of hardship, of firewood in hard winters, of medical help in sickness or injury, were all part and parcel of that tradition. In the seventeenth century, the Verneys retained a protective, paternal attitude towards the villagers of Middle Claydon. However, their help was influenced by their views about the worthiness of the recipients, and by Puritan ideas about the proper forms of charity. There is no evidence that Sir Ralph Verney ever gave indiscriminate alms, indeed early in 1650 William Roades assured him categorically that no families were begging for alms in Middle Claydon although 'many are in need enough'.[109] Yet in East Claydon the lord of the manor still provided regular doles. When Edmund Verney took on that role in 1663 he continued that tradition for several years to establish himself in the squire's role. However in December 1669, just before Christmas, he called in the seven families to whom he had been giving regular support, plied them with beer, gave each a shilling and announced that he would no longer give them alms. In the uproar that followed a wealthy East Claydon farmer, John Millward, led protests in which the families complained that they would not be able to subsist without this help. Interestingly, fifty years later, in 1722, when new owners came to East Claydon they announced that they were restoring doles.[110]

Sir Ralph Verney and his son Sir John provided a selective range of assistance to village families that reflected their priorities and values, and promoted an image of benevolent and enlightened paternalism. It complemented the increasingly important part played by the poor law and parish officers in providing for the poor. It was also fiercely protective of the Verneys' right to determine parish policy free of county interference and national legislation. For instance, the statutory requirement to 'badge' the poor under the later Stuarts was ignored in Middle Claydon, as widely elsewhere, until after the famine year 1709. The

---

[108] eb to srv 15 February 1676/7 CIH 4/5/29.   [109] wr to srv 26 January 1649/50 R10.
[110] ev to srv 20 and 27 December 1669, R23; cc to rv 16 December 1722, CIH 4/5/68.

Abells of East Claydon then used it as an issue in a continuing conflict with the Verneys. As Lady Fermanagh wrote: 'our poor of our parish is all badged yesterday, for Abell turned informer'.[111] Verney policy combined a strictly economic attitude to rents and estate income with a generous paternalism towards those tenants in what they considered genuine need. Poverty was not shameful in itself, but fathers of large families were encouraged to set their children to work early to supplement family income.

The Verneys provided vital help in times of crisis. When Sir Ralph Verney was away in London in the cold days of March 1674, Edward Butterfield wrote to him: 'the poor want you extremely'. Sir Ralph frequently gave his own money during extreme weather, illness, and disaster, prompted either by his steward or the parson's advice, or in response to direct letters of request. In January 1684, he ordered that firewood should be distributed to four poor families in extremely cold weather. In January 1695, he sent down 5s to be distributed amongst those in most need.[112] Other gifts included 1s to help a sick ex-servant, linked with an instruction to the overseer of the poor that she should 'want for nothing that is fit for a poor body'. When Judith May was so poor that she did not have enough wood at Christmas, Edmund Verney gave her 6d a week. Judith then 'says she hath enough and hopes not to be troublesome to the parish'. These gifts helped people avoid claiming parish relief. In Jane Long's case in 1674, the overseers had paid her three weeks' poor rate to look after her sick daughter, but when they reduced the amount the Verneys and Edward Butterfield provided gifts totalling 5s 6d because they considered her 'the poorest in the parish'.[113] The Verneys occasionally relaxed their strict estate management policies to ease poverty. In 1684, Sir Ralph Verney was persuaded not to evict one farmer because his six children would then have to be supported by the parish. Verney held that the tenant 'cannot reasonably expect to keep a family of so many small children (that can earn nothing) out of a bargain of about three score pounds a year, especially if he goes to the alehouse'. In 1688, sixteen holdings out of forty-nine in Middle Claydon paid less than £5 a year in rent, and seven of these paid no rent at all 'by reason of their poverty'.[114]

The Verneys controlled other aspects of parish life to benefit the poor. Sir Ralph allowed only one alehouse in Middle Claydon, and granted it to a widow or family to keep them off the parish. William Guttridge wrote that he was poor, had insufficient work to pay his debts, and feared his creditors would imprison

---

[111] Elizabeth Verney to sjv 23 March 1711/12 R54.

[112] eb to srv 2 March 1673/4 ClH 4/5/26; srv to wc 28 January 1683/4 4/5/36; 7 and 23 January 1694/5 4/5/47.

[113] srv to wc 20 November 1684 ClH 4/5/37; eb to srv 9 January 1669/70 4/5/22 and 13 January 1672/3 4/5/25.

[114] wc to srv 27 January 1683/4 ClH 4/5/36; srv to wc 3 December 1684 4/5/37; Middle Claydon Rentals in 4/3/78–109, and in BCRO D/X 337.

him, forcing his wife and children onto the parish, but Sir Ralph would not allow him to run an additional licensed alehouse. Sir Ralph and his successors gave gifts of firewood to poor families in winter in lieu of the common rights to gather firewood that had been extinguished in the enclosures of the 1620s and 1654–6. The poor were still allowed to take wood from what was left over after wood sales, but wood stealing, either from the woods or the hedgerows, became a recurrent problem for the Verneys and their stewards in the seventeenth and eighteenth centuries.

The Verneys also used their contacts and expertise to help sick villagers and those who faced chronic disabilities. In 1679 Sir Ralph tried to find a cure for his carpenter's blindness. In 1675 he provided Ralph Roades with spectacles. In 1695 Thomas Hicks became 'lunatic again' and money was immediately given to care for him. At first he was kept bound in his bed, watched constantly by two men. Later the smith made special irons to keep his hands tied. However barbaric that seems from a twenty-first century perspective, William Coleman saw these measures differently, reporting that 'neighbours [were] very kind in watching with him, and everyone, as far as I find will be as careful of him as they can'.[115] In the previous year, William Rose's daughter was paralysed and had lost the use of both hands and sought help to find a hospital place. William Coleman supported her case with Sir Ralph, noting that otherwise she would become a burden on the poor rate.[116]

The Verneys oversaw family crises in the village community particularly after bereavements. They helped provide for orphaned children, and protected dead villagers' estates and possessions particularly after a single or widowed person died. Creditors wanted to ensure that their debts were paid first. Relatives frequently tried to make off with valuables before the will (if any) was read and proved. In such cases, the Verneys intervened through their agents, the bailiffs, or the parson, but not always as disinterested parties. In 1732, Francis Meaks died owing both William Butterfield and the first earl money. Butterfield felt forced to ask his master's help because 'the people about him and relations . . . are for making off with the goods in the house'. When Barton Franklin died in 1700, Sir John Verney was quick to instruct the parson to ensure that his children did not divide the property until his debt of £20 4s had been paid. In 1648 William Roades reported a case where a man's son and executor reached his house only after rascals had stolen most of his goods. He blamed the problem on the 'many at the town next to them that are masterless'.[117]

The greatest problems arose when dependent children or grandchildren were beneficiaries. In May 1678, an impoverished gentleman, Mr Scarlet, died

---

[115] srv to wc 18 Feb 1679/80 CIH 4/5/32; wc to srv 12 January 1673/4 4/5/26; wc to srv 25 April 1695 4/5/48; wb to srv 28 April 1695 4/5/48.

[116] srv to wc 3 May 1695 CIH 4/5/48; wc to srv 15 July 1694 4/5/47.

[117] wb to rv 7 March 1731/2 CIH 4/5/74; wr to srv 20 December 1648 R9.

leaving a grandchild who was lodging with Thomas Tattam, one of the Verneys' tenants. Middle Claydon's overseer, Henry Scott, wanted to know what to do with the child. He reported that 30s of Scarlet's money, and 'a little bacon left, which would have kept the child a little while' had been carried off by a Mr Percivall, one of Scarlet's creditors. On the other hand, he thought there were goods worth four or five pounds, which would be enough to make it possible to place out the grandchild. Sir Ralph then ordered his steward, William Coleman, to secure Scarlet's possessions, and Henry Scott to look after the child. The child needed clothes, and the goods and bedding in Scarlet's house had to be washed and cleaned. Scott was also ordered to make a full inventory. The child was settled eventually with one Hall, in Adstock, three miles away, on condition that all Scarlet's goods should be handed over to him.[118]

Village deaths were not always conducive to neighbourliness. When Biser Emberton died intestate in 1663, the parson, Edward Butterfield, heard her last wishes and tried to carry them out. The woman's sister was the main beneficiary, but there was also an orphaned niece to be supported. Butterfield secured the £14 in cash in the house by handing it to the bailiff's wife, Mrs Holmes, for safekeeping. Emberton's sister was persuaded to give up £8 of the inheritance to support the child, but retracted, demanding the whole legacy, but Butterfield retained possession of the £8 to help the child.[119] In 1655 William Roades sought his master's help over his own orphaned grandchild. The boy had lived with William Roades and his wife since birth. Now that his mother had died the boy inherited land worth £20 a year, and William Roades wanted to become his legal guardian. The child was only five, and his aunts would inherit the land if he died. Roades presumably feared for the child's welfare, and even safety, if anyone else became guardian.[120]

In the absence of money from relatives and family, the overseers had to find an appropriate placement for an orphan at least cost to the parish. When Tom King died in 1677 he left two daughters, Elizabeth and Ann, who were seven and five. His wife Elizabeth had died giving birth to Ann. No relatives took any interest in the children, but Ralph Roades agreed to take them in for seven years on payment of £24, and part of this was raised by an auction of Tom King's goods.[121] When Widow Warner died in 1684 after being ostracised following accusations of theft, Sir Ralph mused that the two boys were perhaps old enough to go into service at Lady Day, while the girls might be put out to learn lacemaking. The only sympathetic relative lived in Windsor and took charge, for the eldest boy was only sixteen, so could not administer his mother's estate. In all these cases intervention by the Verneys was an important influence.[122]

[118] srv to wc 6 June 1678 ClH 4/5/31; wc to srv 30 May and 3, 6, and 10 June 1678 4/5/31.
[119] eb to srv 14 December 1663 ClH 4/5/16.   [120] wr to srv 13 February 1655 R13.
[121] srv to wc 25 January 1676/7 ClH 4/5/24.
[122] wc to srv 17 and 22 February 1683/4 ClH 4/5/36; srv to wc 20 February 1683/4 4/5/36.

Traditional personal charity dealt rapidly and directly with major crises by cutting through red tape and village enmities but was administered in ways that suited the Verney family. In 1676 William Taylor's house burnt down. Sir Ralph sent condolences and offers of help but wrote:

I will provide him another house which shall be better than this that's burnt, and I will do it at my own charge for him, but I will set it where I please, and I will give him a load of my faggots such as I bring into my yard. Therefore see it done, also give him a barrel of beer, and a bushell of salt, and six pounds of candles presently.[123]

This kind of help was one advantage of living in an estate village with a resident squire. Other forms of traditional charity survived through the seventeenth and eighteenth centuries. Just before Christmas, on St Thomas's Day, the family gave a bull to the parish. It was slaughtered, and the meat cut up and distributed to the poor. The Verneys and their agents carefully selected the recipients and gave different amounts of meat according to their perceived needs. In 1669 five families received 24 lb, 20 lb, 18 lb, 16 lb and 16 lb respectively, and a further seventeen people received 8 lb of meat each. Presumably most of the meat was then salted and cured to supplement the meagre diets of the poor during the harshest weather of the year.[124]

This approach to food distribution was very different from the traditional food gifts from the 'great house', when the poor received left-over food from the kitchen. The Verney family frowned upon this practice as indiscriminate charity, and their attitude hardened during the eighteenth century. In 1698 a man stole and killed a turkey from the kitchen yard at Claydon. The theft was blamed on the cook's practice of relieving people at the kitchen door, and she was forbidden to continue the practice. The second earl was much harsher eighty years later and instantly dismissed one of his servants caught giving food to a poor man.[125]

Individual charitable acts supplemented doles from several institutional charities. Middle Claydon had more charities than East and Steeple Claydon. By the early nineteenth century there were six trusts for the benefit of the poor of Middle Claydon, which produced £47 8s 8d a year, compared with £13 2s in East Claydon, and £5 0s 6d for Steeple Claydon. The available charitable funds in the three villages were in inverse proportion to their needs.[126] Most charities paid out money to the poor between Christmas and Easter during the harshest weather when under-employment was highest. The poor could expect relatively full stomachs in Middle Claydon at Christmas, and reflect, incidentally, that this bounty came from their social betters. Twenty poor families received 1s each

---

[123] srv to wc 1 February 1676/7 CIH 4/5/29.   [124] wc to srv 26 December 1669 CIH 4/5/22.
[125] Elizabeth Verney to wc 27 December 1698 R50. Undated letter (c. 1770) from an ex-housemaid to Ralph, second Earl Verney about dismissal for giving food to a poor man, CIH 5/1/1.
[126] For Coleman's bequest see BCRO D/A/ We/48/131.

from the Gifford charity while another charity provided bread. At Christmas 1722 the four people in the almshouses each received 8 lb of meat, 1s for bread, and 1s in cash. A bushel and a half of grist were made into nine loaves of bread, and all were given away. In 1749 two bulls were divided between the poor of the three Claydons, and ten of the poorer families in Middle Claydon received between 8 and 10 lb of meat. On Candlemas Day (2 February), the poor received doles paid from the interest from the town stock. In 1705 William Coleman left the parish 10s a year for the poor to provide bread on Ash Wednesday, and Good Friday.[127]

The Verneys also controlled the 'Town Stock', a fund consolidating generations of single donations to the poor from the Verneys and the wealthier local farmers. When Sir John Verney died in 1717 he left £20 to Middle Claydon poor stock, £5 to Steeple Claydon poor stock, while £1 was to be distributed in Adstock. In 1686 he asked his father to add £5 from him to the Middle Claydon stock, and planned to start a similar institution in Wasing. Town Stocks were found in many English parishes in the seventeenth century; one estimate of their total funds suggests a million pounds nationally.[128] The capital in Middle Claydon's rose from £38 in 1650 to £65 in 1674. During the seventeenth century it was usually lent to a number of local farmers to spread the risk, and the annual interest was paid out to the poor.[129] In 1688, Sir Ralph used the capital to buy Steeple Claydon land, probably adding his own money. The land was bought in his own name and produced an income of £6 5s a year.[130]

The Verneys also decided who should benefit from this money, in consultation with the parson and the poor overseer about eligible recipients. Many poor families received something every year, and as they moved away or died, new families were added to the list. Families received cash from the Town Stock according to their perceived needs, unlike the Gifford Charity, which provided a fixed amount per family. In 1680, Sir Ralph decided that all the interest should be used to try to find a cure for his carpenter's blindness, and the man was sent off to London for treatment. A typical extract from 1682 illustrates the flavour of the discussion:

---

[127] cc to rv 6 December 1722 ClH 4/5/68; Middle Claydon overseers a/cs 1749 BCRO PR 52/12/3.

[128] E. G. James, 'Charity endowments as sources of local credit in 17th and 18th century England', *Journal of Economic History* 8 (1948), pp. 153–70; wr to srv 25 January 1649/50 R10; see also Middle Claydon overseers' accounts for 1674. John Verney to srv 24 June 1686 R41; receipts for money paid from Sir John Verney's executors September 1717 and 21 November 1717 R56.

[129] During the Civil War the money was split amongst the wealthier farmers in the parish, wr to srv 26 January 1649/50 R10. Later in the century, various East Claydon and North Marston farmers held the money, either on bond or on mortgage e.g. eb to srv 28 December 1668 ClH 4/5/21.

[130] wc to srv 27 February 1687/8 ClH 4/5/40; the purchase in Sir Ralph's name is dated 15 May 1688 ClH 2/499 a, b.

Widow Bates being dead, there is 2s for Old Harding who I suppose hath need and I think Will Rose may be abated one shilling, and one shilling apiece out of John Roades' wife and Widd. Long's, and I think Widd. Roades hath need of none at all, so then there will be 7s abated off what was given last year.[131]

Charities provided help to the Middle Claydon poor in winter need and did not carry the stigma of poor relief. Accounting and administration were not always strong, and by 1820 the origins of the funds had often been forgotten. Charity money was often applied to appropriate uses rather than the letter of the donor's wishes, and accounted for along with parish relief money. Some charity accounts were written up in the churchwardens' accounts, and charitable funds were sometimes used for purposes normally paid from the poor rate. At one point the Gifford money was used to pay the deficit in the churchwardens' accounts while a rate was used to pay the almspeople and the Gifford bequest. In the later seventeenth century, the churchwardens' accounts show that nothing was received from the Gifford bequest or the Town Stock. When accounts for the Gifford rent charge resumed in 1732 St Thomas's Day doles were charged to it, but so were the weekly almshouse doles that strictly should have come from the Verneys' rent charge.[132] By the late eighteenth century charitable funds were barely distinguishable from parish relief, subsumed in the churchwardens' and overseers' accounts although still properly applied. Town Stock income was also absorbed into the overseers' accounts. When parliamentary enclosure took place in Steeple Claydon in 1795, the Middle Claydon overseers paid their share of the enclosure costs for the Town Stock land from Middle Claydon poor rate. These accounting practices show how charity and poor relief were part of a seamless web of welfare provision, but one shaped significantly by Verney patronage. In 1712 William Butterfield made a visitation return that suggested, incorrectly, that the almshouses were not endowed, since payments to inmates came from a variety of sources.[133]

Sir Ralph Verney had rebuilt the early seventeenth-century almshouse in Middle Claydon in brick to his own meticulous design on his return from exile. Each room was 15 ft by 13 ft. The fireplace was central, the windows (glazed but without casements) were 2 ft 6 in. square. The garden was 40 feet long with a privy at the bottom, while there was a pump in the alley beside the house. In 1686 he endowed it with a rent charge of £15 12s a year that was regularly paid in the eighteenth century. Admission was a regular instrument of estate policy. Inmates were normally paid 4d a week by the churchwardens who

[131] eb to srv 1 December 1673 ClH 4/5/26; srv to wc 19 February 1679/80 4/5/32; wc to srv 9 February 1681/2 4/5/35.

[132] See Middle Claydon parish records in BCRO PR52/12/1-4.

[133] Broad, *Buckinghamshire Dissent*, pp. 204–6.

administered the endowment but the almshouse was rarely used to capacity, with four or five inhabitants in most years.[134] Places went to old and sick widows, or single women, and the youngest recorded was a woman in her late forties.[135] Admission was a matter of patronage. In 1669 Widow Scott was denied a place 'because she refused it when I offered it her, and used me ill in the marriage of her daughter'. Admissions might be part of a bargain with the poor overseers. In 1754 John Blackwell was living rent-free in a cottage and his son had moved in with him. The second earl agreed to take Blackwell into the almshouse and let his son stay in the cottage provided the parish would pay some rent for the cottage from the rates.[136]

Charity was a vital aid to the poor, but poor rates were of increasing importance and raised regularly after 1660, with surviving accounts from 1674. There were two overseers during the Civil War but after 1660 only one was appointed. Practice in that period was for a farmer to hold the post for two or three years but Abraham Teagle remained for seventeen years. After 1727 the post rotated annually amongst the richer tenants, who with a diminishing number of farms, faced a second term after about ten years. Poor rate expenditure from the overseers' accounts is shown in figure 5. It rose sharply at the end of the seventeenth century from an average of £3 16s in the 1670s to £26 11s in the second decade of the eighteenth century. From 1720 to 1775 it stabilised at a decadal mean of between £16 and £20, which concealed considerable annual fluctuations. Decadal means hide wild annual fluctuations with sums frequently doubling from one year to the next. High peaks between 1697 and 1700 and again between 1708 and 1717 can be linked to harvest failures and wartime hardship. That between 1727 and 1730 corresponds to the vicious epidemic which swept the Claydons and most of the country at that time.[137] The relative importance of the poor rate changed between 1660 and the end of the eighteenth century. Personal charity cannot be accurately quantified, but income from charitable trusts at least equalled, and often exceeded rate-based expenditure for much of the seventeenth century. Only at the end of the eighteenth century were the sums raised by rates considerably higher.[138]

Money raised by poor rates paid for the administrative costs of the poor law, and for the long-term poor, the 'pensioners'. The numbers of people receiving

[134] For a detailed description see paper in srv's hand after 31 December 1653 R12; draft endowment deed in August 1663 R19.
[135] This can be shown by linking the burial of an almsperson in the parish to the family reconstitution records.
[136] srv to ev 30 June 1669 R23; John Millward to rvjr 16 May 1754 R60.
[137] See Middle Claydon overseers' accounts in Buckinghamshire CRO PR 52/12/1-4
[138] Cf. John Broad, 'Parish economies of welfare, 1650–1834', *Historical Journal* 42:4 (1999), pp. 985–1006; detailed studies of the particular relationship between charity and poor rates are to be found in D. Eastwood, 'The republic in the village: parish and poor at Bampton, 1780–1834', *Journal of Regional and Local Studies* 12 (1992), pp. 18–28.

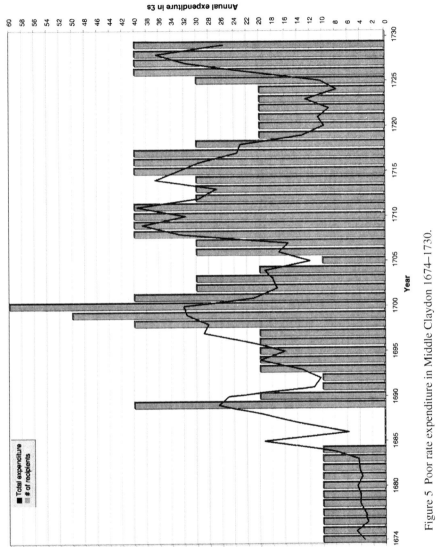

Figure 5 Poor rate expenditure in Middle Claydon 1674–1730.

regular pensions remained small throughout the period from 1660 to 1740. For most of the 1670s and 1680s only one person, Mary Roades, was in regular receipt of an allowance. She was the deserted wife of John Roades, caring for their children. She was destitute (her goods only raised £3 4s 8d when sold to the profit of the overseers' account after her death in 1685), but the parish paid her no more than 1s a week. She was expected to make ends meet by working at lacemaking. One shilling a week seems to have been the standard level of support in the late seventeenth century, and all four households in receipt of regular allowances in 1689–90 received it.[139] The maximum number of families in Middle Claydon receiving year-long allowances seems to have been six in 1729–30, a year of considerable sickness.

The overseers' accounts also supported the travel and legal costs of settlement disputes that went to Quarter Sessions, and were occasionally used for medical purposes. Money was spent burying paupers, providing apprenticeships for poor children, and bringing up orphans. The churchwardens normally made grants to the vagrant poor, and sometimes helped with medicines. Employment schemes for the poor were also paid from the poor rates. Work schemes were used sporadically in the 1660s and 1670s. Flax was bought for the poor to spin in 1663, and Benjamin Bates bought 6 lb of hemp in 1680. However, from 1681 to 1698, while Abraham Teagle was overseer, work materials were provided much more systematically and in greater amounts. Teagle was a prosperous tenant farmer of Puritan, possibly non-conformist beliefs. In the peak year, 1690, he bought in 260 lb of hemp to be spun. In 1688 work was provided for three women, Widow Saunders, Will Scott's wife, and Ralph Howe's wife, and the yarn was then woven by Thomas Hicks. Slightly earlier, Teagle had bought in lace thread for Mary Roades's orphaned children to work at after their mother's death in 1685.[140]

Work schemes at Claydon employed a very few people, and were invariably unprofitable. In 1687–8 Abraham Teagle spent £4 8s 3d on raw hemp, paid £2 19s to the spinners, and £1 11s 2d to the weaver for their labour, and received only £4 13s for all the hempen cloth that had been woven. In the following year, £10 14s 4d was spent on raw materials and labour, but only £7 12s 1d recovered by sale of cloth. Increasing turnover on the poor account in this period can be accounted for almost entirely by the expenditure on work materials. Despite the expense, the Verneys nevertheless supported them. Abraham Teagle's tenure of the overseers' office could not have lasted so long without their encouragement. In 1688 Sir Ralph Verney pressed Abraham Teagle to continue as overseer, even though he had been in office for seven years.[141]

---

[139] See Middle Claydon parish registers and overseers' accounts and eb to srv 9 December 1672 ClH 4/5/25.

[140] srv to hh 11 July 1663 R19. Figures from overseers' accounts.

[141] These figures are based on an analysis of the overseers' accounts.

The Verney family had considerable influence on how money from the poor rate was spent. They approved the appointment of overseers. The overseers' accounts were often written up by William Coleman, and the parson was frequently consulted. However, the overseers were tenant farmers who had their own interests to protect. The poor rate fell on occupiers proportionately to the amount of land they held and, unlike the land tax, could not be passed back to the landlord. The Verneys' tenants paid high rents, and their landlord provided frequent charitable assistance to parishioners. They were unlikely to be generous in their allowances to the poor out of the rates. The bailiff William Roades on one occasion advised his master not to push rent up too much because lower rents would 'encourage your tenants and better enable them to maintain the poor'.[142] How the burden of poverty in Middle Claydon was shared between landlord and farmers was a contentious issue over which the farmers exerted power and influence.

The overseers were reluctant to provide in marginal cases, and might grant insufficient relief. When John Roades returned to his destitute family in 1672, Parson Butterfield tested village opinion and found 'most are willing they should be put to their shifts a while longer'. One result was that the parson and the Verneys were expected to provide for welfare emergencies. When the Claydon housekeeper reported that a local woman and her child were 'pinched with want', she asked Sir Ralph Verney's permission to give her money from the housekeeping funds rather than to approach the overseers for poor relief.[143] In 1672 Widow Long was rapidly becoming destitute as she looked after her sick daughter. On 15 December she had 'already sold her hog and three sheep and spent the money, and hath nothing left but a cow, and that they say goes next'. The parson approached the overseers separately for help and obtained agreement that the woman should be paid 2s 6d a week during the emergency. Once the overseers met, they immediately reduced the sum to 1s 6d. After three weeks, the bailiff reported a further reduction to 1s, though the overseers' accounts say differently. The Verneys and Parson Butterfield were forced to make additional charitable contributions to make up the difference.[144] In May 1711 Thomas Faulkner was receiving sums from three different sources during his final illness. The overseers paid 1s 6d a week, but at the same time the churchwarden was giving the family 4d a week, and the Verneys were paying 9d a week, and briefly an additional 3d loaf of bread.[145]

The overseers often refused to pay as much allowance as the Verneys suggested. The interests of landlord and tenant farmers also conflicted over the eviction of tenants. In 1684, William Coleman successfully persuaded Sir Ralph

[142] srv to wc 11 April 1688 ClH 4/5/41; wr to srv 12 January 1649/50 R10.
[143] eb to srv 23 February 1662/3 ClH 4/5/15/.
[144] eb 15 December 1672 and 13 January 1672/3 ClH 4/5/25; hh to srv 16 December 1672 4/5/25.
[145] cc to sjv 8, 13, 17 and 20 May 1711 ClH 4/5/62.

not to evict Richard Harding, who had six small children, because of the consequences for the poor rate. Harding recovered financially, and was still farming
ten years later, though with a small subsidy from Sir Ralph Verney.[146] In a similar situation in 1715 'the town' – a consensus amongst the leading farmers –
acted rapidly when the Welhead family were about to be evicted. The widow
and her five children would have been left on the parish at an estimated additional cost to the poor rates of £15 a year. The average for the decade was
just over £26, so the rates would have had to increase by over 50 per cent. To
avoid this burden, four or five of the tenants signed an agreement with Sir John
Verney to subsidise Widow Welhead's rent to the tune of about £5 for the rest
of the year.[147]

The leading tenants were given about ten days to persuade the other villagers
to sign it. One farmer was initially reluctant but was forced into line, and the
agreement was regularly renewed. Although originally intended to apply only
until the children were old enough to earn their own livings, the subsidy was
still being paid by the village eleven years later. Indeed, when other farmers
cast covetous eyes on the land in 1724 the steward reported that:

the town don't design to leave that bargain as long as your Lordship will give 'em leave
to go on till the children are put out, which they hope they shall get one of the boys out
at spring to some trade.[148]

The Verneys found other ways of shifting costs to the parish in the early eighteenth century. Sir Ralph Verney had allowed five or six villagers to occupy their
houses rent-free 'by reason of their poverty' in the later seventeenth century.
There were six at Michaelmas 1694, yet none received poor relief. Thirty years
later the poor rates were regularly used to pay house rents for up to four houses.
In 1715 and 1729 the rates also paid for repairs on the houses of those on
relief.[149]

Although the overseers of the poor were subject to outside pressures, the
village had much greater control over the distribution of the poor rate than over
other forms of provision. We know even less of charity between farmers and
labourers. When Taylor's house burnt down in 1677 the village collected £3 10s
to help him and other villages also contributed. The village community regularly
contributed to 'briefs' after disasters, or in good causes. Between 1689 and 1693,
Irish Protestants, Southwark, East Smithfield, Bishops Lavington, St Ives, and
Mr J. Clopton of Norwich, all received sums between 5s and £4 14s, the last

---

[146] wc to srv 27 January 1683/4 ClH 4/5/36.
[147] sjv to rv 29 November and 15 December 1715 R55.
[148] cc to rv 10 and 30 January 1717/8 R56 and 4 August 1726 R57.
[149] See Middle Claydon Rentals ClH 4/3/38-77 and overseers' accounts. Cf. Broad, 'Housing the rural poor', pp. 151–70.

raised for the Irish Protestants. Most informal acts of neighbourliness remain unrecorded.[150]

This analysis of the various strands of help and coercion used to relieve Middle Claydon's poverty demonstrates both the Verney family's power and its limitations. The poor themselves could not be left to starve. A battle of wills and wits between farmers and landlords decided who should take the greatest share of the burden. Parish politics played their part in modifying the Verneys' attitudes to their villagers. There were inherent tensions between a strong paternalism, modified and modernised to accommodate the Puritan ethic, and the economic goals of enlarging farms, re-shaping agriculture, reducing population, and charging high rents for market-oriented farming. This was the formative era of a new and re-defined rural paternalism that differed from both its more self-conscious nineteenth-century idiom, and its residual twentieth-century existence.[151] It made the shaping of the social world of the estate village a complex and fascinating phenomenon.

---

[150] For these see wc to srv 5 February 1676/7 ClH 4/5/29; eb to srv 15 February 1676/7 4/5/29; and for details of amounts raised from briefs see Middle Claydon churchwardens' accounts.

[151] See W. O. Chadwick, *Victorian Miniatures* (London 1960), Havinden, *Estate villages*, and H. Newby, C. Bell, D. Rose, and P. Saunders, *Property, Paternalism and Power: Class and Control in Rural England* (London 1978).

Part III

The great estate and estate communities
c. 1700–1820

8   The rise and fall of Verney fortunes in the eighteenth century 1740–1820

The history of the Verney estates from 1740 to 1820 provides a spectacular example of aristocratic dissipation of wealth, indebtedness, and reconstruction. The second Earl Verney managed not only to consume the £70,000 in portions that he and his brother had received, plus the inheritance that his wife received from her father, but also to put the estate over £100,000 in debt. The management of that debt, and his successor's re-establishment of sound finances, meant that by 1820 a compact but much diminished landed estate remained, and permitted the nineteenth- and twentieth-century Verneys to play an important part in Buckinghamshire society and politics.

The second earl's enormous fortune had been built up over three generations, carefully marshalled by thrifty lifestyles, carefully planned marriages, and obedient elder sons, and brought to fruition by two spectacular heiress marriages. How was it dissipated in a single generation? There was no inherited financial crisis. In 1740 the Verneys were solvent, with resources spread between land and sound paper investments. Nor were there hidden family charges, liabilities to younger brothers and sisters, or crippling jointures, though there was the substantial family liability of £1,600 a year to John Verney's widow, and the prospect of raising a £20,000 dowry for her daughter. Yet £70,000 of new money more than compensated for this. Not all of it was instantly accessible. Of Mary Nicholson's £40,000, £20,000 was in cash, but the remainder was only payable on her father's death. Of Mary Herring's £30,000, only £7,000 was in cash, but £20,000 was in East India stock that could be easily sold.

Until the second half of the 1750s there is no indication that the Verneys were spending heavily at all. Indeed, all the major damage was inflicted on the family finances in the seventeen years between 1754 and 1771. It coincided with the period after the death of his father in 1752 in which Ralph, the second Earl Verney, sought to make a name for himself in Buckinghamshire society and national politics, building extensively, buying himself a political interest, and engaging in a variety of financial and commercial schemes. It represented a major reversal in the family's policy of unostentatious aggrandisement and detachment from national office or political intrigue. Once drawn into that world, Verney could not alter his lifestyle to match his resources. During the 1770s, when his finances were already shaky, his responses to crisis were self-deceiving, in-adequate, and often counter-productive, making his eventual bankruptcy even more pathetic.

Yet Ralph, second Earl Verney, was not a profligate rake. His downfall un-doubtedly reflected elements in his character that made him less steadfast to the iron grip of dynastic advancement and power than his predecessors. He was the younger son, and his parents' fourth child. When family friends, dependants, and more particularly servants, sent reports about the behaviour of any child in their care, the results cannot be taken at face value, but as a six- and seven-year-old Ralph Verney was regarded as of 'sweet temper, vivacity, innocence'. He was 'a trouble to none' and took philosophically the loss of a drum and fiddle sent down as presents but smashed in the wagon. He was educated at school in Fulham near his parents' London residence. In 1732 he thought of travelling abroad, but rejected the idea and went to Christ's College Cambridge from 1732 to 1735, where he was regarded as a diligent scholar and took his degree in December 1735. He was intended for the church, but on graduation declared his intention of studying law at the Temple for the next term insisting that it would be 'no hindrance to my taking Holy Orders at any time'.[1] During his childhood, the Verneys spent an increasing part of the year in London, at a house leased in Little Chelsea, close to their Palmer relatives. Yet when his brother died in 1737 Ralph immediately took on his mantle, throwing himself into learning about estate management, spending much time at Claydon, tak-ing full control of the management of the enclosure of East Claydon. All this suggests a man as malleable to the family purpose as any of his siblings. No great attempt seems to have been made to find marriage partners for his sisters. Elizabeth did not marry until 1748, when she was thirty-eight, and her husband was Lord Sherard, heir to the Earl of Harborough. However, she survived for only eight years, and had no children, suffering several miscarriages. Catherine never married and her family nickname was 'Lady Mouse'. She died in 1750.[2] By 1756, Ralph had few living blood relatives on his father's side. His aunt Elizabeth who died in 1767, and his niece and heir, Mary Verney, were the closest, and there were Caves and Lovetts, but they were no longer close. On his wife's side, her parents had died, and there remained a sister.

The underlying explanation for the second earl's dramatic spending and de-bacle must lie in the failure of his generation to provide a male heir. By the time the first earl died in 1752, he must have been all too aware that his elder son John's posthumous daughter, Mary, was his only likely grandchild, for Ralph's wife Mary Herring proved to be unable to carry a child to term. Less than two years after her marriage in 1740, she was pregnant but miscarried. There must have been several further episodes, for by September 1748 she was described as

[1] M. M. Verney, *Verney Letters*, II, pp. 173–80.   [2] *Ibid.*, II, pp. 235–45.

suffering 'her old complaint which 'tis impossible to remedy', and the doctors had given up all hope, not even bothering to tell her to take to her bed.[3]

During his lifetime, the first earl (raised to that rank in 1743) continued to act as the creator of a dynastic power base, using the new wealth from the two great dowries to enhance the family's financial position, and increasingly to turn that wealth into political power. Between 1740 and 1752 Ralph played the dutiful son to his father, running the estate at Claydon. In that time he and his father bought land with the dowry money in fulfilment of the terms of the marriage settlements of 1736 and 1740, choosing properties within striking distance of the Claydon estates.

Most of the £70,000 available was spent between 1740 and 1752 when the first earl died. They selected properties carefully, discussing and rejecting many possibilities. The first purchase was that of East Claydon tithes and rectory from John Duncombe. This cost £3,700 and was recorded in the 1740 marriage contract. Between 1740 and 1749 they bought small village properties in East and Steeple Claydon, as well as farms in the adjoining parishes of Hogshaw and Grandborough for a cost of some £5,000. In 1744 they bought compact enclosed estates with dairying tenants in the rural townships of the parish of Buckingham, Bourton, and Lenborough for £22,500 and £14,000. Smaller purchases at Thornborough in 1747 and Singleborough in Great Horwood in 1752 lay between the two groups of properties.[4] Properties were bought at Wendover to consolidate political control there, and further small estates there and in East Claydon were purchased in the early 1750s. However, the major addition at that time was of Biddlesden, to the north-west of Buckingham, beyond Stowe. The main estate cost £16,226, but was followed by consolidating small purchases soon afterwards.[5] This new centre around Biddlesden was further developed by the purchase of a substantial estate in Wappenham, just across the Northamptonshire border, from Lord Pomfret for £12,400 in 1759, and some small properties in the adjoining parishes of Abthorpe and Syresham.[6]

By 1767, when the second earl made a major new family settlement, he was able to show that he had spent £70,000 on land to add to the settled estate according to the terms of the marriage settlements of 1736 and 1740. By that time, he was virtually the sole owner of East Claydon as well as Middle Claydon, buying out the last substantial estate from the Duncombes in 1766. It is difficult

[3] *Ibid.*, II, pp. 241–2.

[4] For Thornborough see CIH 2/1380. The Singleborough purchases were made in the early 1750s and when sold in 1797 for £3,100 totalled something over five yardlands, and a sixth share of the manor. See BCRO D/X/584 and CIH 2/1266 and 2/1268.

[5] Details of these purchases are found amongst the Claydon House deeds. Apart from those transactions detailed in the deeds, the clearest list is in BL Egerton MS 2353. However this covers only the settled estate, and by 1780 land worth about £2,000 a year was excluded from this.

[6] CIH 2/2021 dated 21 July 1759.

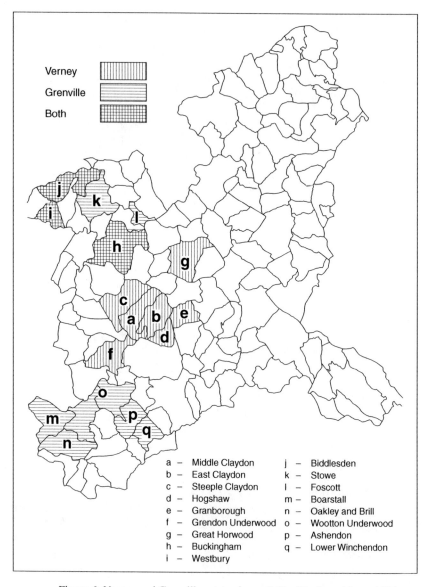

Figure 6 Verney and Grenville estates in north Buckinghamshire *c.* 1770.

to be certain of the second earl's landed income at this period, as there is no full estate rental, but the gross total was probably between £8,500 and £10,000.

The other major investment made by the Verneys before 1752 aimed at building a political power base in Buckinghamshire, particularly in Wendover. This pre-dated the influx of money from marriage settlements. In the years after 1731, the first earl began to buy up Lord Limerick's property there. By 1741 the Verneys had 110 properties and were able to take over the Limerick interest and control one of the parliamentary seats, where the first earl sat until his death in 1752.[7] The Hampden family also had political interests in Wendover but was financially embarrassed after losses in the South Sea Bubble. The Verneys bought them out during the 1740s, and after Hampden's death in 1753 controlled both seats.[8] The cost of building this borough interest is unclear, but it was sold in 1794 for £35,000.[9]

In the first earl's last years his son Ralph was often the model son, but father and son were not always at one in their views. The first earl was parsimonious in the extreme. He strongly opposed his son's proposal to set up a separate London establishment in the mid-1740s, but Ralph and Mary did eventually set up a London home in Bond Street. At one point the first earl wanted to save money by closing down Claydon House, and suggested that his son took up residence in the house on a newly purchased property at Thornborough. Ralph parried his father cleverly, by saying that his father-in-law, Henry Herring, loved to come down to Claydon to stay. He warned that Henry Herring's will, which currently benefited Ralph's wife, might be re-written if he was displeased. Once again, the son seems to have resisted his father's schemes successfully.[10]

During his lifetime, the first earl conserved family resources to advantage the prospects of future generations, still hoping for a male heir to carry on the line. At his death in 1752, the Verneys were solvent, with substantial estates in the county, few debts, and good lines of credit through their new marriages and older commercial networks. Politically they controlled the two Wendover borough seats, and this entry into politics was another stage in repositioning the family socially. An assessment of the first earl by Lord Egmont around 1750 was that he 'lives a close sort of life, does not know very much of the world, and seems a man to be gained with what will cost very little'.[11]

---

[7] R. Sedgwick, *The History of Parliament: The House of Commons, 1715–54* (2 vols. London 1970), entry for Wendover. CIH 1/155, 2/1480, 4/6/65.

[8] On the Hampden financial embarrassment see Habakkuk, *Marriage, Debt and the Estate System*, pp. 323–5.

[9] CIH 2/1413. Originally it was sold to J. B. Church (who had previously lent money secured on it) for £25,600, but after a court case Lady Fermanagh was able to buy it back for £30,000, and re-sell immediately for £35,000. See CIH 1/338 and 2/1404.

[10] M. M. Verney, *Verney Letters*, II, pp. 186, 193.

[11] Sedgwick, *House of Commons, 1715–54*, entries for Ralph Verney and for Wendover.

After his father's death, the second earl began expansive projects on many fronts. The broad outline of events is reasonably clear, but the nature of the archives at Claydon changes in the mid-eighteenth century and makes precision about costs, income, and expenditure extremely rare. Instead of long runs of correspondence, interspersed with accounts, lists of properties, debts, and the usual range of estate documents, we find legal case papers and their supporting documentation predominating.

In the absence of an heir, the second earl used the family assets for more immediate purposes of pleasure and power. When his father died he made 31/32 Curzon St in Mayfair his London home for the rest of his life. It is a rather plain and severe Georgian house formed by linking two adjoining houses that dated from the 1730s, but its austerity was not reflected in many of the second Earl's other activities.[12] Money was spent rebuilding Claydon House. The stable and workshop square beside the house still stands, and proudly displays the date 1754. The building of the new Claydon House is shrouded in a mystery that the Claydon archive does little to unravel. A wrapper marked 'Verney vs. Lightfoot' that must once have contained the papers for a court case between Verney and his builder is tantalisingly empty. Lindsay Boynton's article based on Chancery records in the Public Record office reveals as much as the Claydon papers.

The story is that while Verney was refurbishing his Curzon St house in 1757 a London carver, Luke Lightfoot, replaced a chimneypiece. Verney took to Lightfoot, who became the managing builder at Claydon House. Lightfoot is otherwise unknown as an architect and builder. The overall design was probably Verney's own, and the undistinguished exterior of the house lends credence to this idea. A new two-block house was planned, facing westwards, with an entrance portico between the two buildings. The first, and surviving, block was enmeshed at every level with the existing, south-facing, Tudor house. Lightfoot quickly gained Verney's confidence and after the first year's work little account of the costs was kept for ten years. Much of the present eighteenth-century house was constructed and Lightfoot filled it with the extravagant rococo carvings that are one of the house's lasting claims to fame. Lightfoot continued to work until 1767, by which time the shell of the grand portico and the north wing, with its ballroom, were also well under way.[13]

Most of our information about Lightfoot's work comes from a hostile source. In 1766 the second earl brought in a friend and business associate, Sir Thomas Robinson, to examine progress at Claydon. Robinson was something of an

---

[12] I would like to thank Robert Thorne for help in tracking down details of the house. Some evidence of its earlier owner is found in ClH 2/1957–8.

[13] L. Boynton, 'Luke Lightfoot (?1722–1789)', *Furniture History* 2 (1966), pp. 7–17; PRO C12/532/29 and C12/1519/83; other Lightfoot material at Claydon in scarce but is mainly found in ClH 2/2019 4/6/80 5/2/82 5/2/83 5/2/88 5/2/92 5/2/94/1-11 5/2/96/1-2 5/3/86-8.

architect, and well known as a man-about-town of extravagant tastes. He had persuaded Verney to buy shares in the Ranelagh pleasure gardens in Chelsea. At Claydon he began to accuse Lightfoot of waste and extravagance. His correspondence with Verney suggests that Lightfoot had received £50 weekly on account over the previous ten years, a total of some £30,000. Robinson valued the work at Claydon at some £7,000, insinuating that Lightfoot was defrauding Verney rather than merely being wasteful. Eventually Verney sued Lightfoot for repayment of moneys advanced.[14]

Robinson was not a disinterested friend. When Lightfoot was dismissed, Robinson took over and replaced Claydon's rococo flamboyance with a more restrained classicism found in the salon, which was decorated in plaster rather than wood, and in the grand staircase. He brought in Italian plasterers, one of whom, Giovanni Padrola, remained at Claydon until work was halted in 1783. Robinson worked at Claydon until 1771, battling with sagging foundations and an over-heavy roof in his attempts to finish the ballroom. At this point he and Verney quarrelled and Verney carried on the work at Claydon helped by William Donn, despite his growing financial troubles.[15] New plasterers were engaged in 1777, and Verney ordered painted panels for the ballroom from an Italian painter in 1780. When the finances reached crisis point in 1783 there were still nineteen men employed on the house. All were dismissed and sent back to their villages, while the Italian Padrola remained at Claydon, supported out of the poor rates until 1791.[16]

Claydon House was constructed without much heed of cost, with a new designer halfway through, and probably largely according to the whims and prejudices of Verney and his builders rather than to a well-developed plan. We are unlikely to know the cost, but it was not cheap. A contemporary estimated a figure of £70,000, which is not implausible if Lightfoot received £30,000 on account up to 1767, and building works went on for fifteen years after he had been dismissed.[17]

We do not know whether the resplendent new house was ever in full use. Verney lived there at times during the 1770s and 1780s, although he also resided at Biddlesden. By 1780 it was certainly inhabitable, and a considerable amount of furniture was sold from it in 1783. But it seems unlikely that it was ever used as the centre of a political and social empire, with balls and pageants on the model of Stowe. By the mid-eighties Verney could no longer afford such grandeur. In 1784 he was forced to leave for the continent when he lost his seat

---

[14] CIH 5/3/86-8.   [15] For Donn see CIH 12/2/12-14.

[16] M. M. Verney and Patrick Abercrombie (eds.), 'Letters of an eighteenth-century Architect', *Architectural Review*, 59–60 (June–September 1926). References to John Padrola are to be found in the eighteenth-century Middle Claydon poor accounts BCRO PR52/12/4.

[17] The figure of £70,000 is given in an estate particular dated 1786 and a mortgage deed of 1790 CIH 1/170.

in parliament and thus immunity from his creditors. When he died, the Baroness Fermanagh decided that the ballroom and portico were unnecessary, and pulled them down.[18] Earl Verney's energies as builder and developer were largely confined to Claydon. He financed two small urban property developments. One, with Luke Lightfoot, was in Bermondsey; the other, with Oakley Halford, an apothecary, in Pimlico. He made no money from either enterprise. At the time of his financial collapse in 1783, the Earl owned houses at Claydon and Biddlesden, his town house in Curzon Street, Mayfair, and a fashionable seaside retreat at Ramsgate.[19]

Verney poured large amounts of time and money into politics. His main aim would appear to be to gain some recognition for his position and the power of his money. In the 1750s he worked with the administration, offering Newcastle access to his parliamentary patronage in 1754 and 1761. Later he supported Fox over the Peace of Paris, seconding the Address on the Peace preliminaries, regularly attending the whole session, and then applying to him for a British peerage. Later he attached himself to the Grenvilles and Grafton, and then to the Rockingham administration. His relationship with the Grenvilles was a strangely schizophrenic one. George Grenville and Verney apparently had no liking for each other, and they were electoral rivals in the county. Verney and his father had fed rivalry between the families by buying estates in and around Buckingham, encroaching on the Stowe estates, including one confrontation on the ground in 1748 about adjoining stone pits between Buckingham and Stowe where the Verneys' agents threw spoil into the Grenville pits.[20] Verney never seriously challenged the Grenvilles' hold on their pocket borough in Buckingham, but bought considerable property in the parish and borough. In 1777 Verney gave land to rebuild the dilapidated church on a site on Castle Hill that would mortify Grenville 'as that part does not answer for a view through the centre of his arch, up the flight of steps, the middle of his House, as where he intended building it'.[21] From the late 1750s Verney compounded his land purchase strategy by moving his country residence from Claydon to Biddlesden, adjoining Stowe parish, while the new Claydon House was being built.

In the early 1760s the two families briefly worked together closely in common interest over John Wilkes, the radical MP for Aylesbury who became notorious for his attacks on Lord Bute and George III. Grenville and Verney both became Governors of the Foundling Hospital at the very time Wilkes was setting up his Aylesbury branch establishment, which he was later shown to

---

[18] Details of the various contents of Claydon and Curzon St in the 1780s are found in sale catalogues in ClH 4/7/83/25 27, 1/271-7, 5/5/28/18-20.

[19] For Halford see ClH 5/3/2-5; for Bermondsey ClH 1/282, 2/2197, 2/2208, 5/3/87-8, 4/6/80.

[20] M. M. Verney, *Verney Letters*, II, p. 243 and 4/6/62/1-22.

[21] ClH 5/1/23 for correspondence and the private Act of parliament.

have defrauded.[22] Verney and Grenville were also patrons of the rising political star, Edmund Burke, but it was Verney who provided William with a parliamentary seat at Great Bedwyn from 1764 and Edmund with one at Wendover in 1765 where he remained MP for nine years. Contemporaries believed William Burke's influence over Verney was considerable, and one wrote 'he had as great a sway with Lord Verney as I ever knew one man have with another'. Edmund almost certainly composed much of *Thoughts on the Cause of Present Discontents* at Biddlesden in 1769. When Verney went bankrupt, Burke was embarrassed to have to look for new patrons and paid his benefactor a high compliment: 'if ever I have been able to attempt anything in a public way . . . it is wholly owing to him'.[23]

Yet for all his wealth and patronage, Verney never achieved office, and his only reward was admission to the Privy Council in 1763, even though he was not a minister. Verney–Grenville relations were often strained. In 1769 Burke and Verney worked with Grenville to help John Wilkes, and met to draw up a petition and discuss tactics, but did not eat together. Instead Verney and his supporters retired to Biddlesden. In the late 1770s Grenville and Verney both attended Aylesbury races but neither would acknowledge nor even raise a hat to the other. Nevertheless, Verney built support across the county so successfully that he was nominated for the county seat in 1768, holding it unopposed through to 1784, when against the political tide he lost by only twenty-four votes. The Grenvilles did not oppose him then or in 1790 when, despite his poverty and advancing years, he was returned for the county unopposed. His popularity was perhaps linked to his radical stance on a number of issues, including parliamentary reform and Fox's East India Bill.[24] But he also developed an increasingly sophisticated political organisation at county level. Richard W. Davis detected its origins in the aftermath of the 1784 election defeat, but it was apparently already in being in 1778, and in 1782 Verney's supporters produced a most elaborately printed invitation card for their London dinner. Political organisation and fundraising became much more important as Verney's finances declined. Two of Verney's oldest political allies, Joseph Bullock and Sir John Lovett, played a prominent part, while its Treasurer and Secretary in 1790 was George Minshull, who had also loaned Verney large sums of money.[25]

[22] P. D. G. Thomas, *John Wilkes: A Friend of Liberty* (Oxford 1996), ch. 1 and R. K. McClure, *Coram's Children: The London Foundling Hospital in the Eighteenth Century* (Newhaven and London 1981), pp. 121, 123, 141.

[23] See particularly the *History of Parliament* articles on Verney, Edmund Burke, and William Burke, and more generally in T. W. Copeland (eds.), *The Correspondence of Edmund Burke*, 10 vols. (Cambridge 1958–78), vols. I and II.

[24] L. Namier, and J. Brooke, *The History of Parliament, The House of Commons 1754–1790* (3 vols. London 1964), III, pp. 580–2.

[25] R. W. Davis, *Political Change and Continuity 1760–1885: A Buckinghamshire Study* (Newton Abbot 1972), pp. 38–9.

Before 1768, Verney also spent money and effort making an interest in borough seats outside Buckinghamshire. He sold his influence in the Wiltshire borough of Great Bedwyn to Lord Bruce in 1766 for £18,000, and also secured an interest in Carmarthen borough where he was MP from 1761–8.[26] No accurate account of Verney's overall political spending is possible, but very considerable amounts of money were spent buying and cultivating interests in his chosen seats, and on election campaigns themselves. Yet Verney failed to turn his influence and political loyalty into office or lasting recognition. A review of his wider social and business activities in the 1750s and 1760s suggests some reasons why he was regarded as a political lightweight.

When Verney's obituary in the *Gentleman's Magazine* described him as a 'man of great plainness', it meant his direct and open approach to all matters, and lack of guile and intrigue, not his physical appearance. His renowned generosity left him open to fraudulent schemes. He took people at their own valuation, and was patron of a range of struggling and unknown writers as well as the Burkes. One such was Samuel Rogers, who spent his time translating Swift and Goldsmith into Latin verse. Perhaps he lacked sophistication, or even intelligence. His adult signature remained very plain and childlike. Yet he had large amounts of money, and wanted to make his mark. From a family without wide social and political networks, he was an isolated figure, yet one who attracted great loyalty from those in his inner circle.

We know surprisingly little about Verney's social habits and expenditure from the Verney manuscripts, and much more from contemporary commentators. Buckinghamshire's county historian, Lipscomb, wrote that he was:

One of the last of the English nobility who, to the splendour of a gorgeous equipage, attached musicians, constantly attendant upon him, not only on state occasions but in his journeys and visits: a brace of tall Negroes with silver French-horns behind his coach and six perpetually making a noise.

He probably employed far more servants than his antecedents. He is said to have loved music, though the existence of a harpsichord and hand organ in the inventory of one room of his house, and a passing reference to his organising a series of musical entertainments, are the only solid evidence. He subscribed to numerous publications and in 1783 his library consisted of some 3,000 volumes in nine mahogany bookcases. They included such standard items as Dugdale, Holinshed, and Speed, as well as a general dictionary and various vellum manuscripts concerning ship money. Many of the books were classical texts, and Samuel Rogers declared Verney to be 'a perfect master of the [Latin]

---

[26] See Sedgwick, *The House of Commons, 1715–54* on Great Bedwyn, and for 1754 leases CIH 2/2247-57.

language'.[27] His range of interests befitted a well-rounded eighteenth-century aristocrat. He became a Fellow of the Royal Society. In 1790 a Royal command requested him, with twenty-one other gentlemen, to evaluate a new remedy for tree diseases. He took an interest in charitable works and became a Governor of the Foundling Hospital. He liked horse racing, and had use of a house at Epsom during race week. He probably owned racehorses, and perhaps racing pigeons.[28]

Verney invested in many business ventures in the 1750s and 1760s. Sir Thomas Robinson persuaded him to become a shareholder in the Ranelagh Gardens in London.[29] He was an easy target for speculators and swindlers in the 1760s. One was the English Linen Company, which Negley Harte has described as 'one of the most audacious smuggling projects of the century'. Verney helped the bill to set it up through Parliament, but only a year later the scheme collapsed. The major loser was Verney, who although only a minor shareholder had actually paid up his shares, unlike Sir George Colebrooke, the mastermind behind the scheme, and his colleagues, who never actually put up their capital. Verney had been duped, and found himself liable for £2,000 in 1775.[30]

He was equally out of his depth in coal mining. In 1764 he obtained a grant of the Honour of Pontefract, including Leeds and Bradford, to exploit the residual rights over minerals and waste lands. Verney began mining at Purston near Featherstone, investing some £4,000 to install a steam engine and dig shafts between 1765 and 1769, yet the mine produced no more than £569 worth of coal partly because he was attempting to manage it at a distance with little knowledge or experience. He also used the Honour to make claims on wastelands, opposing enclosure acts to extract compensation. Verney then allowed the appointment of a new steward in 1775, who permitted one of Verney's competitors to fill up the mine and break up the roads. Overall, the Honour proved an expensive and unprofitable speculation.[31] Another speculation involving coal mines in Cumberland during the 1760s arose out of a legacy meant to satisfy unpaid

[27] G. Lipscomb, *The History and Antiquities of the County of Buckingham* (London 1847), vol. I, pp. 183–4. Inventory of books dated 4 May 1781 CIH 5/4/26/8; there is also a list of over 1,000 books at Curzon Street in 2/1959; S. Rodgers to rvjr 21 August 1784 5/5/8.

[28] Request dated 29 November 1790 CIH 5/5/28/7; Oakley Halford to rvjr 21 June 1763, 1 August 1772 5/3/2; ? to rvjr 29 November 1790 5/5/26–8.

[29] CIH 5/1/30/3-5, 5/5/21/4, 5/5/28/12.

[30] Details of the Linen Company scheme come mainly from papers concerning Colebrook vs. Verney in CIH 6/17/1, 2; cf. PRO PC 1/7/95 and BL Add. MS 38446 fo. 18. For an account of the scheme see N. Harte in N. B. Harte, and K. G. Ponting, *Textile History and Economic History, Essays in Honour of Miss Julia de Laey Mann* (Manchester 1973), pp. 84ff.

[31] Evidence on the Yorkshire enterprises is found in CIH 2/2283-4, 4/6/82, 5/2/35-55, 6/31/1-4; cf. PRO DL 5/46 49/43 and BL Add. MSS 38446, fo. 18. I would like to thank John Goodchild, Archivist of Wakefield Metropolitan District Council, for local information.

debts to Verney. How Verney became involved with the mines, Great and Little Clifton, that were let to James Lowther, is unclear. Again, the luckless Verney made nothing of his claims.[32]

All Verney's 'industrial' investments were disastrous, often for lack of supervision of enterprises at a great distance from London. They were speculative, aimed at quick profits, and, in at least one instance, fraudulent. Perhaps during the 1760s Verney invested in them because his estates lacked the urban land or mineral resources that were increasingly important contributors to the incomes of great estates.[33] During the 1760s he spent both capital and income, and ran up very considerable debts. He increased his available resources by tapping his wife's fortune, and re-settling the family estates, but operated largely on credit, raising money on bonds, notes, and bills, and running up large bills with shopkeepers, trades people, and all kinds of suppliers. Those around him presumed that he wanted money all the time. On one occasion a broker employed to sell some shares failed to find a buyer immediately, so automatically borrowed some money in Verney's name, assuming that he needed cash. Verney's accounting systems give little clue to the scale of his investments and commitments at this time, and he probably had very little idea of his overall financial position. His credit rested on his reputation, and the fame of his dowries and until 1771 he could always raise cash easily. In part he was spending his money because he had no heirs to pass it on to.

It was a supreme irony that, after the first earl patiently built up his estates and fortune, forged a political interest, and arranged spectacular matches for both his sons, the male Verney blood line ended with the death of Ralph, the second earl in 1791. The first earl became resigned to Mary Herring's childlessness before his death, and wrote a final codicil to his will directing that, in default of sons, the estate should descend in the female line. His granddaughter, Mary Verney, would eventually succeed.

The second earl had a complex relationship with his widowed sister-in-law, Mary Nicholson. Mary was guardian of her daughter, Mary Verney, but the second earl was executor of his brother's will, which carried significant powers. Mary Nicholson remarried Richard Calvert, a member of a London brewing family like her own, with estates in Hertfordshire. Her sister and co-heiress, Christian, had also married a Calvert, binding the Nicholsons and Calverts closer. Mary Nicholson received the handsome jointure of £1,600 a year until her death in 1789, and this was never disputed. Yet the second earl spent some

---

[32] The full story of Verney's Cumberland involvement is highly complex, and at one point Verney was bequeathed the interests in the mines of both parties in a legal dispute Ord vs. Salkeld. This case eventually turned on whether an English Catholic nun in a French convent had died before or after her brother. The mother superior was not very obliging in her answer. CIH 2/1552-59, 5/2/1-33, 5/5/14, 19, 22.

[33] See, e.g. J. V. Beckett, *The Aristocracy in England 1660–1914* (1986), chs. 6–7.

eight years contesting liabilities to his niece Mary Verney in Chancery until 1761.

There were two issues. One was two legacies of £1,000 each that the first earl left his granddaughter in the third codicil to his will. More significant was Mary Verney's portion of £20,000, determined in the 1736 marriage settlement and surely intended to be paid when a suitable match was arranged. Yet Earl Verney and his lawyers argued that the words in the marriage settlement: 'if the daughter attains her age in her father or mother's lifetime her portion shall be paid within one year after the decease of the survivor', meant that the portion was only payable at her mother's death. Chancery agreed with their arguments. Mary Verney was forty-nine when her mother died in 1789, and received her portion only two years before she inherited the whole of the Verney estates.

Despite this, Mary Verney was no pauper and could easily have married advantageously. Her grandfather Josias Nicholson left her £7,871 in 1745, payable at the age of twenty-one in 1758. In 1761 she received a further £2,000 from Verney when Chancery forced him to pay the legacies in his father's will. In bringing the suit against her uncle, Mary Verney faced immense difficulties. Because Verney was executor of her father's will she required parliamentary permission through a private Act to sue him in Chancery.[34] Verney appeared determined to bring the matter to trial, but Mary Verney and the Calverts would have preferred a quiet family agreement. Yet there is no evidence that Mary Verney felt deeply embittered against her uncle. In 1759 she wrote to her lawyer: 'I trust to you to proceed in this affair in every respect the best for my advantage in the gentlest manner possible.' There were ambiguities on Verney's side too, for as he began the suit against his niece, his electoral influence provided John Calvert with a parliamentary seat at Wendover in 1754.[35]

Why did Earl Verney not feel as generous towards his nearest relative? The major reason may well have been the codicil in his father's will confirming female succession to the estates in default of the male line and specifically naming Mary and her heirs male and female. Verney therefore had no say in the final disposition of his estate. The dynastic imperative and patriarchal power remained supreme to the last. After the court case he acknowledged Mary Verney's right to succession in a grand family settlement in 1767.[36]

Verney's spendthrift habits reflected ingrained dynastic ambition left without purpose, just as the Duke of Newcastle's lack of an heir led him to dedicate his

[34] The private act is in 31 Geo II (1758) Private c13 but is not so much concerned with this case as with the Herring estate and additional money from it.
[35] For details of the case including pleadings and correspondence see CIH 5/1/32/1-6 and 6/62-72 esp. 6/69. For Calvert at Wendover see Sedgwick, *The House of Commons, 1715–54*.
[36] The 1767 settlement exists in BL MS Egerton 2353; it was organised by Robert Harper (see his letter of 1766 5/514) and fo. 28 notes the codicil to the first Earl's will in favour of heirs female made on 20 September 1752. For Harper see S. Lambert, *Bills and Acts: Legislative Procedure in Eighteenth-century England* (Cambridge 1971), ch. 1.

life to politics.[37] Verney was endowed with considerable wealth yet made little impact in political or public life and had every incentive to spend his money. There was something of the spoilt child in him. He combined a most unworldly, childlike trust in humanity in general and his friends in particular, with a frustration at not getting his own way. This helps explain how his reputation for generosity in the political and artistic worlds paralleled stubbornly litigious dealings with his family on financial matters and with his creditors in later years. His preoccupation with legal process was, as with so many other aspects of his life, completely at odds with three previous generations of Verneys who avoided litigation wherever possible.

He continually sought new sources of money to support his lifestyle. One lay with his wife's family. Mary Herring was one of three sisters. Henrietta Maria married Kenrick Clayton, son of Sir William Clayton in 1735, while Sarah never married, and died in 1757.[38] At marriage Mary and Henrietta Maria were endowed with money, as well as a third share of properties in London, Southwark, and Middlesex. They were also granted the reversion of Exchequer annuities worth almost £300 a year. In Mary's case this was put into a trust for her own rather than her husband's use. In 1744 a trust was also set up to hold annuities for the third daughter, Sarah. When Henry Herring died in October 1752 he left Mary a further £13,202 in bank stock in his will. Although earmarked 'for her separate use', there is no evidence that Mary ever asserted separate rights in it. When Sarah died in 1757, the Verneys and Claytons went to law to secure Sarah's property for themselves and eventually tapped tens of thousands of pounds, but only after lengthy and costly litigation.

Verney also came to believe that he had claims on various properties. Most of these had been used by others to secure debts they owed to Verney. Thus Verney claimed several estates in the West Indies as a result of his dealings with Luke Lightfoot and the Earl of Shelburne, while a claim to Cumberland coal mines ultimately derived from another unpaid debt. Expectations from these properties enabled Verney to spend above his means throughout the 1760s. He also tended to ignore the impact of considerable financial obligations such as the handsome jointure of £1,600 a year payable to Mary Nicholson, his brother's widow. When his sister Elizabeth married her dowry of £5,000 was not paid and instead she agreed to take interest on it amounting to £250 a year. When she died in 1756 that capital sum fell due.[39] Another Elizabeth, his aunt, was also paid £150 a year in lieu of her dowry, and when she died in 1766 he was forced to find £1,000 to pay bequests.[40] Even Verney's court victory against the Calverts in 1761 only delayed the payment of Mary Verney's £20,000 which would become due at her mother's death.

[37] R. A. Kelch, *Newcastle, a Duke without Money: Thomas Pelham-Holles, 1693–1768* (Berkeley, CA and London 1974).
[38] For the various settlements see CIH1/530-42.   [39] CIH 5/5/22/1.   [40] CIH 1/169.

Verney had no means of knowing his true financial position for the best part of twenty years because he failed to set up financial management and control systems suitable for his expanded enterprises and cash flow. It was unimportant up to 1770. He had access to bank stock as well as landed income and was able to treat the Verney estates as a bank, allowing his bills of hand to circulate freely, and when necessary discounting them. In 1786 over £6,000 worth of his bills were in circulation or outstanding. It was a simple practice, and quite painless. He may well have learnt the technique from his father-in-law, Henry Herring, whose notebooks show him listing his 'running' money in the 1720s, and 1730s, in amounts totalling up to £20,000 at any one time.[41] There is no evidence that Verney ever kept a tally of his own bills.

This is the family and financial context of the downfall of the second Earl Verney. The collapse was set in train by East India Company dealings in the late 1760s. It reached a climax in 1783–4 when he effectively became bankrupt. Although he had been spending beyond his means for many years only a spectacular speculative disaster overrode the access to numerous interlocking sources of wealth that had made his credit apparently limitless.

Verney's losses in the various schemes he engaged in during the 1760s were tiny compared with those that triggered his financial ruin. In 1769 he became liable for losses of over £50,000 on the Amsterdam futures market in English East India Company stock. When the scale of the debt became widely known, Verney found it difficult to raise credit and could not adjust his lifestyle and expenditure to pay the debt off. Over fourteen years the debts increased until eventually his creditors' patience was exhausted. The second earl suffered the humiliation of seeing his furniture and books seized, and his tenants' stock impounded. When he lost his seat in parliament in the 1784 election, at least partly because of lack of finance, he was forced to flee to the continent to avoid imprisonment for debt. During the next eight years, trustees gradually put the estates in order, but it was only after Earl Verney's death that the amazing ramifications of the debt were set in order by his niece and heir, Mary Verney, who became Baroness Fermanagh.

The great East India speculation was a direct result of British success in the Seven Years War and the spectacular territorial gains in India confirmed in 1763. The immediate beneficiary was the East India Company, which experienced a huge surge in its profits. The battle for control of those profits spilled into English politics. Three linked processes interacted. One, within the East India Company, set the nabobs and company agents in India against the London directors, primarily over the question of how far the windfall profits should be reflected in higher dividends. At the same time the company and the government debated the company's role in governing India. Various political

---

[41] Herring's notebook, which covers the period 1707–52 is in CIH 7/81.

factions took the battle into the company by buying East India stock, in attempts to alter the Board of Directors and change policy. Verney was a member of a partnership with Lauchlin Macleane and William Burke, buying stock, and at a later stage dealing in the Amsterdam futures market in English East India stock. Finally the price of East India stock began to rise dramatically, driven by the combination of windfall profits in India, and political intrigue in England. Speculators and disinterested financiers began to invest in the stock purely for capital gains.[42]

Verney played a small part in the political battles, but became deeply involved financially. As part of the political faction around Shelburne he bought East India stock and then sub-divided the holdings to multiply the shareholders to vote in a new Board of Directors willing to raise dividends. At a later stage he was tempted to use the rising price of the stock to make capital gains. Sutherland found evidence from legal cases that Verney was already more than £70,000 in debt by 1769. Most of Verney's mortgages were raised in the period from 1766 to 1769 when he was actively involved in this East India Company scheme.[43]

Although £70,000 was a very considerable sum, it was not large enough to embarrass Verney publicly. It was probably to recoup some of his losses that he entered into a foolhardy scheme with the impoverished William Burke. Verney and Burke went into a fifty-fifty partnership to speculate in East India Company futures. Sutherland has shown that Verney and William Burke were already involved in these speculations in 1766. At first they made profits, and Burke claimed to have made £12,000 at one stage. Burke managed the final speculation, but Verney put up all the money. Since he was trading on margins, this simply meant putting his credit on the line. For Burke it meant a half share of any profits for no capital outlay.[44]

Burke and Verney began their collaborative speculation as the boom ended. Between May and November 1769 the share price fell from 278¼ to 226, some 18.7 per cent. Burke and Verney were speculating on such a scale that this fall meant a loss of £38,000 for them. They held on in hope of a recovery, but the shares fell further, and they eventually lost almost £52,000. Since William Burke had no substantial resources of his own, the Amsterdam broker Van Jever, sued Verney for the whole sum. The loss was one that Verney could not sustain and he vainly attempted to recover money from Burke. The episode

---

[42] L. S. Sutherland, *The East India Company in Eighteenth-century Politics* (Oxford 1952), provides the best overview.

[43] L. S. Sutherland, and John A. Wood, 'The East India speculations of William Burke', *Proceedings of the Leeds Philosophical Society – Literary and Historical Section* II, pt vii (1966), pp. 183–216, provides much detail on Verney's involvement with William Burke; p. 215 Appendix IV provides a picture of Verney mortgages that is generally confirmed by CIH 1/231-51.

[44] See rvjr to Van Jever 4 December 1768 CIH 5/5/10 and 6/40/1-5.

ruined William's career and ironically led him to leave for India later to try and make his fortune there. Verney used delaying tactics to avoid paying the debt, making an issue of whether the case should be heard in London or Amsterdam, and claiming that he had ordered the purchase of shares, not options for future purchase. Final judgement came only in 1771, but the court ordered him to pay off £47,000 by annual instalments of £5,000. It was a crippling burden, costing Verney more than half his annual income at a time when his debts were already large and his lifestyle extravagant.[45]

There were other losses from the East India Company speculation. At one point Verney lent Lauchlin Macleane money with which to buy additional stock on a rising market. At the time of the crash in 1769, he was owed money by Macleane, and also £22,500 by the syndicate's broker, De La Fontaine. Verney held a mortgage for over £15,000 on West Indian estates in Grenada as security, but this proved worthless as the property was already security for other mortgages totalling over £40,000 and the estate was producing insufficient to cover the arrears of interest due.[46]

These huge debts entirely altered the complexion of the Verney finances. When the court ruled against him his credit rating instantly fell. News of his embarrassment had reached the press in July 1769, when it was claimed that 'a certain Irish Peer had been given up by his Brokers for refusing to pay his Differences'. A carefully worded statement from the brokers had shored up their credit as well as his during the crisis in the financial markets, and Verney's true position remained unknown to all but a few insiders.[47] After the 1771 court judgement, creditors rushed to secure their debts by taking out judgements for their bonds and other credit instruments. In the vast debt lists that pepper the Verney papers of the 1780s, the first lists of judgements taken out in Common Pleas and Exchequer against the Verney estates came in 1771 and their numbers accelerated towards the end of the decade.[48]

Verney might have been able to pay off the debts if he had been willing to make instant retrenchment and change his lifestyle in 1770 and 1771. He chose instead to fight all claims on fairly spurious grounds, and delay repayment. This was fatal to his long-term solvency. At the point when the final judgement made him repay £47,000 in yearly instalments of £5,000, London, and

[45] CIH 6/40/1-5 papers from Van Jever vs. Verney 1771; these include Van Jever's account with Verney, 1771–87, which shows how the money was paid to his executors even after his death in 1775.

[46] CIH 5/2/56-61 'Grenada' for Verney's attempts to recover something from the West Indian mortgage. One document /d gives an account of estate income and interest due which concludes 'the value of which [the residual income] were it to be sold is not equal to the arrears of interest due'; an audit of 1773 shows very little income and huge outlay.

[47] Sutherland, and Wood, 'The East India speculations of William Burke', pp. 199–200.

[48] Judgements listed in CIH 1/327, 5/6/2/1-4, 5/6/17/1-4, and Sutherland and Wood, 'The East India speculations of William Burke', p. 215.

indeed England, was just entering a wider financial crisis. Julian Hoppit has described the crisis of 1772 as the first financial crisis with a national dimension across private as well as public credit, linked to mounting economic growth, and causing bankruptcies in trade and industry nation-wide.[49] The paper-credit system based on circulating bills partially failed when banks in London and Ayr collapsed, triggered by the failure of Alexander Fordyce, a London banker who had been speculating in East India stock and fled to France when his bills were not honoured. This technique which Adam Smith described as 'swivelling', exactly paralleled Verney's own methods of financing his lifestyle throughout the 1760s. Verney also had links with Sir George Colebrooke's attempt to corner the world's supply of alum, crucial to textile finishing, which also collapsed in the 1772 crisis. Colebrooke was earlier central to the English Linen Company scheme with Verney, and also in the attempts to manipulate the East India Company, gaining a position on the board primarily for speculative reasons.[50] Verney never regained his financial credit, and was forced to ever more desperate measures to survive.

Verney made no sustained attempt to cut expenses or plan expenditure. He continued to spend freely, with many new tradesmens' bills amongst the papers for the 1780s. As late as 1781, when Verney was close to final disaster, he ordered servants' clothes to the value of over £129 in a period of eighteen months at one shop alone. In 1780 he ordered a series of eighty-eight paintings from Italy for the ballroom at Claydon House. Others were well aware of the situation. In 1774 Edmund Burke recognised that Verney's financial plight 'made it necessary for me either to quit publick life or find some other avenue to parliament than his interest'. Verney naturally tried to hide his financial embarrassments from general knowledge. When Earl Temple and he were feuding over the rebuilding of Buckingham church in 1777 Temple generously wrote that he was convinced that 'his [Verney's] present conduct is actuated by the unwillingness to make that state public then by an Intention of opposition to me'. Verney refused to accept that his affairs would not recover, but his activities during the 1770s made his financial situation worse, not better.[51]

Verney could still raise money because until 1766 he had no significant funded debts and he could secure loans on the estate. After 1776 these became general

[49] J. Hoppit, 'Financial crises in eighteenth-century England', *Economic History Review* 2nd series 39 (1986), pp. 39–58 esp. pp. 50–4; see also his *Risk and Failure in English Business 1700–1800* (Cambridge 1987), esp. ch. 8. For an older overview see T. S. Ashton, *Economic Fluctuations in England* (Oxford 1959), ch. 5.

[50] Hoppit, 'Financial crises', p. 53, and L. S. Sutherland, 'Sir George Colebrooke's world corner in alum, 1771–3', *Economic History* (1936), pp. 237–58 esp. p. 238.

[51] Bills June 1781–November 1782 ClH5/1/6/1-8, 5/2/78, 5/6/7, 5/6/29, 5/7; agreement with Colomba dated 15 July 1780 ClH 5/1/29/1; Copeland, *The Correspondence of Edmund Burke*, III pp. 32–33 (September 1774); IV, pp. 130–2 Burke to Portland 25 September 1779; Lord Temple to Mr Box [copy] 23 August 1777 ClH 5/1/23/1-41.

mortgages on the whole estate, suggesting an increasingly difficult situation. When he could raise no further mortgages he sold annuities for cash, a device used by the eighteenth-century aristocracy in desperation. This instrument rapidly became popular after 1773 after a favourable legal judgement, and an Act of Parliament of 1777 went no further than to require their registration.[52] These were additional to the family annuities already totalling £1,630 a year from the estate. In 1772–4 and 1778–80 annuities involving payments of £3,984 a year were sold.[53] The life element made annuities a gambling investment, because the commitment ended when the annuitant died. Verney sold annuities on his own life, but also, unusually for this period, on the life of the buyer, which was only possible on unsettled estates. The terms were based on the age and health of the purchaser, but reflected the declining state of Verney's credit too. They also enabled lenders to charge above the legal maximum rate of interest of 5 per cent. Thus one annuity in 1774 was based on two lives, and if treated as a straight loan with interest represented an interest rate of 5.88 per cent. In 1779, as the finances became worse, another paid £150 a year for a payment of only £720, equivalent to 21 per cent interest. The general drift of the situation was well put in one letter in 1782 when one of Verney's correspondents wrote: 'People who have Money now will not part with it at the simple Interest of £5 per cent when they can have near of quite £15 per cent.'[54]

Verney also found new ways of continuing his old practice of discounting accommodation bills. By 1778 Verney was discounting bills in the country because he could no longer do so in town. To float his bills he needed accomplices who would accept them, and recruited a number of failing businessmen to enable him to continue his 'swivelling'. The simplest case involved a Buckinghamshire laceman named Thompson Pater whose trade with the Eastern counties – particularly Cambridge and Norwich – was decaying during the 1770s. Verney accepted Pater's bills, and Pater in turn accepted Verney's. All went well until in 1778 Pater used Verney's bills as security for other loans without telling Verney, and then went bankrupt. Verney now had two problems – how to pass his bills, and how to pay the bills that had been used as security. Other bills were also drawn in London on Ralph Verney Knight, addressed to him at the house of Verney's apothecary friend and adviser, Oakley Halford. Who was Knight? The bills drawn on him by Verney appear to be signed by the same hand that accepted them. Initially I assumed that Verney had created a fictitious partner specifically for this purpose. However, Knight existed, whether or not he knew

[52] Habakkuk, *Marriage, Debt and the Estates System* (1994), ch. 4, esp. pp. 264–8.
[53] CIH 1/279–89, 1/312.
[54] CIH 1/287 lives of James Brown and Thomas Collinson of Lombard St, London, bankers; CIH 2/2197 Grant of Annuity 12 January 1779 to Benjamin Pope. The best overall view of the various debts and annuities in the period 1770–86 is the annotated debt list of 5 July 1786 CIH 5/1/3; C. Woodhouse to rvjr August 1782 CIH 5/3/57.

that Verney was using him as an accomplice on his financial schemes. He was probably an illegitimate child, and he and two sisters were provided for with annuities, while Knight was mentioned in Verney's will.[55]

Verney also found partners in Cornish tin mining to circulate his bills. His interest in tin mining began in about 1768 when he was apparently drawn into partnership with two merchants, Thomas and Vezian, by the lure of a patent to a new and faster tin-flagg grinding machine. The partnership took shares in a tin mine, Weal Ruth, near Penzance, intending to exploit the new invention with modern technology including steam engines. Verney's main contribution was to allow bills to be drawn on him in London, originally up to the value of £24,000. The mine produced little profit. When the whole system collapsed, Vezian sued Verney for £6,000, but could recover nothing. Later, in desperation, Verney accepted Vezian's offer to raise a loan of £24,000 for him in Holland on mortgage of the reversion of the fee simple of Middle Claydon, with Vezian taking a commission of £5,000 on the operation. Vezian failed to raise the sum, but held on to Verney's deeds as security for his original claim. By this stage Verney was using dubious expedients on the fringes of finance and trade, where he was quite out of his depth.[56]

These financial operations show how desperate Verney's plight became during the 1770s. From about 1777 Verney was unable to pay interest on many of his debts, and even on some of his annuities. New sources of credit gradually dried up. In 1774 Lady Verney released the bank stock she had been left by her father as security for more loans. Silver was sold in 1776 and diamonds and plate in 1781 and 1782. In 1779 to pay off a judgement against him by one Jacob Solomons of Islington for £500, Verney agreed to let Solomans have the next half-year's rent of six of his Buckinghamshire tenants. Timber sales were planned in Essex and Buckinghamshire.

Verney was gradually persuaded that he needed to manage the debt. He found it convenient to pay someone to seek new loans and consolidate and sort out the debts. It also put him at one remove from the clamour, and deflected the demands on someone else.[57] Two men attempted to rescue the Verney finances between 1775 and 1783, by negotiating prepayments and restructuring of the debt. Both failed because their activities required that they alone were managing the debt, yet the second earl constantly undermined them by raising money separately. Between 1775 and 1780 Christopher Hargrave, a London lawyer who specialised in this service, acted for Verney, who agreed to pay him regular sums from estate income to service the debt while Hargrave negotiated a

---

[55] On discounting bills see 5/5/2-5 (Hargrave letter of 1778); scepticism of Verney credit is also indicated by his dealings with Mr Skinner 1777–9 CIH 5/1/1-18; on Pater see CIH 5/4/27; on Knight see CIH 6/76-7, 5/4/3-13.

[56] On Vezian see CIH 1/306-8, 5/2/6-13, 5/5/12, 6/4/1.

[57] Correspondence of C. Hargrave and rvjr CIH 5/5/1-5 shows annuities behind, and the arrears on the East India speculation debt. On the bank stock see C. Hargrave to rvjr 10 March 1777. For plate and jewel sales see CIH 5/3/55-7 and for Jacob Solomon see CIH 5/5/1.

major restructuring. Verney failed his side of the bargain. In 1777 Hargrave had to travel to Middle Claydon in search of money, and by 1780 had borrowed £4,000 on his own security, and accepted Verney's bills for cash, putting his own credit in danger. Hargrave expected rapid repayment as a matter of honour, but instead Verney turned on him, publicly (and falsely) accusing him of withholding money. Hargrave's credit was undermined and after 1780 the two men had no further dealings.[58]

In 1781–3 Sir John Lovett, a distant kinsman, close political ally, and Buckinghamshire neighbour attempted another restructuring of the debt. He focused on Mary Verney's claims on the estate. These were inhibiting new mortgages or any land sales needed for any major debt settlement. In 1782 he planned to establish a trust to sell portions of both settled and unsettled estates totalling £3,900 a year and raise £97,000 to pay off debts. In July 1783 he believed a 'Grand Settlement' was imminent, but once again Verney destroyed the negotiation by offering the reversion of Middle Claydon to another leading creditor, and then writing directly to Mary Verney claiming he had only ever had one offer from her. Lovett was rightly outraged at Verney, writing that 'your Lordship might have devised some other means than the sacrifice of my character to apologise for your own conduct'.[59]

Verney used both Hargrave and Lovett duplicitously. Whether consciously or not their function was to keep creditors at arm's length, rather as the second Duke of Buckingham behaved in the 1840s.[60] Lovett later accused Verney of asking him to undertake the work only 'to please my Lady Verney and so get rid of the subject'. Both Hargrave and Lovett claimed Verney had given them his word to make no private financial deals without consulting them. Both were appalled at his behaviour and the way he betrayed them.

Most of his creditors felt the crueller side of Verney's character as financial disaster approached. Verney staved off the day of reckoning by refusing to acknowledge his debts. For almost every large judgement and debt, there was a counter-suit, claiming that the money was not owed, or had been paid. At any one time in the late 1770s and early 1780s, Verney had twenty or thirty such

---

[58] On Hargrave see particularly his correspondence in CIH5/5/1-5; Andy Federer found evidence that Hargrave specialised in such operations and was doing similar work for other aristocratic clients; see Copeland, *The Correspondence of Edmund Burke*, III, p. 372 for some biographical details. In particular see letters dated 4 January 1776, 22 March 1777, 15 September 1777, 31 October 1777, 13 March 1779, 4 June 1780, 7 July 1780, 14 November 1780. Samuel Rogers to rvjr 27 September 1787 5/5/8 states that Hargrave had just died while Verney was still claiming to be a creditor and took out letters of administration after his death in 1791, see 5/3/91. Heselrige vs Verney papers CIH 6/27/1-12; C. Hargrave to rvjr 1 March 1779, 5 February 1778 CIH 5/5/1-5.

[59] Mr Darby to J. Lovett 27 July 1782 CIH 5/5/6. CIH 5/5/6 J. Lovett to rvjr 10 September 1782, 19 January 1783, Prevost to rvjr 30 July 1783, 13 August 1783, Lovett to rvjr 13 November 1783, 25 November 1783, 4 December 1783, 22 December 1783. Verney could legally offer the reversion of the estate after his own and his niece's deaths provided she had no heirs, which seemed very likely.

[60] J. V. Beckett, *The Rise and Fall of the Grenvilles* (Manchester 1994), ch. 7.

suits pending. Verney acted in disbelief and despair, hitting out both at those who had undoubtedly conned, cheated, or led him into unwise speculations, and everyone else connected with his financial affairs. He turned on those like Hargrave, Oakley Halford, and Pater Thompson who although not totally disinterested, believed they were primarily, if not disinterestedly, doing him some kind of service. When Verney finally collapsed, they were dragged down with him, threatened with suits alleging moneys owed.

While professionals and friends who attempted to help the second earl were sacrificed for short-term gain, it took an unscrupulous rogue to bring about his ultimate downfall. Verney's largest creditor was a man named Arthur Jones of Newhaven in Sussex to whom he owed £19,387 by July 1779. Jones died in January 1780, leaving his estate to his under-age daughter, who soon after married a man named John MacNamara of Hereford St Westminster. The couple quickly contacted Verney, as he later wrote in a court submission:

At the latter end of 1780 Mrs MacNamara made an unexpected visit to Curzon St and desired to introduce Mr MacNamara who was at that time a perfect stranger. Lord Verney was not at home but Mr MacNamara assured Lady Verney that the sole motive of his visit was to make a tender of his services to extricate Lord Verney from his difficulties in the same manner had been agreed to be done by the late Mr Jones at the time of his death. He then assumed the character of a Gentleman and friend and did not come to offer himself as a steward or agent with an expectancy of being paid for which he might do, but as a disinterested friend. Lord Verney some days afterwards returned the visit when the same professions of friendship were repeated, and the same assertions of immense wealth as had before been made to Lady Verney, viz that he should have £100,000 the day his wife came of age at his own disposal, £30,000 left him by an uncle who died at Montserrat (whom Lord Verney has since learnt died insolvent), the expectancy of £50,000 from Mr Francis on his return from India, £80,000 from Lord Porchester, as considerable sum from Mr Berwick, Banker at Worcester, and to this curious list was soon afterwards added as curious an item of £20,000 from Mr Stackpole. In consequence of the above and other assurances Lord Verney was induced to accept of his proposed services. Accordingly several engagements were entered into on both sides and soon afterwards it but too apparently appeared that Mr MacNamara's immense wealth had totally vanished, and finding himself unable to perform his engagements he took underhand means to make Lord Verney a Martyr to his folly.

Verney took up MacNamara's offer to manage his debts and gradually became totally dependent on him. By a deed of May 1781, renewed in the following year, he made over the running of his estates and the management of the debt to trustees including Lovett, Heslop, and Bullock, his own friends and allies, but effectively run by MacNamara. In return he was to receive an assured income of £2,000 a year.[61]

---

[61] For the origins of this large debt see Jones vs. Verney 1783 CIH 6/47; Verney's account of his first meeting with MacNamara, who later became known in his circle as 'the badger' is in CIH

MacNamara was no mere estate manager, but took possession of the estate. He began to lord it over the unfortunate earl, at one point charging him £400 a year to use Claydon, and advising him to give up living in Curzon Street because he could not afford it. MacNamara dominated Verney's affairs, and deliberately insulted Verney's social sensitivities. He invited Verney down to Claydon as a visitor, and expressed surprise when Verney did not come. He wrote condescendingly to the earl, avowing friendship, but lecturing Verney forthrightly on his position and attitudes:

For God's sake, my Dear Lord, why will you so constantly shut yourself up. I well know the weight of Business you have on your Hands, but it does not, it ought not, to follow from this that you should not sometimes unbend your mind . . . you are now stewing yourself and shutting yourself up (like Diogenes in his Tub) at a time when you are in a better situation than you have been in these ten years past and what vexes more than all I fear you fret about what cannot be helped and is past – you surely ought to consider that you may command everything I can do for you and ought to esteem yourself extremely fortunate in not having been completely ruined by the infamous villains by whose chains you have been bound for twelve years past.

MacNamara posed as the only man to solve Verney's difficulties, and actually wrote to him: 'I consider your Lordship to be very helpless and totally in my power.' Although MacNamara gained even greater powers in 1782 and 1783, he was no more able to deal with the debts than his predecessors, if indeed he ever intended to. Verney obstructed his access to estate income, and when MacNamara went to Claydon the agent there, Webb, refused to act for him. Other creditors took direct action. Mrs Calvert, the earl's sister-in-law, began to collect her own rents when her £1,600 a year annuity remained unpaid. Verney found it difficult to live on £2,000 a year, and began to claim that MacNamara was not paying him enough, and was cheating him. While MacNamara was supposedly clearing the huge debt, Verney tried to raise fresh loans through a lawyer, using diamonds as security. At a later stage, MacNamara claimed that Verney sent his own agents to collect rents from his Buckinghamshire tenants for his own use. These cross-currents were bound to lead to confrontation with catastrophic consequences for Verney's lifestyle and reputation in the late spring of 1783.[62]

As the two men traded recriminations MacNamara prepared inventories to sell Verney's goods, beginning with the contents of the Curzon Street house, followed by Verney's book collection, which he moved to his own house. He threatened a sale unless he was immediately paid £1,000 plus the cost of

6/47-61. See also MacNamara to rvjr 22 October 1783. For details of the 1781 trust to pay Verney £2,000 a year and Mrs Calvert £1,600 a year and keep down and pay off debts, and its later replacements, see CIH 1/311, 1/318-19, 1/326.

[62] MacNamara to rvjr 23 December 1781, 5 November 1783, 4 and 14 November 1782, 20 September 1783 CIH 6/47.

preparing the sale. When Verney refused, MacNamara used Christies to conduct sales, both in London and at Claydon House. Verney's books were sold on 30 May. Verney was a broken man. In one of his few surviving letters, written the day before the sale, he wrote:

The apathy of my Mind is such that if the malignant influence of the most diabolical Beings under the Sun was to fall upon me alone it would not interrupt my Felicity or break my Rest. I have always acted the part of an honest man and claim'd no man's property wrongfully. I can't suppose that you claim in earnest any part of my Personal Estate. I from my soul believe you have as just a right to it as you have to the Crown of England. You have made the same compensation for one as you have done for the other. You fetched my Property from Pall Mall and without my Knowledge and to use your own Phrase to me in writing, out of disinterested Friendship and pure Love. This Baseness will soon be elucidated by the strongest Evidence. In your Letter a Demand is made for £1,000. Have you received my Rents without ever discharging the Obligations you so faithfully promised punctually to perform? From whence was I to raise the money except by trying my Luck upon the Highway or by Gambling?[63]

The Claydon sale was widely advertised in the press for 11 June, and news of it spread rapidly, soon reaching Verney's old friend the Revd Samuel Rogers in the West Country.

The two sales finally toppled Verney's credit and reputation, and he could no longer pretend that there was no financial embarrassment. MacNamara and Verney continued bitterly at odds. In October 1783 MacNamara threatened to put the whole Verney estate up for sale unless he was paid all his money and spoke of an 'infamous, ungentlemanlike letter (written, I fear by your authority)' in which Verney planned his arrest for arrears of his yearly £2,000. On 5 November he wrote:

I am informed that you report publicly that I will not pay you a 'just debt' and that I refuse to give you 'any account &c &c.' It would be very unbecoming in your Lordship to propagate so false a Report as this and I conceive it would be exceedingly improper in me to suffer such base Insinuations against my Character to be spread abroad most particularly as I consider your Lordship to be very helpless and totally in my Power.

MacNamara now began to exploit the estates more fully to recoup his losses. Already in February he had announced his intention to raise Claydon rents at Lady Day, and took bills of sale from a number of tenants in arrears. At the end

---

[63] MacNamara to rvjr 12 January, 9 February, 13 and 14 March, 20 May 1783, CIH6/48. Inventories and details of the Curzon Street sale in CIH 6/57. See also the bill of sale dated 4 May 1781. The books had originally been pledged by Verney in November 1779 but the pledge passed through at least two hands before MacNamara acquired it in 1781; rvjr to MacNamara 29 May 1783 6/48. S. Rogers to rvjr 9 June 1783 CIH5/5/8. *Jackson's Oxford Journal* advertised the March 1784 sale at Aylesbury. Final settlement of Verney vs. MacNamara dated 2 May 1786 involved Verney paying £2,815 13s 6d to MacNamara in return for a disclaimer for all interest or debt apart from the original mortgages.

of November he ordered the Claydon bailiff, Sewell, to minimise expenditure at Biddlesden farms, and to prepare to cut timber in the park for sale. Verney tried a diversion by allowing George Minschull, a creditor, but also a close political ally, to take possession of parts of the Claydon estate. Once the damage had been done, he too began to exploit the estate resources.[64]

Verney's position was destroyed by the dissolution of parliament and the general election early in 1784. He fought the county seat despite financial weakness, and lost by only twenty-four votes at the last gasp. His personal popularity, and support for his radical views nearly secured victory. He had also stood in his pocket borough of Wendover as a failsafe. He could not pay the expected gratuities, and the electors took advantage of it to ignore his candidature and voted him out. Without a parliamentary seat Verney lost the vital immunity from imprisonment for debt that had enabled him to prolong the debt crisis for so many years. For the next six years, until his return at the next general election, he was forced to spend much time on the continent, mainly in the channel ports. His wife remained in England, often in real poverty:

my Lady and her [maid] have got no money and can scarce get victuals to eat and when they do cannot get coals to dress it and are obliged to drink water. My Lord cannot be in a much better state as he had only twenty eight pounds when he went. I wish you would send some money to my Lady who will send it to my Lord and get you a receipt for it. I can't bear to hear of their Distress. I went and borrowed forty pounds and have sent it to my Lady and likewise some provision.[65]

The battle between MacNamara and Verney continued in the courts. A Chancery order of 1 April 1784 was intended to prevent Verney's tenants paying rent to MacNamara but had little effect, for Sewell, the bailiff, wrote in May that 'there are but few of the tenants that have not paid to Mr MacNamara'. In May 1784, a further sale of furnishings and other effects from Claydon House took place in Aylesbury. In November further injunctions were needed to prevent MacNamara felling trees on the estates. Eventually a Receiver acceptable to both sides in the dispute was installed. Both MacNamara and Verney claimed that each had been defrauded by the other and these claims and counterclaims went to court. When the case was eventually settled in 1786 Verney was found to owe MacNamara over £2,800.[66]

During the Chancery case both parties took whatever income they could from the Claydon tenants making 'sad havoc of the place'. While MacNamara had

[64] MacNamara to rvjr 23 October and 5 November 1783; MacNamara to Sewell 29 November 1783 CIH 6/48. On Minschull see CIH5/3/26 and 5/6/17. Minschull became Treasurer and Secretary of the political club that provided financial backing for Verney's election campaign.
[65] Sewell to Bryant 20 May 1783 and 8 August 1784 CIH 6/55 and 6/5/20-6; R. W. Davis, *Political Change and Continuity*, pp. 33–9.
[66] Chancery order of 1 April, 19 November and 19 December 1784 CIH6/50-1. Sale Catalogue of 3 May 1784 CIH 4/7/83/27 and 4/7/86.

an interest in the estate, nothing could be done about debt repayments, and the debt interest mounted. Verney's three friends on MacNamara's trust, though largely powerless, sought a more general debt settlement. Creditors' meetings were held in London from the summer of 1784 onwards, and in 1786 forms were printed in large numbers ready for a general settlement. Unfortunately only sixteen out of eighty creditors were prepared to believe that this attempt was any more real than earlier ones, and the blank forms survive in pristine condition to this day. Once MacNamara had been removed from the scene in 1786, recovery was possible.[67] Verney's finances had now reached their lowest point, and for the last six years of his life, his affairs were in the hands of men who were long-time friends and allies. More important, he recognised that he could no longer go behind their backs to forge his own deals. An old and broken man in his seventies, he allowed his trustees to do their work.

A new trust was set up on 5 July 1786, with Sir Jonathan Lovett, Joseph Bullock, and Archdeacon Heslop, all old friends, as trustees. They took a much more down-to-earth view of the finances. Estate accounts for 1787 show that Verney's net income was closer to £8,500 than the figure of £13,000 gross that had so often been claimed. Debt lists and estimates of income abound from this period, as well as schemes for paying off the debts by selling land. One overview in 1786 shows the estate income, including interest from Lady Verney's bank stock and other city investments, was £10,979 4s 2d. Interest and annuities payable amounted to some £12,000, including the annual payments of £1,600 to Mrs Calvert, and an allowance of £2,000 a year to Lord Verney. The debt was estimated at £140,095, including £100,000 on mortgage, £22,500 on bond, with notes of hand and simple contract debts between £2,500 and £3,000 each. The various annuities that Lord Verney had agreed to, mainly during the seventies, were valued at £12,320. Between 1786 and 1791 careful management transformed the picture. The interest on mortgages and other debts had been reduced to about £5,500 a year, and many annuitants had been bought out, reducing their charge from £2,400 a year to under £700.[68]

Income and expenditure were both strictly controlled. Timber worth over £1,000 was sold in both 1787 and 1788. In the year ending 1 April 1790 there was a balance on the income account of over £2,000 even after Verney's annuity had been paid. An undated statement of the same period claimed that 'Lord Verney paid out of his annuity sundry bonds and Debts amounting with interest to £4,700 and upwards.' Either Verney had at last realised he had to take personal responsibility, or in his miserable existence on the continent he no longer had the inclination to spend what money he had. Other factors helped the trustees.

[67] Sewell to Bryant 8 August 1784 CIH 6/55. Creditors' propositions dated 22 May 1786; minutes of creditors' meetings for 1784–5 CIH 5/1/4 and 5.

[68] The state of the debts after 1786 is well covered in a series of estimates and accounts, and in the trustees' accounts for 1786–9, CIH 5/1/4, 5/1/5, 5/1/7.

In 1789 Mary Calvert had died, releasing her jointure annuity of £1,600 a year. However, the estate was now liable for the immediate payment of her daughter's dowry which Verney had managed to delay for more than thirty years. The trustees had so improved the financial climate that it was not difficult to raise a new mortgage and promptly pay the £20,000.[69]

The trustees gradually gained the confidence of Verney's creditors during the late 1780s. The various propositions for a general settlement, rejected in 1785 and 1786, eventually became acceptable, and all the creditors signed an agreement in 1790. This exchanged all existing claims on the estate for interest-bearing debentures signed by Verney and his trustees, and assignable by endorsement. In the case of mortgages, arrears of interest from a given date were to be included in the principal stated on the debenture.[70]

The trustees created a new confidence amongst creditors by promising land sales. In 1787 detailed particulars of large amounts of Buckinghamshire land were printed and distributed. Some potential purchasers were wary of the settled estate and interested only in those farms not 'subject to the life in- terest of someone aged forty-nine', that is, Mary Verney. There was land to the value of £2,500 a year or more outside the settled estate that was easiest to sell. Carlton in Lincolnshire, which Verney had received in settlement of one of his few successful legal actions, was sold without too much difficulty, raising just over £5,000. Wendover's value was easy to sell for its electoral advantages, but Verney shrewdly refused early bids, to the frustration of his trustees, eventually receiving four or five thousand pounds more in 1789 than originally offered. The £25,552 it raised paid off the mortgage secured on the property.[71]

Carlton, Wendover, and a few small properties such as Hogshaw were sold between 1788 and 1790. The creditors' agreement of 1790 enabled Verney to return to England where he successfully contested the Buckinghamshire county election and as an MP regained his immunity from arrest for debt. This was a signal for the remaining creditors to come to terms. Many of the annuitants were now being bought out, and mortgage lenders were paid off one by one as cash became available. The estate finances were on an even keel, even if the vessel was low in the water. Nevertheless, Verney's situation was hardly ideal. He was now seventy-seven and much remained to be done. Claydon House was uninhabitable, presumably mainly because unfurnished. When he visited his native county in 1790, he stayed at Liscombe with Sir Jonathan Lovett.

[69] Mortgage to Culling Smith CIH 1/170 dated 30 January 1790.
[70] Terms were agreed at a creditors' meeting of 27 August 1790 and a whole bundle of signed agreements has survived in CIH 5/6/1, 5/6/5-8, 5/6/17, 5/6/29/17-20,
[71] For Norton see L. Heslop to J. Forster 16 September 1787 CIH 5/1/15. The general particular of the sale gives full details of farms, tenants, acreages, and rents for 3,786 acres of land producing old rents valued at £2,822 a year 'capable of great augmentation' CIH5/1/15. On Carlton see CIH 2/1873-9 and on Wendover 2/1404/2-13; see also L. Heslop to J. Forster 16 October 1787 CIH5/1/15 and letters in 5/1/26/2-12, 5/6/31.

When his wife died early in 1791, Verney lost his major support through all his troubles, and his death followed soon afterwards on 31 March.

At his death Verney's dreams were unfulfilled, his house empty, his political patronage destroyed. The Buckinghamshire electorate had nevertheless confirmed his personal electoral popularity in the previous year. His financial affairs had been righted, although the humiliations of 1781 to 1785 could never be erased. The long crisis that had begun in 1769 had certainly taken its toll. It had brought out character traits in Verney that were ugly. He displayed the paranoia of a man overwhelmed by events. In his last years Richard Burke found him 'so obdurate and apparently selfish at the same time so vindictive, so wrapped up and perplext with his own interests, and the intricacies of his affairs, his mind so sordid with perpetual money dealing, and so soured by difficulties'.[72] He constantly sought quick and easy solutions at the risk of betraying the hard work of friends and employees around him. His continuing litigiousness when faced with claims on his estate meant that he was repeatedly contradicting himself and those around him. In 1781 he had thirty-six suits or counter-suits in progress. Perhaps worst of all was his treatment of those he had earlier supported and helped: men like Oakley Halford, whom he committed to the King's Bench gaol for debt after Halford had been an important source of floating credit by providing a covering address for Ralph Verney Knight. Halford had been associated with Verney since 1759 in a wide range of enterprises before he was used to provide credit. In March 1783 he wrote from gaol claiming that Verney would neither pay him the 2s 4d a week due under statute to every prisoner held on a writ of execution, nor allow him bail. He died later that year, and Verney took out administration of his affairs as a creditor. Verney's obligations to Thompson Pater were rather less, yet once again both men had benefited from the system they had set up to bolster each other's credit.[73]

Such acts are far removed from the flamboyant and generous character portrayed in easier times. Nor should they be allowed to detract from the continuing personal loyalty that men like Edmund Burke, Jonathan Lovett, and the freeholders of Buckinghamshire showed him over many years. Perhaps, though ostensibly a man of the world, he was simply not worldly enough. Though his career ended in disarray, he left monuments both tangible and intangible, in the rococo glories of Claydon House, and in his patronage and nurturing of Edmund Burke in his formative years.

At his death, the Claydon estate and the financial problems passed to his niece, Mary Verney who was subsequently granted the title Baroness Fermanagh in her own right. She had many advantages in settling the debts. She had some money of her own, both from the Verney estate and from her maternal grandfather. She

---

[72] Copeland, *The Correspondence of Edmund Burke*, VII, p. 141.
[73] For Pater see 5/4/28; Oakley Halford to rvjr 26 March 1783 5/3/2-3 and 5/1/4.

could do more or less as she wished, for she was the last direct heir to the Verney fortune, and was not restricted by family settlements designed to keep the estate intact. She set about clearing the debts with all haste. Within two months of Lord Verney's death the sale of Abthorpe, Buckingham, and his houses in Curzon Street and Ramsgate had been completed and raised over £15,000. Major sales followed in the following year with most of Lord Verney's great purchases passing out of the family. Biddlesden, Syresham, Abthorpe, Lenborough, and Bourton together with odd properties in Winslow, London, and claims on the Cornish tin mine, were all disposed of for a further £88,860. With the money it was possible to pay off many of the long-standing mortgages, including those to Van Jever, Minschull, and the mortgage which had enabled MacNamara to take over the estate ten years earlier. There was sufficient cash left over to pay off hundreds of small sums and trade bills which cover six pages of accounts. By the end of 1792, the back of the problem had been broken, though there were further sales during the decade.

Lady Fermanagh's swift actions were a tribute to the groundwork laid by the trustees. Every creditor appears to have been paid in full, although perhaps some lost part of their arrears of interest when they took debentures in 1790. She also pursued Earl Verney's financial claims on the various West Indian estates arising from disputes with Luke Lightfoot and Lauchlin Macleane. The legal paperwork in these cases was formidable. William Burke was also hounded for his share of the East India Company gamble.[74] In businesslike fashion she pulled down the grandiose ballroom and central cupola of Claydon House.[75] These symbols of her uncle's aspirations, were ironically, and perhaps typically, never used for their intended purposes. What remained to her was considerable. The fine south wing of the house was the centrepiece of a still considerable estate. The Claydons remained intact as Verney domains. The land-tax records for the 1790s show her to be the sole proprietor in East and Middle Claydon, and owner of more than one third of Steeple Claydon, yet according to Lysons she 'resides during the greater part of the year at a villa in Kent'.[76] There were also some other small properties in Buckinghamshire – the Grandborough enclosure award for 1798 for instance shows her holding land there. However the Claydons were the only substantial estate. What Lady Fermanagh saved formed the bulk of the Verney estates during the nineteenth and twentieth centuries, and much has been retained to this day. It is also not so very different from what the second earl had begun with. Now at least it was on firm foundations.

---

[74] Copeland, *The Correspondence of Edmund Burke*, IX, pp. 350–60.
[75] CIH 4/5/100 notes the progress of pulling down parts of the house.
[76] D. Lysons and S. Lysons, *Magna Britannia; Being a Concise Topographical Account of the Several Counties of Great Britain*, 6 vols. (1806–22).

9   Transforming the Claydons in
       the eighteenth century

As the Verneys expanded their estates during the eighteenth century, they extended their social and economic control beyond Middle Claydon to the adjoining parishes of East and Steeple Claydon. This chapter examines the extent
to which changes in Middle Claydon in the period 1660 to 1740 were extended elsewhere in the Claydons during the eighteenth century. After 1730
the Claydon correspondence becomes less compendious, and after 1752 frag-
mentary, dominated by material relating to court cases about the second earl's
debts and business affairs. Material about the running of the Claydon estates
is episodic, with no long runs of letters, so this analysis is more dependent
on conventional sources about rents, farm sizes, and tenants, the structure of
landholding and tenancy, and rich occupational data, linked where possible to
parish reconstitution.

These changes after 1750 mirror a shift in the second Earl Verney's concerns and priorities. His life became London-based and he spent much time on
politics and business schemes. Although he rebuilt Claydon, it is doubtful if
he lived there for long periods, particularly between 1760 and 1780, when he
used Biddlesden House near Stowe and Buckingham as his Buckinghamshire
residence. He spent more time in London, following the pattern set by his father
and mother after 1721 when they established a permanent residence in Little
Chelsea, rather than using the central London lodgings as had been customary
for Sir Ralph and Sir John Verney. For a period after his marriage in 1740 the
second earl spent much time at Claydon, taking on the estate management role
devolved on him by his brother John's death. He worked diligently, and successfully enclosed East Claydon, but always hankered after his own London
residence and establishment. Even when after 1750 the second earl's attention
shifted to politics and London life, he did not neglect his estates. He signed
most of the annual Claydon parish accounts. Surviving material records spas-
modic concern and intervention, but not much evidence of a continuing zeal for
agricultural experiment and improvement. In part this reflected the agricultural
and management systems on the Verney estates.

The Verneys ran their Buckinghamshire estates in the eighteenth century
to make administration easy and maximise income. The family primarily

purchased properties close to Middle Claydon and intended to produce rental income. Figure 8 shows the location of parishes in north Buckinghamshire where the Verney properties lay. Their land was either in substantial blocks in a parish, or in adjoining parishes adjacent to existing landholdings. At Middle Claydon, major acquisitions in East and Steeple Claydon were supplemented by smaller purchases in Grendon Underwood, Hogshaw, and Grandborough. Two other compact estates were also developed. One was in the parish of Buckingham, where substantial enclosed estates in the rural townships of Lenborough and Bourton produced more income than the small amounts of land in the borough. Adjacent to Bourton lay Thornborough, where land and manorial rights were also acquired, while there were small properties in Singleborough in Great Horwood. The other estate centred on Biddlesden to the north-west of Buckingham, where the second earl often lived during the 1750s and 1760s while building Claydon House. Most of their land was in Biddlesden, but they also acquired farms and rights in nearby Syresham, Abthorpe, and Wappenham, just over the Northamptonshire border. All these properties were within twelve miles of Claydon, enabling estate officials to supervise tenants and estate work without difficulty.

The Verneys acquired properties with predominantly enclosed farms devoted to pastoral agriculture on permanent pasture. The farmers were primarily 'dairymen', keeping cows for their milk that was turned into cheese, and increasingly butter. Sheep were also kept, and pigs were fed from the skimmed milk and whey left over after the dairy had taken what it needed. Enclosed pastoral estates were a deliberate choice. When the first earl was seeking out land purchases with his sons' dowries in the early 1740s he secretly sent his steward to look at an estate in Water Stratford, close to Buckingham, and asked him to consider whether

It might be turned into dairy bargains and hold rent, and all, or all but trifle, laid down, for surely if near half is ploughed, or but one fourth of it, must needs have many barns and outbuildings to it which are great incumbrances.[1]

Water Stratford was not bought even though it had been largely enclosed since 1720. When in 1741 the Verneys were offered some open-field land in Grandborough near Claydon, the second earl wrote to his father: 'I believed you did not care to meddle with an open field estate.'[2]

Lenborough, Bourton, and Biddlesden were already enclosed and run as pasture farms. Pasture farms were preferred because they yielded much higher rents per acre than arable or mixed farms. Improved permanent grass in the midlands in the early eighteenth century was treated as the equivalent of meadow

[1] rv to John Millward 27 January 1743/4 ClH 4/5/75.
[2] rvjr to rv 25 June 1741 R58. Further evidence of a bias towards enclosed land is found in rv to J. Millward 6 January 1737/8 R58 and J. Millward to rv 19 November 1738 R58.

land, mowed in rotation to provide winter fodder, and streams or ponds were diverted to ensure sufficient water for livestock in dry summers. During the late seventeenth century enclosed pasture of reasonable quality across north Buckinghamshire was let for between 15s and 25s an acre on a variety of estates, while most open-field arable produced 5s to 9s an acre, and enclosed mixed farms somewhat more. In 1810 St John Priest estimated Buckinghamshire Vale pasture rents averaged £2 an acre, where arable land would not exceed £1 an acre even where enclosed.[3]

On the heavy clays of Buckinghamshire, permanent pasture gave the best returns to landlords and had other benefits. Concentration on a single type of agriculture allowed the Verneys' steward with a limited range of farming skills to manage tenants effectively. More importantly, no tenant could take on a dairy farm of any size without considerable initial capital laid out in livestock. Most of a farmer's capital lay in their livestock, and stock on a farm was a good measure of the financial viability of the tenant. A failing farmer's assets in livestock could be seized as security for rent, or sold off easily.

The writers of the *Agricultural Reports* in the period 1790 to 1820 noted that good returns from permanent pastures lasted for a few decades, but long-term management was difficult. They advocated careful short-term rotation of arable and pastures as was happening on much newly enclosed land in an era of high grain prices. But although the crop returns confirm that more land was ploughed for fodder crops, the proportion of pasture remained high, and many practical men believed that permanent pasture remained the most profitable and was damaged by ploughing. For eighteenth-century landlords, dairy farming on midland permanent pastures retained more advantages than drawbacks.

On the Verney estates farms were enlarged and those smaller than about seventy-five acres gradually eliminated. The process described in Middle Claydon in chapter 6 continued there and was extended to other properties through the eighteenth century. In the second half of the century dairy farms of more than 150 acres became common in Middle Claydon, but the process was rarely socially disruptive. In that village, farm enlargement was at a more advanced stage than elsewhere on the estates. Comparisons of farm sizes in 1810 shown in table 9.1 suggest a rough correlation between the reduction of cottager numbers and the length of time the property had been in Verney hands.[4]

The process of enlargement also increased the working capital required by dairymen taking on farms, and meant they were more likely to have resources, including freehold land, to secure their rents and enterprises. Larger farms meant more secure rents for the landlords and fewer tenants with whom to haggle and bargain, and from whom to extract rents.

[3] Priest, *General View of the Agriculture of Buckinghamshire*, pp. 71, 249–51; Broad, 'Alternate husbandry and permanent pasture', pp. 77–89.
[4] Priest, *General View of the Agriculture of Buckinghamshire*, pp. 383–6.

Table 9.1 *Farmers and cottagers on the Verney estates, c. 1810*

	Date of purchase/ enclosure	Parkinson 1810 Nos. of farmers	Parkinson 1810 Nos. of cottagers	Crop return 1801 % acreage cropped
Middle Claydon	1620/57	7	1	4.0
East Claydon	1729/42	14	20	4.0
Steeple Claydon	1706/97	14	67	13.0
Biddlesden	1754	4	12	n.a.

Estate policy dealt with relatively uniform agrarian and agricultural structures within a narrow geographical confine. Potential for improvement was limited to incremental increases in farm sizes, improvements to farm buildings, drainage, and water supply, and modest improvements in stock. Rents per acre for enclosed improved pasture land were as good as anywhere in the country, and exceeded only by those paid by specialist nurserymen and market gardeners. The eighteenth-century Verneys bought new land that was already enclosed and rarely needed major reorganisation. But they also wanted to expand their estates around Middle Claydon where East and Steeple Claydon remained unenclosed in 1736. Enclosure was therefore an important tool of estate management to re-model the landscape around the Verneys' seat and consolidate their authority and presence.

Policy implementation was monitored in a constant flow of letters between Claydon and London when the family were away, though few letters have survived after 1750. The very simple management system did not allow the development of bureaucratic structures and systems that could run effectively without an active landlord. Hands-on management, with the head of the family or his eldest son intimately involved with day-to-day detail had been central to the Verney tradition since 1630. There is less evidence of agricultural experiment and improvement amongst the later Verneys, yet they remained careful guardians of their estates, and shrewd decision-makers and negotiators. Their long-serving estate stewards acted primarily as the trusted voices and information providers for their masters rather than as instigators of improvement.

In the seventeenth century the appointment of William Coleman showed the rising social status of the Verneys' agents at Claydon. Charles Chaloner's appointment in 1705 confirmed this. Chaloner was the son of a declining gentry family, whose manor of Steeple Claydon had just been bought by the Verneys. His new role firmly helped to transfer village loyalty from the Chaloners who had benefited strongly from it in the 1660s to the new and previously antagonistic owners. It was also part of a string of minor gentry connections and placements that linked the Verneys to local notables and provided channels of communication and patronage. Charles's brother, Edmund, became a clergyman, and was found a benefice at Drayton Beauchamp, the seat of Lord Cheyne, Sir John Verney's political patron and ally in the county, some fifteen miles from Claydon.[5]

Chaloner died in December 1727, his last letters recording his struggle to continue his duties while succumbing to what was probably the most potent epidemic of the eighteenth century. John Millward, his successor, also came from a long-established minor gentry/freeholder family who had owned property in East Claydon since at least 1379. Millward also took on his post just as his family sold off substantial property to the Verneys.[6] Two years previously, at the age of twenty-five, he married the youngest daughter of William Butterfield, the third Butterfield rector of Middle Claydon, and two years older than her husband. This was not a new kinship. An earlier Millward had married Edward Butterfield, while a later Millward, Edmund, was to become rector of Middle Claydon when William Butterfield died, and remained in post there and in East Claydon for forty-seven years.[7] John and Ann Millward's one surviving daughter in turn married a John Butterfield (of Brackley) in 1757.

The Millwards were firmly entrenched in local gentry society. Edmund was a JP for the county in the 1760s and attended Quarter Sessions on several occasions.[8] The appointment of clergy and estate stewards as JPs increased during the eighteenth century as their patrons withdrew from active participation in Quarter Sessions. Only five titled JPs attended the forty Buckinghamshire Quarter Sessions between 1736 and 1745, and there was never more than one at a session.[9] John Millward remained in the Verneys' service for over thirty years until his death in 1761, and his many letters up to 1754 indicate a continuity of activities and concerns. Estate management was not restructured to cope with the estate's expansion in the mid-eighteenth century.

After 1754, details of estate management become sparse despite the work of supervising the rebuilding of Claydon House and re-planning of the park. Occasional letters, especially in the 1780s when the estate was in the hands of trustees, reveal little of estate management practices. At one time a leading Claydon tenant, Charles Webb, had major responsibilities in the house and on the estate, and he may have run a home farm 'exercising his talents in husbandry, buying and selling cattle'. Later in the 1780s William Sewell had responsibilities

[5] Drayton Beauchamp was one of the two Cheyne seats in Buckinghamshire – the other was Chesham Bois.

[6] The earliest deeds of the Millward family are in ClH 2/141. The house, 2 cottages, and $3\frac{1}{2}$ yardlands sold in 1728/9 (2/219-36) included Millward's expected inheritance from his father (who died in 1730) as well as land he currently held in possession. The property was already heavily mortgaged to the Verneys.

[7] He, or another Edmund Millward, was also appointed to Biddlesden chapelry in 1768 ClH11/43.

[8] Buckinghamshire CRO Q/SO/18. He attended four consecutive Quarter Sessions in 1766–7.

[9] See Buckinghamshire CRO Q/SO/14. There were no clergy active either; indeed there were only two to seven justices listed as in attendance at Quarter Sessions in this period apart from three sessions – Easter 1741–18, Easter 1736–10; Midsummer 1736–9.

covering both Biddlesden and Claydon but his duties went little further than rent collecting, and farm repairs were neglected.[10]

Verney estate policy and purchases consolidated a high-rent, permanent pasture regime with dairy farmers already in place, rather than speculating in 'improveable' estates. There was no 'agricultural revolution' of a traditional kind on these north Buckinghamshire estates. The regime of dairy farming in north-west Buckinghamshire became standard practice for many farms and parishes from the Restoration to the Second World War, probably giving the most efficient return on capital for owners, and tenants, provided the condition of the pastures was maintained. Its high rents and increasing farm sizes are testament to a modest managerial revolution, and the system spread as more parishes enclosed.

Before 1736 the Verneys had used enclosure widely to raise their rentals and streamline farm management. Middle Claydon was sandwiched between two open-field parishes, East and Steeple Claydon, that were both mainly unenclosed in 1700, and fully enclosed a century later. In the first half of the seventeenth century the Verneys had enclosed land wherever feasible. Enclosure increased estate income by bringing fallow and marginal lands into cultivation, and by conversion to higher value pasture where suitable. Yet after 1665 the Verneys undertook no further major enclosures for seventy-five years. Joan Thirsk has argued that in the period 1660 to 1740 there were fewer enclosures because falling prices and rents made them less profitable for landowners.[11] On the Verney estates there were few lucrative enclosure opportunities in this period, and estate policy illustrates another reason for a reduction in enclosure nationally. By 1665 the Verneys had sold all their outlying properties. They became the largest landowners in East Claydon in 1663, but there was a significant body of freeholders and copyholders who remained independent of them, including the gentry Duncombe family.[12]

The Verneys were more concerned to defend their own assets – the enclosed pastures of Middle Claydon, where their rents were considerably higher than on the open-field land and waste of nearby villages. While rents were falling, they feared that their rental income would be reduced if adjoining parishes were enclosed and converted to permanent pasture and twice intervened to prevent neighbours' enclosures. In Steeple Claydon the Chaloner family planned an enclosure of the common fields by agreement to restore their finances. By the early 1670s they controlled three-quarters of the parish – 60 out of 80 yardlands. Sir Ralph pressed his son Edmund to prevent enclosure. Knowing Edmund was

---

[10] CIH 5/1/20/11-14. This was in 1784/5, but he was also dealing with Claydon estate matters in 1791/2 after Verney's death CIH 4/5/100.

[11] Thirsk, 'Changing attitudes to enclosure', pp. 517–43.

[12] PRO E179/80/333 shows Thomas Duncombe Esq. being assessed for the Free and Voluntary Present of 1661 at £10, the same rate as the Abells whose estate the Verneys annexed by marriage.

more interested in hunting and rural sports than agricultural rents and improved agriculture, Sir Ralph pointed out that the enclosure:

might not only cloak up your estate in point of hunting, hawking, coursing, riding and other pleasures . . . but it needs be a great loss to you in letting your grounds.

The Verneys needed to purchase property in Steeple Claydon. A land purchase in the open fields would not prevent the enclosure because it could be excluded from the enclosure agreement and ignored. They had to acquire common rights of pasturage over the open fields, first confirming that cow commons could be bought separately from field land. Edmund eventually bought one yardland and half a cow common in separate deals. His father concluded that the purchase was 'enough to prevent an enclosure, which is all you aim at'. These purchases destroyed the Chaloners' plans, but Sir Ralph warned his son to be vigilant in managing the land, to ensure that it was not let to the owner of adjoining open-field strips, or for more than two years. He feared that if either occurred, Chaloner could buy up the lease and proceed with enclosure.[13]

The cow common cost £7, and the yardland (bought in two separate deals) £167 10s. These small purchases prevented enclosure in Steeple Claydon for 120 years and altered the development of landholding, farming, social structure, and indeed the whole fabric of village life. Within eight years the Chaloners decided to sell the Steeple Claydon estate. They offered it to the Verneys at a high price. Sir Ralph wanted to buy it to consolidate his estates, but could not raise the money.[14]

Selling the estate as a single lot would bring the best price, but the Verneys were the only realistic purchasers as they would not allow anyone else to enclose Steeple Claydon. The only solution was to break up the estate and offer it for sale in smallholdings and farms. The sale took place in two blocks in 1683–4. Just over half the open-field land, 40.5 yardlands, was put on the local market and sold to twenty-five buyers, fifteen of them Steeple Claydon farmers or current occupiers. Most of the land went to men of modest means who wanted to occupy and work the land themselves. They included two of Sir Ralph Verney's tenants in Middle Claydon.[15] When the Verneys finally bought the manor from the Chaloners in 1704 they received only the eight and a half yardlands that remained of the sixty consolidated by 1675. Steeple Claydon was not fully enclosed until 1795, by which time the Verneys had only managed to acquire approximately one third of the land in the parish.

The Verneys also prevented enclosure of the inter-commoned waste between East Claydon and Quainton by the Dormer family in 1673. Edmund Verney owned insufficient land in the parish to engineer a total enclosure of the open fields there by agreement and therefore opposed the enclosure of common

---

[13] srv to ev 13 and 20 February 1672/3 R25; ev to srv 17 February 1672/3 R25. CIH 2/487–96.
[14] see above ch. 5, p. 105.   [15] Broad, 'The fate of the midland yeoman', p. 15.

waste by an outsider. But within the village he sided with those substantial farmers who did not want manorial courts to be held any more, and attacked other unsubstantiated common rights, including the Vicar's right to cow commons. Later, when East Claydon was firmly under the Verneys' control, they proceeded to enclose the same intercommoned waste and then undertook a full enclosure themselves. Interfering with neighbouring enclosures to protect one's own economic interest was not exclusive to the Verneys. They hoped that Sir John Busby, the landlord of the neighbouring enclosed parish of Addington would buy land in Shipton Lee (part of Winslow parish) to prevent the Lowndes family enclosing parts of that, and Sir John Verney wrote that Busby 'did wrong not to buy somewhat there' in 1711.[16]

The defensive actions of landlords who blocked their neighbours' enclosures to maintain their own rents reduced the number of successful enclosures between 1660 and 1740. Enclosure by agreement required the unanimous agreement of freeholders and provided ample opportunity for disruption of this kind. Enclosure by parliamentary act during the eighteenth century required the consent of the owners of only two thirds of the land. No longer could the meddling landowner or the stubborn peasant farmer with his small freehold plot hold up a village enclosure.

However, even though the Grenvilles used a parliamentary act to enclose nearby Ashendon in 1738–9, and Wotton Underwood in 1742–3, the enclosure of East Claydon after 1737 was a private agreement, as was the Wenmans' enclosure of Twyford at the same period.[17] Early in 1740 Lord Fermanagh had the 'property of the place entirely to himself' and declared he had no intention of using an Act of parliament.[18] The timing of the East Claydon enclosure reflected the family's financial situation. When they purchased the large estate there in 1729 they made substantial borrowings. Only after receiving the considerable dowry brought by Mary Nicholson's marriage to John Verney in 1736 did the family become cash rich, just as the Grenvilles began the enclosure of Ashendon and Wotton soon after Richard Grenville married Anna Chambers with a dowry of £50,000 in May 1737.[19] Another factor was the death of John Duncombe, the other major freeholder in East Claydon. His heirs kept their enclosed lands at East Claydon and elsewhere, but sold the Verneys the open-field land, common rights, and tithes for some £3,600.[20]

---

[16] Broad, 'The Verneys as enclosing landlords', pp. 18–19, and see below p. 240; Lowndes was himself accused of fomenting opposition during the East Claydon enclosure.

[17] For the Wotton and Ashendon Acts and Awards see copies in BCRO D/T/1.

[18] Christ Church, Oxford archives MS Estates 7/316 Philip Barton to Dr John Conybeare 12 January 1739/40.

[19] J. V. Beckett, *The Rise and Fall of the Grenvilles* (Manchester 1994), pp. 36–7.

[20] Duncombe's probate was granted 27 April 1737 (copy in CIH 2/303) and the sale completed in July 1737 2/308. The deal was done through the intermediary of Lady Fermanagh's sister, Mrs Stone, in London, and the Duncombes' Oxfordshire lawyer John North. Mrs Stone's husband's lands were in Oxfordshire. M. Stone to rv 4 April 1737 R58; rv to M. Stone 21 July 1737 R58. A terrier of the Duncombe field land has survived in the letters for November 1737 R58.

The first earl first discussed enclosure in a letter to his steward in September 1737. Within six weeks an enclosure agreement had been drawn up and new reduced stints for cottagers' cow and sheep commons (one and five per cottage respectively) agreed. One freeholder, Thomas Thame, did not want to join in enclosure, and was allowed to enclose his own lands concurrently, provided he paid his share of the general enclosure costs, and that he should

> have some good and some bad land as well as other people, he is not to pick and choose some here and some there for the sake of good land.

As in many north-west Buckinghamshire parishes, piecemeal enclosure had already eroded the open fields, and the intercommoned waste between Middle and East Claydon had been divided in 1611. In 1741 the second earl estimated the acreage of open-field land left to enclose at about 1,660 acres, about two thirds of the parish area.[21]

The re-allocation of land, digging of ditches, and erecting of fences in East Claydon did not begin until 1741. There is no clear reason for the delay. Most of the freeholders and copyholders had acquiesced in the agreement proposed in 1737, but discussion of the parson's compensation was still in progress in 1739. In many eighteenth-century villages freeholders and copyholders sold their lands at enclosure. It was an opportunity to get a good price for those in debt who could not afford the share of the enclosure costs, or disliked adapting to new farming practices, or depended on access to common pasture rights. Yet the Verneys bought very little land in East Claydon during the period of enclosure. They spent £1,860 on field and cottage property in East Claydon between 1730 and 1750, but only £383 of this between 1737 and 1743. The seven purchases were cottage properties, a number of small closes, and open-field land totalling only just over one yardland. They also made two small property exchanges to facilitate enclosure. After the enclosure sporadic purchases went on through to the mid-1760s. By 1798, the Verneys owned everything except the parson's freehold in East Claydon parish, and the small Christ Church estate that they leased.[22]

The slow preparation helped to smooth out conflicts and accustom the villagers to a changing environment. However, a more likely cause of the delay was the Verneys' preoccupation with Ralph Verney's marriage to Mary Herring in 1740 and the first earl's attempt to re-enter parliament in May 1741.[23] By the summer of 1741 enclosure was back on the agenda. Meanwhile, John Millward

---

[21] This was based on a comparison with the Grenville enclosure at Wotton at the same time, which was measured at 1,664 acres – see BCRO Q/SO/14.

[22] CIH 2/266, 2/273/ 2/327/ 2/332, 2/340, 2/345, 2/350. The exchanges are 2/276 and 2/333. Cf. M. E. Turner, 'Parliamentary enclosure and landownership change in Buckinghamshire', *Economic History Review* 2nd series, 28 (1975), 565–81.

[23] T. Bishop to rv 16 April 1741 R58; Sir T. Cave to rv 11 May 1741 R58.

had gained first-hand experience of enclosure by serving as a commissioner for the Ashendon enclosure in 1738. The Grenvilles used parliamentary procedures at Ashendon and again at Wotton in 1742–3 because the acts also allowed the Grenvilles to raise mortgages on their settled estates to undertake exchanges of Oxford college leasehold lands. However the first earl wanted a private enclosure even though there were college lands in East Claydon. He cited Lord Wenman's plans at nearby Twyford and folk memory of Hillesden enclosure in the 1650s, where college land was enclosed without difficulty.[24]

When Ralph Verney and John Millward enclosed East Claydon's farms they had one eye on what was going on at Wotton and Twyford. Their plan was to survey the land and set out the new fields immediately after the 1741 harvest. The bumper wheat harvest of 1741 which the Verneys' old rival, Richard Abell, claimed was giving yields of 12:1 for wheat and 8:1 for barley also stirred up feelings in East Claydon and was the prelude to further negotiations between the Verneys and the farmers and cottagers.[25] The enclosers wanted to combine enclosure with laying down the whole to grass and letting it off as pasture farms. Ideally, sowing grass seed over the whole area would raise some kind of sward by the following summer. As the second earl wrote

I think it will be best to lay all three fields down in one year and then we may enclose two or all three as we find it convenient. Besides then every Tenant will [unreadable] into immediate business and will know his own lands and we shall avoid a great many quarrels and disputes.

However, conflicts soon arose. Grazing and dairy tenants had been lined up to take on at least a third of the newly enclosed land, but plenty of existing open-field tenants and owners wanted to continue growing grain. The Verneys' solution was to undersow barley with grass seed in what would customarily have been the 'tilth field', suggesting barley because it allowed the grass to grow much better. However, the tenants preferred wheat, which promised higher yields and a better price.[26]

The Verneys thought this was a ruse by villagers to get better terms for agreeing to enclosure. They did everything possible to conceal the scale of their newly acquired dowries from local people to minimise the cost of buying out village rights.[27] In late August 1741 the villagers were very divided as to when

[24] H. Davies, 'The making of a modern landscape: Wotton Underwood 1649–1743', unpublished MA thesis, University of Reading 1983, pp. 46–9; rv to J. Millward 24 January 1737/8 R58. Curthoys, 'Land, settlement and enclosure in Hillesden, Buckinghamshire'. I would like to thank Judith Curthoys for allowing me to see this. Christ Church, Oxford MS Estates 7/316–24 gives some idea of how the Verneys effectively ignored the small Christ Church estate during the enclosure.

[25] rvjr to rv, 2, 4, and 9 August 1741 R58.   [26] rvjr to rv 4 August 1741 R58.

[27] Cf. J. V. Beckett, M. Turner, and B. Cowell, 'Farming through enclosure', *Rural History* 9 (2) (1998), pp. 144–55; rvjr to rv 3 September 1741 R58.

the open-field system should end and enclosure take place, and the second earl concluded that

> They insist on so much that I believe it will be impossible to bring 'em all into a reasonable agreement this year nor will it be done ye next year unless we draw up an agreement and have it under hand and seal, and those that will not sign it must be ordered to quit.[28]

A scheme was proposed on 27 August 1741 that the 'wheat' field remain un-ploughed until the following spring because it easily became waterlogged. Existing tenants could have use of the new-sown grass until Lady Day 1743 – fully eighteen months away and after hedging and ditching should be completed.[29] By 8 September all but two tenants had agreed to the proposal. One very obstinate tenant refused even after four hours of wrangling but since he was two years in arrears with his rent, the second earl waited until he had sowed his winter wheat, and then threatened bankruptcy by taking a bill of sale. The villagers were clearly divided. One man threatened to sow all his land with wheat, but others petitioned the Verneys for a rapid enclosure.[30]

The enclosure went ahead, surveying began, and in October the second earl was estimating the types, quantities, and costs of fencing and hedging. The surveyor, Lee, was called home to Essex where his wife was ill and thereafter two local surveyors took on specific tasks and disputes. The second earl delayed a planned trip to Bath until December, by which time the hedging and ditching had begun. Men were digging boundary ditches in mid-November. A total of £80 was spent on ploughing the fields, and the types of hedges to be planted were agreed. Crab grew quickly and was mixed with aspen (a type of poplar) on the wettest parts of the estate. Elsewhere elm sets were mixed with crab, and a young oak tree was planted every two or three poles. The plants came from a hedge nursery two miles from Syresham, just over the Northamptonshire border, and cost 3d a pole. Ditching was also under way on the Grandborough side of the parish. Eleven men were employed to dig a ditch 4ft wide and 3 ft deep at a piece rate of 7d the 18 ft pole, a cost which Verney proudly announced 'is the lowest price it was ever done for in this county'.[31]

A new problem emerged at this time because the simultaneous enclosures of Wotton and Twyford for pasture required large quantities of grass seed. The Verneys had made some advance provision by leaving a meadow on their Bourton estate, which remained unlet in 1741, uncut for seed, 'it being better for the ground and more profitable for we shall need a great deal for the enclosure'.

[28] rvjr to rv 23 August 1741 R58.
[29] rvjr to rv 27 August 1741 R58 and Agreement of same date.
[30] rv to John Millward 8 September 1741 CIH 4/5/75.
[31] rvjr to rv 18 and 22 October 1741 R58; 17 and 24 November 1741 R58; rv to Lee October 1741 CIH 4/5/75.

By Christmas 1741 the second earl feared that 'Grass seed will be the worst article in the whole enclosure. They ask one guinea per quarter for rye grass and trefoil mixed together.' He sought seed at Brackley and Bicester markets to the north, but also asked his father about grass-seed prices near the Verneys' small Canvey Island estate in Essex. Clover was considered as an alternative, but the tenants were very resistant to it because 'they say it has a venom in the bite of a sheep which stops its growth, and that seed lasts the least time of any'.[32]

The price of grass seed remained high through January and February. The Grenvilles had agents posted at Bicester and Buckingham markets, and the price of a guinea a quarter was standard there. In early February the second earl sent John Millward to Tring, Hemel Hempstead, and St Albans in Hertfordshire, knowing there was plenty of grass seed there and that the Grenvilles' agents did not operate there. Millward found that the north Buckinghamshire enclosures were fully discounted in the price there, and estimates of the total quantity of grass seed required in each parish were circulating. A dealer (an 'engrosser') offered him a mix of one quarter rye grass and three quarters trefoil at 16s a quarter, and this was before significant carriage costs. Very little grass was available on the open market.[33]

East Claydon enclosure took a long time to prepare after 1737, but the actual process went relatively smoothly. It is difficult to work out the overall cost. The Verneys bought off their tenants more cheaply and with fewer concessions than the Grenvilles made at Wotton and the ditching had been keenly priced. After the existing tenants had been allowed to use the new grass over the summer of 1742 at their old rents, the farms were let on yearly tenancies so no leases survive. The Grenvilles apparently had plenty of land to let at Wotton in October 1742, but we do not know what proportion of East Claydon's newly enclosed lands were immediately let. The Verneys felt they dealt more successfully than the Grenvilles with their existing tenants in smoothing the transition to a pastoral economy. At Wotton most tenants were given nine-year leases, with one of twelve and another of twenty-one years. Only two tenants held 'at will'. One tenant's agreement required him to lay his 165 acres down to grass, but other tenancies left farmers free to make their own husbandry decisions providing the land was laid down to grass at the end of the lease. At East Claydon tenants could grow crops in the summer of 1742 but the fields were all undersown with grass. This grass became available as common grazing during the autumn and winter of 1742–3 before the whole parish was available to let as enclosed farms at Lady Day 1743. The very use of Lady Day as the year start for tenancies is symbolic of the primacy of a pastoral economy.[34]

---

[32] rvjr to rv 25 June 1741 R58; 13 and 27 December 1741 R58.
[33] rvjr to rv 28 January 1741/2 and 2 February 1741/2 R58.
[34] rvjr to rv 29 January 1742/3 R58; H. Davies, 'Wotton Underwood', p. 55.

The surviving Verney letters suggest that the majority of villagers supported or acquiesced at enclosure but negotiated tenaciously for the best deal. Verney believed that he could deal with recalcitrants by threatening to evict them. Even Thomas Thame, who demanded the separate enclosure of his freehold land, seems to have acquiesced, but died in 1744. Yet there are some indications of dissent and surreptitious opposition. In August 1745, just after the beginnings of the Jacobite rebellion, an alehouse keeper pulled down a 'new dead Hedge at East Claydon field' and abused Verney's workmen who tried to intervene. Sir Charles Tyrell provided the second earl with a warrant for his arrest, and the East Claydon constable served it, but 'being afraid of Sir Charles Tyrell', took the man to Justice Lowndes of Winslow, who told them 'the Hedges were put up without an Act of parliament and Justices had nothing to do with such unwarrantable Proceedings' and promptly discharged him. Verney regarded this as complicity, for Lowndes had a reputation of opposing the Verneys: 'Winslow law is always against Claydon.' The man who had pulled down the hedges was from Singleborough, five miles from East Claydon, and the other side of Winslow. The second earl felt an exemplary punishment was in order, arguing that:

Unless the Fellow is very contrite & makes humble submission, I must bring an Action against him at the next Assize, otherwise all my Fences will be thrown down, for L[ownde]s has given all the Encouragement possible to set people at Work.[35]

The enclosure of East Claydon was an efficient operation that allowed the Verneys to shift farming to the pastoral mould they preferred. It seems likely that dairying was fully established within twenty years and universal by the end of the century. The Verneys achieved a monopoly of landownership in the parish, and a parallel transformation in East Claydon's social and economic life by 1800, comparable with what happened to Middle Claydon after 1660.

The Verneys planned the enclosure of East Claydon as a profitable means of raising estate income. In marriage negotiations with Henry Herring in 1740 the figure of an extra £350 a year in rental income was used.[36] During the enclosure Ralph Verney tried to keep accurate accounts, and was pressed to see how they compared with the situation at Wotton, but they have not survived. Prevailing wisdom was that the pastures would yield the best return in the early years of enclosure and laying to grass, which made the Verneys try especially hard to let their enclosed lands quickly. Yet in 1746 the second earl pronounced that 'as to the improvement of East Claydon, the expenses attending the enclosure do yearly exceed the improvement as the books will make appear'. A partial rent account in 1747 suggests that the rents of the various fields of the new

---

[35] M. M. Verney, *Verney Letters*, II, p. 2119.

[36] BCRO PR 52/5/1 Notes at the back of Middle Claydon churchwardens' accounts 1724–81 in Herring's hand.

enclosure varied widely, from 8s an acre for 'Lord's Moor' to 22s per acre for some meadow ground. The variation was much wider than for the longer-enclosed Middle Claydon pastures. The Verneys may have felt that they had a poor return from their investment in enclosure. This did not mean their decision to lay the land down to grass was a misjudgement, for grain prices remained low. However, cattle plague ravaged cattle all over the country from 1745, bankrupting some farmers, while many landlords found themselves supporting and helping their tenants.[37] The outbreak made finding well-capitalised and dynamic tenants more difficult. Even in the 1780s East Claydon's farms were let at a lower average acreage rent per acre than in Middle Claydon. But by 1813 rents had risen markedly and apart from two farms on what had once been intercommoned waste and rough pasture, rent levels were much more comparable.[38]

Although the Verneys mainly bought ready enclosed estates in the eighteenth century, the second earl would always enclose to increase his land and income where he found opportunities. Several occurred around his purchases at Biddlesden and Syresham, on the Buckinghamshire/Northamptonshire border, close to Whittlewood Forest. When Westbury, which adjoined Biddlesden, was being enclosed by parliamentary act in 1764, he seized and enclosed woodlands previously intercommoned by the two parishes, and excluded Westbury commoners' livestock.[39] At Syresham where he owned a small amount of land, Verney claimed some twenty of the thirty-six acres of waste included in the Act, exaggerating his rights and deliberately increasing the numbers of his own livestock pastured there.[40] In 1765 he led a posse of gentry who charged 'levellers' who were attempting to dismantle the fencing of the enclosures at Warkworth, a Northamptonshire village near Banbury.[41] During the 1760s and 1770s he was also active on the scrutinising committees for the enclosure bills for the Buckinghamshire parishes of Little Horwood, Shalstone, Grendon Underwood, and Soulbury, all in the north of the county.

Very soon after the second earl's death in 1791 his successor, Lady Fermanagh, was engaged in preliminaries and negotiations to enclose Steeple Claydon. There is no correspondence to clarify Lady Fermanagh's part in instigating the enclosure. One account suggests that George Harding, a London lawyer and MP for Old Sarum, and descendant of one of the land purchasers in 1683/4, had unsuccessfully canvassed an enclosure in 1785, and pushed the bill

---

[37] rvjr to rv 6 October 1736 R59; Account dated 1747 in papers at end 1749 R59; J. Broad, 'The cattle plague in eighteenth century England', *Agricultural History Review* 31 (1983), pp. 104–15.

[38] 1780s rental in CIH 4/3/3–25; BCRO D/AF/106 gives rental valuations for a planned marriage of Catherine Verney and Thomas Aubrey of Boarstall. These may have been inflated rents, but it is unlikely that relativities between farms were distorted.

[39] CIH 5/5/17-18.

[40] Broad, 'The Verneys as enclosing landlords', p. 45 n. 25b; CIH 2/2283-4; 4/6/82; 5/2/37-55.

[41] Broad, 'The Verneys as enclosing landlords', p. 45 n. 25a.

through parliament in 1795.[42] However, the timing, soon after Lady Fermanagh began the vigorous reorganisation of the Claydon estate, makes it likely that she played some part.

The rapidly rising population of Steeple Claydon during the eighteenth century had increased pressure on grazing. There were relatively small changes to the stints in the field orders made between 1635, when three cows, two horses, and thirty sheep per yardland were the limit, and 1792, when the only reduction was to twenty sheep. However, other court orders allowed cottagers only one pig in the common fields, and in 1669 an order forbade the keeping of geese on the common. More interesting is the upper limit of 120 sheep per person, irrespective of their holdings.[43] The 1792 Court rolls illustrate other pressures on the land, with one presentment for enclosing from the waste, and seven for building on the waste. In the autumn of 1791, a meeting of common field occupiers was called under the aegis of the 1773 Act 'for the better Cultivation, Improvement, and Regulation of the Commonable fields, wastes and common of pasture'. It took place in Steeple Claydon schoolhouse on the afternoon of Tuesday 29 November, supposedly at the instigation of fifteen occupiers who between them farmed sixty-two and three-quarters of the eighty and a half yardlands. Letters agreeing to enclosure from five owners controlling seventeen yardlands are on file for 1791–2.[44]

Steeple Claydon's enclosure took place during the second wave of Buckinghamshire enclosure between 1790 and 1814, and it seems to have had support from the farming population from the outset. One of Mary Fermanagh's leading tenants at Middle Claydon, Charles Webb, was a significant landowner in Steeple Claydon but not amongst those Steeple Claydon landowners who wrote letters of agreement in 1791–2. On the other hand two of her own tenants in Steeple Claydon, Thomas and William Roades, who were also landowners there, wrote in support. The only indication of local opposition to enclosure lies in the report of the House of Commons Committee on the enclosure bill, which noted that one freeholder with two yardlands had objected, but had not come to parliament to press his views. No provision for the poor was made in the enclosure allotments, which covered under 1,800 of the 3,300 acres – just over half (54 per cent) of the parish area. The rest was old enclosure, much of it to the south and south-east of the parish where the woods lay, and adjoining Middle Claydon. The parliamentary bill was presented in Mary Fermanagh's name early in February 1795, and with James Grenville on the committee in the House of Commons, and the Marquess of Buckingham in the Lords, it passed quickly through all stages and received the Royal Assent on 28 April.[45] Few details

---

[42] W. James and J. Malcolm, *A General View of the Agriculture of Buckinghamshire*, p. 30.
[43] CIH 3/14/1-9.   [44] CIH 3/14/13.
[45] *CJ* L pp. 124, 291, 340; *LJ* XL pp. 345, 348, 357.

of the implementation survive except the enclosure map and award. However, enclosure was quickly followed by conversion to a pastoral farm economy, as it had been at East and Middle Claydon. The crop returns made in 1801 show only 433 acres, or 13 per cent of the parish under crops of any kind. The main crops were fodder crops, oats and beans, and made up 63.5 per cent of the sown acreage. Parkinson's enquiry in 1810 found 'beef and butter increased; grain decreased'. This implies that not just the Verneys but other owners thought pasture farms gave the best returns, even at a time of exceptionally high grain prices.[46] By 1800 the Verneys' estates were concentrated in adjoining parishes in north Buckinghamshire, and all had been enclosed. A modern estate regime, dominated by large, market oriented, tenant farms, was in place. What was the impact of these changes on the farmers and their farming, the social and economic structure of the Claydons, and the people and their welfare?

Enclosing landlords across north Buckinghamshire and much of the south midlands frequently turned newly enclosed parishes into permanent pasture farms after 1660. The famed 650-acre Creslow pastures north of Aylesbury had long been managed as great sheep runs, but after the Restoration the banker of Edward Backwell switched to grazing cattle there. He introduced similar farming on his land at Tyringham, to the north-east where other early-enclosed parishes included Chicheley, Weston Underwood, Filgrave, Hardmead, Clifton Reynes, and Petsoe.[47] Further west, Doddershall, Hogshaw, and Stowe, and the famous fattening grounds north-west of Aylesbury in Quarrendon, Hardwick, Blagrave, and Fleet Marston were also enclosed before 1650 while the disafforestation of Bernwood in 1632 resulted in large-scale conversion of enclosed farms, first for fattening, and then for dairying. Parkinson found a marked shift to dairying across north-west Buckinghamshire in his survey of the effects of enclosure on agriculture in 1810.[48]

After 1654–6 Middle Claydon had become an enclosed parish with newly laid out pasture farms and farmhouses and buildings away from the village centre. Almost simultaneously, the Dentons enclosed nearby Hillesden, refashioning farming layout and moving farm buildings in a similar way.[49] After 1670 the negative impact of the Irish Cattle Act on fattening encouraged farmers to change to dairying. Dairy farmers initially concentrated on cheesemaking, but

[46] Priest, *General View of the Agriculture of Buckinghamshire*, p. 403. M. E. Turner, 'The 1801 crop returns for Buckinghamshire', pp. 471–82.

[47] For Backwell's farming enterprises see his banking ledgers at Glyn Mills Bank, Lombard St, where his farming accounts were held as if bank accounts, under Creslow and Tyringham.

[48] A. C. Chibnall, *Sherington*, pp. 99–200 points out that this left the villages of Sherington, Emberton, and Lathbury surrounded by wholly or substantially enclosed communities. Defoe, *A Tour through the Whole Island*, II, p. 14. The estate papers for these parishes near Aylesbury are in Oxon CRO Dillon MSS esp. xb, d, g-l, xiic, xivb, d, h; Broad and Hoyle, *Bernwood*, pp. 79–81. Priest, *General View*, Appendix 10, pp. 401–4.

[49] Curthoys, 'Land, settlement and enclosure in Hillesden, Buckinghamshire'.

after 1750 they switched increasingly to butter production. Cheese became a delicacy enjoyed by the elite in the Restoration period where previously the poor had eaten it as a substitute for meat. The advantages of dairying for farmers and landlords alike were increasingly discussed.[50] Two examples of its adoption in north Buckinghamshire occurred at Hillesden and at Beachampton. Hillesden's enclosure in 1658 was supervised by Dr William Denton. Denton enthused about dairying as the most dependable form of farming: 'any other way I must run the hazard of a fool and a knave, and this way I only hazard the knave'. He consulted dairymen and calculated turnover and profit for cheesemaking, including not just what could be produced for market, but the residual whey that could be consumed in the household as butter, or by pigs. He even asked Sir Ralph Verney to recommend 'poor tenants' Verney felt insufficient for Claydon's post-enclosure farms so that he could offer them share-farming partnerships at Hillesden.[51] Browne Willis's father moved from Dorset to Beachampton in 1684 to improve the management of his estate. Initially he was 'feeding large oxen and weathers, and western ewes and selling them at Smithfield, but finding the Price of Cattle to sink, he thought it expedient to build dairy houses in the Grounds, that being the most probable way to make the rent in any times, and therefore in 1689 he build [2] house[s] . . . and the Lady Day following set them to sufficient tenants'.[52] At Middle Claydon the switch into dairying came in the 1670s and 1680s when Sir Ralph built additional cow houses and appropriate farm buildings for in-coming tenants at a time of falling rents. Initially dairying was taken up by middling tenants, and the highest rented fields on Knowl Hill were still generally let to gentlemen graziers such as Francis Rogers, or Joseph Churchill.

On smaller farms in the later seventeenth century some tenants combined pastoral farming with other trades. There were always farming tailors in Middle Claydon at that time, while the smith was often also a tenant. Declining smallholders and cottagers might carry on a carting trade. John Dixon did this after his dubious grazing enterprise failed in the mid-1660s. Others, like John Hicks, had weaving skills. Female skills and trades altered the dynamics of the household economy in more concealed ways. A number of women were lacemakers, and took on female apprentices on their own account. Lacemaking was the commonest women's work. Spenceley found it and straw-plaiting in open arable villages in Bedfordshire and Buckinghamshire because in enclosed pastoral villages dairying fully involved the farmer's wife. Her skills in cheese and buttermaking determined the success of the enterprise. Increasing farm sizes on enclosed estates encouraged specialisation in dairying for the whole household. In 1677 George Haynes of Middle Claydon was forced to give up

---

[50] Thirsk, *Alternative Agriculture*, pp. 165–7.   [51] wd to srv 14 and 22 October 1658 R16.
[52] BL Add. MS 5821 fo. 225b.

his farm because his wife was too ill to work, and five years later he was doing odd jobs on the estate. In the early eighteenth century dairy skills made the wife's ability as important as her husband's when choosing a tenant. In 1722 Wallis's bid for a tenancy in Middle Claydon was granted because his wife was deemed to 'understand a dairy very well', although he was not considered a 'very understanding man'.[53]

Eighteenth-century agricultural writers emphasised women's vital part in dairying, but also the increasing influence of cheese and butter factors over the trade. Deborah Valenze has argued that men used doubtful claims of rational and scientific progress to exclude women from cheese and butter production between 1780 and 1850. However, few male writers strongly supported this idea, rather more realising that it did not reflect the practicalities of contemporary dairying. In Buckinghamshire, and certainly in the Claydons, female roles in the industry were reinforced well into the nineteenth century.[54]

In late eighteenth-century north Buckinghamshire employment opportunities changed. Demand for male labour fell as larger farms became more common, and needed less labour. Simultaneously employment in lacemaking, and, near the Bedfordshire border, straw-plaiting, increased. These trades required women's nimble fingers and also employed large numbers of children, both boys and girls.[55] Joseph Mayett's autobiography shows how this Quainton labourer's son learnt lacemaking at a very young age to boost family income. More significantly, when he worked as a farm servant he often milked cows and carried butter, stereotypically female occupations.[56] Mayett was not unusual for the agricultural reports remark how uncommon it was to find women doing the milking in Buckinghamshire, though normal in the rest of the country.[57]

Farmers found it difficult to hire female servants as dairy maids when lace and straw provided better returns for day and piecework, but women retained their primacy in buttermaking. Successive female owners (Baroness Fermanagh and Catherine Verney) of the Verney estates between 1791 and 1820 were active estate managers and favoured female tenants. In East Claydon, a high proportion of dairy tenants in the first two decades of the nineteenth century were women.

[53] On Haynes see wc to srv 4 February 1677/8 ClH 4/5/30; For Wallis see cc to rv 15 December 1722 ClH 4/5/68. Wallis appears to have been selling up his land in Steeple Claydon to take on a tenanted farm, cf. Broad, 'The fate of the midland yeoman', pp. 325–47.

[54] D. Valenze, 'The art of women and the business of men: women's work and the dairy industry c. 1740–1840', *Past and Present* 130 (1991), pp. 142–69.

[55] On these trades see A. Buck, 'Middlemen in the Bedfordshire lace industry', *Bedfordshire, Historical Record Society* 57 (1978), pp. 31–58; P. Horn, 'Child workers in the pillow lace and straw plait trades of Victorian Buckinghamshire and Bedfordshire', *Historical Journal* 17 (1974), pp. 779–97; G. F. R. Spenceley, 'The origins of the English pillow lace industry', *Agricultural History Review* 21 (1973), pp. 81–93.

[56] Kussmaul, *The Autobiography of Joseph Mayett of Quainton*, pp. 1, 7.

[57] W. James and J. Malcolm, *A General View of the Agriculture of Buckinghamshire*, p. 15; Priest, *General View*, p. 289.

Five of the fourteen farms in an 1813 rental had female tenants all farming between 100 and 150 acres. The land tax returns between 1795 and 1814 show even more, with 50 per cent of farm occupiers female in 1805, 1810, and 1812. Many were widows, some described as managing farms with their sons, and had retained their husband's tenancies. However, Sarah Stevens's new tenancy of a farm in 1811 appears unconnected with any male death, and she may well have been a single woman entrusted with a farm by her female landowning patron.[58]

Dairying was widespread and substantial across north Buckinghamshire, south-west Northamptonshire, parts of Oxfordshire (around Thame and Bicester), and Warwickshire. Farmers remained committed to a permanent grass system, with only a few farmers tilling more than 10 per cent of their land on the Verney estates in the late eighteenth century. Those in Addington, Winslow, and Hoggeston ploughed from 0 to 15 per cent. Few cows were taken off the land in winter and stall fed. James and Malcolm wrote of outbuildings 'methodically arranged over the farm' to prevent damage to the farmstead from dairy animals. Yet farm and herd sizes in the south midlands were considerably larger than in other dairying areas. In Cheshire, evidence from rentals and agricultural reports between 1750 and 1800 suggests that farm sizes averaged between sixty and ninety acres, with most dairy farms around Arley Hall of about this acreage, but devoting up to one third of the land to crops. Average herd sizes were about ten cows. This matches available information about herd sizes during the mid-eighteenth-century cattle plague.[59] A similar pattern is apparent in Wiltshire and Somerset where in 1798 Billingsley used a dairy farm of sixty acres and twenty cows as his example. He reckoned dairying much more profitable than grazing, and saw a 200-acre grazing farm better divided up to provide four fifty-acre dairying enterprises. Thomas Davis expressed a similar view about Wiltshire dairying.[60]

In late eighteenth-century Buckinghamshire, dairying farms of 100 to 250 acres were typical, with those between 100 and 150 acres predominant. There were farms at East and Middle Claydon over 300 acres in size devoted to dairying, and an 1813 rental shows that two of these were combined from earlier separate farms. At Wotton in 1813 there were more farms of 200 to 300 acres than between 100 and 200 acres, while across the whole Grenville estate in 1811 there were several dairy farms of more than 400 acres. Of eight dairy

---

[58] BCRO D/AF/106 1813 rental of Verney estates part of marriage negotiations; East Claydon Land tax return duplicates 1793–1814: BCRO Q/RPL/1/14-35.

[59] C. F. Foster, *Cheshire Cheese and Farming in the North West in the 17th and 18th Centuries* (Arley Hall 1998), chs. 5 and 6, pp. 71–82; H. Holland, *A General View of the Agriculture of Cheshire* (London 1808), pp. 91–2.

[60] J. Billingsley, *General View of the Agriculture of Somerset* (3rd edn London 1798), p. 251; T. Davis, *General View of the Agriculture of Wiltshire* (London 1794), pp. 118–48.

farms at Lee Grange, adjoining the Claydons, for sale in 1788 four were of 200 to 300 acres, two between 100 and 200, and two less than 100 acres.[61] This compares with William Marshall's calculation that the average farm size in the county was 161 acres. Reckoning at four acres per cow, this implies herd sizes of up to eighty, with some sheep and a few pigs fed on the milk residues. St John Priest noted herds of 50 to 70 cows on farms near Claydon in 1810.[62]

Five surviving Buckinghamshire probate inventories from the period 1720 to 1730 show that most of those described as graziers were in fact dairy farmers. Four had goods and stock worth over £350. One, John Reeve, lived in Grendon Underwood, but his impressive enterprise covered three parishes, with much of the land in Middle Claydon. He had seventy-eight cows and calves, with a bull, some forty-two sheep and nine pigs. The value of his cattle at £312 10s was almost half of his total probate valuation. In early September 1727 he had almost two and a half tons of cheese in store, valued at £50. His total moveable assets of £653 11s 5d included £97 in money lent out on bond, while he owned properties in Steeple Claydon let out for rent. Despite the presence of horses, wagon and cart, and plough harrow and harness, the only crop on the farm when the inventory was taken in early September was hay. Reeve exemplifies the new way of life for the adapting yeoman farmer – no longer referred to as a yeoman – in the eighteenth century.[63] Three farmers' inventories for 1726–7 made on the Verney estate to secure rent or debt at death or bankruptcy were not so large, but substantial amounts of cheese were in store – one ton, one and a half tons, and two and a half tons. They had a similar range of farm stock and equipment, but fewer cows, and valuations of £177, £333, and £356. Thomas Grimes had a freehold farm worth £35 to £40 a year in Steeple Claydon, bought about thirty years before, which he was now forced to sell through debt and near bankruptcy.[64] Landed wealth was becoming less important, and a high percentage of his working capital was tied up in animals and maturing cheese.

There are too few inventories to chart the transition from cheesemaking to the predominantly butter-producing economy described in the second half of the eighteenth century. At Middle Claydon a creditor who took bills of sale on farm livestock in 1787 to recoup annuity arrears found a range and balance of

[61] Huntington STGM 14/12, 14/20 and 6/9.
[62] W. Marshall, *The Review and Abstract of the County Reports to the Board of Agriculture*, IV (Newton Abbot 1969), p. 524; Priest, *General View*, pp. 53–7.
[63] Buckinghamshire RO D/A/Wf/75/137 dated 1 September 1727; cf. 1722 Middle Claydon rental showing Reeve as tenant of Knowl Hill and its meadow for £90 per year. In 1727 he also had fields in Fimore, amongst the woods bordering Claydon and Grendon. On the change from landowning yeoman to tenant farmer see Broad, 'The fate of the midland yeoman', pp. 325–47, esp. pp. 331–7. The remaining inventories show differing ratios of sheep to cattle, with sheep predominating in two from Weston Turville near the Chiltern edge, but dairy cattle on the heavy clays to the north.
[64] CIH 4/5/73 cc to Ralph Verney 21 September 1727, 5 October 1727; CIH 4/5/74 Inventory of Robert Markham dated 25 November 1726.

livestock not dissimilar to that at the beginning of the century. On one 120-acre farm there were 35 cows, 44 sheep, and 12 pigs, while another of 160 acres held 14 cows, 1 bull, 54 ewes, and 1 ram when the bailiff arrived to take possession.[65] There was no attempt to value crops, but also no evidence of maturing cheese on the premises. At Biddlesden, there is evidence to suggest a long-term shift to pasture, though the tradition of a more mixed regime remained, with one farmer in 1790 requesting Verney to let him rent more arable land to grow corn for grain and straw.[66] The size and layout of farm buildings also suggest specialisation there, with cow sheds and pig-sties listed amongst outstanding repairs in 1787, and the building of a cow house for thirty-eight cows in 1791 evidence of a possible move towards winter stall feeding.[67] The predominance was even greater at Bourton where in 1792 only 88 out of *c*. 1,350 acres were arable, and all but 12 of these on one farm.

The 1801 crop returns show that both East and Middle Claydon had less than 5 per cent of their land under crops, while even recently enclosed Steeple Claydon had less than 14 per cent. The absence of a return for Biddlesden, as for Boarstall, another closed parish under pasture, probably indicates there were no arable crops to account for. Other returns made specific mentions of the importance of grassland agriculture, including Hillesden, Worminghall, Hoggeston, and Milton Keynes, described as 'chiefly pasture', while Lillingston Dayrell and Dorton had a very low acreage under crop. Beachampton produced 'great quantities of butter most of which is sent off weekly to London' with less than 100 of its 1,450 acres under tillage.[68]

Cheesemaking equipment was widespread in all the early inventories, as were churns and leads which were used in butter production. Butter and cheese were probably made concurrently in the first half of the century, and whey butter was made for local consumption after cheesemaking. The absence of butter from inventories almost certainly reflects its rapid movement to market while cheese matured on the farm. The decline of cheesemaking reflected changing tastes and the lack of distinctive branding for Buckinghamshire cheese, in a market closely controlled by the London factors. Buttermaking capitalised on improving transport services that allowed wicker baskets of butter to sell in London the day after they left the farm. Rapid sales also released capital tied up in storing maturing cheese, which in John Reeve's case constituted almost 8 per cent of his total inventory, and perhaps 10 per cent of his working capital.[69]

---

[65] Bills of sale dated 14 September 1787 CIH5/1/4/5; cf. Michaelmas rental 1787 in 4/3/9 and 5/1/29.

[66] CIH 4/6/56 for 1730s and 1740s; 5/1/20 for 1790 correspondence, while the 1786/7 estate particular is in 5/1/5.

[67] CIH 4/6/13, 5/1/20.   [68] PRO HO67/15.   [69] CIH 4/6/56.

The lifestyle of the well-capitalised tenant farmer increasingly separated him from the general run of village families. There were fewer farming tenants as farm sizes expanded, while rising rural population after 1780 brought new pressures on housing and jobs. Substantial tenant farmers may have made a reasonable, even a good living, but were also vulnerable, with so much capital tied up in livestock. Animal disease was always a threat and the cattle plague (rinderpest) of 1745 to 1757 could affect whole herds, with only limited compensation. The epidemic may have fostered the switch into butter, with its better cash flow. However the weaker farmers quickly became dependent on the butter factors, who by 1800 were delaying payment to farmers for three months or more. As tenant farmers, the dairymen understandably sank their capital into productive assets. The eighteenth-century farmhouses of north Buckinghamshire remained insubstantial, as landlords felt no need to provide more. Pasture Farm in Boarstall, built for dairying in the 1690s, is a modest structure. Its most impressive room is the stone-flagged cellar, suitable for keeping dairy products cool. Sion Hill Farm, built in the 1740s at East Claydon in the aftermath of enclosure, is also modest, though the second earl's three later farmhouses were rather more substantial. By contrast, the splendid eighteenth-century farmhouses on the Cheshire plain were attached to farms of 60 to 100 acres which in north Buckinghamshire were unviable dairy units.[70]

While the Buckinghamshire dairymen adapted their product and farming to economic circumstances, we know little of their profitability or use of labour. Did expanding farm sizes and the switch to butter increase the efficiency of labour use? It seems unlikely that farms of 300 acres and herds of 60, 80, or 100 cows were as easily managed by a farmer and his wife as one of 60 to 80 acres. The Posse Comitatus of 1798 shows a higher proportion of living-in servants on farms in those parishes where enclosure and conversion had taken place, or where there were low or null returns of crops in 1801, but accounts only for male servants.[71] Bigger farms certainly meant fewer farmers in the villages and more families employed as labourers or seeking work in the service and artisan sectors of the economy. These groups, and the effects of economic and agricultural change on the social world of the Claydons, are the subject of the remainder of this chapter.

Farming changes were only one element in the process of social change in the three Claydon parishes during the eighteenth century. Comparisons of

---

[70] Airs and Broad, 'The management of rural building', pp. 43–56; Plans for Sion Hill farm c. 1740 in Verney microfilm R59. Cf. Foster, *Cheshire Cheese and Farming*, pp. 37–47.

[71] I. F. W. Beckett, *The Buckinghamshire Posses Comitatus of 1798*, Buckinghamshire Record Society 22 (1985).

Table 9.2 *Wealth in the Restoration Claydons from the Hearth Tax returns 1662/71*

	Exempt	1 hearth	2 hearths	3–5 hearths	6 hearths	Total houses	Total hearths
Middle Claydon	14	8	9	2	3	36	109
East Claydon	25	15	15	12	7	74	168
Steeple Claydon	23	27	19	10	1	80	105

Table 9.3 *Percentage of houses in parish by number of hearths*

	1 hearth and exempt	2 hearths	3–5 hearths	6+ hearths	Total houses	Total hearths
Middle Claydon	61	25	5.5	8.3	36	109
East Claydon	54	20.3	16.2	9.4	74	168
Steeple Claydon	62.5	23.75	12.5	1.25	80	105

population, landownership, and social structure in the late seventeenth century and at the end of the eighteenth century elucidate patterns and shifts that are less visible in the family archives after 1752. The Hearth Tax provides an indication of social structure around 1660. The mutilated returns for the Claydons make it difficult to link individual houses to hearths. However, a plausible reconstruction of comparative social structure is possible following conventional group categories (1 hearth, 2 hearths, 3–5 hearths and 6+ hearths) and in the case of the larger houses, some assumed mean hearth number per house.[72] These figures in percentage terms are shown in table 9.3.

The different social structures of the three villages expand the picture of community characteristics suggested by letters and accounts. Claydon House, with its forty-six hearths, dominated Middle Claydon. Indeed it had more hearths than any other house in north Buckinghamshire. The parsonage and Fimer Lodge, a hunting lodge in the woods that had been the Verneys' bailiff's residence, were the only other houses of any size. Two houses had three hearths, and over 60 per cent had only one hearth. The housing structure already reflected the concentrated ownership of land in the parish: even apparently wealthy tenant

---

[72] The mutilated state of the only surviving Hearth Tax return gives total numbers of houses, exempt houses, and of hearths, but in Middle Claydon, and even more substantially in East Claydon, it is not possible to read the names, or the number of hearths, for some of the houses. It was therefore necessary to attempt an estimate of how the numbers of hearths not attributable to readable names were distributed. For discussion of hearth/wealth relationships see Spufford, *Contrasting Communities*, pp. 37–45.

farmers lived in relatively insubstantial houses. The number of exempt houses exceeded the taxpaying single-hearth homes, suggesting that the widowed poor remained in the village, while the able-bodied and enterprising without farming capital migrated to villages and towns with greater opportunities.

Steeple Claydon had a very similar proportion of houses of three hearths and above, but only one was over six hearths. The Chaloner family was the biggest landowner in 1660, but after their failed enclosure and subsequent piecemeal sale, the parish became a typical open village, with no resident landowners of elite status, many small owners, and an active land market through the eighteenth century. The Verneys became manorial lords in 1704, but only slowly accumulated land, selecting mainly enclosed land adjoining Middle Claydon. East Claydon's social structure in 1660 is the most difficult to reconstruct from the Hearth Tax record. However a tentative conclusion is that there was a more even distribution of wealth, with over one quarter of the houses of three hearths or more, and almost 10 per cent with six hearths or more. Perhaps the presence of a major route from London to the west midlands, and at least one inn offering overnight accommodation, accounts for some larger houses. However, a higher proportion of resident gentry and yeoman families was probably more important. In the 1660s the Abells and Duncombes were both resident on modest gentry estates in the village. Several other yeoman families hovered close to gentility. In the 1713 and 1722 elections a dozen freeholders cast their vote.

The occupational structure of the three Restoration communities did not vary markedly. There were yeomen and husbandmen in all three parishes, though in Middle Claydon they were all tenant farmers, of whom the most prosperous owned freeholds or copyholds elsewhere. A combination of parish registers, militia surveys, court cases, and correspondence also indicates a good range of trades in all three parishes. Smiths and tailors were present in each parish. Weaving skills were fairly widespread, and hemp spinning and weaving employed the poor. There was a baker, an innkeeper, and a carrier in East Claydon. By 1715 Steeple Claydon's parish register recorded a shopkeeper and a baker, while a one-acre market garden producing fruit and vegetables provides evidence of agricultural diversity. Lacemaking was common in all three villages, hidden from formal records by the predominance of female and child labour in the work.

In 1600, the three Claydon parishes had varied profiles, but were not obviously dissimilar types of community. All three had open fields, manorial courts, copyhold and freehold estates owned by yeomen and husbandmen. Middle Claydon had its great house and extensive demesnes, but these were let out on a long lease. Even in 1660 populations and occupational structures in the three parishes were not very different, although the landscape and ownership of Middle Claydon had been transformed. The social impact on Middle Claydon

Table 9.4 *Population estimates for the Claydon parishes 1603–1811*

Parish	Year					
	1603	1662/71	1676	1706–12	1801	1811
Middle Claydon	200–16	200–37	217	206	103	129
East Claydon	200–16	296–351	301	340–80	299	309
Steeple Claydon	315–91	332–94	n.a.	314–50	646	704

was discussed in chapter 7. The eighteenth-century divergence of the three parishes is the subject of the remainder of this section.

By 1800 much had changed in all three parishes, and the most obvious indicator of that change is the number of inhabitants at different periods shown in table 9.4. Middle Claydon's population fell by over 50 per cent, while East Claydon's remained stable and Steeple Claydon's virtually doubled. The figures for East and Steeple Claydon reflect the trends in baptisms, marriages, and burials in their parish register shown in figures 4b and 4c. East Claydon appears to have suffered a severe crisis after the epidemic of 1727–9. All three series show a rapid falling away from peaks in 1727 to 1735, to much lower levels in the 1740s. A partial recovery from the 1750s to 1780s still left annual totals well below those for the early seventeenth and early eighteenth centuries, and subdued levels of births and marriages until the century's end. These figures reflect a combination of epidemics, the economic impact of the loss of the main road, and the effects of enclosure. Steeple Claydon mirrors East Claydon in several respects, with baptisms showing a long period of decline from the 1660s to 1720s, and a strong long-term rise from then until 1800, while only in the 1720s and 1730s were there high levels of mortality. From 1745 baptisms rose to unprecedented heights, only briefly checked in the 1770s, and well above burial levels. Steeple Claydon's population rose strongly in the second half of the eighteenth century with considerably fewer burials than baptisms.

Middle Claydon's declining population was accompanied by agricultural specialisation. Apart from one cordwainer, there were no non-farming occupations amongst active adult males in 1798. The seven farmers were all described as dairymen. In the same period Steeple Claydon's 172 males were in agricultural and general work, with 24 farmers, 39 servants, and 80 labourers, and the remainder in a wide variety of trades. There were traditional village trades – blacksmith, tailors, and cordwainers (shoemakers), as well as one remaining weaver, a butcher, and a baker. There were also two shopkeepers, a pig dealer, seven bricklayers, a maltster, and three coopers. With over 600 inhabitants it was large enough to support a range of trades, and attract custom from surrounding villages. Within ten miles, Whitchurch and Tingewick were of a similar size, and Tingewick had a greater variety of trades. Brill, Quainton, and Waddesdon were rather larger, but only Brill, with a long semi-urban tradition of rural service functions, had a significantly wider range of trades.[73]

East Claydon was in an intermediate position in 1798. It retained non-agricultural trades: a dealer, five joiners and carpenters, a blacksmith and a wheelwright, together with two tailors and two weavers, but the range was smaller than one hundred years earlier. Some of the same process of 'closure' that had engulfed Middle Claydon over 140 years and reflected a monopoly of landownership affected the village. East Claydon landownership patterns changed most during the eighteenth century. By 1798 the Verneys were effectively sole proprietors, as they had long been in Middle Claydon. In Steeple Claydon where the Verneys came to own about one third of the land, they never wielded the same day-to-day influence. The dominant influence of the Verney family changed East Claydon as profoundly after 1740 as it had Middle Claydon in the previous eighty years. In Steeple Claydon, where the family's control was much less, many characteristics of an 'open' village developed. A lack of active governance permitted in-migration, and led to an occupational profile including a large pool of general labour, together with a significant range of craft and service occupations that were absent from landowner-dominated communities. Up until 1795 common land helped augment incomes from smallholdings and service and artisan occupations, and additional housing was erected on the waste.[74]

Eighteenth-century Steeple Claydon's social dynamics are revealed only by snapshots of particular moments of interest or tension. Settlement examinations and other surviving poor law documents point to growing under-employment after 1750, which coincided both with rising baptisms in the parish, and the enclosure and tightening of settlement in East Claydon. The roundsman system had been introduced into the parish by 1785 to reduce poor rates by encouraging farmers to use additional labour.[75] The village's community harmony had been fractured by the money-grabbing activities of the regicide Thomas Chaloner at the Restoration, and the subsequent attempts of Sir William Smith and Richard Lane to seize the Chaloner estates by force. Following the Chaloners' recovery of the land after 1668, unsuccessful attempt to consolidate and enclose the parish in the 1670s, and piecemeal sale of their estate in 1683–4, the parish was left with a diffuse pattern of landownership. The parish had a mentally unstable

[73] I. F. W. Beckett, *The Buckinghamshire Posses Comitatus of 1798*.
[74] CIH 3/14/7-14 Steeple Claydon Court Rolls show presentments for cottages on the waste in eighteenth-century Steeple Claydon.
[75] Huntington STGM Box 9 (11); cf. BCRO QS/M vol. 21 1787.

vicar for much of the late seventeenth century, and lacked an alternative focus for community leadership.[76]

These tensions and discontents are well illustrated by the history of the school. In 1657 Thomas Chaloner built and endowed a schoolhouse with a rent charge of £12 a year to pay a schoolmaster to teach pupils for no charge, and keep the building in repair.[77] This community enterprise involved least two village yeomen carrying bricks and timber for the work, and Chaloner giving a dinner for those villagers and neighbours who had assisted. John Berry was employed to teach at the school, and received his salary for one and a half years. After the Restoration Sir William Smith and Richard Lane seized the lands, and refused to pay the annuity. Berry's wife insisted that 'her husband should not teach school any longer for nothing'.[78] There was an outcry at the time, and a petition to the Commission of Charitable Uses in 1668. In 1689 villagers petitioned Sir Ralph Verney as the sole surviving trustee to nominate five new trustees and soon afterward further efforts were made to resume payment of the rent charge.[79] The new owner of the land from which it was paid, Penelope Lane, was almost certainly a relative of Richard. She contested payment because Chaloner had been a Regicide, rendering any charity deed null and void. A Chancery Commission examined the case and found for the school, assessing arrears at £70. However, Lane took the matter to Chancery where the Lord Keeper, Lord Somers, upheld her view and thereby deprived the school of all future income.[80]

In the early 1720s the village was the centre of a deer-stealing gang with a strong sense of community awareness and defensiveness against outsiders. It successfully prevented Judge Denton of Hillesden from dealing harshly with a gang member. The leader of the gang was also an agricultural innovator, whose adoption of turnips as a field crop raised questions about the extension of tithes. A few years earlier the villagers prevented a Hillesden tailor settling in the village because 'there are five tailors there already', evidence that the diversifying occupational structure was not economically prosperous.[81] In 1722 Charles Chaloner remarked that 'Steeple Claydon people are an uneasy sort of people'.[82] Steeple Claydon's abundance of labour made it very different from

---

[76] On the battles over Steeple Claydon lands in the 1660s see my forthcoming article 'The battle for regicide land in Steeple Claydon, Buckinghamshire, 1660–1700'; for the failed enclosure and land sale see Broad, 'The fate of the midland yeoman', pp. 337–44; for evidence of the state of pastoral leadership see Broad, 'Buckinghamshire dissent', pp. 90–1.

[77] CIH 2/995 20 June 1657.

[78] PRO C91/21/16 Depositions to Commission to enquire into the Charity September 1693.

[79] Charles Cheyne to srv 12 July 1664 R19; petition dated 23 September 1668 R22; Petition dated 16 October 1689 R43.

[80] PRO C90/26a February 1693/4; for the various actions in the 1680s see CIH 2/997.

[81] For further details see ch. 7 above, pp. 180–1; CIH 4/5/1/67-70.

[82] cc to rv 18 December 1722 4/5/68.

East and Middle Claydon, or indeed from the enclosed villages of Hillesden and Addington to the north and east of it, both of which also lost population between 1660 and 1801. For much of the eighteenth century the existence of extensive common in the south-west of the parish, adjoining Poundon common, and more in the east beside the old Aylesbury to Buckingham road provided fuel and pasturage for the inhabitants. The enclosure of 1795, which eliminated this asset, must have been a hard blow at a time of expanding population and rising prices.

Middle Claydon after 1740 saw rising farm sizes, and a reduction in farm numbers, while the population of the parish fell. The small village population in 1801 lived in five or six houses around the parsonage, while the remainder lived at Claydon House, or in farmhouses out in the enclosed fields.[83] The building of the new Claydon House between c. 1759 and 1783 used a good deal of labour, but the permanent Claydon-based staff was small – housekeeper and/or steward, a small farm staff, gamekeeper, woodman, and a few assistants were all that were needed. Apart from the farmers themselves there were just nine families in cottages in 1787, and several of these may have been working for the house on a permanent or semi-permanent basis. Something of the experience of the less fortunate inhabitants is revealed in the poor law records after 1740. Up until 1776 the overseers' accounts show extremely modest payments, never exceeding £36 a year – less than 15s a week – and often much lower. From 1741 to 1750 the total sum was between £10 and £15 in two years and the pattern continued for thirty years. The numbers receiving year-round support were small. In 1749 only Ann Roades received such payments, though John Roades was paid 2 guineas 'for keeping a poor boy a year'. Only one house rent was paid. In the 1730s two or three people had received money throughout the year, and three or four had their house rent paid. Those receiving benefit were normally paid 1s 6d to 2s 6d a week, and there is no evidence that certificated families in other parishes were being supported. These long years of frugal expenditure reflected the Verneys' successful policies of encouraging out-migration, excluding potential settlers in the village, and keeping a tight rein on village affairs. They also provided a good deal of support from their own pockets to supplement the poor rate.

From 1777, patterns of relief changed abruptly as can be seen in figure 7b. In that year £44 was spent, rising to £69 in 1779, £83 in 1784, and only twice falling below £50 between 1777 and 1800. Expenditure rose for two main reasons. Firstly, the amounts paid to those in permanent receipt of pensions rose sharply, with John Norcutt receiving 4s 6d a week regularly from 1780, and 6s 6d on some occasions. In 1779 Middle Claydon failed to remove the Loveridge family to East Claydon. The legal costs of the case fell on the rates,

---

[83] This pattern is visible on both Jeffreys's map of 1768 and Bryant's of 1824, see *Buckinghamshire in the 1760s and 1820s* as well as on the Ordinance Survey map of 1814.

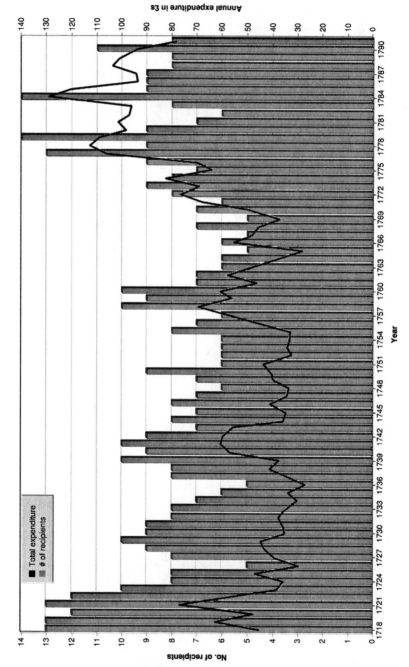

Figure 7a East Claydon poor rate expenditure 1718–91.

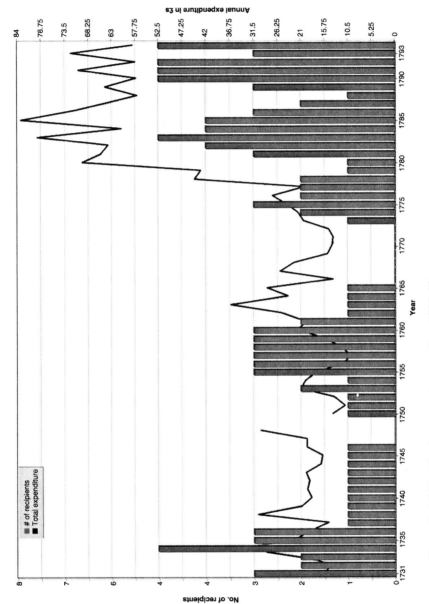

Figure 7b Middle Claydon poor rate expenditure 1730–93.

as did continuing pensions (Moses Loveridge was still receiving 5s 6d a week in 1800) and apprenticeship costs for a child in 1782. Renewed attempts to provide work materials and tools for the poor were also costly, with a linen wheel bought in 1779, while hemp was spun and woven throughout the 1780s and 1790s. A jackass and a grinding wheel were purchased in 1782. In 1797 70 lb of hemp were bought and 5 ells of cloth sold. During the period 1730 to 1775 there were no equivalent costs.[84]

This abrupt change coincided with the collapse of the second earl's finances, suggesting that his personal charity had been important for the poor. He was known for his generosity in Buckinghamshire, and as county MP was keen to display it. As his financial power and his political influence crumbled, he could no longer support the parish in the same way. Before the 1770s there are no records of payments in settlement cases, or other legal costs that elsewhere formed a considerable proportion of overseers' outgoings. When the Loveridge settlement case between East and Middle Claydon went to court and was lost, it was indicative of his failing political influence. Between 1660 and 1770 few cases went to court, and the Verneys generally arbitrated between parishes. The sudden doubling of the standard rate of weekly relief also suggests that Verney had previously made regular payments to the poor. The case of Giovanni Padrola, a plasterer and key craftsman in the construction of the new house at Claydon, is symptomatic. When the financial crisis came the parish supported him and paid him relief of 5s a week from 1785 to 1791, perhaps continuing his work with whatever materials were on site. He disappeared from the records soon after Earl Verney's death.

The collapse of Verney power in the late 1770s put more power into the hands of the large farmers who tenanted the estate. In the thirty years from 1771 to 1801 only twelve men acted as overseer, and four of these acted only once. Thomas Roades held office seven times in 1771, 1776, 1780–1, 1787, 1794, and 1801, and Joseph Stevens and William Hinton four times each.[85] This parish elite was even more closely knit than these figures suggest. There were only six surnames amongst them, with three Roadeses and Stevenses and two Hintons and Webbs. This nevertheless represents a greater measure of rotation of office than had occurred between 1674 and 1730 when Abraham Teagle held office for seventeen years, and five others for three or more years. These same men also had to rotate the office of churchwarden.[86] What is difficult to gauge is whether this late eighteenth-century parish elite were the initiators of new policies or whether the various work schemes had existed before but been funded by Verney himself. After 1791 the firm hand of Baroness Fermanagh may be seen in the decision to make the poor rate pay for the enclosure of the

[84] BCRO PR52/12/1-4.   [85] BCRO PR52/12/4.   [86] BCRO PR52/5/1, 3-4.

parish charity lands in Steeple Claydon in 1795. It may also have instigated the short-lived attempt to reduce the standard rate of relief to 3s 6d per week in 1798, only possible until the famine year of 1800.

Welfare policy in Middle Claydon shows a continuing relationship between lordly personal charity and the work of the overseers, but there is less evidence of the tensions in the village community which is not surprising in a closed and regulated parish. East Claydon's parish affairs show rivalries between competing gentry families before it too came into the tight grip of the Verney family in the later eighteenth century. Up to 1730 three gentry families had land and lived in East Claydon. The main rivalry was between the Abells and the Verneys. The Abells had owned land there since the first half of the seventeenth century, and rather surprisingly retained it into the eighteenth, after Mary Verney (née Abell) died without children to inherit and the estate reverted to her cousins instead of passing to the Verneys. Mary lived on until 1715, and the Verneys eventually bought the estate back in 1729. But in the later seventeenth century Edmund Verney had also bought a small numbers of farms and cottages in East Claydon to augment his estate there, which did not pass to his widow. They gave the Verneys a continuing landed presence in the parish, which Sir John Verney and his son Ralph increased by further purchases, particularly after 1717.

Whatever anti-Verney sentiment existed in East Claydon in the early eighteenth century was reinforced by public awareness of the lunacy of Mary Abell. Her condition was considered to have been aggravated by her awkward and uncouth husband's behaviour, and open sexual misdemeanours in the locality – he employed pretty servant girls to care for his wife and kept them as his mistresses. In 1714 William Abell endowed a new charity for the poor in the parish, paying doles on a specific day to commemorate the death of his wife. In 1716 he added a further sum and day to remember 'Mary Abell alias Verney . . . who for several years was very melancholy during her husband's life.' The Abells attempted to gain popularity among the villagers in less subtle ways by restoring personal alms giving in 1722, more than fifty years after the Verneys had abandoned them.[87] Even when they sold their estates, the Abells remained in the village as tenants of their manor house.

From 1700 to 1725 power in East Claydon was widely distributed. The parson, resident landowners, and the farming freeholders and cottagers held stakes. Charitable provision was modest and recent. Apart from the Abell bequest there was a late seventeenth-century gift for the poor by a long-resident parson, Mr Griffith. The total disposable income was estimated at £13 2s in the early nineteenth century, and around 1720 it was probably nearer £5 than £10. This compared with £47 for Middle Claydon and nothing for Steeple Claydon. The

---

[87] BCRO PR51/12/1 inside front cover.

poor on relief were benignly treated during the period 1718 to 1722. Twelve or thirteen individuals received regular relief in a range from 1s to 5s per week, and some householders had their rent paid. Expenditure ranged from £45 to £65 per year with a peak in 1721. Extraordinary charges included payments for three midwives in an unsuccessful attempt to save Thomas Miller's wife and child, and the rebuilding of the poor house.

The tone of vestry decisions changed in 1723. The ten pensioners of 1723 fell to five in 1726, and total expenditure from £57 in 1722 to £29 in 1726. Vestry decisions about pensions for the able-bodied in 1723 include phrases such as 'until he is better able to subsist' and 'till she can shift without'. A vestry resolution of 12 April 1724 agreed only eight regular pensions of 1s to 2s, and six of the recipients were widows. These changes came immediately after the Abells sold their estate to the land-jobbers and bankers, Snow and Paltock, who in December 1722 had sent in bailiffs to recover all arrears from tenants. Vestry policy may reflect the tightened circumstances of the farmers making vestry decisions, passing on their own financial woes to the poor. The harshness was soon modified and five pensions were raised by the end of June. A generally tighter regime continued through the 1720s and 1730s, with fewer regular recipients until 1739 (except during the epidemic year 1729), the highest weekly pension paid exceeding 2s in only two years, and the total expenditure topped £40 in only three. In the mid-1730s the number of regular recipients fell as low as five, but rent was paid for two or three parishioners (see fig. 7a).

Weekly pensions were only one component of available parish resources for the poor, and the village elite used charitable resources in tandem with them. The Abell and Griffith charity regulations both limited eligibility to those 'who received no collection', and this was adhered to up to 1722. In 1718–19 the money from both charities went to the same group of people. After Abell died in 1721 the parish decided to pay the charity money in three tranches, in January, February, and June (to commemorate William Abell's death). The Town Stock money was paid at Christmas, and the Griffith charity at Candlemas and Easter, allowing the marginally poor to receive money at regular intervals during the hardest months of the year.

However, when the vestry cut weekly pensions and the numbers of people receiving them they found other ways of providing for the poor. They bought clothes and shoes regularly in the 1720s, paying some rent for villagers, and in 1737 they 'paid for cow commons for Thomas Holtom' who was otherwise unsupported from rates or charities and three years later began to receive charity money for the first time. Charitable income was also distributed more flexibly. Between 1724–5 and 1729, after pensions had been lowered, charitable payments were made to those on permanent relief in contravention of the bequests. In the late 1730s and 1740s, the rent from the church lands was used to supplement the overseers' income. Despite the more stringent parish regime, the poor house was kept in repair. Substantial work was done in 1721, a chimney and oven built in 1725, and the roof re-thatched in 1733.

From the late 1720s when the Verneys bought and consolidated their East Claydon estate, the villagers faced two economic changes of great consequence. The passing road traffic on a main route from London to the midlands had supported the inn at East Claydon (the Swan), and brought money into the village. A carrier based his enterprise in the village.[88] However in the early 1720s the road from Aylesbury to Buckingham was turnpiked along a route that by-passed the Claydons to the east through Winslow. The old road fell into disuse, and much of it is now a bridle path across the fields of East Claydon. There are no allusions to loss of traffic in the correspondence, but by the 1740s the Verneys considered East Claydon a 'poor town'.

East Claydon people needed even more alternative employment after the enclosure of 1742–3. The gradual disappearance of freehold cottage property over the next twenty-five years reflects the declining prosperity of small free-holders in the village. The parish's population stabilised during the second half of the eighteenth century, while Steeple Claydon's rose. This reflected falling employment opportunities, but also the increasing use of the same controls on migration and housing that had been used in Middle Claydon. Enclosure had a rapid impact on poor relief. Between 1737 and 1742 the number of people regularly receiving relief increased from five, six, or seven, to nine or ten, and the overseers' expenditure to £60 or more from under £40. Part of the overseers' expenditure was for ditching work in 1740, when six or seven poor men were set to work. They included Thomas Holtom, who in 1737 had his cow's common paid for by the parish. Was this work partial short-term compensation for those losing common rights? Soon after enclosure parish work schemes were introduced, with hemp bought for spinning between 1743 and 1751. The overseers bought wood for fuel for three women in 1747. Before the enclosure they would have gathered it themselves.

However the numbers regularly receiving relief soon fell back to earlier levels. Apart from the period from 1758 to 1760, there was no rise until after 1778, when the Verney finances collapsed. Expenditure rose to around £100 until the 1790s. However other aspects of policy affected the cost of poor relief. As they enclosed East Claydon, the Verneys used settlement laws to remove five families from the parish, two in 1740, one in 1742, and two in 1743. Only one other removal from East Claydon is recorded in the whole eighteenth century. Three families were removed from other parishes to East Claydon in the course of the century, but all other cases were dealt with by the use of settlement

---

[88] Ogilby, *Britannia*; John Taylor, *The Carriers Cosmographie* (London 1637); J. A. Chartres, 'Road carrying in England in the seventeenth century: myth and reality', *Economic History Review* 2nd series, 30 (1), pp. 73–94. J. Chibnall, 'The roads of Buckinghamshire, 1675–1913', unpublished MSc thesis, University of London 1963.

certificates with payments made to distant parishes.[89] In 1740 two people's goods were sold up. The year 1750 also saw two children apprenticed well away from the parish using charitable funds effectively in the grant of the Verneys. For the rest of the century, the welfare provision in East Claydon was similar to that in Middle Claydon, suggesting that Verney benevolence subsidised the poor rate until 1778. As in Middle Claydon, when the Verney finances collapsed, not only did the number and cost of the poor rise, the maximum amount paid weekly also rose to 4s or 5s, even before inflation began to bite seriously in the 1790s.

Data about landownership, population, and occupation around 1800 allows useful comparisons across the three Claydon parishes, even though the estate material is poorer. There were real differences in the timing and scale of changes after 1660 and marked differences in social structure at the end of the eighteenth century. However, by 1800 the parish was no longer the sole unit for discussing social and economic dynamics. It remained the basic unit of administration and politics and played a vital role in the lives of the poor. But as the Verneys consolidated power and land ownership in East Claydon along lines already established in Middle Claydon, they began to consider the area as a single entity. In all three parishes they controlled two of the three major levers of power – the church and parson, and the lordship of the manor. In East and Middle Claydon they were also sole proprietors, while in Steeple Claydon the one third of the parish that they owned was concentrated close to Middle Claydon. Middle Claydon House was the centre of an area in which there were no strong competing claims to power. The disappearance of manorial courts after enclosure allowed the uniqueness of each village's customs and tenures to disappear. Farmers agreed to similar kinds of tenancy agreements across the whole estate. Although the farmers of each village formed the vestry elite who made decisions about the housing and relief of the poor, they were always in the sights of the estate stewards, and ultimately of the landowning family.

There were other ways in which the Verneys treated the estate as a single unit. In 1820 the gamekeeper was licensed for the estate as a whole, covering the manors of East, Middle, and Steeple Claydon.[90] In 1767 Edmund Millward, rector of Middle Claydon, became the parson of East Claydon, and unified religious influence in the two parishes. His successors also held both parishes until the permanent amalgamation of the two ecclesiastical parishes in 1821. More interestingly they redirected the charities of Middle Claydon to where need was greatest. From the late eighteenth century onwards, money from the Gifford charity was given across all three parishes, according to a note in the

[89] BCRO PR51/10/1; cf. N. Landau, 'Who was subjected to the laws of settlement? Procedure under the settlement laws in eighteenth-century England', *Agricultural History Review*, 43 (1995), pp. 139–59.
[90] CIH 3/2/32 deputation of gamekeeper 3 June 1820.

Middle Claydon churchwardens' accounts. In the same way, the St Thomas's day grant of alms and bread became a feature of all three parishes. In 1793, two years after she inherited the estate, Baroness Fermanagh endowed two new rent charges of £4 10s for the poor of Steeple and East Claydon. By 1813 the Charity Commissioners reported that the Middle Claydon churchwardens made a gift of half a guinea to the poor of Steeple Claydon, parallel to a similar gift to the Middle Claydon poor.[91] The Verneys had completed the process of bringing their own stamp to the parishes where they lived, owned their estates, and wielded power. The Claydons were truly estate villages.

[91] BCRO PR 52/5/1; PP1837–8 xxvii, pp. 15, 18, 69.

10   Conclusion

This study has looked at medium- and long-term changes in family fortunes and in rural landscape and society through a detailed case study. The many elements and linkages, and the range of themes explored encouraged an artificial subdivision into periods to ensure coherence. Although comparative studies have been drawn into the argument, it has concentrated on the internal dynamics of the Verney family and estates. What long-term trends and conclusions can be drawn from the various strands in the context of English social and rural history?

The Verney family's success in establishing themselves in the Claydons after losing most of their estates and their country seat in the first years of the seventeenth century was built on a single-minded dedication to the dynastic imperative over four generations. The heiress marriage was a vital and recurrent aspect of their aggrandisement. Four successive generations of Verneys married women with great financial assets in land or money, but without high social connections. This enabled them to build up their landed estate. But it took much more than that. Younger children, though few in number after the first generation, were never granted a substantial share of the growing wealth. When a younger son, Sir John Verney had been apprenticed to a Levant merchant, he was told to make his own way, and not to expect any landed endowment. Ralph, his younger grandson who became the second Earl Verney, was directed towards the church as a career, but preferred the law, and had no settled income whatsoever, even though his father made small provisions in land and cash in various wills. Daughters were never used as instruments of social advance. The social connections derived from Sir Edmund's six daughters' marriages reflected their relatively modest dowries but more importantly the disruption of normal social life during the Civil War when they were looking for husbands. Two of Sir John Verney's daughters found love matches in which their father was interested only in ensuring a reasonable jointure provision. Mary's marriage was modest but happy. Margaret's elopement with Sir Thomas Cave allowed her to receive a jointure far larger than the dowry her father had allotted would have bought.[1] Elizabeth never married. In the next generation neither daughter

---

[1] Whyman, *Sociability and Power*, pp. 131–2.

played a conventional part in the marriage market. Elizabeth was well into her late thirties when she married Lord Sherrard, while Catherine never married. Both had portions of £5,000, which were respectable for their day, but unlikely to attract a fortune seeker.

The Verneys concentrated their estate-building efforts on their eldest sons. The men of the family took first place at all times, and the patriarchal pressures on other members of the family were strong. Susan Whyman's conclusion that the women of the Verney family had to find modes of expressing power in their own domestic life and as 'gatekeepers of sociability' rings true.[2] However, the important strand that runs through successive generations of Verneys is the closeness of the marriages, and the strength of the conjugal bond. Verney wives appear to have been genuinely attached to their husbands and their hopes and desires. Perhaps in the case of Elizabeth Baker's marriage with Sir John this was less obviously true, but she was a third wife, and had no children. Even then she acted conscientiously as wife and stepmother, and promoted her husband's political career and social position. Catherine Paschall and Mary Herring, wives of the first and second earls, do not figure strongly in the Verney correspondence, which probably reflects the high degree of time spent in their husbands' company. Men brought up to follow the family tradition of patriarchy and paternalism, and married to socially inferior and submissive wives whom they respected, provided for the possibility of companionship and domestic content. It is a pattern alien to modern eyes, but one that also saw children successfully brought up to follow and accept the family's priorities of dynastic advancement. Catherine and Mary lived in the period from 1710 to 1750 when their husbands preferred domesticity to public office and political participation. There are sufficient numbers of letters that show their interests and opinions to suggest that neither were ciphers. When the family acquired a permanent London base in the 1720s it was in the semi-rural environment of Little Chelsea. London was in easy reach, yet explored from the outside for its entertainment and diversions, rather than fully participated in. When John Verney married, in 1736, his bride came from Clapham, another suburban spot of its time, and a number of letters speak of home entertainment in that quiet environment.

It was from a milieu of comfortable near-metropolitan networks that the eighteenth-century Verneys worked. Despite their peerage, the last three generations of Verneys were non-participants in London high society for long periods. Their heiresses brought them money, but not high-status links. Their daughters married for love, not connection. These forces made it more difficult for the second earl to turn his fortune into political power or even influence. But Verney women could act with strength and decisiveness, of which there are only hints in each generation, perhaps most obviously in the case of Sir Ralph Verney's wife,

---

[2] *Ibid.*, p. 140.

Mary. Her namesake 150 years later, Baroness Fermanagh, was to show that when male power had withered away, a single woman of wealth and character could act swiftly to save the family estates.

The early seventeenth-century Verneys followed a family tradition of more than 200 years in which they used court connections to further family interests and wealth. Sir Edmund's achievement in raising his family to a substantial position amongst the Buckinghamshire gentry from the ruins of his half-brother's rebellion and indebtedness relied on the contacts, positions, and profitable deals available at the court of James I and Charles I. But he was always on a financial knife-edge, balancing considerable current borrowings against future financial gain. The trauma of the Civil War for the Verneys was considerable, as this clever house of cards built on multilateral deals and assistance collapsed leaving little substance. Yet recovery was possible and William Denton's tough negotiations enabled Sir Ralph to put the finances on an even keel by 1655. His son's profitable marriage aided that process, not by paying off the debts, but by removing his obligation to provide jointure from his own lands. He was then able to pay off the debts by selling his own (heiress) wife's lands, and by good financial management. But while the male family line emerged successfully from the mid-century crisis, Sir Ralph's younger siblings were major losers. Not only did his sisters make poor marriages but also his younger brothers did not find successful careers. Soldiering had a much less certain future than a professional or merchant career. While Sir Ralph always did what was proper for an elder brother, and head of the family, it never amounted to generosity. He was scarred by the Civil War experience, particularly in his dread of debt and of reciprocal financial obligations. He used social contacts built up from pre-Civil War days and his own friendships in France, acting as trustee for the Earl of Rochester, and for members of the Denton and Gaudy families, as well as adviser to many others, but never allowed himself to become financially embroiled with them. Furthermore he did not seek out court or government office as a means to raise his family, as the Temples and Cheynes were happy to do in the late seventeenth century. It was a lesson he impressed on his sons, and they may have passed it on to the next generation. Did it play any part in their limited ability to build elite social contacts that paralleled their increasing wealth? The Verney experience confirms many of Lawrence Stone's findings about companionate elite marriages and family life in the eighteenth century. At the same time it casts doubt on his views about the openness of elite families to commercial and financial interests. The Verneys appear to have absorbed commercial and financial values into their social world as they took its money to expand their estates. Ultimately when the Verney blood line failed, their name, estates, and traditions were taken over by the Calvert family, whose wealth had come from brewing and distilling.[3]

---

[3] Stone, *The Family, Sex and Marriage in England 1500–1800*; Stone and Stone, *An Open Elite?*

From Sir John Verney's stewardship of the Verney fortunes onwards, the family retained close links with the commercial, professional, and financial elite in London, and never ignored the marriage links they made with such families. It gave them access to financial expertise, and they invested in government stock and trading company shares. Yet their main source of income remained the land. Commercial and financial links gave them a comfortable cushion of liquidity, but they preferred landed rents, and the creation of a substantial landed estate, even as they spent a higher proportion of their time in a permanent London home. This appears to reflect the first earl's ambitions for the family whose apotheosis in the two great heiress marriages of 1736 and 1740, was dashed by the failure of the male line thereafter. The absence of any discussion about these ambitions and aims comparable to that found in Sir Ralph's intimate letters to his friends, particularly William Denton and Sir Roger Burgoyne, is amongst the most frustrating aspects of the later Verney correspondence. The expansion of the Buckinghamshire estates and the building of a political interest were two essential components. Even the second earl's marriage settlement channelled most of the money into land. Although in his many schemes he became involved in manufacture, mining, and urban development as well as the stock market, they were always marginal enhancements to his income. A high level of expenditure, together with the cost of building Claydon House, triggered the financial disaster that followed his one major foray into stock market speculation. Although the Verneys were well versed in financial markets and investment opportunities, and invested in them throughout the eighteenth century, the landed estate remained the prime source of income.

The way in which the Verneys built up their estates gave them a greater flexibility in shaping its growth than many of their contemporaries. The land at a distance from Claydon brought into the family by two heiress marriages was sold off within forty years and replaced with land closer to the main estate. The purchase of East Claydon in 1729 was a natural prelude to the sale of the remaining Blacknall and Paschall estates to pay for it. The Verneys spent over twenty years finding suitable properties for their large cash dowries after 1740. Leaving aside acquisitions in Wendover, and to a lesser extent Buckingham and Carmarthen to gain political influence, purchases were narrowly concentrated on enclosed pasture farms easily managed from Claydon.

This complemented the simple, inexpensive, and un-bureaucratic estate management techniques used by the family throughout the period. They developed no Estate Office on the model of the Russells, Egertons, or Ashburnhams. Each eldest son was brought up to learn estate management, and when younger sons – Sir John Verney and the second earl – found themselves heirs, they diligently took up the challenge. Hands-on estate management was an essential element in the Verney family tradition. Although Sir Ralph Verney had a keen eye for agricultural innovation, and undertook a variety of experiments on his estates, there is little evidence that the Verneys' farming initiatives significantly raised output or productivity. Sir Ralph's investment in new dairying building in the 1680s facilitated a shift from fattening and sheep farming to dairying, but was primarily a response to low rents and a method of keeping his nominal rent roll as high as possible even while tenants fell into arrears.

The family's most important contribution to changing the complexion of farming came from enclosure and gradual farm enlargement. For all the detailed correspondence on such matters, their long-term financial significance is difficult to gauge. The chance survival of a costing for the enclosure of a twenty-acre field in Middle Claydon in 1648 suggests that high rates of return were available from seventeenth-century enclosure – perhaps 50 per cent per annum. At £1 per acre the costs were so much lower than for parliamentary enclosures 150 years later, which were closer to £4 an acre, that it was an excellent investment with immediate returns.[4] Yet Turner's figures for average costs per acre in the 1760s were less, so the enclosure of East Claydon in the 1740s may not have been markedly more expensive. The second earl believed that the returns in the early years were not great, and rents were only generally comparable with Middle Claydon at the end of the century. The rentals cannot provide a satisfactory quantitative estimate, and are distorted by many small purchases in the parish up to 1765.

The economic benefits of farm enlargement to the Verneys were more qualitative. Highly capitalised farmers probably paid their rents more readily and were less likely to go bankrupt. The correspondence sheds only partial light on whether the pressure to enlarge farms came from the farmers. Small incremental changes, adding fields here and there, are more commonly found than proposals to merge whole farms. The negative side was the changing structure of village society that went with it, with fewer families supported on their own farms, more from labouring and ancillary trades. Their plight influenced the social policies of landlords and farmers through poor law and charity administration.

Landlord investment in farms and buildings on the Claydon estate was unsystematic but certain patterns emerge. Major farm building was associated with the enclosure of Middle Claydon in the 1620s and again in the 1650s. Incoming tenants sometimes paid for new farmhouses and buildings on newly ring-fenced farms, but by the 1650s the cost fell exclusively on the Verneys. Later in the 1680s and 1720s there is evidence of extensive rebuilding works on farmhouses. They reflect problems with holding tenants and keeping up rents rather than enlightened and forward-looking investment. They also tell us something important about the life expectancy of the thatched buildings constructed of wattle and daub on stone footings that were typical on the estate up to 1750. Investment in farm buildings also followed the enclosure at East Claydon,

[4] M. E. Turner, *English Parliamentary Enclosure: Its Historical Geography and Economic History* (Folkestone 1980), pp. 130–4.

where detailed plans of Sion Farm survive. Architectural evidence also suggests that the second earl rebuilt three farms in brick in Middle Claydon and across the border of Steeple Claydon in the 1770s.[5] While the landlord increasingly provided basic farmhouses and outbuildings, any specialist buildings, such as those required by the potash-makers, were constructed by tenants at their own cost, and taken away with them, or sold on, when they left.

Within the parameters of the farming systems used on the Verneys' Buckinghamshire estates in the seventeenth and eighteenth centuries, it is difficult to see how further investment would have increased their returns. Enclosed pasture farming gave the highest possible rent per acre on clay soil fifty miles from London throughout the eighteenth century. Only late in that century did agricultural writers suggest ploughing a small proportion of the land to allay the long-term deterioration in permanent pastures. The growth of fodder crops supplemented natural grasses, and increased nitrogen inputs on the soil, while cleaning the fields of their thistles and molehills, and allowing re-seeding with higher quality grass seed. Some areas of southern England were beginning to invest in winter quarters for dairy cattle by 1800, but in Buckinghamshire these came considerably later, as did the government-inspired under-draining of fields in the mid-nineteenth century. Buckinghamshire farmers marketed their produce as grass-fed, and a change that increased production would have undermined this selling point. Larger farms on enclosed estates were probably the most efficient way of dairying at a distance from London. The most recent analysis of livestock changes in the eighteenth and nineteenth centuries does not suggest that the size of cattle and sheep rose markedly before the nineteenth century. It provides no data on milk yields or changes in the quality or conversion rates of butter and cheese.[6] Rent levels on the Middle Claydon estate where comparable data are available for most of the 200 years of the study show that enclosed pasture lost some value after peaking in the mid-seventeenth century, and only rose substantially in the last quarter of the eighteenth century. It confirms patterns found on the Lee, Temple, and Grenville estates in Buckinghamshire and Oxfordshire for the same period, which are markedly at variance with the recently produced rent index for England, particularly in the period from 1690–1750.[7]

---

[5] N. Pevsner, and E. Williamson, *The Buildings of England: Buckinghamshire*, 2nd edn (London 1994), p. 645. Catherine Farm in Middle Claydon should be bracketed with Rosehill and Blackmorehill Farms in Steeple Claydon.

[6] M. Turner, J. Beckett, and B. Afton, *Farm Production in England 1700–1914* (Oxford 2001), pp. 95–115 and ch. 6.

[7] M. Turner, J. Beckett, and B. Afton, *Agricultural Rent in England 1690–1915* (Cambridge 1997), pp. 155–76. In the 1690 to 1750 period the index figures are distorted by the narrowness of selection criteria and the overwhelming weighting for the Castle Howard estate. These show a rapid rise in the late seventeenth century and again in the 1720s that has no counterpart in southern England.

Pasture farming, as carried out on the Verney and neighbouring estates in the seventeenth and eighteenth centuries, was probably reasonably profitable for those who remained tenants for considerable periods. Some farmers lost money through poor management, or bad luck, and there was a long-term turnover of farmers, but there is no evidence that Claydon rent levels were markedly higher than on equivalent farms in the neighbourhood. The landowner's preference for pasture farming systems maximised estate incomes while allowing their tenants to make a living. As tenants also had to provide considerably more working capital, in the form of their livestock, than they would on an arable farm, the landlord was asking more from his tenant. But there is no evidence of endemic tenant hardship. Increasing farm sizes argues that tenants used economies of scale on larger units to offset the squeeze on their incomes and profitability. From this point of view, the system employed by the Verneys encouraged efficient farming practices amongst their tenants. It promoted the growth of a class of well-capitalised tenant farmers who became the predominant voice of English agriculture in the nineteenth century.

These findings are very different from Robert Allen's whose large-scale statistical analysis of the south midlands argued that pasture systems were less productive and working at lower profitability than mixed and open-field systems.[8] Unfortunately, his only data on pasture farming systems came from Huntingdonshire and Rutland in the early nineteenth century, outside his 'pasture' area and at the end of the period under study here. Even his figures suggest that only farms on old-enclosed pastures in Rutland were making a good surplus.[9] His other pasture farms look extremely suspect, since they had slightly more, and in one case less, money invested in livestock than his open-field farms.

Whatever the profitability of grassland systems in the eighteenth century, there is no doubt that the ways the Verneys managed their estates after 1600 drastically transformed the landscape of the Claydons, and the methods employed by farmers. In doing so they maximised their income, but did not raise land productivity markedly. This was a transformation in management, not an agricultural revolution. But it encouraged efficient, cost-conscious tenant farmers with capital, characteristic of English farming for the next 150 years.

Beyond family dynamics and the management of estates and farming practices on grassland systems, the novelty of this study lies in its analysis of the changes in the rural society of villages undergoing landlord-inspired enclosure, and a subsequent reorganisation of farms and farming. The existence of village typologies of 'closed' and 'open', and various stages in between, has long interested rural historians. However, they have usually been part of a static analysis

---

[8] Allen, *Enclosure and the Yeoman.*
[9] *Ibid.*, pp. 176–9; compare his map of soil types, p. 33.

of counties and 'pays' from information about landownership, farm sizes, population change, and other indicators at a single date. This study has shown the process by which parishes were transformed, and the subtle dynamics of the social processes involved. It is not a prescriptive model for the process of 'closing' large areas of southern and eastern England, but many of its features have parallels on other estates without the same range of sources to analyse the process. Owen Chadwick neatly described the nineteenth-century estate village over forty years ago in an essay about the Boileau estates in Norfolk where he depicts the ideal:

Model cottages were built and moderate rents were charged, employment and wages were good on the estate, and there was an efficient village school. In return the villagers were expected to behave well; cottagers were not allowed to take lodgers and their parents had to send their children to school until the age of twelve or they were not found employment later on. The village, together with its villagers, were regarded as his property.[10]

This picture of a mid-nineteenth-century community has some echoes at Claydon in the same period where the Verneys also built cottages, schools, and public libraries. Such self-conscious re-creation of the rural community was not an eighteenth-century phenomenon. Chadwick's description was, however, very much from the landlord's point of view, and the predominance of estate sources for the Claydons makes this study potentially lopsided. Yet the richness of the sources makes it possible to discount a great deal of that to reveal a substantial element of the tensions, negotiations, and interactions that went on in the transformation of rural society. The nature of landlord villages means that some sources exploited in recent village studies, particularly court cases, are very scarce for the Claydons. In closed communities, landlord power brought the settlement of community disputes into the landowner's domain. The small numbers of probate inventories for the Claydons, however, reflects a county-wide deficiency, not an estate bias. This study has always been aware of the problems of point of view implicit in its major source, but the richness revealed in the Verney papers more than compensates for the slant they inevitably bring with them.

Studies of village communities over the last fifty years have concentrated on communities with larger numbers of landowners, often with enduring open-field systems. In part this reflects their continuing interest in the problem of the disappearance of the small landowner, and the decline of rural independence which has been a theme of rural and agricultural history since the late nineteenth century. It also brings to the fore the actions and exploits of communities that were not dominated by powerful landed elites, and where the 'middling sorts'

[10] O. Chadwick, *Victorian Miniatures* (London 1960), pp. 70ff.

were able to exercise power and influence. One feature of a number of such communities was the importance of religious diversity – whether in the influence of Puritanism in Keith Wrightson and David Levine's works, or of dissenting groups in Margaret Spufford's studies. One element that often went with the creation of estate villages and 'closed' communities was the exclusion of non-conformity, or at the very least disapproval of it. In 1712 William Butterfield made a return to the Bishop of Lincoln stating that 150 out of Middle Claydon's population of 206 had taken communion – almost as high a percentage of villagers as was possible. In the early eighteenth century there were few parishes in the south midlands or indeed in the diocese of Lincoln, stretching from the Thames to the Humber, with as high a proportion of communicants, and many with poor attendance at church and negligible taking of communion. It was part and parcel of the enclosed estate community, not actively fostered, but built into estate expectations of tenants and parishioners. Yet the absence of religious dissent in the estate village does not imply abject conformity, simply that the permissible limits of the expression of dissent were more tightly drawn and more difficult for outsiders (and historians) to become aware of.

At the beginning of this book, I noted how over half the land of England was in the hands of the gentry and aristocracy by 1873, and probably not much less in 1820. Not every substantial landowner had estates as concentrated in a small number of parishes as the Verneys, or moulded the landscape and community to the same extent. However, the impact of estate villages on the texture of English rural life in the eighteenth and nineteenth centuries was considerable, particularly in those counties within a hundred miles of London. Their numbers are difficult to pinpoint accurately, as is the extent of conformity to a Claydon-like model of control. By the end of the eighteenth century the area around Claydon, Ashendon hundred, had many parishes with a high concentration of landownership. In thirty-four out of its thirty-seven parishes more than two thirds of the land tax was paid by one or two owners in 1798, while in more than one in three parishes a single landowner paid more than 90 per cent of assessed tax. In three of the four hundreds of north Buckinghamshire more than half the parishes had as high a proportion of elite landownership (see figure 8).[11] Other areas of the south midlands were not as intensively bought up by landowners, but the impact of concentrated landownership was substantial. By 1815 the writers of the various county agricultural reports found that year-to-year tenancies were the norm in Bedfordshire, Buckinghamshire, Oxfordshire, and Northamptonshire, as well as further afield.[12]

During the eighteenth century, many such villages grew only slowly in population, squeezing families into their 'open' neighbours, or further afield to

[11] Broad, 'Alternate husbandry and permanent pasture', p. 83.
[12] Allen, *Enclosure and the Yeoman*, p. 79.

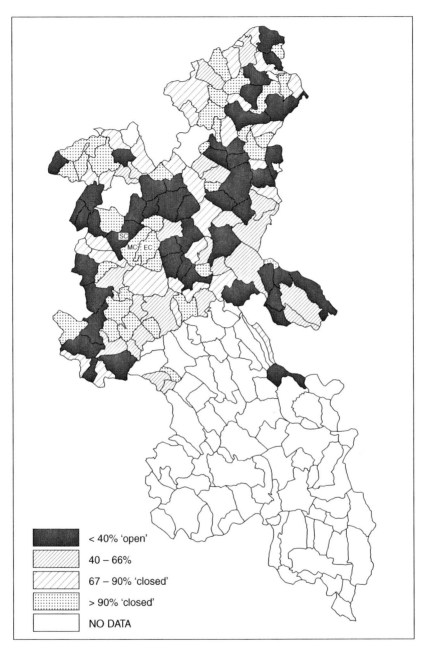

Figure 8 Landownership concentration in north Buckinghamshire *c*. 1798.

towns and London. In early nineteenth-century southern England most rural settlements expanded in numbers and temporarily increased the pressures on all country communities, before the flight to the towns became more rapid after 1870. Estate villages grew in numbers because they rarely reverted to wider landownership and looser control. Demand for country estates from the wealthy did not slacken in the nineteenth century. Yet estate villages probably contained a lower percentage of the rural population even as they increased in number.

The considerable scale of the transformation brought about by the creation of estate villages was a significant feature of English rural history in the eighteenth and nineteenth centuries. This study has shown how patterns of 'open' and 'closed' villages could emerge through a combination of circumstances. The Verneys only briefly created a 'great estate' and challenged for entry into the premier league of the landowning aristocracy. But their lasting legacy was the forging of the Claydons into a group of estate villages whose farming and landscape patterns, and social relationships endured into the twentieth century, and are still strongly visible in the twenty-first.

Appendix A
Sir Ralph Verney's confessional letter of 1650[1]

But to return again to the matter of rents. I shall clearly tell you what course I was wont to take in the letting of my land, and what Rules I went by. After I had received up the parcels I commonly made my demand, somewhat above what I meant to take, and seldom or never gave any other reasons why I valued it at such rate but that I thought others would give about that price for it which I conceive they would not do but that it was really worth it.

And then again I can truly say that if any tenant found his rent too high and was desirous (leaving house and land in the condition he found it) to quit his bargain, I never refused to take it, though by bond and lease I might have compelled him to hold it many years longer. And furthermore I have found an honest poor labouring man that perhaps paid (not more. than another, but more than he was able to give, though I have not abated. that lest others (who are better able) should require the same abatement, yet I let him another thing 20 or 30 shillings under the true value, and so one helped the other. And this I took to be as well for the tenant, and better for me, than if I had made the abatement in the other way. This I did in the case of Joseph Bates (that hath 10 or 11 children) who paid £15 rent for 2 yardlands, his house and picle which 20 would give if he would leave it. But to ease him somewhat he had the Riding at £3 10s 0d which is worth at least £5 rent and yet this poor man is behind. I know not how many years rent, therefore he cannot justly complain, but if he do, this (and all that ever let at Claydon) being let in my fathers time, when I reaped no present profit by it, but as it were his bailiff made the most of it for him, certainly it doth alter the case as to me.

One thing I must tell you, I ever was and still am of opinion that no man is bound to suffer his tenants to reap the benefit of his land, because they are poor that were a ready way indeed to make them rich, and him poor: nor is any man tied to let his land (unless it be of a great value) as his tenant with his family may live upon the profits of it, for – perhaps a man (as Joseph Bates) that takes a farm of £20 rent hath a wife and 10 children and by that time he and they are fed and clothed (though very plainly) I believe there will rest but small pittance for

[1] srv to wd 2/12 June 1650 R10.

his landlord. If so tenants were in a much better condition than their landlords, for they would be sure to have food and raiment when the landlords might be in hazard to want both. But on the other side I do believe a landlord is obliged to take but an equitable rent for his land, so as the tenant by God's ordinary providence and blessing upon his honest endeavours may be a gainer by it. And to my knowledge I never broke this rule but 'tis an easy matter to be too partial in this point, therefore (as from your self and without discovering why) I pray discourse with the Parson and William Roades about this and wherever find that any holds either house or land at too dear a rent (and hath no other parcel at an inferior rate to help out his bargain) if you please to present the name of the person with the particulars of his case at large, I assure your self 'twill be a favour no less acceptable to me than charitable to the poor man, and both of us will be bound to bless you for your pains therein. By this I hope it will appear that what I wrote before was neither to maintain nor justify my former actions, but rather to give you a more clear full information of my proceedings and the rules I walked by, which I shall as willingly amend, as acknowledge, being well assured that if I confess and forsake my faults I shall find mercy.

Appendix B
The genealogy of the Verney family

THE VERNEY FAMILY IN THE SEVENTEENTH CENTURY

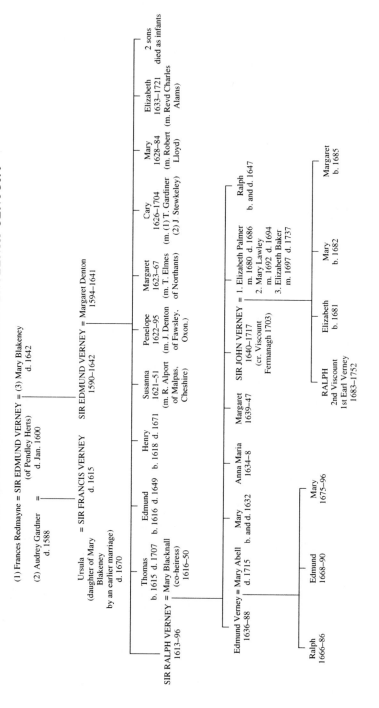

THE VERNEY FAMILY IN THE EIGHTEENTH CENTURY

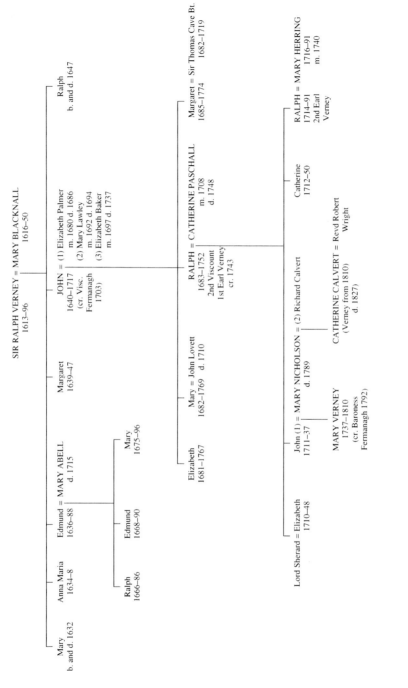

Bibliography

PRINCIPAL PRIMARY SOURCES

CLAYDON HOUSE, BUCKINGHAMSHIRE

The Verney papers divided between:
The Verney Letters microfilmed in 60 reels *c.* 1960, references by reel number
e.g. R47
The Verney Papers – recently catalogued by S. Ranson, references by ClH and
catalogue number

BODLEIAN LIBRARY, OXFORD

From the Gough, Tanner, and Rawlinson series

BRITISH LIBRARY MSS

Primarily from the Additional Stowe and Egerton series

CENTRE FOR BUCKINGHAMSHIRE STUDIES, AYLESBURY
(FORMERLY BUCKINGHAMSHIRE COUNTY RECORD OFFICE)

From the PR, QS, D/X, and various family papers series

HOUSE OF LORDS RECORD OFFICE

H. E. HUNTINGTON LIBRARY, SAN MARINO, CALIFORNIA

Primarily from the Stowe and Ellesmere MSS

PUBLIC RECORD OFFICE (NOW NATIONAL ARCHIVES)

A variety of records from the SP, HO, E, W, C, and other classes

SECONDARY SOURCES

Airs, M. and Broad, J. 'The management of rural building in seventeenth-century
Buckinghamshire', *Vernacular Architecture* 29 (1998), pp. 43–56
Allen, R. C. *Enclosure and the Yeoman: The Agricultural Development of the South
Midlands 1450–1850* (Oxford 1992)

280

Amussen, S. D. *An Ordered Society: Gender and Class in Early Modern England* (Oxford 1988)

Andrew, D. *Philanthropy and Police: London Charity in the Eighteenth Century* (Princeton 1989)

Ashton, T. S. *Economic Fluctuations in England* (Oxford 1959)

Aylmer, G. E. 'The meaning and definition of "property" in seventeenth-century England', *Past and Present* 86 (1980), pp. 87–97

Baker, A. R. H. 'Evidence from the "Nonarum Inquisitions" of contracting arable lands during the early fourteenth century', *Economic History Review* 2nd series, 19 (1966), pp. 518–32

Banks, S. 'Nineteenth-century scandal or twentieth-century model? A new look at "open" and "closed" parishes', *Economic History Review* 2nd series, 41 (1989), pp. 51–73

Bateson, F. N. W. *A Short History of Steeple Claydon* (n.p. 1939)

Beckett, I. F. W. (ed.) *The Buckinghamshire Posse Comitatus of 1798* Buckinghamshire Record Society 22 (1985)

Beckett, J. V. *The Aristocracy in England 1660–1914* (1986)
The Rise and Fall of the Grenvilles (Manchester 1994)

Beckett, J. V., Turner, M., and Cowell, B. 'Farming through enclosure', *Rural History* 9:2 (1998), pp. 144–55

Bennet, M. *The Civil Wars in Britain and Ireland 1638–51* (1997)

Beresford, M. W. *The Lost Villages of England* (London 1954)
'The beginning of retail tobacco licences 1632–41', *Yorkshire Bulletin of Economic & Social Research* 7:2 (1955), pp. 128–43

Billingsley, J. *General View of the Agriculture of Somerset*, 3rd edn (London 1798)

Bonfield, L. 'Marriage settlements and the "rise of great estates": the demographic aspect', *Economic History Review* 2nd series, 32 (1979), pp. 483–93
Marriage Settlements 1601–1740: The Adoption of the Strict Settlement (Cambridge 1983)
'Marriage, property and the "affective family"', *Law and History Review* 1:2 (1983), pp. 297–312

Boynton, L. 'Luke Lightfoot (?1722–1789)', *Furniture History* 2 (1966), pp. 7–17

Brinkworth, E. C. R. 'The Laudian Church in Buckinghamshire', *University of Birmingham Historical Journal* 5 (1955), pp. 31–50

Broad, J. 'Sir Ralph Verney and his estates 1630–96', Oxford University DPhil thesis 1973
'Gentry finances and the Civil War: the case of the Buckinghamshire Verneys', *Economic History Review* 2nd series, 32 (1979), pp. 183–200
'Alternate husbandry and permanent pasture in the midlands, 1650–1800', *Agricultural History Review* 28 (1980), pp. 77–89
'The cattle plague in eighteenth century England', *Agricultural History Review* 31 (1983), pp. 104–15
'Sir John Verney and Buckinghamshire elections, 1696–1715', *Bulletin of the Institute of Historical Research* 61 (1983), pp. 195–204
'The Verneys and the sequestrators in the civil wars 1642–56', *Records of Buckinghamshire* 27 (1985), pp. 1–9
'Whigs and deer-stealers in other guises: a return to the origins of the Black Act', *Past and Present* 119 (1988), pp. 56–72

Broad, J. 'The Verneys as enclosing landlords, 1600–1800' in J. Chartres, and D. Hey, (eds.), *English Rural Society, 1500–1800: Essays in Honour of Joan Thirsk* (Cambridge 1990), pp. 27–53

    'The fate of the midland yeoman: tenants, copyholders, and freeholders as farmers in north Buckinghamshire 1620–1800', *Continuity and Change* 14:3 (1999), pp. 325–47

    'Parish economies of welfare, 1650–1834', *Historical Journal* 42:4 (1999), pp. 985–1006

    'Housing the rural poor in southern England, 1650–1850', *Agricultural History Review* 48:2 (2000), pp. 151–70

Broad J. (ed.), *Buckinghamshire Dissent and Parish Life 1669–1712*, Buckinghamshire Record Society 28 (1993)

Broad, J. and Hoyle, R. W. (eds.) *Bernwood: The Life and Afterlife of a Forest* (Preston, 1997)

Bruce, John. *Letters and Papers of the Verney Family down to the End of the Year 1639*, Camden Society 56 (1853)

Buck, A. 'Middlemen in the Bedfordshire lace industry', *Bedfordshire Historical Record Society* 57 (1978), pp. 31–58

Buckinghamshire in the 1760s and 1820s: The County Maps of Jeffreys and Bryant, Buckinghamshire Archaeological Society (2000)

Chadwick, O. *Victorian Miniatures* (London 1960)

Chartres, J. A. 'Road carrying in England in the seventeenth century: myth and reality', *Economic History Review* 2nd series, 30:1, pp. 73–94

    'City and towns, farmers and economic change in the 18th century', *Historical Research* 64 (1991), pp. 138–55

    'Market integration and agricultural output in seventeenth-, eighteenth-, and early nineteenth-century England', *Agricultural History Review* 43 (1995), pp. 117–38

Chartres, J. and Hey D. (eds.) *English Rural Society, 1500–1800: Essays in Honour of John Thirsk* (Cambridge 1990)

Chibnall, A. C. *Sherington: Fiefs and Fields of a Buckinghamshire Village* (Cambridge 1965)

Chibnall, J. 'The roads of Buckinghamshire, 1675–1913', unpublished MSc thesis, University of London 1963

Clarendon, Earl of. *History of the Great Rebellion*, 6 vols. (1704–6)

Clark, A. A. (ed.) *The Life and Times of Anthony Wood*, 5 vols. (Oxford 1891–5)

Clay, C. 'The price of freehold land in the seventeenth and eighteenth centuries', *Economic History Review* 27 (1974), pp. 173–89

Cliffe, J. T. *The Puritan Gentry* (1984)

    Puritans in Conflict: The Puritan Gentry during and after the Civil War (London 1988)

Copeland, T. W. (ed.) *The Correspondence of Edmund Burke*, 10 vols. (Cambridge 1958–78)

Crittall, E. (ed.) *The Justicing Notebook of William Hunt, 1744–9*, Wiltshire Record Society 37 (1982)

Curthoys, Judith. 'Land, settlement and enclosure in Hillesden, Buckinghamshire', unpublished MStudies thesis, University of Oxford 1997

Davies, H. 'The making of a modern landscape: Wotton Underwood 1649–1743',
    unpublished MA thesis, University of Reading 1983
Davies, M. G. 'Country gentry and payments to London, 1650–1714', *Economic
    History Review* 2nd series, 24 (1971), pp. 15–36
  'Country gentry and falling rents in the 1660s and 1670s', *Midland History* 4
    (1977), pp. 86–96
Davis, R. W. *Political Change and Continuity 1760–1885: A Buckinghamshire Study*
    (Newton Abbot 1972)
Davis, T. *General View of the Agriculture of Wiltshire* (London 1794)
Defoe, D. *A Tour through the Whole Island of Great Britain* (London and Toronto
    1928)
Dickson, P. G. M. *The Financial Revolution in England* (Oxford 1967)
Dietz, F. C. *English Public Finance 1558–1641* (New York 1932)
Eastwood, D. 'The republic in the village: parish and poor at Bampton, 1780–1834',
    Journal of Regional and Local Studies 12 (1992), pp. 18–28
  Government and Community in the English Provinces, 1700–1870 (London and
    Basingstoke 1997)
Edwards P. R. *The Horse Trade of Tudor and Stuart England* (Cambridge 1988)
  'The decline of the small farmer: the case of Rushock, Worcestershire', *Midland
    History* 21 (1996), pp. 73–100
Edwards, P. *Dealing in Death: The Arms Trade and the British Civil Wars* (Stroud
    2000)
Eland, G. 'A Hillesden account book 1661–7', *Records of Buckinghamshire* 11
    (1919–26), pp. 135–44
  Papers from an Iron Chest at Doddershall, Bucks (Aylesbury 1937)
Ellis, Monica. *Ice and Icehouses through the Ages*, Southampton University Industrial
    Archaeology Group (1982)
Ellis, W. *Chiltern and Vale Farming Explained* (London 1733)
Erikson, A. L. 'Common law versus common practice: the use of marriage settlements
    in early modern England', *Economic History Review* 43 (1990), pp. 21–39
  Women and Property in Early Modern England (London 1993)
Everitt, A. *Change in the Provinces: The 17th Century*, Leicester University
    Department of English Local History, Occasional Papers, 2nd series (Leicester
    1969)
Firth, C. H. 'A chronological survey of the Civil War in Oxfordshire, Buckinghamshire
    and Bedfordshire 1642–6', *Proceedings of the Oxfordshire Archaeological
    Society* new series, 5 (1896–8), pp. 280–92
Firth, C. H. and Rait, R. S. *Acts and Ordinances of the Interregnum*, 2 vols. (London
    1911)
Fletcher, A. J. 'The enforcement of the Conventicle Acts 1664–1679.' In *Persecution
    and Toleration*, Studies in Church History 21, ed. W. J. Sheils (Oxford 1984),
    pp. 235–46
  'Men's dilemma: the future of patriarchy in England 1560–1660', *Transactions of
    the Royal Historical Society* 6th series, 4 (1994), pp. 61–81
Fletcher, A. J. and Stevenson, J. (eds.) *Order and Disorder in Early Modern England*
    (Cambridge 1985)
Forster, J. *England's Happiness Increased* (1664)

Foster, C. F. *Cheshire Cheese and Farming in the North West in the 17th and 18th Centuries* (Arley Hall 1998)

French, H. R. and Hoyle, R. W. 'The land market of a Pennine manor: Slaidburn, 1650–1780', *Continuity and Change* 14 (1999), pp. 349–83

Gairdner, J. and others. *Letters and Papers, Foreign and Domestic, Henry VIII*, 21 vols. and 2 vols. of addenda (1862–1932)

Gardiner, S. R. *History of the Great Civil War 1642–9*, 3 vols. (London 1886–91)

Gay, E. F. 'The temples of Stowe and their debts, 1603–53', *Huntington Library Quarterly* 2:4 (1939), pp. 399–438

  'Sir Richard Temple: The debt settlement and estate litigation 1653–75', *Huntington Library Quarterly* 6:3 (1943), pp. 255–91

Girouard, M. *Life in the English Country House: A Social and Architectural History* (Harmondsworth 1980)

Goodacre, J. *The Transformation of a Peasant Economy: Townspeople and Villagers in the Lutterworth Area 1500–1700* (Aldershot 1994)

Gough, R. *The History of Myddle*, ed. D Hey (Harmondsworth 1981)

Gunther, R. T. (ed.) *The Architecture of Sir Roger Pratt* (Oxford 1928)

Habakkuk, H. J. 'Marriage settlements in the eighteenth century', *Transactions of the Royal Historical Society* 4th series, 32 (1950), pp. 15–30

  'Landowners and the Civil War', *Economic History Review*, 2nd series, 18:1 (1965), pp. 130–51

  Marriage, Debt, and the Estates System: English Landownership, 1650–1950 (Oxford 1994)

Hainsworth, D. R. 'The mediator: a link between national and provincial society in seventeenth-century England', *Parergon*, new series, 6 (1988), pp. 89–102

  Stewards, Lords, and People: The Estate Steward and his World in Later Stuart England (Cambridge 1992)

Hanley, H. 'The inclosure of Pitstone Common Wood, 1612', *Records of Buckinghamshire*, 29 (1987), pp. 175–204

Harte, N. B. and Ponting, K. G. *Textile History and Economic History: Essays in Honour of Miss Julia de Lacy Mann* (Manchester 1973)

Hasler, P. W. (ed.) *History of Parliament: The House of Commons, 1558–1603* (London 1981)

Havinden, M. A. *Estate Villages: A study of the Berkshire Villages of Ardington and Lockinge* (London 1966)

Heal, F. *Hospitality in Early Modern England* (Oxford 1990)

Heal, F. and Holmes, C. *The Gentry in England and Wales, 1500–1700* (London 1994)

Hey, D. G. *An English Rural Community: Myddle under the Tudors and Stuarts* (Leicester 1974)

Hindle S., 'Persuasion and protest in the Caddington Common enclosure dispute, 1635–1639', *Past and Present* 158 (1998), pp. 37–78

  'Power, poor relief, and social relations in Holland fen, *c.* 1600–1800', *Historical Journal* 41 (1998), pp. 67–96

  'The problem of pauper marriage in seventeenth-century England', *Transactions of the Royal Historical Society* 6th series, 8 (1998), pp. 71–89

  The Birthpangs of Welfare: Poor Relief and Parish Governance in seventeenth-century Warwickshire, Dugdale Society Occasional Papers 40 (2000)

Hockliffe, E. (ed.) *The Diary of Ralph Josselin*, Camden Society, 3rd series 15 (1908)
Holderness, B. A. '"Open" and "close" parishes in England in the eighteenth and nineteenth centuries', *Agricultural History Review* 20 (1972), pp. 126–39
Holland, H. *A General View of the Agriculture of Cheshire* (London 1808)
Hollingsworth, T. H. *The Demography of the British Peerage*, supplement to *Population Studies* 18:2 (1964), pp. 1–108
Hopkins, E. 'The Bridgewater estates in north Shropshire during the Civil War', *Transactions of the Salop Archaeological Society* 56:3 (1961), pp. 308–13
Hoppit, J. 'Financial crises in eighteenth-century England', *Economic History Review* 2nd series, 39 (1986), pp. 39–58
Risk and Failure in English Business 1700–1800 (Cambridge 1987)
Horn, P. 'Child workers in the pillow lace and straw plait trades of Victorian Buckinghamshire and Bedfordshire', *Historical Journal* 17 (1974), pp. 779–97
Hoskins, W. G. *Midland Peasant* (London 1957)
Hoyle, R. W. (ed.) *The Estates of the English Crown, 1558–1640* (Cambridge 1992)
Houghton, J. *Collections for the Improvement of Husbandry and Trade* (London 1681–3 and 1691–1703)
Hughes, A. *Politics, Society and Civil War in Warwickshire 1620–1660* (Cambridge 1987)
Hull, F. 'The Tufton sequestration papers', *A Seventeenth-century Miscellany*, Kent Records Society 17 (1960)
James, E. G. 'Charity endowments as sources of local credit in 17th and 18th century England', *Journal of Economic History* 8 (1948), pp. 153–70
James, W. and Malcolm, J. *A General View of the Agriculture of Buckinghamshire* (1794)
Johnson, A. M. 'Buckinghamshire 1640–60', unpublished MA thesis, University of Wales, 1960
Jones, E. L. 'Agriculture and economic growth in England, 1660–1750: agricultural change', *Journal of Economic History* 25 (1965), pp. 1–18
Kelch, R. A. *Newcastle, a Duke without Money: Thomas Pelham-Holles, 1693–1768* (Berkeley, CA and London 1974)
Kent, J. R. 'The centre and the localities: state formation and parish government in England circa 1640–1740', *Historical Journal* 38 (1995), pp. 363–404
Kerridge, E. *The Agricultural Revolution* (London 1967)
King, P. 'Prosecution associations and their impact in eighteenth-century Essex'. In Hay, D. and Snyder, F. (eds.), *Policing and Prosecution in Britain, 1750–1850* (Oxford 1989)
Kussmaul, A. *Servants in Husbandry* (Cambridge 1980)
A General View of the Rural Economy of England 1538–1840 (Cambridge 1990)
Kussmaul, A. (ed.) *The Autobiography of Joseph Mayett of Quainton 1783–1839*, Buckinghamshire Record Society 21 (1986)
Lambert, S. *Bills and Acts: Legislative Procedure in Eighteenth-century England* (Cambridge 1971)
Landau, N. 'Who was subjected to the laws of settlement? Procedure under the settlement laws in eighteenth-century England', *Agricultural History Review* 43 (1995), pp. 139–59
Lane, C. 'The development of pastures and meadows during the sixteenth and seventeenth centuries', *Agricultural History Review* 28 (1980), pp. 18–30

Larminie, V. *Wealth, Kinship and Culture: The Seventeenth-century Newdigates of Arbury and their World* (Woodbridge 1995)

Laurence, Edward. *The Duty of a Steward to his Lord* (1727)

Le Hardy, W. and Reckitt, G. Ll. *Calendar of Buckinghamshire Quarter Sessions Records*, 9 vols. (Aylesbury 1934–58)

Le Muet, P. *Traicté des Galleries, Entrées, Salles, Antichambres et Chambres, etc.* (1645)

   Manière de bien bastir pour toutes sortes de personnes . . . Augmentée et enrichie en cette seconde edition de plusieurs figures, etc. (Augmentations de nouveaux bastimens faits en France), 12 pts (1647)

Lennard, R. *Rural Northamptonshire under the Commonwealth: A Study Based Principally upon the Parliamentary Surveys of Royal Estates*, Oxford Studies in Social and Legal History 5 (Oxford 1916)

Levine, D. *Family Formation in an Age of Nascent Capitalism* (New York 1977)

Levine, D. and Wrightson, K. *The Making of an Industrial Society: Whickham, 1560–1765* (Oxford 1991)

Lipscomb, G. *The History and Antiquities of the County of Buckingham*, 4 vols. (London 1847)

Loades, D. M. *Two Tudor Conspiracies*, 2nd edn (Bangor 1992)

Lysons D. and Lysons, S. *Magna Britannia; Being a Concise Topographical Account of the Several Counties of Great Britain*, 6 vols. (1806–22)

McClure, R. K. *Coram's Children: The London Foundling Hospital in the Eighteenth Century* (Newhaven and London 1981)

Marshall, W. *The Review and Abstract of the County Reports to the Board of Agriculture*, 4 vols. (Newton Abbot 1969)

Melton, F. *Sir Robert Clayton and the Origins of English Deposit Banking* (Cambridge 1986)

Mendelson, S. H. 'Debate', *Past and Present* 85 (1979), pp. 126–35

Mills, D. *Lord and Peasant in Nineteenth-century Britain* (1980)

Mingay, G. E. *English Landed Society in the Eighteenth Century* (London 1963)

   'The eighteenth-century land steward'. In Chambers, J. D. and Mingay, G. E. *Land, Labour, and Population in the Industrial Revolution* (London 1967), pp. 6–12

Morrill, J. S. *Cheshire 1630–60* (Oxford 1974)

Munby, L. M. *The Hertfordshire Landscape* (London 1977)

Nair, G. *Highley 1660–1880* (Oxford 1988)

Namier, L. and Brooke, J. *The House of Commons 1754–1790*, 3 vols. (London 1964)

Neeson, J. M. *Commoners: Common Right, Enclosure and Social Change in England, 1700–1820* (Cambridge 1993)

Newby, H., Bell, C., Rose, D., and Saunders, P. *Property, Paternalism and Power: Class and Control in Rural England* (London 1978)

North, R. *An Account of the Different Kinds of Grasses Propagated in England . . .* (London 1759)

Ogilby, John. *Britannia: By a Geographical and Historical Description of the Principal Roads Thereof* (London 1675)

Overton, M. *Agricultural Revolution England: The Transformation of the Agrarian Economy, 1500–1850*, Cambridge Studies in Historical Geography 23 (Cambridge 1996)

Paley, Ruth (ed.) *Justice in 18th Century Hackney: The Justicing Notebook of Henry Norris and the Hackney Petty Sessions Book*, London Record Society 28 (1991)

Peck, L. L. *Court Patronage and Corruption in Early Stuart England* (London 1990)

Pevsner, N. and Williamson, E. *The Buildings of England: Buckinghamshire*, 2nd edn (London 1994)

Pollock, L. 'Rethinking patriarchy and family life', *Journal of Family History* 23 (1998), pp. 3–27

Prest, W. R. 'Judicial corruption in early modern England', *Past and Present*, 133 (1991), pp. 67–95

Priest, St J. *A General View of the Agriculture of Buckinghamshire* (London 1810)

Ranson, S. R. 'The Verney papers: a catalogue' (t.s. 1994)

Reed, M. 'Enclosure in north Buckinghamshire, 1500–1750', *Agricultural History Review* 32:2 (1984), pp. 133–44

    Buckinghamshire Glebe Terriers 1580–1640, Buckinghamshire Record Society 30 (1997)

Rosenheim, J. M. *The Townsends of Raynham: Nobility in Transition in Restoration and Early Hanoverian England* (Middletown, CT, 1989)

Roots I. A. *The Great Rebellion 1642–60* (London 1966)

Sainfoin Improved (1674)

Seaver, S. S. *The Puritan Lectureships: The Politics of Religious Dissent 1560–1662* (Stanford 1970)

Sedgwick, R. *The History of Parliament: The House of Commons, 1715–54*, 2 vols. (London 1970)

Sharp, B. *In Contempt of All Authority: Rural Artisans and Riot in the West of England, 1586–1660* (Berkeley, CA and London 1980)

Sharpe, J. A. 'Enforcing the law in the 17th century English village' In V. A. C. Gatrell, *Crime and the Law, the Social History of Crime in Western Europe since 1500* (London c. 1980)

Sharpe, K. *The Personal Rule of Charles I* (New Haven, CT and London 1992)

Shaw-Taylor, L. 'Labourers, cows, common rights and parliamentary enclosure: the evidence of contemporary comment c. 1760–1810', *Past and Present* 171 (2001), pp. 95–126

    'Parliamentary enclosure and the emergence of an English agricultural proletariat', *Journal of Economic History* (2001), pp. 640–62

Shoemaker, R. B. *Prosecution and Punishment: Petty Crime and the Law in London and Rural Middlesex 1660–1725* (Cambridge 1991)

Slack, P. *Poverty and Policy in Tudor and Stuart England* (London 1988)

Slater, M. 'The weightiest business: marriage in an upper gentry family in seventeenth century England', *Past and Present* 72 (1976), pp. 25–54

    Family Life in the Seventeenth Century: The Verneys of Claydon House (London 1984)

Smith, R. M. (ed.) *Land, Kinship and Life-cycle* (Cambridge 1984)

Speck, W. A. *Tory and Whig: The Struggle in the Constituencies 1701–15* (London 1970)

Spenceley, G. F. R. 'The origins of the English pillow lace industry', *Agricultural History Review* 21 (1973), pp. 81–93

Spring, E. *Law, Land, and Family: Aristocratic Inheritance in England, 1300 to 1800* (Chapel Hill, NC 1993)

Spufford, M., *Contrasting Communities: English Villagers in the Sixteenth and Seventeenth Centuries* (Cambridge 1974)

Spufford, Margaret (ed.) *The World of Rural Dissenters, 1520–1725* (Cambridge 1995)

Spurr, J. 'A profane history of early modern oaths', *Transactions of the Royal Historical Society* 6th series, 9 (2001)

Stone, L. 'The Verney tomb at Claydon', *Records of Buckinghamshire* 16 (1953–60), pp. 67–82

  An Elizabethan: Sir Horatio Palavicino (Oxford 1956)

  The Crisis of the Aristocracy (Oxford 1965)

  Family and Fortune: Studies in Aristocratic Finance in the 16th and 17th Centuries (Oxford 1973)

  The Family, Sex and Marriage in England 1500–1800 (London 1977)

Stone, L. and Stone, J. C. F. *An Open Elite?* (Oxford 1984)

Sutherland, L. S., 'Sir George Colebrooke's world corner in Alum, 1771–3', *Economic History* (1936), pp. 237–58

  The East India Company in Eighteenth-century Politics (Oxford 1952)

Sutherland, L. S. and Wood, J. A. 'The East India speculations of William Burke', *Proceedings of the Leeds Philosophical Society – Literary and Historical Section* 11, pt vii (1966), pp. 183–216

Taylor, J. *The Carriers Cosmographie* (London 1637)

Tennant, P. *Edgehill and Beyond: The People's War in the South Midlands 1642–5* (Stroud 1992)

The Humble Petition of Sir Ralph Verney, Nathaniel Hobart and Others . . . (1660)

Thick, M. 'Garden seeds in England before the late eighteenth century, part 2: the trade in seeds to 1760', *Agricultural History Review* 38 (1990), pp. 105–16

Thirsk, J. 'Agrarian history 1540–1940', *VCH Leics*, II (1954), pp. 199–264

  Economic Policy and Projects (Oxford 1978)

  'Changing attitudes to enclosure in the seventeenth century', *Festschrift for Professor Ju Hwan Oh Taegu* (Toegu, Korea 1991)

  Alternative Agriculture (Oxford 1997)

Thirsk, J. (ed.) *The Agrarian History of England and Wales*, vols. IV and V, (Cambridge 1967, 1984)

Thomas, P. D. G. *John Wilkes: A Friend of Liberty* (Oxford 1996)

Thompson, E. P. *Whigs and Hunters* (London 1975)

Thompson, F. M. L. 'The social distribution of landed property in England since the sixteenth century', *Economic History Review* 2nd series, 16 (1966), pp. 505–18

  Chartered Surveyors, the Growth of a Profession (London 1968)

Turner, M. E. 'The cost of parliamentary enclosure in Buckinghamshire', *Agricultural History Review* 21 (1973), pp. 35–46

  'The 1801 crop returns for Buckinghamshire', *Records of Buckinghamshire* 19:4 (1974), pp. 471–82

  'Parliamentary enclosure and landownership change in Buckinghamshire' *Economic History Review* 2nd series, 28 (1975), pp. 565–81

  English Parliamentary Enclosure: Its Historical Geography and Economic History (Folkestone 1980)

'Cost, finance and parliamentary enclosure', *Economic History Review* 2nd series, 34 (1981), pp. 236–48

'Economic protest in rural society: opposition to parliamentary enclosure in Buckinghamshire', *Southern History* 10 (1988), pp. 94–128

Turner, M., Beckett, J., and Afton, B. *Agricultural Rent in England 1690–1915* (Cambridge 1997)

Farm Production in England 1700–1914 (Oxford 2001)

Turner, R. W. *Equity of Redemption* (Cambridge 1931)

Valenze, D. 'The art of women and the business of men: women's work and the dairy industry *c.* 1740–1840', *Past and Present* 130 (1991), pp. 142–69

Verney, F. P. and Verney, M. M. *Verney Memoirs of the Seventeenth Century*, 4 vols. (London 1892–6)

Verney, M. M. *Verney Letters of the Eighteenth Century*, 2 vols. (London 1930)

Verney, M. M. and Abercrombie, P. (eds.) 'Letters of an eighteenth-century architect', *Architectural Review*, 59–60 (June–September 1926)

Verney, P. *The Standard Bearer: The Story of Sir Edmund Verney, Knight-Marshal to King Charles I* (London 1963)

Wales, Tim. 'Poverty, poor relief and the life-cycle: some evidence from seventeenth-century Norfolk'. In R. M. Smith (ed.), *Land, Kinship and Life-cycle* (Cambridge 1985), pp. 351–404

Warner, G. F. (ed.) *The Nicholas Papers*, Camden Society new series, 40, 50, 57, and 3rd series, 31 (1886)

Whiteman, E. A. (ed.) *The Compton Census of 1676*, British Academy Records of Social and Economic History, new series 10 (1986)

Whyman, S. *Sociability and Power in Late-Stuart England: The Cultural Worlds of the Verneys 1660–1720* (Oxford 1999)

Williams, N. J. 'Two documents concerning the new draperies', *Economic History Review* 2nd series, 4:3 (1952), pp. 353–8

'Wotton Underwood in 1657', *Records of Buckinghamshire* 14 (1942), pp. 133–48

Wrightson, K. 'Two concepts of order' in J. Brewer, and J. Styles, (eds.), *An Ungovernable People: The English and Their Law in the Seventeenth and Eighteenth Centuries* (1980)

Wrightson, K. and Levine, D. *Poverty and Piety in an English Village: Terling 1525–1700*. rev. edn (Oxford 1995)

Wrightston, K. and Levine, D. *The Making of an Industrial Society: Whickham, 1560–1765* (Oxford 1991)

Wrigley, E. A. and Schofield, R. S. *The Population History of England 1538–1871* (Cambridge 1981)

Wrigley, E. A., Davies, R. S., Oeppen J. E., and Schofield, R. S. *English Population History from Family Reconstitution 1580–1837* (Cambridge 1997)

Index

16. Marjorie Keniston Mcintosh *A Community Transformed: The Manor and Liberty of Havering-atte-Bower 1500–1620*
hardback 0 521 38142 8 paperback 0 521 89328 3
17. Richard T. Vann and David Eversley *Friends in Life and Death: The British and Irish Quakers in the Demographic Transition*
hardback 0 521 39201 2 paperback 0 521 52664 7
18. L. R. Poos *A Rural Society after the Black Death: Essex 1350–1525*
hardback 0 521 38260 2 paperback 0 521 53127 6
19. L. D. Schwarz *London in the Age of Industrialisation: Entrepreneurs, Labour Force and Living Conditions 1700–1850*
hardback 0 521 40365 0
20. John Landers *Death and the Metropolis: Studies in the Demographic History of London 1670–1830*
hardback 0 521 35599 0
21. Angelique Janssens *Family and Social Change: The Household as a Process in an Industrializing Community*
hardback 0 521 41611 6 paperback 0 521 89215 5
22. Michael Zell *Industry in the Countryside: Wealden Society in the Sixteenth Century*
hardback 0 521 44541 8 paperback 0 521 89306 2
23. Roger S. Bagnall and Bruce W. Frier *The Demography of Roman Egypt*
hardback 0 521 46123 5
24. Anne Digby *Making a Medical Living: Doctors and Patients in the English Market for Medicine, 1720–1911*
hardback 0 521 34526 X paperback 0 521 52451 2
25. Richard P. Saller *Patriarchy, Property and Death in the Roman Family*
hardback 0 521 32603 6 paperback 0 521 59978 4
26. Donald Woodward *Men at Work: Labourers and Building Craftsmen in the Towns of Northern England, 1450–1750*
hardback 0 521 47246 6 paperback 0 521 89096 9
27. Simon Szreter *Fertility, Class and Gender in Britain, 1860–1940*
hardback 0 521 34343 7 paperback 0 521 52868 2
28. Carl Ipsen *Dictating Demography: The Problem of Population in Fascist Italy*
hardback 0 521 55452 7 paperback 0 521 89425 5
29. Mary Dobson *Contours of Death and Disease in Early Modern England*
hardback 0 521 40464 9 paperback 0 521 89288 0
30. Barry Reay *Microhistories: Demography, Society and Culture in Rural England, 1800–1930*
hardback 0 521 57028 X paperback 0 521 89222 8
31. James Lee and Cameron Campbell *Fate and Fortune in Rural China: Social Organization and Population Behavior in Liaoning, 1774–1873*
hardback 0 521 58119 2
32. E. A. Wrigley, R. S. Davies, J. E. Oeppen, and R. S. Schofield *English Population History from Family Reconstitution, 1580–1837*
hardback 0 521 59015 9
33. Sheilagh Ogilvie *State Corporatism and Proto-Industry: The Württemberg Black Forest, 1580–1797*
hardback 0 521 37209 7

34. Marjorie Keniston Mcintosh *Controlling Misbehavior in England, 1370–1600*
hardback 0 521 62177 1 paperback 0 521 89404 2
35. Robert Woods *The Demography of Victorian England and Wales*
hardback 0 521 78254 6
36. Eilidh Garrett, Alice Reid, Kevin Schürer, and Simon Szreter *Population Change in Context: Place, Class and Demography in England and Wales, 1891–1911*
hardback 0 521 80153 2
37. Katherine Lynch *Individuals, Families and Communities in Europe, 1200–1800: The Urban Foundations of Western Society*
hardback 0 521 64235 3 paperback 0 521 645417
38. Robert Fogel *The Escape from Hunger and Premature Death*
hardback 0 521 80878 2
39. Susannah Ottaway *The Decline of Life: Old Age in Eighteenth-Century England*
hardback 0 521 81580 0
40. John Broad *Transforming English Rural Society: The Verneys and the Claydons, 1600–1820*
hardback 0 521 82933 X